The Lady Vanishes

Subjectivity and
Representation in
Castiglione and
Ariosto

The Lady Vanishes

Subjectivity and Representation in
Castiglione and Ariosto

VALERIA FINUCCI

Stanford University Press
Stanford, California
1992

Stanford University Press
Stanford, California
© 1992 by the Board of Trustees
of the Leland Stanford Junior University
Printed in the United States of America

CIP data are at the end of the book

A mia madre
e in memoria
di mio padre

ACKNOWLEDGMENTS

Many friends provided the intellectual milieu that made working on the Renaissance a fun thing to do and read parts of the book at various stages of its development. I thank Giuseppe Mazzotta, Elissa Weaver, Kevin Brownlee, Constance Jordan, Daniel Javitch, Marina Zancan, Olga Zorzi-Pugliese, Juliana Schiesari, Deanna Shemek, Joseph Lowenstein, and Sergio Zatti. Back home I have greatly benefited from a number of stimulating conversations with the members of the North Carolina Research Group on Medieval and Early Modern Women. Jean O'Barr, Regina Schwartz, Joan Hinde Stewart, Philip Stewart, Mary Ann Frese Witt, and Ronald Witt spurred me on and offered emotional support. Elizabeth Clark was always there, entertained me endlessly, and made me grow, literally, into a scholar. I owe her more than these words can tell. Rosamaria Preparata and Carmel Mullin checked on me from far away, and Lee Lourdeaux kept me being me.

In the past four years I have received grant support from a number of sources, which I gratefully acknowledge here. First of all, I thank the Women's Studies Program of Duke University for a summer grant in 1990 and the Duke Research Council for a faculty summer grant in 1987 and for research grants in the following years. An NEH Summer Institute on Ariosto and Tasso at Northwestern University offered me the chance to refine my ideas on chivalric romances. I thank its directors, Albert Ascoli and David Quint, for giving generously of their time, and Elizabeth J. Bellamy and Joy Potter for a summer of endless discussions on more than epics. I am also very grateful to the members of the Romance Studies Department of Duke University for their encouragement; I especially thank my chairman, Jean Jacques Thomas, for repeatedly showing his support of junior faculty members. Finally, I should mention my students Catherine Maggio and Christy Constabile and the staff of the Interlibrary Loan Office of Duke University for their ready willingness to track down even the most exotic requests.

Helen Tartar's enthusiasm and skill swept me, literally, through the pitfalls of publishing. I consider myself fortunate for having met her. I particularly thank her for assigning me the most wonderful editor an author can hope to have, John Ziemer, who could read my mind even when scanning my writing. He made me laugh through my revisions.

A much earlier version of Chapter 1 appeared in Italian as "La dama di corte: discorso istituzionale e realtà ne *Il libro del cortegiano*" in *Annali d'Italianistica* 7 (1989): 88–103. A shorter version of Chapter 3 appeared in *Exemplaria* 4.1 (1992): 51–77; reprinted by permission of MRTS, SUNY, Binghamton, New York.

V. F.

Contents

NOTE ON TEXTS AND
TRANSLATIONS

Il libro del cortegiano and *Orlando furioso* are quoted in the original, followed by translations in parentheses. Citations of Castiglione list first the book, then the section, and finally the page of the passage in the Italian version, all in arabic numerals. They are from the 1972 edition by Ettore Bonora, which reproduces the text of Bruno Maier, still the most authoritative until a definitive critical version becomes available. The English version is from George Bull's translation. Citations of Ariosto list first the canto and then the appropriate octave, both in arabic numerals. The English version is from Guido Waldman's translation. Petrarch is given in English in Durling's translation. All other translations, unless otherwise noted, are mine.

The Lady Vanishes

Subjectivity and
Representation in
Castiglione and
Ariosto

Subjectivity, Representation, and the Construction of Femininity

THE MANY upheavals that marked the transition from the fifteenth to the sixteenth century in Italy—the French invasion, the collapse of Medici prestige in Florence, the power struggles in Lombardy—advanced the influence of courts and the prestige of courtly culture. Thanks to the printing press and the expansion of education among both the thriving urban bourgeoisie and the aristocracy, courtly ideology spread rapidly.[1] Two of the most influential representatives of courtly culture, Baldassarre Castiglione (1478–1529) and Ludovico Ariosto (1474–1533), lived at court as intellectuals and diplomats. It was a fairly quiet existence for Ariosto, who refused to move to Hungary when his patron demanded it, and a more active one for Castiglione, who died in Spain as the papal envoy at the court of Emperor Charles V.

Both Castiglione's *Il libro del cortegiano* (The book of the courtier) and Ariosto's *Orlando furioso* appeared during the same period after a lengthy gestation. Begun around 1508, about the same time Ariosto started writing his romance epic, Castiglione's text circulated in manuscript for a number of years before its publication in 1528. Three editions of the *Furioso* appeared during Ariosto's lifetime: two were printed before Castiglione's treatise (1516 and 1521) and one after (1532). Ariosto knew of Castiglione's work firsthand; he seems to have been present at the Gonzaga court in Urbino in 1507 for the conversations recorded in *Il libro del cortegiano* in fictional form. He also refers to Castiglione twice in *Orlando furioso* ("chi / ha tal i cortigian formati"; "he who depicted courtiers" [37, 8]; also 42, 87) and once in the *Satire* (III, 91).[2] Castiglione records neither Ariosto's presence (his name is not among the participants) nor his point of view, but dedicates Book 4 of the treatise to Ariosto's cousin Alfonso Ariosto.[3] The success of both works was remarkable. Enthusiastically received in every court, *Il libro del cortegiano* was soon translated into several European languages; *Orlando furioso* underwent no fewer than 150 printings by the turn of the century, 70 of them between 1536 and 1560 alone.[4]

Castiglione and Ariosto stand among the best representatives in the literary world of the values associated with the Renaissance. The historian Jacob Burckhardt would have hailed their sense of history, their approach to politics (matched by a shrewd understanding of statehood and nationhood and by an open distance from the clergy), their assertion of self-identity, and their consciousness of merit as characteristic of the spirit of the period. This holds true even though the contemporary sociopolitical configuration of Italy retained elements of feudal customs, a sense of nationhood was at best a yearning, and economic decline severely tested the individual's aspiration for self-empowerment. *Il libro del cortegiano* and *Orlando furioso* reflect both the cultural constructs and contradictions of their time and the social and political arrangements of the courts at which their authors lived.

My project is to examine the construction of identities in Castiglione and Ariosto. Specifically, I aim to explore how the authors of the most influential prescriptive (Castiglione's treatise) and descriptive (Ariosto's romance epic) texts of the High Italian Renaissance construct and problematize feminine identities and occasionally male ones. The problematic of subjectivity in relation to gender and of gender in relation to culture is rewarding when applied to Renaissance literature, for although much has been written about selfhood in that period and its links with a protocapitalist society of ubiquitous merchants, this selfhood was essentially celebrated in or even advocated only for men. I contend that although Ariosto and Castiglione offer a number of questionable self-identities (and the idea of a contradictory selfhood formed by and through discourse is essential to my deconstructive readings of paradigmatic episodes), they also move toward the representation of the unified subject needed by ideology, one who takes his/her place in society and culture on a specific side of the gender division.

Representation, it has been said many times, goes hand in hand with ideology. Althusser ("Ideology") sees ideology as a system of representations, representations that are both real (they match the real relationships of people to their culture) and imaginary (some ways in which these relationships are related to social arrangements cannot be understood). Althusser speaks from a post-Marxian point of view, but it is clear that given the weight of patronage and their often didactic purposes, texts of the Early Modern period are even more grounded in their social and political world than are present-day works, which are more self-consciously literary.[5] When reading from his work at the Estes court, for instance, Ariosto could ill afford to displease his prince or alienate his courtly audience by writing of unsavory topics and destabilizing choices. And Castiglione could offer his vision of an idealized counselor-courtier only by being selectively blind to the all-too-visible power struggles and quarrels on the sidelines.[6] The *Cortegiano* not only foregrounded, in an idealized form, the status of the courtier in Renaissance courts and the discourses that positioned him and his ruler in those courts but also produced an ideology that other courtiers and patrons found easy to accept. The representation of an ordered court at a time when there were many courts but little order and of a mobile group of individuals ascending to power through self-promotion was bound to please many readers, from the prince interested in order to the parvenu interested in admittance. Not surprisingly, time and again in the *Cortegiano* and the *Furioso*, the fictional characters recognize themselves in the discursive practices being furthered and endorse them (as in the case of the court ladies discussed in my first two chapters), for ideology—Althusser insists—by interpellating individuals as subjects, assures them a place within culture.

For Althusser, it is impossible to escape the ideological apparatus, but it is possible to understand how it works (*For Marx*).[7] At times, readers from different generations and different backgrounds are able to approach a literary text subversively because ideological assumptions have changed from the period in which the work was written; at others, what is said still rings so true that opposition is difficult. To give an example of shifting cultural responses, the final cantos of the revised *Furioso* have disappointed modern readers because they seem to endorse "bourgeois" values, but the lack of such a criticism in the sixteenth century confirms that the period was satisfied with that representation. Ariosto's contemporaries actively read the *Furioso* as a moral and serious narrative, although later critics have steadily complained about an array of immoral and hardly serious episodes.[8]

A literary text, of course, is not directly bound to an ideology: a work of art endures because it somehow transcends the cultural constructions that inform its background. Fredric Jameson assures the autonomy of the text by applying Greimas's semiotic square, which he uses to read both what is manifest and what is not in a text, "a relationship of tension between presence and absence" (*Political Unconscious*, 49). Althusser asserts that art also "presupposes a *retreat*, an *internal distantiation*, from the very ideology" that engenders it ("Letter on Art," 222–23). Gramsci emphasizes that a hegemonic discourse is not all-comprehensive in a deterministic way; subordinate groups may challenge a particular ideology and constitute a subculture that questions, resists, or renegotiates current ideological tenets. It is in these gaps that women and minorities have often been able to insert their voices.

The very works that seem to reconfirm the pervasiveness of current ideological tenets are often subversive, sometimes without the author's awareness. Castiglione praises his duke for having "l'affabilità e piacevolezza congiunta ancor la cognizione d'infinite cose" ("an affable and charming nature, an infinite range of knowledge" [1, 3, 35]) while he constructs a position of authority for his courtier in Book 4 that in many ways undermines the power and autonomy of the prince under whom he is working. Ariosto dedicates his book to his patron, Ippolito d'Este, but chastises the prince's lukewarm sponsorship of poets and poetry (35, 23). More dangerously, he frames his praises of Ippolito and the House of Este with critical readings of the historical events in which they participated; his spokesman, San Giovanni, for example, claims that poets can change and rearrange history and do not necessarily have to accept as a duty the furthering of dynastic purposes (35, 25–27).[9] No wonder that Tasso, a writer much more interested in the historicity of his work, sharply refuted this statement in his *Discorsi* (*Prose*, 367).[10] Ironically, since San Giovanni's declaration is made on the moon, it could be argued that it has no subversive message.

That the ideological aim of representation is the construction of fixed identities in an ordered world is especially clear in the genres that Castiglione and Ariosto used. The pedagogical aim of conduct books is to mold men and women for the roles they are supposed to assume, roles that are gender-specific and suitably respectful of power relations. Similarly, epic narratives construct exemplary rulers by linking the fashioning of selves to the fashioning of kingdoms. Just as Castiglione creates an idealized courtier moving through the ranks by conforming to rules of etiquette, Ariosto invents an idealized prince moving with a good dose of luck toward his destiny, which coincides with the founding of the family of Ariosto's patron. In Castiglione, the procedure of subsuming the private self to public strategies seems at times perfectly sutured, as disruptions are recuperated through poise or gentle laughter and the protean courtier is forever given the chance to offer another interpretation of his (masked) self, another alteration of his public image. In Ariosto, the process is less smooth and the divisions less discrete; too often, the values of the feudal world Ariosto is recreating resist an easy assimilation into the more individualistic, power-driven culture that is the author's own, and divine providence is challenged by the whims of Fortuna.

Paradoxically, narrative ambiguities in both works have often been dismissed in the name of order. The overall sense of a controlled structure and of a playful, decorous atmosphere often attracted readers to the *Cortegiano*, but the book is full of contradictions, badly mended breaks (for instance, the one separating the last book from the first three), and unresolved conflicts between the idealized world recreated inside and political reality outside. No matter: the text was read fanatically as a homogenous, unified, serene work, a master narrative subsequently reproduced in countless how-to textbooks, from those extolling the art of riding a horse to those advising on ways of dueling, eating, and behaving.[11] Like Castiglione, Ariosto was thought to be oblivious of the practical requirements of daily life at court and personally unchallenged by the numerous contemporary social and political upheavals. Fostered by influential studies by De Sanctis and Croce, the tradition of an aloof, ironic, measured, all-knowing poet presenting his court with an escapist and self-referential chivalric romance has been difficult to counter. Recently, however, a number of critical works have increasingly historicized the *Furioso* and read it intertextually. Barberi-Squarotti looks at the historical events that took place during the writing of the first edition

(1509–15) and sees the book as mirroring a new sense of cosmic disharmony (109). More specifically, the added episodes of the 1532 edition are understood as exemplifying a new authorial somberness; the laws of courtesy that earlier motivated the best knights to selfless deeds seem to make room now for the reality of vice, power, and institutionalized wickedness.[12] Finally, the *Cinque canti* and the *Satire* show even more deeply how events were disturbing Ariosto.[13]

Representation also goes hand in hand with subjectivity, if one understands identity production not (or not simply) as a philosophical construct but as the product of a discourse. Subjectivity, specifically male subjectivity, was a primary concern of Renaissance theorists, as in many ways it still is today. In *De dignitate hominis*, for example, Pico della Mirandola grandly casts aside Aristotelian and Scholastic ideas on man's fixed identity and argues for a self adept at fashioning itself into any desired shape or form ("thou mayest fashion thyself in whatever shape thou shalt prefer" [225], God says to Adam). It is debatable whether, as Pico and other humanists claimed, a truly self-sufficient, harmonious self capable of ordering the world can really exist, or whether, as the new historicists insist, the subject is always dispersed within ideology, always subjected to power relations. To be sure, Burckhardt praises man's ability to shape his identity even in the face of a benevolent despotism: "The private man, indifferent to politics, and busied partly with serious pursuits, partly with the interests of a dilettante, seems to have been first fully formed in these despotisms of the fourteenth century" (99). But Stephen Greenblatt, although agreeing with Burckhardt in claiming that the free individual of the Early Modern period had to fashion a persona in order to better cope with power relations (*Renaissance Self-fashioning*, 162), finds little resolute individuality even in this new shrewd individual: "The human subject itself began to seem remarkably unfree, the ideological product of the relations of power in a particular society. Whenever I focused sharply upon a moment of apparently autonomous self-fashioning, I found not an epiphany of identity freely chosen but a cultural artifact. If there remained traces of free choice, the choice was among possibilities whose range was strictly delineated by the social and ideological system in force" (256).[14]

By the time the *Cortegiano* and the *Furioso* appeared, courtly rhetoric was substantially endangering the humanist model.[15] Unlike humanist ideology, courtly ideology is meant to foster the power of the ruling house and to legitimate the position of those who aspire to sit among the powerful as well as that of the prince whom they serve in administrative and legislative faculties. It does not promote a democratic discourse for the intellectual of any social class, but an exclusionary discourse for people who belong, or want to belong, to the group in power either because of hereditary right or, as was increasingly becoming the norm, because of individual merit. As Heinrich Plett puts it, "Where the humanistic rhetoric strives toward an ethical renewal of man by way of persuasion (*genus deliberativum*), the courtly seeks primarily a stabilization of the political regime through the praise (*genus demonstrativum*) of its leading representative, the ruler. Where the humanist rhetoric envisages a moralizing of social being, the courtly aims to aestheticize it" (599). Courtly ideology therefore posits a less flexible self than does humanism. Machiavelli, for one, is quite pessimistic about man's ability to perfect his selfhood in the face of fortune's interventions and disruptions. The same could be said for Ariosto: in the *Furioso*, no goal is forever reached, and no relationship is forever stable.[16]

Castiglione makes the chief quality of the court intellectual not intelligence or a clear philosophical stand, but grace, nonchalance, and flexibility; in short, he praises his courtier for what amounts to a style of naturalized artfulness. In the *Cortegiano*, a "true" self is the product of careful construction: the courtier's purpose in public life, the author writes, is to form an identity ("vestirsi un altra persona") that is the product of a social and political discourse, "a pure commodity," as Frank Whigham puts it, "generated (however self-consciously) for conversational consumption" (631). Nowhere was human pliability more debated than in the many treatises on men, women, princes, courtiers, and lovers of the period, treatises that might have been written to fix individuals in given roles, Thomas Greene argues, but that actually did not, because it was thought that anyone could ascend the ladder of perfection through education ("Flexibility," 251). Castiglione's courtier may indeed have perceived his self-construction as empowering, rather than as a response to the social requirements and practical politics that dictated it, but he was no less a prisoner of power relations. This quasi-theatrical identity, moreover, must have caused some sense of self-estrangement or alienation; nevertheless, he chose not to reveal it.

The pliable self that constitutes so much a characteristic of the successful courtier is formed in language, Castiglione states, as a result of politically correct and commendable individual traits: "Vorrei . . . che si elegesse uno della compagnia ed a questo si desse carico di formar con parole un perfetto cortegiano" ("I would like . . . that one of us should be chosen and given the task of depicting in words a perfect courtier" [1, 12, 45]). This sentence is echoed in the other genre under consideration in this study, the romance epic, though interestingly not in Ariosto but in Tasso, who in his *Discorsi dell'arte poetica* aims at forming the idea of a perfect knight ("formar l'idea d'un perfetto cavaliero," *Prose*, 356). The notion of a shapable knightly self also informs the *Furioso* and constitutes its outward aim, but it has problematic connotations; Ariosto's men often seem to deviate from, or more or less consciously to resist, the epic's natural design of relating the assumption of power to the historical/imperial destiny being narrated.[17] The world in which these knights move seems too often out of joint; after all, the author's purpose is not to create the "perfectus vir," as the humanist Cristoforo Landino calls Aeneas, the prototypical hero of any epic (1:215), but instead to tell how his exemplary hero erred from the path of reason and duty and lost his selfhood: "per amor venne in furore e matto, / d'uom che sì saggio era stimato prima" ("driven raving mad by love—and he a man who had been always esteemed for his great prudence" [1, 2]).

Francesco De Sanctis is only partially correct, then, in writing that Ariosto's world is characterized by individualism and that each knight voluntarily obeys self-imposed laws of honor and love (492). I find the Ariostan hero much more constrained, his rationality often floundering when confronted with passions and his empowerment illusory. I also see the process of becoming a unified, coherent subject and of successfully integrating the psychic and the social, the goals of any epic hero, as being quite thorny in the *Furioso*, where social harmony is reachable only through leaps of the imagination. At times the split between inner demands and outer duties achieves grandiose proportions, as when a shaky self in Orlando becomes monstrous or nonexistent ("Non son, non sono io quel che paio in viso"; "I am not who my face proclaims me" [23, 128]). In other instances, the resistance to prescriptive behavior is dramatized through experiments in role reversal and cross-dressing, for difference is not posited *a priori* as natural and immediately visible (as Bradamante contends, "Ma chi dirà . . . s'io sono o s'io non son quel ch'è costei?"; "Who shall say . . . whether or not I am of the same sex as she?" [32, 102]), and identity can even be stolen (as in the case of Ricciardetto disguised as his twin sister). Yet in other moments, disunity and self-loss within the subject find violent expression in rituals of boasting and carnage or in self-reflective moments of isolation and thoughts of suicide. As chance buffets each character and makes a joke of everyone's best intentions, furor replaces self-control and desperation takes the place of reason. In Bartlett Giamatti's words, characters become "radically divided against, and within" themselves (*"Sfrenatura,"* 37). In the end, as Giuseppe Mazzotta ("Power and Play") insists, only the metaphor of play can dedramatize situations and give a certain order to this encircling madness: play as an enjoyable sequence of duels, jousts, and war games; play as a humorous display of human shortcomings and illusions; and, finally, play as the only exercise of the imagination capable of imparting a sense of sanity and purpose to a world in perpetual movement and conflict.[18]

The questioning of subjectivity, specifically of a subjectivity always in flux, always divided and dispersed, is also central to psychoanalysis. In this study I argue that, just as there is no place for the individual outside society, there is no place for the subject outside an Oedipal framework and a patriarchal organization of life, for entrance into language means entrance into the symbolic and into ideology. Psychoanalysis is an important tool for me, first because it stresses gender in the formation of one's identity, and second because it enables me to focus on the repression, dispersion, and alienation of an individual's psyche at the precise moment in which that individual's subjectivity is being celebrated. My intention is to foreground the instances of instability and dispersion of the subject as well as the moments of friction, defiance, and dissent that surface before a "correct" ending is superimposed and the characters subject themselves to social arrangements.

Psychic processes can easily be examined in the romance portion of Ariosto's *Furioso* (as Frye points out, the structure of the romance is not without links to the unconscious) [19] by chronicling, for example, the responses of his unsteady characters toward desire and the conflicts between self and other. As for Castiglione, his sense of the formation of the self duplicates the Lacanian concept of the self as a linguistic construction. Freud himself applies his theories to the Italian Renaissance from time to time, both in art (da Vinci and Michelangelo) and in the epic (Tasso's Tancredi and Clorinda episode). He also refers specifically to Ariosto in discussing the sources from which consciously or unconsciously a creative writer draws his material. [20]

No matter how consuming the process of reclaiming one's subjectivity was in the Renaissance, there is no question that women failed by and large to achieve the status of selves either by claiming a core identity or by publicizing a constructed "I" of their own. [21] Given their historical position, any individuality for women would have been the product not only of a social, public self subject to the authority of the ruler/prince but also of a private self subject to the authority of the father/husband in the privacy of the home. It was woman's dependence on man—his authority and his utterances (whether she was the object of a discourse on her self, as in Castiglione, or the object of a desire, as in Ariosto)—that in a sense allowed man to cast himself as a unified social being. In this construction, woman was the necessary non-self man needed in representation to define both who he was and who he was not (or did not want to appear to be). Ironically, this was the period in which discourse on woman, elaborated in countless treatises, became most fashionable. But with the exceptions of Moderata Fonte's treatise *Il merito delle donne* and Lucrezia Marinelli's *Nobiltà e eccellenza delle donne*, published much later in the century, this discourse was articulated exclusively by men, with the understood aim of constructing a normative woman for themselves and their society.

My assumption is that any representation of femininity reflects a construction of femininity anchored in cultural conventions and disciplined by them, as well as by an epistemological tradition that privileges man. This tradition places woman securely under male authority, since it conceptualizes a somewhat ordered society in which man stands as a rational being to whom woman is hierarchically subject through a socially and institutionally promoted heterosexual contract. By tracing the link between ideology and discourse and between discourse and the (always gendered) subject, I propose to explicate why Castiglione and Ariosto employ certain strategies in constructing identities and how their discursive practices end by investing the phallus with value.

Perhaps more directly than other genres, the treatise and the epic place men on the side of truth and knowledge and inscribe a set of homosocial and narcissistic ties that bind them to each other and to their male-oriented society. Customarily, treatises are devoted to philosophical, ethical, and political issues, traditionally the domain of men, for women have been excluded from participation in their construction both by custom and by ideology. Lionardo Bruni was clear on this point in "De studiis et litteris": "Rhetoric in all its forms," he argued, "—public discussion, forensic argument, logical fence, and the like—lies outside the province of woman" (126). The epic chronicles the growth into adulthood of a male hero of uncertain allegiances but good moral background, who gains understanding through deeds of courage and valor and is rewarded at maturity with a kingdom and a wife.[22] Women in epic narratives are usually cast on the "wrong" side of culture and progress: they are associated with losers (unless they function as rewards for winners) or, more generally, with transgression and turmoil.[23] When depicted as warriors, they are either represented as Amazon-like (thus not quite women) or described as temporarily engaged in warfare before fully embracing their femininity. Their reward for valor may be a husband (provided their virginity is not in doubt), and often land or a city, but never a kingdom, unless of course in the comic mode (Marfisa in the *Furioso* has already conquered India before joining the war). More often than not, women warriors are killed before the distribution of rewards, as with Virgil's Camilla.

Yet Castiglione and Ariosto can hardly be faulted for their attitudes toward women. Misogynist attacks were the norm in their century; the decades in which they published were, moreover, famous for producing lively manifestations of the *querelle des femmes,* although not in the virulent forms that the polemic took toward the end of the century. Still, both authors layered their works with praise of contemporary women and gave sympathetic renderings of fictional female characters.[24] As a result, *Il libro del cortegiano* is often taken as an early feminist treatise and read as a quasi-historical representation of the position of women in Renaissance Italy. Similarly, Ariosto's lady knights are firmly placed within the pantheon of liberated, assertive females. The *Furioso* even opens with a modified Virgilian *incipit* in which women are added to the traditional pairing of men and arms: "Le donne, i cavallier, l'arme, gli amori" ("ladies, knights, arms, and love" [1, 1]). Finally, both Castiglione and Ariosto openly complain about the treatment of women in literature. Castiglione attributes female obscurity to male writers' envy (3, 76, 281); Ariosto blames the same culprit but claims that the problem is finally being redressed (37, 2).

My study chastises neither author for his approach to the problematic status of women. On the contrary, I examine the construction of femininity in the *Cortegiano* and the *Furioso* precisely because Castiglione and Ariosto are open-minded toward women, because they give women positive roles, and because they have written some of the most celebrated passages in praise of this gender to appear before, during, or after the sixteenth century. It is precisely because they are perceived as protofeminists (although they are sometimes explicitly antifeminist)—as well as because they enjoy a canonical status—that they provide a rewarding forum for studying the role of cultural compromises in the formation of subjectivity.

What Castiglione and Ariosto create, I argue, are fictional constructs, even when they use real names and characteristics based on the historical individuals bearing those names. These constructs are not mimetic but ideological, religious, mythical, rhetorical, and political offerings that reflect the authors' cultural and intellectual tastes. Representation does not capture truth but constructs it, just as Zeuxis, an ever-present figure in Renaissance texts, paints an image of the ideal woman from the body parts of five women chosen for their representative beauty.[25] This collage of fragments is made to stand, then, for reality and its representation, for the object and its illustration. But it is a personal construction, for it reflects the artist's will to represent his view and his desire at a specific historical and cultural moment. It is a construction that denies the individuality of each female subject even as it makes woman a metaphor. It is a construction based on sexual difference and therefore "naturally" places woman in a hierarchical position in relation to man. Finally, it takes woman's own specificity and historicity away from her through assimilation into a current idea of Woman. This universalized Woman is then offered as a normative exemplar for real women, one both desirable to imitate because endowed with traditional qualities and impossible to imitate because too perfect.

The point therefore is not whether Castiglione and Ariosto portray good or bad female characters, or whether they naturalize certain female characteristics and espouse a phallocentric or a feminist system of representation. Rather, it is that the women they present have little historical verisimilitude. Even historical verisimilitude has, in any case, to be understood as construed by the individuals who control signifying practices (i.e., men) and who, like women, being informed by the ideology specific to their historical situation, can respond only in gendered ways. In this context, the court lady is not more real than the woman warrior because she existed and the female warrior perhaps did not. Both are male representations of femininity, and both are produced through a discourse on femininity.

As is often the case, there is a discrepancy in the *Cortegiano* and in the *Furioso* between what the text says and what the subtext reveals.[26] I work at the interstices of this double discourse, in the gap between the superficial, polite, appreciative, and celebrative discourse on womanhood, and the less evident discourse on woman that often intrudes into both works to reverse or question the dominant representation of femininity. My hypothesis is that since the representation of women in literature reflects and legitimizes ideological constructions of their gender and since this in turn rationalizes a certain metaphysics of order, women (like men) must be presented as securely positioned within structures of power. How Castiglione and Ariosto imbed these structures in their works is worth examining. My thesis is that Castiglione opts to include women within his ordered, courtly world and has them participate, paradoxically but cunningly, in the enunciation of the very argument that eliminates them as subjects. Thus, no matter how progressive the discourse on the court ladies is per se, the *Cortegiano* does not undermine the social order by empowering women. Unlike Castiglione, Ariosto portrays iconoclastic female characters and experiments with gender reversals, transvestism, and cross-dressing. Nonetheless, he too recontains disorder by reaffirming the need for alignment through normalization (marriage) or elimination (death or displacement to mythical lands) of the different female characters. To be sure, Castiglione and Ariosto are not ideologues bent on fostering women's status quo. Still, because of the genres they use, they need to end their narratives by reaffirming the values of their society. Whatever is improper has to be distanced or harnessed, marginalized or legitimized, in the cases both of women and of men. For women, legitimation means not only social but also sexual conformity.

In his study of the Italian Renaissance, Burckhardt marvels at the power Italian women seemed to have in their society and, as confirmation, focuses on texts in which women were highly praised and their contributions recognized. The problem I see with this reading is that Burckhardt confuses literary representations of fictional women with real women and interprets the Renaissance controversy on woman's worth as progressive (provided that the author rejected an openly misogynist stance) rather than as an exercise in ideological gymnastics. Thus his conclusion that the freedom women seemed to enjoy in Castiglione and Ariosto's texts reflects the freedom real women had in Renaissance Italy seems faulty to me.[27] There were, of course, women in positions of power and authority in the courts of the time, and some historical women, such as Caterina Sforza, fought in wars and directed warfare. But they were few and often assumed power by default. They took their husband's place during the minority of their heir, but only temporarily; similarly, they substituted for their mate at war and in times of illness, but again only briefly.

As many cultural historians have pointed out, the Early Modern period experienced an increasingly explicit division between the workplace and the home, probably as a result of the crumbling of feudal traditions and the flourishing of capitalist enterprises. This dichotomization of spheres of action into public and private, rulers and citizens, employers and employees, seems to have brought a clearer separation between the role of the husband and that of the wife. The "bourgeois sex-role system," as Joan Kelly-Gadol calls it, was in place (38). Man came to be identified with production and the outside world (the business place, the market, the office), and woman with reproduction and the domestic (the household, the nursery).[28] Society as a whole was understood to be ordered according to a dualism in which the subordinate relation of man to God, subject to ruler, child to father, and wife to husband, was hierarchically correct and helped maintain a workable status quo. The monogamous family reproduced this ideology, consumed it, and constructed subjects reflecting it. Embedded in history, literature could only recast this state of being, this new view of subjectivity and individuality, with its concurrent canonization of patriarchal interests.

The image of the domesticated woman exemplified prevailing thinking about femininity within the family.[29] In drawing the ideal court lady, Castiglione invites the courtier to be practical rather than idealistic and to fix his mind on a marriageable woman, a lady of a social status and background comparable to his. The woman to admire is thus neither the most beautiful nor the most forbidden, but rather the most steadfast, chaste, and available; she is not individualistic, but companionable. In short, Castiglione enforces contemporary boundaries of permissible sexuality, although he seemingly espouses the precepts of courtly love. Ariosto deploys many chivalric ideals in the *Furioso*, but he funnels them perceptibly toward a notion of a decorous marriage sustained by a form of romantic love rather than toward an adulterous tie, as in the famous Breton antecedents of Tristan-Iseult and Guinevere-Lancelot.

The normalization and domestication of women were concurrent with the disciplining of sexual life. Ideas on female sexuality were mainly Aristotelian: since women were physically weaker than men (*De generatione animalium*) and rationally inferior to them (*Politics*), they needed to be guided and restrained.[30] The varied literary genres of the time, from the treatise to the epic to the novella to the love poem, consistently investigated the sexualized female body in order to appropriate it as "right" (in which case they idealized it) or as "wrong" (in which case they described it as problematic or grotesque). Surprisingly, even the right body could at times be eliminated because it was too unapproachable (as in the case of Ariosto's Isabella), and the wrong body (for example, Bradamante dressed as a man) could be recuperated, as long as

the woman underwent a process of feminization and domestica-
tion. A third approach to the female body sometimes appeared. It
presented it as neither good nor bad, but as having an essentially
allegorical function and thus no narrative weight. It was easy to
empower an allegorical woman since she was not real, although
even in this case her energies were directed toward helping the
male hero. Logistilla's function in the *Furioso*, for example, is to
make sure that Ruggiero mends his ways and becomes a Christian
man and a true epic hero.[31]

My general argument is that women as court ladies are highly
regarded in Castiglione's *Cortegiano* because they are indispensable.
They preside over the book's lengthy conversations; indeed, there
would be no conversation without them. Yet this role is hardly
more than ceremonial, since women's task is not to converse but
to listen. As it turns out, the court ladies are necessary, not be-
cause they contribute to the discussion but because in order to
universalize the representation of an ideal courtier and his com-
panion, both sexes must be present. This allows for criticism to
remain within the group, which explains the need both for the
women's presence and for their silence. Positioned as the subject
of a discourse but not as the speaking "I," the court lady finds
herself presiding mutely over the circuitous demise of her sub-
jectivity. The courtier, in contrast, has the opportunity to present
himself as the classical, coherent, socially adjusted man of reason,
a man engaged throughout the text in narcissistically talking about
himself and staking out a territory.

Once the court ladies accept that it is right for them to exist in
conversation as bodies—literally—they cannot raise themselves to
the place of the subject, to the same level as the assured, ever-witty,
and authoritative male voice that moves the narrative forward.
What guarantees men's power is that the court ladies do not merely
accept that the courtiers can appropriate them for the construction
of their own identity or simply consent to their own positioning as
silent listeners within the diegesis of the text. They are also oblig-
ingly made to agree with what is being said about them in the
mimesis, because they have so fully internalized the principle that
others can speak for them that they are even left to wonder why
so many good stories about their gender are known only by men.

Finally, the court ladies are made to support the explanation that their nonparticipation is to their personal advantage ("commodità") since, unlike the courtiers, they can refuse unwanted duties ("fatica"). Thus, a connection is established between women and leisure, and a new set of values reconfirms society's claim that it is undesirable for the court ladies to pursue intellectual activities by paradoxically presenting this non-choice as a personal choice and as a powerful tool in their hands.

Ariosto reaches narrative harmony vis-à-vis women by subsuming them to culture and society and thus sealing off disorder. In this process, the woman who eventually acquiesces finds her presence in the text easily legitimized; rebellion and resentment, although at times portrayed as empowering, entail expurgation from the plot. To be sure, the length of the *Furioso* allows numerous possibilities of self-definition for women, including transgression. For instance, Angelica, the text's elusive object of desire, is represented as a never-ending threat to the knights' customary loyalty toward their king. However, when she chooses a man of lower rank and thus stops reflecting the desires that the men project onto her, she is dispatched to the mythical land of Cathay. What causes her movement from the utmost signifier of desire to a redundant object within the ethos of the epic? Put more generally, what would allow woman to be accommodated within the Law-of-the-Father? I argue that as Ariosto shifts the narrative of *Orlando furioso* from romance to epic and moves from digressive plots to ethically coherent goals, as he eliminates the father figure of Atlante and espouses the father figure of Merlino,[32] he also chooses to consign Angelica, the prototypical romance heroine, to oblivion and to reward Bradamante, the prototypical epic heroine, with married bliss. Angelica is identified with romance and deviation (she comes from the East, after all), and Bradamante with epic and closure; her determination to find and marry the man of her choice is eventually made to stand against Angelica's futile and sterile flight from any choice.

Transgression can indeed not only be recuperated but also be rewritten as useful to institutional strategies. Olimpia, for example, is essentially restored to her society after she starts to behave in expected feminine ways. Even when women are allowed to go so far beyond the limitations of their sex as to experiment with cross-dressing (Bradamante) and possibly unorthodox longings (Fiordispina), their behavior is normalized in the end when they are given more strictly defined gender positions for the sake of social harmony and political needs.

As in Castiglione, representations of female desire in Ariosto are strongly informed by current social values regarding what is correct and incorrect for women to desire. These representations tend to fall into one of two categories: the sexual, in which the desiring women are punished (Alcina, Dalinda, and Fiordispina); and the asexual, in which they are rewarded (Isabella). When desire does not fall neatly into either category, it is left out (Marfisa) or subsumed to that of man (the second part of the Olimpia story, Angelica before her encounter with Medoro). Willfully choosing to escape man's desire is sadistically condemned (Lidia burns in Hell) or religiously praised (Isabella ascends to Heaven), but in either case it requires the woman's death and thus puts her beyond desire altogether. Running away from the Law-of-the-Father, as Isabella does, is not really a choice, for this course of action also ends with the woman's death. Having neither father nor any substitute for his law is also pernicious and needs to be corrected (as in the cases of Olimpia's abandonment and the Mankilling women). Women in Ariosto do not at first accept this normalizing phallocentrism as wholeheartedly as Castiglione's court ladies do, but eventually they too learn their social role and the reason for their education into femininity; at this point their story ends.

I devote three chapters to Castiglione and five to Ariosto. In Chapter 1, "The Production of Discourse, or How to Be Left Out by Staying In," I first examine the interplay between linguistic marginalization and the construction of identities and then explore how ideological assumptions about femaleness and femininity legitimate the displacement of woman as speaking subject. My aim is to show how the strategy of seeming to give the court ladies control of a discourse in which only men talk works to frame the ladies' agreement to what is being said. This reinforces the hegemonic discourse and pre-empts women's chances of providing a different, personal, and perhaps subversive, point of view.

In Chapter 2, "Cutting and Sewing: The Representation of the Court Lady," I pursue the investigation further, contrasting the unofficial discourse on woman that occasionally intrudes into the text with the official, progressive discourse on the court lady that runs through Book 3. The unofficial discourse presents a more threatening (because more real) woman, who is often the object of an array of misogynistic attacks; the official discourse creates Woman, a construction of normative femininity based on current social and culture-related practices. Ironically, this fictional product best exposes the institutional duplicity of a politics of order that associates women with disorder while retaining mythological examples of correct womanhood as positive and easy to imitate.

In Chapter 3, the last on the *Cortegiano*, "The Comic Bond: Castiglione on Jokes Via Freud," I concentrate on Castiglione's *facezie* on women in Book 2 and apply Freudian insights to the triangular structure of the dirty joke. My aim is to show what happens when woman is not allowed to be the teller of a joke and what positions are available to the court lady when she is the object of sexual humor. I also review a number of specific strategies (such as point of view and subject position) used in the construction of sexual identities and speculate on how woman—both as a character and as a reader—is persuaded to accept the constructions offered.

I move to Ariosto in Chapter 4, "The Narcissistic Woman: Angelica and the Mystique of Femininity." Here I use themes from Freud's "On Narcissism" and Sarah Kofman's critique of this essay in *The Enigma of Woman* to explain Angelica's appeal to the men pursuing her, as well as their fetishistic use of structures of avowal/disavowal to counteract the threat of her narcissistic nature.

The next two chapters center on Olimpia and Isabella; both their destinies are marked by an undying faithfulness to their freely chosen companions. But here their stories diverge, not because of any change in the two women or even in their characterization (blond hair, beautiful face, noble status), but rather because Bireno, Olimpia's beloved, is faithless and Zerbino, Isabella's fiancé, is a paragon of faithfulness. No matter: both women lose. Olimpia is abandoned, although she is later rescued in a problematic fairy tale finale, and Isabella has a tragic and definitely undeserved ending. In Chapter 5, "Ego Games / Body Games: The Representation of Olimpia," I examine the portrayal of woman as disorder by concentrating on the shift in Olimpia's characterization from imperious and articulate to acquiescent and silent. In

Chapter 6, "(Dis)Orderly Death, or How to Be In by Being Out: The Case of Isabella," I investigate the connections between power and sex and between self-identity and self-loss. My aim is to show where a politics of rape leads and how a dead woman can be used to refashion a man's sense of self-worth.

Freudian and Lacanian theories on sexual identity and gender identification bear on an episode of male potency and self-assurance in Chapter 7, "Transvestite Love: Gender Troubles in the Fiordispina Story." Here I follow the progress of the Bradamante-Fiordispina-Ricciardetto triangle from a moment of undifferentiated sexuality fostered by cross-dressing to a reaffirmation of sexual difference to an alignment with the law to a remastering of woman.

The last chapter, "Un-dressing the Warrior / Re-dressing the Woman: The Education of Bradamante," incorporates the strands from the chapters on Angelica (order/disorder), Olimpia (empowerment/disempowerment), Isabella (faithfulness/faithlessness), and Fiordispina (dressing/cross-dressing). Here I apply psychoanalytical insights on the feminine to examine the strategies the author uses in his normalization of femininity. Ariosto's program requires that Bradamante slowly give up her desire for independence to allow her to epitomize the best in womanhood. As a result, her cross-dressing as a woman warrior is represented as temporary: it is not so much a transgressive posture as one that is in the past and thus justified for a woman pressured to pursue her beloved even into the woods in order to reach her goal of progenitrix and further the institutional purposes of the epic.

As the examples of Castiglione and Ariosto indicate, the discourse on Woman and women in the Renaissance is articulated within an array of genres, philosophical positions, and intellectual postures. In this discourse, women are cast in both assertive and docile roles, and in both complex and simpleminded plots. They often add voices of discord. They are at times represented as capable of overcoming all constraints; at other times they are positioned by their culture as obstacles. Their feminization often replicates, even as it hides, the very feminization that their authors had to experience vis-à-vis their own relationship with the prince/patron at court. No matter how they are characterized, however, they end up recontained (even happily recontained, as in

Bradamante's case) or expelled (again sometimes happily so, as in Angelica's case), at one with the hierarchical and enclosing society that could envision a freer order but in the final analysis could not allow women to be too different.

Does this mean that there is little room for a female reader to enjoy the two texts without masochistically accepting her own marginal position in it (in the case of Castiglione's work) or her own reinscription into the Law-of-the-Father (in the case of Ariosto)? Although I only occasionally take this topic up, I would argue that both works offer moments of disruption and ironic reversal, what Bakhtin would call *heteroglossia,* to justify some pleasurable connivance with the teller on the part of the female reader.[33] Two examples will suffice. In a humorous rebuttal in the *Cortegiano,* Emilia Pio questions the terms of the Magnifico's defense of her sex: "Or non intendemo già in che modo voi ci diffendiate" ("Now we can't at all understand your way of defending us" [3, 17, 223]). The response can be read in at least two ways. First, it can be seen as a confirmation of the fact that women are incapable of understanding, let alone engaging in, intellectual conversations. In this reading, Pio complains because the level of the talk is too high for her. The response can also be read as a humorous attack on the uselessness of intellectual conversations about a subject—woman—of which men know little, but on which they love to expound. It is clearly this position that most engages a female reader.

Similarly, there is a scene in Ariosto's Canto 12 in which Angelica plays a trick on Orlando and Ferraù, who are locked in combat, by hiding Orlando's helmet. Here, too, the action can be read in at least two ways. First, it can be seen as a restatement of the fact that women are frivolous and irresponsible. In this reading, Angelica confirms that she is as childish as the men desiring her want her to be. The scene can also be read as a humorous rebuttal of the seriousness of men's triangular desires, desires that cause them to fight for the love of a woman-object (as in the Girardian plot) or for each other's understanding and respect (as in the Kofman / Sedgwick rewriting). Again, this last position is more fruitful and more pleasurable for the female reader.

A woman reader may also find points of identification with women described as still searching for a unified gender identity

(Fiordispina and Bradamante) or whose involvement in discourse is not specifically sexual (the court ladies enjoying being laughed at in the section on puns in Book 2). Although stable, normative subject positions are enforced at the end, it is the resistance detectable in the gaps that provides pleasure. In this respect, a process of Gramscian negotiation between what the text represents and the sociocultural, aesthetic, and political codes a reader brings to the reading may offer more fluid modes of identification and a more active position for a female reader pondering the ambiguities of the narrative and the shifts in representation.

PART

I

Castiglione

CHAPTER ONE

The Production of Discourse, or How to Be Left Out by Staying In

I have plenty of evidence to assume that no woman, as opposed to male, has ever failed to enjoy the possibly mortifying experience of being reorganized in the course of incarnating my vision of her.
—Josef von Sternberg, *Fun in a Chinese Laundry*,
120

I N *Il libro del cortegiano*, a group of intellectuals associated with the Gonzaga court at Urbino gathers one evening to discuss how to present a perfect image of the court through the courtiers that constitute it. This company of noblemen (poets, philosophers, musicians, and politicians) soon discovers the subject to be unexpectedly rich. Their conversation lasts for five evenings or perhaps more; four of these are transcribed by the company's fictional scribe, Baldassarre Castiglione.

The courtiers start by affirming their distinctive position in the social order and the importance of their common cultural background. They then offer themselves as models of good judgment ("bon giudicio") and as evidence of the gracious values of the court they are celebrating.[1] In time, the discourse would prove important not only for the participants but also for those whose ideal image the text inscribes. Castiglione's rhetorically self-created courtier became the aesthetic, cultural, political, moral, and even religious model for any would-be courtier in Europe,[2] and *Il libro del cortegiano*, published twenty years after the original ideas were first put on paper, grew into one of the most widely circulated Renaissance texts.[3]

The second longest section of the *Cortegiano*, Book 3, centers on the "institution" of the court lady.[4] Through his court spokesmen, Castiglione acknowledges the value of the "donna di palazzo," offers her practical counsel on how better to fulfill her role, and provides her with examples of virtuous femininity on which she is quietly advised to fashion, or refashion, herself. Every critic agrees that the female figure is of unusual importance in this text and that her influence is not limited to the pages in which she is the official object of conversation. Ghino Ghinassi hypothesizes that Castig-

lione had planned to introduce a lengthy discourse on femininity
in the first draft, even though it appeared extraneous to the topic
defined by the title. He also suggests that Castiglione may have
originally intended to write an independent defense of the female
sex and decided later to incorporate his ideas on womankind into
the text instituting the courtier.[5]

Given the times, Castiglione's attitudes toward women are sur-
prisingly open. Like the German Cornelius Agrippa (1486–1535),
who wrote a celebrated conduct book on this gender, Castiglione
is well aware of the pressure that social conventions exert in en-
forcing female submission; like the Spanish humanist Juan Vives
(1492–1540), another influential writer of treatises, he emphasizes
the formative value of education and asks that his court lady "abbia
notizie di lettere, di musica, di pittura e sappia danzar e festeggiare"
("be knowledgeable about literature and painting, . . . [and] know
how to dance and play games" [3, 9, 216]).[6] Moreover, although
the text offers a comparable amount of space to arguments for and
against women's worth, the general impression is that misogynis-
tic views do not carry the same weight as progressive ones. To start
with, the tasks of choosing the topic of conversation and of direct-
ing it are assigned to a woman, Emilia Pio, and the dialogue owes
its existence to another woman, the duchess Elisabetta Gonzaga,
who presides over it in the welcoming ambience of her rooms
away from her husband's inhibiting presence. Finally, the later re-
ception of the text would lead us to believe that it was thanks to the
numerous allusions to women that the *Cortegiano* enjoyed such a
wide readership. A number of European authors (Montaigne, for
example) used the book as a reference manual and as a catalogue
of *exempla* of femininity; some "educators" even dedicated the text
to women because they considered it a work on and for them.[7]

Could things have been so good for women in the Renaissance?
Was perhaps Burckhardt not overly optimistic when he declared
that "there was no question of 'woman's rights' or 'female eman-
cipation,'" during the period "because the thing itself was a matter
of course" (251)?[8] It is my intention in these pages to contest the
idea that a woman is important to a text simply because she is in it
or is indispensable to a conversation because she is allowed to sit
among the discussants. My aim is not to catalogue Castiglione's
interventions in favor of or against women or to rebut the argu-

ments of the various detractors of womankind. I propose, instead, to concentrate on the place reserved in the text for the court lady as a real figure outside the discourse that institutes her as an ideal figure. A study of the discursive practices of *Il libro del cortegiano* should allow us to see how woman is presented in a text that so absolutely, so continuously, and so willingly requires her presence. In view of the essential function of discourse in the formation of the "I," an examination of the crystallization of the speakable and of the spoken in the *Cortegiano* should prove both challenging and fruitful.

Castiglione uses a number of discursive tactics throughout his text to exclude woman from a theoretical construction while seemingly including her by assigning her the selection and direction of the conversation. After reviewing them, I will concentrate specifically on the first two, with occasional references to the other three.[9] The first is to have woman absent as "instituter" of the dialogue even as the courtiers institute her as a necessary presence in courtly life. In this construction, woman finds herself implicated both physically as messenger between two men and structurally as personification of order. Her participation is in any case exterior, because the order of the discourse does not belong to her.

The second is to demonstrate that woman is too incoherent to be discursively present because she is incapable of talking about herself rationally and can only inadequately represent herself as she is or should be. This incoherence is underlined at a key moment in the narrative by her inability to reply verbally to an invitation to speak; she has to resort, as we will see in the next chapter, to hysterical and excessive gestures. Unable to express desires, she is erased as a desiring subject and projected as a desired object; unable to tell the "truth" about herself, she is assimilated into falsity and dissimulation.

Castiglione's third strategy is to declare woman non-representable and radically different, neither real nor reconstructable on the model of the court ladies present at the conversation. Soon after, however, the discussants assume the task of representing her visually and culturally in a phantasmatic manner and through a process of mystification and fetishization. In this way, woman better reflects the person creating her and is better absorbed into the unitary system of her creator.

The fourth strategy is to freeze woman in a perfect pictorial, sculptural, and literary image and to make her a symbol of beauty for the use of the courtiers describing her. In the same breath, it becomes necessary for the courtiers to speak negatively of some marked, and thus dangerous, sexual characteristics in her.

The fifth strategy is to equip woman with a collection of narratives for her own consumption, mini-stories that reflect her construction as sexual object, so that both the discourse that molds her at court and the tales that piece her together as a mythical entity present an identical person. This person knows and understands the patriarchal values around which her exemplary image is being codified and acquiesces to that imposition because of the elements of immutability and of order present in every ideological construct. Woman can then mirror herself in this ideal self either narcissistically (if she identifies with the enunciator of the discourse, who foregrounds her by speaking about her) or masochistically (if she identifies—as a woman—with the enunciated, that is, with the desires of the enunciator of the discourse, conventionally a man, who creates her in this fashion).

For the first time in vernacular literature, Piero Floriani writes of the *Cortegiano*, the courtiers talk as peers ("un ambiente di *pares*," 131) and represent themselves as living exemplars of the model of courtiership they are proposing. Floriani has no doubt about the identity of the *pares* of the courtiers' discourse. Castiglione himself provides a list of noble and talented men, among whom are Ottaviano Fregoso, his brother Federico, the Magnifico Juliano de' Medici, Pietro Bembo, Cesare Gonzaga, Count Ludovico da Canossa, Gasparo Pallavicino, Ludovico Pio, Morello da Ortona, Pietro da Napoli, Roberto da Bari, Bernardo Bibbiena, Unico Aretino, Ioanni Cristoforo Romano, Pietro Monte, Anton Maria Terpandro, and Nicolò Frisio (1, 5, 37). Other characters appear later, such as Serafino Aquilano, mentioned a few pages on, and more important, the prefect Francesco Maria della Rovere, Duke Guidubaldo's adopted son, who is absent for most of the first evening but very much present in successive gatherings. These are the gentlemen of the house ("i gentilomini della casa," 1, 5, 36), who assemble at night in the duchess's private apartment for a few hours of pleasing entertainment.

Gentlewomen are not mentioned, but we know that sitting in

a circle were "un omo ed una donna, fin che donne v'erano, chè quasi sempre il numero degli omini era molto maggiore" ("alternately one man and one woman, as long as there were women, for invariably they were outnumbered by the men" [1, 6, 38]). Apart from the duchess, three women are named: Emilia Pio, her sister-in-law; Constanza Fregoso, sister of the loquacious Ottaviano and Federico; and Margherita Gonzaga. They are not listed at the beginning but introduced as necessary to the mimesis of the text. Even though there are clearly fewer women than the seventeen men named, four are quite an underrepresentation. How does one explain this omission in Castiglione? "Language—like all semiotic systems—has," Umberto Eco writes, "the ability to render present what is not present (even if only in the possible world circumscribed by our assertions). Because of this, says Abelard, the expression 'nulla rosa est' ('there is no rose,' 'such a thing like a rose has never existed') in some manner brings to our mind the rose" (258). To name the court ladies present at the meeting or even to say that they are not named would make their absence inconceivable. But forgetting to name them means that women are not intellectually present, that they are not *pares* and certainly not considered such by the men engaged in conversation. Since they are not protagonists, they cannot, to follow up on Floriani's point, represent themselves as living examples of the model being proposed.

Yet they are present, necessarily present. The conversation itself could not develop without them, since they are appointed to give order to it and to make it proceed satisfactorily. Such is the explicit role that Castiglione assigns to the duchess and Emilia Pio: that of creating a place where a discourse of power can be held. The duchess is potent in this case, not because she is cast against an impotent husband (and Guidubaldo's sexual impotence, textualized as known by everybody, opens up a larger discourse on other psychical and political impotencies in Urbino), but because as a key alternative representative of the court, she better illustrates the feasibility or the permissibility of the arguments that develop under her direction. Moreover, the women are present because they are indispensable to the familiar social and political world the author portrays and idealizes, a world whose realistic representation requires their inclusion. But they are present and valuable only as long as they assent to remain within the limits of the discourse that forms them in this way. As Foucault writes ("The Subject and Power," 428), a relationship of power is possible only when it is understood that the individuals over whom power is exerted are free subjects. And the reason that individuals freely submit to the dominant ideology, according to Althusser, is that it represents their current position and beliefs in the world in which they live.[10] The court ladies could confirm this point, for they are represented throughout the book as free subjects freely subjecting themselves to power relations with which they seem to live comfortably.

On a typical evening at the Urbino court, Castiglione writes, the courtiers would spend time not only dancing and playing music but also conversing. We do not know why the subject of the ideal courtier is chosen over the others suggested, since each topic seems equally propitious. Apart from Gonzaga's proposal to discuss madness, the various submissions concern love and the skirmishes between the sexes. All are typical arguments of courtly love literature and also, in a revised context, of humanistic culture. Gasparo Pallavicino suggests discussing the deceptions or illusions created by love; Ottaviano Fregoso proposes the sufferings and amorous outbursts of anger, a submission Bembo backs up with a recommendation that they explore the slights of love ("sdegni d'amore," 1, 11, 44). Two proposals centering on women are immediately eliminated: one, quite obscene, by Serafino Aquilano, and one on women's cruelty and ingratitude, by Aretino. All recommendations are rejected except the "game" proposed by Federico Fregoso on how to institute/constitute a courtier.[11] Emilia Pio assigns the development of the subject to Ludovico da Canossa, not because she thinks he knows how to expound it better than the others, but because his style guarantees controversies and, therefore, can better engender the sequence of *confirmatio* and *refutatio* necessary to a stimulating conversation.

Women do not participate in any of these proposals. It is thus emblematic that from the start Emilia Pio chooses not to propose a subject because she wants to avoid the trouble: "Delibero proporre un gioco, del quale penso dover aver poco biasmo e men fatica; e questo sarà ch'ognun proponga secondo il parer suo un gioco non più fatto" ("I want to suggest a game which I think will cause me little criticism and even less trouble. And this is that each one of us should suggest some game he likes that has not been played before" [1, 6, 38]). Even when Pallavicino asks her the reasons for this voluntary silence, Pio avoids the question and takes refuge in the duchess's authority by calling on Elisabetta Gonzaga to ratify her desire not to speak.

In the first draft of the *Cortegiano*, each woman excludes herself from the conversation by naming a substitute courtier ("procuratore") to talk for her, a decision that Bernardo Bibbiena reiterates when it seems to come under question: "Non sapete voi, signora madonna Constanza—disse—che le donne questa sera non hanno da parlare?" (Don't you know, my lady Constanza, he said, that women this evening should not talk? [*Cort.* I, f. 17]). In the final edition, when it comes time for Constanza Fregoso to offer a proposal, the duchess intervenes to impose silence on women, since "madonna Emilia non vole affaticarsi in trovar gioco alcuno, sarebbe pur ragione che l'altre donne partecipassino di questa commodità, ed esse ancor fussino esente di tal fatica per questa sera" ("signora Emilia is unwilling to give herself the trouble of thinking of a game, it is only right for the other ladies to enjoy the same privilege and also be exempt from making any effort this evening" [1, 7, 39]).

When the duchess indicates that speaking of important matters is a burden, she gets an interesting answer in response. "E che gran peso è però questo?" Aretino comments to her remark. "Chi è tanto sciocco che quando sa fare una cosa non la faccia a tempo conveniente?" ("But what is this great burden? Who is so foolish, when he knows how to do something, as not to do it in his own good time?" [2, 5, 109]). One can infer that, given the same onus, women know neither how to talk nor how to talk in a suitable way, and thus, being irrational and loquacious, they need to hold their tongues. Even the duchess is playfully silenced soon thereafter. At the very moment she gets ready to answer Aretino's query on the meaning of the letter "S" on her diadem, her interlocutor suddenly asks her to keep quiet, although he himself invited her to reply: "Non parlate, Signora, che non è ora il vostro loco di parlare" ("No, madam, it is not your turn to speak now" [1, 9, 42]). The sentence is also present in the first draft (f. 16), though in a slightly more colloquial tone (in the final edition "signora" replaces "figliola bella" [my beautiful child]).

When is it woman's turn to speak? As we have seen, the possibility of speaking is taken away from both named and unnamed women, and the duchess and her deputy intervene only in their role of normalizing and dedramatizing content and context. The duchess's first intrusion, for example, is to reproach Bibbiena for not respecting the agreed-on sequence of proof and disproof. The second interruption is similar; it too is made to recall the order of enunciation and not to form the order of what is enunciated, for the duchess urges the company not to stray from the original intention: the institution of the courtier (1, 32, 70). Only those who know can depict through words ("formar con parole") in this treatise, only those possessing subjectivity and rationality can speak. The point is reiterated by Canossa: "Quello adunque che principalmente importa ed è necessario al cortegiano per parlare e scriver bene, estimo io che sia e sapere; perchè chi non sa e nell'animo non ha cosa che meriti essere intesa, non po nè dirla nè scriverla" ("What the courtier especially requires in order to speak and write well, therefore, is knowledge, because the man who lacks knowledge and has nothing in his mind worth hearing has nothing worth writing or speaking" [1, 33, 72]).

Since speaking expresses one's "I" and one's desires, those unable to speak cannot constitute themselves as social and sexual beings.[12] In *Il libro del cortegiano* woman is not pushed aside for her individual peculiarities, which are denied her in the process that assimilates womanhood into the discourse of oneness linking the court lady to the courtier. Rather, she is excluded for a number of intellectual, political, and philosophical reasons that predicate femininity as *physis*, matter and body (and thus spontaneously assimilable to what Lacan calls the Imaginary), and masculinity as *logos*, mind and spirit (and thus naturally associable to the Lacanian symbolic). In other words, woman is removed from the intellectual circuit and canceled from the verbal sphere, not because she is other *than* man, but because she is other *from* man. If her subjectivity were fully accepted, she could prove destabilizing to the person who needs to create her as a mirror of himself or who would rather project her outside history by seeing her, for example, as a sign of beauty.

The problem, then, is not that the court lady is not allowed to talk—she does talk at times—but that her comments are irrelevant to the discourse. She has spoken in other places and on other occasions, but since we cannot judge the seriousness of the conversation, this is a moot issue. Yet, she must be present, because, through her silent association with the hegemonic discourse, she helps maintain the desired order within the group, an order dependent on her acquiescence.

There is, of course, something quite valuable in being assigned to preside over the production of a text. But the image created inside the circle is much more important than silently presiding over that image. It is the topic of conversation, not the ambience surrounding that conversation, that forms the courtier and *Il libro del cortegiano*. The court lady has no access to this construction; the rational order of the discourse does not belong to her anywhere, no matter the topic. This is in tune with the general position of women in a period in which men were busy questioning their own identity and in the process also codified that of others. As Catherine Belsey reflects, "From the discourses defining power relations in the state women were simply absent; in the definition of power relations within the family their position was inconsistent and to some degree contradictory. While the autonomous subject of liberalism was in the making, women had no single or stable place from which to define themselves as independent beings. In this sense they both were and were not subjects" (*Subject of Tragedy*, 149–50).

There is more to this exclusion of women's voices. From the start the courtiers' conversation is defined as a pastime, a moment of relaxation and mirth for busy courtiers spending, as Wayne Rebhorn wittily writes, "night after night in the self-contained playground of Urbino's palazzo" (196). One would think that women could excel in discussing inconsequential topics, in mocking others' statements, or in directing salacious remarks, since they have often been reproached for engaging in these activities and associated culturally with leisure and escapism. But play can also be a subversive activity; serious, codified beliefs may be destabilized under the pretense that the courtiers' exercise is just a game. Thomas Greene notices, for example, that a good number of speeches begin with the participle *ridendo*, "laughing" ("*Il cortegiano*," 9), as if it were imperative for the group to emphasize playfulness even in the most serious moments.

It is precisely their playful mood, of course, that allows the courtiers to rewrite their role at court, not once but twice, first in Books 1 and 2 and then, in a quite far-reaching move of empowerment, in Book 4, when even the Magnifico complains that they have elevated themselves too far, or too dangerously, above their status. To create this powerful role, it is necessary that a tight rein be kept on both the mimesis and the diegesis of the text. If the courtiers' game were one of self-understanding, for instance, the court ladies' input would only complicate matters by opening up a space for different, perhaps differing, views. Or worse, the ladies could reveal the men's game as precisely that, so that no matter how much the courtiers' professional image were improved in conversation, it would be understood that nothing substantive could change in their everyday life or in their relations of submission to the prince. Thus, the court ladies' task needs to be a specific, well-defined, and official one, that of facilitating the passage of words spoken and approved by other people, from the initial concept to the formulation of an ideology to which everybody, men and women, eventually subscribes.

This exclusion from the conversation is maintained not only when a general topic is expounded (humor, divine love), but also, paradoxically, when the court lady herself is the subject of conversation, as in Book 3. Here again it pays to look at the strategy of exclusion by inclusion. In constructing the male figure, the courtier's discourse is self-referential, for the necessity of a courtier's existence at court is never questioned. Canossa declares, for example, that the man after whom he fashions his courtier reflects more the person he himself wants to be than an absolutely ideal courtier, but he still recognizes that his argument is built on observations of specific courtiers ("Non posso laudar se non quella sorte di cortegiani ch'io più apprezzo"; "I can only praise courtiers of the kind I esteem myself" [1, 13, 47]). The court lady, however, is not indispensable at court. She is necessary to the courtier's physical and civic well-being, as Gonzaga points out ("S'è dimostrato quanto esse siano necessarie non solamente all'esser ma ancor al ben esser nostro"; "it has already been adequately shown how essential they are not only to our being here at all, but to our well-being once we are" [3, 40, 246]), and perhaps necessary to courtly life, but not to the prince or to court politics. She is there because she is related to the courtier, and she lives inside a system created for him and within the limits of a discourse of power that he, and not she, is engaged in codifying for both of them. The result is that the newly defined courtier functions as signifier (ideal) of a signified (real), because he is created with characteristics that, although idealized, are also realistically identifiable, or approximatable, in the persons drawing his image. The ideal court lady, by contrast, is important not for the way she is, since she is not drafted on present figures or even on the person representing her hierarchically—the duchess—but for the way she should be, a metaphor and a sign of the man representing her with his needs and his cultural prerogatives.[13] If her function is iconic, his is diegetic, because only the person manipulating discourse can construe himself narratively.

Woman is therefore a mirror of a mirror: a mirror, that is, of an ideal courtier about whom men theorize as a mirror of themselves, real courtiers in a court celebrating its grace and power. In this sense, the Magnifico is right. The woman that is the object of his speculation is not necessarily real, but she is functional to her society. Because she can be drawn and made readable, and thus representable, she is a reflection of others' fantasies. Sperone Speroni wrote a few years later, in *Il dialogo della cura familiare* (1535), that woman needs to behave like Echo, who never starts a conversation but always happily answers to any voice.[14] The *Cortegiano* similarly casts women as new figures of Echo's punished loquacity. In a later treatise, Stefano Guazzo's *La civil conversatione* (Venice, 1575), the term *conversatione* has acquired a strong sexual overtone when applied to the conversation between men and women. With women, the speaker argues, one uses hands ("si giuoca alle braccia," 1: 290): women who speak have become loose women.[15]

Still, since what is being codified in the conversation is common opinion ("commune opinione"), the content necessarily has value for everybody. Thus, even if we were to admit that neither the perfect courtier nor the perfect woman of the palace exists and therefore that the very courtiers providing an abstract construction of themselves can also provide one for the other subject, the result does not change. The hypothesis that a comprehensive discourse of all that is speakable may be proposed with no regard to sexual differences is itself discriminatory, because culturally and historically the order of the discourse has been gendered, no matter how

often it has been put forth as universal.[16] Woman knows that she is
praised if she stays in her place and agrees to repress the most feared
aspects of her personality (sexuality, for example) and to empha-
size those sides of herself perceived as more becoming (modesty,
chastity). Thus, only in a conceptual ambit in which femininity is
not defined as radically different (from the one, the norm, Truth,
Being) and reason is not assimilated into the subject (which is by
convention masculine) is it possible to associate woman with the
rational, her presence with discourse, and her conversation with
power. Such a move would require that the subject of enunciation
be desexualized and that the construction that posits thinking as
substantially universal, and not as asymmetric and gendered, be
broken. The question of who controls discourse is important, not
only because those who speak can give voice to their personal and
their class power and thus make themselves spokespersons for an
ideology, but also because those who speak can organize desire
and articulate the ways in which they want to represent others or
to represent themselves.

There is no doubt that the *Cortegiano* is sometimes so innova-
tive that one could be tempted to see the treatise as an optimistic
exaltation of womanhood. Unfortunately, what is said and what
the text shows seldom coincide. The same group, for example,
that reiterates through Bibbiena that the human race is a composite
of masculine and feminine elements, each sex imperfect without
its complement, also articulates a discourse and produces points
of view that assimilate complementarity into power and therefore
make it advantageous only to males. The same group that rejects
the Aristotelian theories rescued by Pallavicino and Ottaviano Fre-
goso concerning women's natural physical and moral inferiority
proceeds to select *exempla* that reiterate, and sometimes not just
liminally, those same theories.

All that the court lady can do at this point, excluding rebellion
(which she is unable to consider because she belongs and needs
to belong to the group in power), is to imagine herself as others
prefer to imagine her or to desire herself to be as others desire her
to be. In short, putting questions of subjectivity aside, she agrees
to the dominant fiction, because she is fully aware that she can
remain in the gathering only as long as she accepts the reiteration
of her silence (with her narcissistic association with the image that

constructs her as beautiful as long as she remains speechless) and the masculinization of her position (with her voluntary acceptance of a transvestite identification with the masculinity of the reasoning presented to her).[17] At the same time, with her tacit acceptance of what is being said, she allows the group to recognize a sense of community and of homogeneity in desiring the same things and advocating the same principles.[18]

Originating in a woman's rooms, regulated by a woman embodying vaguely military features ("locotenente"—lieutenant—is how the duchess characterizes Pio), published because of the disobedience of a woman, Vittoria Colonna, who "contra la promessa sua ne aveva fatto transcrivere una gran parte" ("contrary to her promise, had a large part of it written out" [Pref. 1, 23]), *Il libro del cortegiano* nonetheless remains peculiarly and at all levels an Oedipal and homocentric narrative. It is easy to see, in this light, why the discourse on the court woman, continuously postponed because of its difficulty, is in many ways the most polemic and the most sarcastic of the whole book, or why the courtiers' positions in this discourse are particularly dichotomized and the sexism of their rhetoric more realized than elsewhere. To perceive the distance between the other books and Book 3, where woman comes center stage and the gender debate becomes more virulent, one has only to compare the retorts made there with the quieter, less vituperative tone of the books that immediately precede and follow it, the second and especially the fourth, with its long digression on platonic love.

Ironically then, what seems to differentiate this treatise on woman from others in the genre of *de laudibus mulierum* is not its progressive call for female education. What is revolutionary is that Castiglione prescribes woman a new task: to produce discourse and excel in conversation in a heterosexual and charged environment—a task, unfortunately, that he strips away from her in the fiction of the text. In the end, this reversal better illustrates woman's life, with its social restrictions, than the diegetic discourse on the court lady that occupies a hundred pages.[19] As Giovanni Barbaro wrote with a logic all his own in yet another treatise, *De re uxoria* (1513), "Women should believe that they have achieved the glory of eloquence, if they will honor themselves with the outstanding ornament of silence" (206). For Barbaro the act of speaking exposes women to innuendos about their personal lives: "It is proper . . . that not only arms but indeed also the speech of women never be made public; for the speech of a noble woman can be no less dangerous than the nakedness of her limbs" (205).

The first step in constructing a discourse on femininity, once it has been agreed this is a discourse that women cannot make, paradoxically consists of invoking the impossibility of representing femininity. Woman is an enigma, an indecipherable text, unknown or not properly knowable. The Magnifico muses on the quandary ("Di questa non so io da chi pigliarne lo esempio"; "I do not know where to find my model for her" [3, 4, 210]), but bypasses it quickly and starts to represent exactly what he has just pronounced non-representable ("a provar di far quello ancora ch'io non so fare"; "to attempt what I do not even know how to do" [3, 4, 211]). The Magnifico's uneasiness goes beyond a personal impossibility, which Castiglione twice laments, of finding the right words to describe the duchess. The dilemma could be solved by allowing woman to represent herself, if the issue were not more complex.

Let me detour for a moment to Freud, who ponders the issue of the speaking female subject in, among other writings, an article titled "Femininity." "Throughout history," Freud writes, "people have knocked their heads against the riddle of the nature of femininity. . . . Nor will *you* have escaped worrying over this problem—those of you who are men; to those of you who are women this will not apply—you are yourselves the problem" (113).[20] Set in these terms, it is evident that the woman who is the subject of Freud's speculation cannot speak of or for herself, because she is the problem to solve or the question, as Lacan would later say. Of this discourse made about her, but not by her, and from whose enunciation she is excluded, woman is object rather than subject. The result is that the enigma of femininity can be solved only by those who can raise the question, since they are in the position of desiring subjects. Woman's task consists, then, not in examining herself and in offering her own musing, but in assenting to her own removal from the process of signification, because it is implicit that the solution can be found only outside the impasse. The problem, however, is that the explanation of femininity offered at this point is considered appropriate not only for men but for everybody; as I have already noted, this discourse has been defined as sexually indifferent, ungendered, and thus *a priori* applicable to both man and woman.

In the *Cortegiano* woman is similarly visualized as either puzzle or myth. In other words, woman is projected as either destabilizing if she is different or acceptable if she accedes to her own mystification. Those in charge of the dialogue create this construction through the use of two restrictive strategies, one linguistic and the other specular. In the linguistic approach, woman is mastered politically and culturally by inscribing her within a discourse of power as "lady of the palace"; in the specular approach, as will become clearer in the next chapter, she is controlled by being fashioned as a mirror of what the onlooker wants, a projection of others' desires and fantasies, and an embodiment of acceptable sociocultural constructions of femininity. Ultimately, the Magnifico's purpose, which plainly reflects that of the whole company, is not to decipher a woman declared indecipherable and unknowable from the very beginning—a woman who, Lacan writes, cannot be said or represented by men because she is outside both language and the symbolic. However, Lacan adds, men can talk of her or around her, and they can also represent their image of her. This is what our instituters do when they produce a woman fashioned according to their expectations and their desires. They then immediately affirm that this fantasized woman is a true woman, the only one possible in the court they are describing, and the only one worth desiring and thus representing.[21]

But why do the courtiers have such an overriding need to explain, silence, and rewrite woman? Can it be that since they have to adopt "woman's ways" (in Kelly-Gadol's words) in relation to their prince/patron, they also have to cancel, at the verbal level and specifically within their group, the possibility that they themselves have been feminized in their daily lives? If so, the construction of a court lady is imperative, not for the identity of the lady who is asked to mirror herself in the new script but for that of the courtier, since woman needs to be foregrounded precisely to act as a foil for him. In other words, the courtiers have to codify a viable feminine position because only through this process can they posit their own difference.

Another question occurs rather spontaneously at this point: Why is it so easy to induce woman to accept her own exclusion? Furthermore, why does Castiglione make Emilia Pio ask permission not to represent herself? According to Lacan, the female desire for passivity comes from the fact that the passage from the imaginary to the symbolic order presupposes that woman recognizes her passive role and her peripheral "I" in the order of the discourse and masochistically participates in her own presentation in those terms. Reduced to a mere spectator, both when man speaks about her in order to dominate her and when he describes her as an erotic object in order to show her reproducibility and her physical availability, woman finds herself simultaneously possessed and dispossessed.

It is in this light, I believe, that our judgments concerning the importance of the female figure in the *Cortegiano* and the progressiveness of Castiglione's opinions on this gender should be revised. Undoubtedly, Castiglione's woman is important, more acculturated to appreciate the value of nonchalance (*sprezzatura*) than that of the loom. However, this does not mean that cultural dictates regarding women were fostering a progressive representation of femininity during the years in which the author was writing his treatise. Rather, the text examines a court lady, and thus a woman already possessing a specific identity in terms of status and already entering the discursive regime more freely than her counterparts in other social classes. Judged specifically as "lady of the palace," it is easy to see how the role she has, or can claim to have, is thoroughly circumscribed. The light shining on her inevitably comes from the courtier to whom she is related and with whom she has the same hierarchical relationship of power that the courtier has with his prince: one of gracious, courteous, indispensable, codified, and accepted dependency.[22] We will follow the process that step by step produces in these court ladies perfect embodiments of femininity later in Ariosto, who steadily and at times as playfully as Castiglione educates his future bride Bradamante into proper womanhood.

It is possible, of course, to see the court lady as influential vis-à-vis other women, and in this sense her position could be read as constituting a great leap forward for her sex. Yet, with a closer reading, not even Castiglione's "feminist" text on woman's importance confirms Burckhardt's statement that "female emancipation" was "a matter of course" in that period and that women stood "on a footing of perfect equality with men" (250). No law, no recorded cultural convention, no historical source, has ever been found to confirm such a statement.

CHAPTER TWO

Cutting and Sewing: The Representation of the Court Lady

Representation of the world, like the world itself, is the work of men; they describe it from their own point of view, which they confuse with the absolute truth.
  —Simone de Beauvoir, *The Second Sex*, 133

Such duty as the subject owes his prince,
Even such a woman oweth to her husband.
  —Shakespeare, *The Taming of the Shrew*,
      V.ii.155–56

IN THE DISCOURSE on woman and womanhood that constitutes Book 3 of *Il libro del cortegiano*, Castiglione assigns the task of linguistically "instituting" the court lady to the Magnifico Juliano and Cesare Gonzaga, two of the most accomplished courtiers at the Urbino court. Their discourse defines the gentlewoman of the palace as a social asset because of her elitist and multidimensional appeal, even as it decenters, disperses, repositions, rewrites, and polices the woman within the gentlewoman. A double ideology is at work in this representation: the courtiers codify not only a permissible woman—the end result of discourses on women from contemporary philosophical, religious, and social points of view—but also a woman who is good for them as courtiers and for their class interests; a woman, for example, who knows the dangers of speaking freely and the need for circumspection.[1]

Conduct books (in this case a book on how to construct a courtier and a court lady) are political books in that they reproduce ideological givens, culture-related practices, and social assumptions proper to the historical moment in which they circulate. In short, they propagate a dominant fiction. Conduct books for women have the purpose of regulating feminine desire by proposing, and thus promoting, the image of an acceptable desirable woman. The characteristics of desirability shift from region to region, from social class to social class, and from generation to generation, but all tend to essentialize woman by emphasizing stereotypes of femininity as specific to her gender and as grounded in biology. These ideological constructs of womanhood conflate the standards of female attractiveness at a specific time in history with what is manifestly considered normal and then present themselves as coherent and logical.

Women are often unable or unwilling to read past the particular orthodoxy being offered them and end up desiring to be as they are desired to be. Such a desire also leads to a collective need to mirror the image of approved femininity, and at different times women have sincerely aspired, for instance, to Rubensian rotundity or Twiggy-like angularity. In this chapter, I discuss the linguistic construction of femininity—at court and in society at large—the courtiers' strategy in creating it, the discourses they engage in, and their conclusions. I examine both some unauthorized, and as it turns out subversive, discourses on the female sex that appear in the *Cortegiano* before the court lady moves to center stage and the official, highly praised discourse on woman as it is textualized in Books 3 and 4.

The representation of femininity in the *Cortegiano* begins as early as Book 1 with two concepts commonly associated with womanhood. First, a degraded image of femininity associates woman with notions of dissembling, distorting, and disguising. Second, an idealized image of femininity presents woman as the object of male desire, at times dismembered (the better to be fetishized), and at times mystified (the better to be controlled). The two poles of femininity—as horror or as aesthetic representation—are often so intermingled that they can occur on the same page. In Book 1, for instance, soon after the topic of conversation moves to the ideal courtier, Ludovico da Canossa, who bears the burden of constructing this male ideal, suddenly reverts to the female figure to illustrate the concept of artificiality in the context of *sprezzatura*. In this situation, he tells his audience, women can be helpful because they always want to appear beautiful: "Dove la natura in qualche parte in questo è mancata, esse si sforzano di supplir con l'artificio. Quindi nasce l'acconciarsi la faccia con tanto studio e talor pena" ("So when Nature has fallen short in some way, she endeavors to remedy the failure by artificial means. That is why we have women beautifying their faces so carefully and sometimes painfully" [1, 40, 82]).[2] At this point, Constanza Fregoso disobeys the injunction that the court ladies remain silent and interrupts Canossa. She cheerfully suggests that he stay on the subject rather than bring up women for no good reason ("senza proposito"). Her plea goes unheeded: Canossa proceeds to characterize artificiality and its opposite, naturalness, in terms of femaleness. His statement can be considered tacitly approved by the whole company, for no one attempts to refute it.[3]

An excessively attired female body is grotesque and disobedient, Canossa implies; the same can be said of a face so encrusted with cosmetics that it appears masked and so static for fear of cracking it that it cannot express lively emotions ("empiastrata tanto, che paia aversi posto alla faccia una maschera, e non osi ridere per non farsela crepare," I, 40, 82). Woman transgresses social limitations, therefore, at the very moment that she tries to improve her appearance or to conform to current cultural conceptions of feminine beauty. Given male familiarity with female artifices (men after all define what is artificial and what is natural), the result of Canossa's construction is to label ridiculous any women perceived as excessively made-up and overly put together or any women whose "feminine wiles" are scandalously evident to the other's gaze.

Voluntary self-dissimulation, then, is symptomatic of a narcissistic bent in woman that needs to be controlled or of a tendency toward promiscuity and an inclination toward irrational, concupiscent forces that need to be conquered. For Canossa, woman-as-artifice must be chastised not for what she is but for what she says about herself. By looking at this type of woman—and smelling *odor di femmina*—man's fear of castration comes to the surface. The imperative to control both this dread of femininity and the anxiety it generates requires that such a woman be punished by the courtiers through ridicule or that she be demystified through a process of explanation that offers her to the whole court in a more acceptable and commendable fashion. This procedure is present everywhere in representation. Ariosto, for example, offers similar solutions in his romance epic: Alcina and Gabrina, who are portrayed as opposite poles of beauty at the beginning of the text, are ridiculed at the end, but Olimpia, who elects eventually to conceal her assertiveness, gets nicely rewritten as a docile wife.

The woman worthy of admiration because she better represents the courtier's aesthetic ideal in the *Cortegiano* appears two lines later in Canossa's speech. This woman is endowed with the "right" body, a body in which not only normative beauty but also sexuality accord with the ideological requirements of the instituter leading the conversation. "Quanto più poi di tutte piace una, dico," Canossa rationalizes, speaking in the name of the court,

"non brutta, che si conosca chiaramente non aver cosa alcuna in su
la faccia, benchè non sia così bianca nè così rossa, ma col suo color
nativo pallidetta e talor per vergogna o per altro accidente tinta
d'un ingenuo rossore" ("How much more attractive than all the
others is a pretty woman who is quite clearly wearing no make-
up on her face, which is neither too pallid nor too red, and whose
own coloring is natural and sometimes pale [but who occasion-
ally blushes openly from embarrassment or for some other rea-
son]" [1, 40, 82]). The discursive process molding femininity here
both neutralizes and immobilizes woman's form into an ordered
and erotic image, as well as objectifies it through a technique of
descriptive dismemberment. The desire to subject woman to the
regime of the gaze serves mainly to cure the courtiers' sense of
disorder and of non-pleasure that the references to woman as mask
and to the dangers of the flesh produced in them earlier. Wanted as
a pliable mind within a docile body, woman becomes collectively
desired by this group only when imagined as accessible and created
as graceful. Representation, then, moves from woman as source
of danger and cause of confusion (because female seductiveness
hints at possible carnal intemperances) to woman as image frozen
in the simple and the beautiful, an image that is viable because
summarizable and controllable.

Canossa next identifies the erogenous zones through close-ups
of women's bodies, progressing from top to bottom. Teeth are
admired first in this chain of signifiers, then hands, and finally
foot and leg (1, 40, 83). The body fragments that Canossa invento-
ries are all dutifully hidden, gloved, or stockinged in order some-
how to veil more fully a femininity that becomes more valuable
because veiled.[4] Teeth are admired because they are not exposed
("non essendo così scoperti come la faccia"; "hidden from view
most of the time, unlike the rest of the face"), hands because they
also are concealed ("massimamente revestite di guanti"; "especially
after they have been covered again with gloves"), and legs because
they are dressed ("attillata nei suoi chiapinetti di velluto, e calze
polite"; "showing her velvet ribbons and pretty stockings" [1, 40,
83]). Thus, a woman left to herself is transgressive because she has
the potential for being different or for appearing grotesque, but
woman as reconstructed by this group is classical, statuesque, and
proposable as normal. Decorated, woman is dangerous; covered,
she is coveted.

The specific physical parts enclosed or veiled not only confirm the usual praxis of decorporealization of the body practiced by the courtiers throughout the text but also reconfirm Vasari's famous requirements of rule, order, and measure in every facet of life and art. In other words, the Urbino court privileges the image of the classical body over the grotesque body, both for the courtiers (remember Castiglione's emphasis on grace) and for the ladies of the palace, for the group's identity is tied to this ordered image.[5]

The body reviewed, manipulated, and emblematized tells more about woman than she is ever allowed to tell about herself. If the teeth function as an erotic image, a dislocation of other fantasies, then the closed mouth stands for a social exigency (she who doesn't speak, doesn't sin)—in short, it is a sign of chastity. The same holds true for stockinged feet, whose slow-moving description emphasizes Canossa's fetishistic rendering. The other men narcissistically identify with the enunciator of the discourse, find their wants in what he evokes so nicely, read his text through him (a text that gratifies their curiosity and their illusions even further since the object of desire is described as attractive), reduplicate what they read, and start to desire the same desire. They desire, however, not a real woman, but a woman mentally recreated, a woman whose absence from discourse and from representation (made for the most part by the Magnifico, as far as she is concerned) is necessary for desire to be linguistically manifested.

This desire only appears to be directed toward woman, however; as a recreated other, she can do nothing more than narcissistically mirror the heterosexual desires of the group that creates her. Thus, woman unwittingly reconfirms the homosocial ties thoroughly established among these courtly instituters. As object of a libido metaphorically veiled, she serves in the end to guarantee less male libido and more male solidarity, the bonding of the group in which this libido is being excited. There is no need to give this woman an identity; the purpose of the description is not to evoke a specific person but to visualize female beauty. The represented ideal can thus easily erase the real being that has permitted its representation, and woman as physical being can be conveniently removed from woman as summation of an attractiveness aesthetically constructed. Transfixed into an immutable image and set outside history, woman is cast as perfect as long as she witnesses in silence, and from her assigned place, her own reconstruction.

At the same time, as I pointed out in the previous chapter, woman's presence is required within the discourse that prescribes her worth and marks her limits within this court, for her presence assures a certain viability to her image. By assenting to her prescribed roles to cure a vague sense of degradation born from having her identity atomized for aesthetic purposes, woman recognizes herself in the idea of womanhood formed before her eyes and feels pleasure in seeing her body spectated as erotic object and sign of beauty. Her presence in the text requires her automasculinization, her association, that is, as a "man," with the male voice that beguiles her in the act of portraying her. Strangely enough, the feminine position here would be that of subject, although by proxy. A second, opposite choice is for woman to associate narcissistically, as a woman, with the image being presented, an image in which she is asked to annul herself. In this case her position, as usual, would remain that of object.[6] Mirrored by her, the desire of the person who describes her has become by now her own desire.

A third possibility exists. Woman, rather than accepting her representation in the terms mentioned above, would become furious. The court ladies take this position once in the text when, finally invited to vent their feelings, they find themselves unable to express themselves verbally and collectively opt for a gestural reaction: "Allora una gran parte di quelle donne, ben per averle la signora Duchessa fatto così cenno, si levarono in piedi e ridendo tutte corsero verso il signor Gasparo, come per dargli delle busse" ("At this, seeing the Duchess making a sign, a large number of the ladies present rose to their feet and, laughing, they all ran towards signor Gaspare as if to rain blows on him" [2, 96, 202]). It is symptomatic that women lack words when they most need them; a loss of linguistic abilities parallels a loss of identity. To be sure, loquacity and femininity are linked in the text, but only when the act of speaking is synonymous with chatting and not when reason is involved. No wonder that Pallavicino reads this episode as expression and proof of a lack of female ratiocinative capabilities: "Eccovi che per non aver ragione vogliono valersi della forza ed a questo modo finire il ragionamento, dandoci, come si sol dire, una licenzia braccesca" ("There, you see, as they are not in the right they resort to force, wanting to end the discussion with their hands" [2, 97, 202–3, trans. modified]).

To fully perceive the importance of woman as spectacle in the text, it is necessary to examine the second introduction of the subject of "femininity," broached during a debate on the emblematic value of painting. Again the subject is illustrated by making woman the object of a libidinal desire. The discussion centers on the meaning of affection and on the reasons for men's pleasure in seeing a woman. Gonzaga's view is that man cannot have real affection for a woman if she lacks the physical qualities that would inspire such an affection, because "secondo che 'l piacer nasce dalla affezione, così l'affezion nasce dalla bellezza" ("just as pleasure arises from affection, so affection is prompted by beauty" [1, 53, 98]).

Ludovico da Canossa intervenes to offer more psychological reasons, because he is conscious of the transitoriness of beauty. We can extrapolate from his observations that the outer beauty of woman can be represented because it activates the mechanisms of eroticized contemplation, voyeurism, and fetishism. In this act of representation, painters are particularly successful, it is implied, because they are better than others in convincing the eye that reality is being mimetically represented in their work. Affection for a woman, however, although it can arise from exterior beauty, feeds on other reasons not easily summarizable. Canossa mentions "i costumi, il sapere, il parlare, i gesti e mill'altre cose . . . ma sopra tutto il sentirsi essere amato" ("attractive manners, wisdom, speech, gestures and a hundred and one other things . . . but above all, by the feeling that one is loved oneself" [1, 53, 98]). In other words, it is possible to represent a body by idealizing it, but it is not possible to represent a person in all facets. Infatuation with a perfect form is conceivable but insufficient as a true cause of love.

Canossa insists a sign cannot be entirely separated from its referent; if painters are more capable than others of perceiving formal beauty, since they often represent it, they still cannot claim a better understanding or a better representation of a real woman. Unruffled, Gonzaga continues to fantasize both about his ability to understand beauty fully by remembering it and about his talent for surpassing any visual artist in representing what can only be felt psychologically.

The overall subject of conversation here is Alexander the Great's largess. In accordance with classical and medieval traditions, Castiglione's Alexander is magnanimous, vain, and prodigal.[7] Yet his magnanimity can be considered a quality in this story only if we thoroughly accept the view of woman as a commodity, for Alexander gives the painter Apelles his woman, Campaspe, because Apelles happened to fall in love with her while painting her portrait:

Si legge che Alessandro amò sommamente Apelle Efesio e tanto, che avendogli fatto ritrar nuda una sua carissima donna ed intendendo il bon pittore per la maravigliosa bellezza di quella restarne ardentissimamente inamorato, senza rispetto alcuno gliela donò: liberalità veramente degna d'Alessandro, non solamente donar tesori e stati, ma i suoi proprii affetti e desideri; e segno di grandissimo amor verso Apelle, non avendo avuto rispetto, per compiacer a lui, di dispiacere a quella donna che sommamente amava; la qual creder si po che molto si dolesse di cambiar un tanto re con un pittore.

We read that Alexander was so fond of Apelles of Ephesus that once, after he had had him portray one of his favourite mistresses, and then heard that the worthy painter had fallen desperately in love with her marvellous beauty, without a second thought he gave the woman to him: this was an act of generosity truly worthy of Alexander, to give away not only treasures and states but his own affections and desires; and it showed, too, how deeply fond he was of Apelles, to please whom he cared nothing about the displeasure of the lady whom he loved so much himself, and who, we may well believe, was more than grieved to lose so great a king in exchange for a painter.   (I, 52, 96)

We can infer that the woman to love is an imaginable woman, one desired all the more when her image mirrors her creator's desires. Only then does she appear perfect, desired because she is created desirable and because she is the object of a triangular desire.[8] Campaspe is not desired by Apelles for the way she is or for the way she was before her painted portrait took shape. Rather, she is desired because she has been reconstructed by the painter's desire and has been reproduced by his gaze in the immobilized and codifiable form that he prefers in his portraits and for which he is famous.

Alexander, in turn, recognizes Campaspe's iconic value only when he sees someone else in love with her. Thus, rather than making Alexander renounce his libido, his gift to Apelles allows him to consume it in two ways: first, narcissistically, at the level of identification with a person so fascinated by a female image as to be able to enjoy it more aesthetically than he himself can hope to do; second, by proxy, at the level of scopophilic gratification. This sort of continence reappears in the text when Alessandro saves the beautiful women of Darius, his defeated enemy (3, 39, 245), and again his narcissistic or, rather, arrogant thrust is praised for its magnanimous quality. If Apelles's progression is from the person to the portrait he eroticizes in the process of deciphering it, Alexander moves from erotic pleasure to the scopophilic and, finally, to the homosocial.[9]

Desired for her desirability to another man and for the fact that she no longer remains enjoyable after the transfer (thus being a stimulant for an insatiable and unsatisfiable desire), woman is lost in the equation. Not only is she literally transferrable—her passivity spelled out in the assumption that she can only let herself be gazed upon—but her own position in society becomes one of a unifier of two men, the object of a single erotic desire. To be sure, Castiglione does register Campaspe's displeasure at the shift, but he emphasizes loss of status over feelings. In other words, he has Campaspe aware that the transfer makes her lose value as a commodity, an imposition against which she would like to rebel, but he does not make her question that a woman can be given away.

Surprisingly, the misogynist Pallavicino is better able than others to deconstruct the rhetoric of the discourse on woman and to read the language of the libido coded in the Magnifico's text. Rather than forming a court lady for the courtier, as had previously been done, he laments, the Magnifico has described a female object of his desires, and for this reason he has made her more desirable. He has forgotten to make clear, however, this woman's value to the court: "Voi avete veramente, signor Magnifico, molto adornata questa donna e fattola di eccellente condizione . . . e nominato in lei alcune cose tanto grandi, che credo vi siate vergognato di chiarirle; e più presto le avete desiderate . . . che insegnate" ("You have indeed, signor Magnifico, beautifully adorned this lady and made her of excellent character . . . and have mentioned qualities so impressive that I think you were ashamed to spell them out; and . . . rather than explain them you have simply wished them into existence" [3, 7, 214]).

Zeuxis's composite portrait is admired next. By putting together five women for a unique pictorial vision of feminine perfection and by denying each woman represented her own alterity, Zeuxis erases in this process of multiple composition all the real individuals who have posed for the painting. Such dispersion and reconstruction, however, are exactly what make his models so desired: "Furono celebrate da molti poeti, come quelle che per belle erano state approvate da colui, che perfettissimo giudicio di bellezza aver dovea" ("[They] were celebrated by many poets because their beauty had won the approbation of one who must have been the most perfect judge" [1, 53, 98]).[10] Zeuxis's women are praised because they are readable—a collectivized, cannibalized image of femininity correlated with beauty, and of beauty with the sublime. Denounced more than once in the text as non-representable, femininity ironically comes to be represented as a figure of the non-representable, with the assimilation of woman to the idea of the sublime. Although subjects of the representation, Zeuxis's models become objects of the represented, illustrations of a "reality" that the artist consistently needs to improve so as to better represent his ideal. The portrait is never totally mimetic—notwithstanding the fame as reproducer of reality on which Zeuxis built his reputation—because the women shown on the canvas, despite their beauty, have some natural imperfections that the painter must erase in representation.

A letter Raphael sent to Castiglione in answer to his praises of the *Triumph of Galatea* at the Farnesina reiterates this idea. In order to paint a beautiful woman, Raphael writes, he should see many beautiful ones, but since there are not many around, he usually follows his own ideas on the subject.[11] Raphael thus agrees with Zeuxis in seeing the representation of female beauty as the universalization, idealization, and, at times, the spiritualization of an idea of beauty drawn from a number of representative beauties. Yet, as Elizabeth Cropper notices, in no known Renaissance male portrait is the purpose simply to represent beauty as beauty.[12]

A similar representative female beauty is present *en abîme* in the woman the Magnifico creates. The court lady is drawn not from a particular, and thus real, figure but from a sum of female figures gathered in her creator's imagination. The Magnifico is clear here: "dirò di questa donna eccellente come io la vorrei; e formata ch'io l'averò a modo mio, non potendo poi averne altra, terrolla come mia a guisa di Pigmalione" ("I shall describe this excellent lady as I would wish her to be. And when I have fashioned her to my own liking, since I may have no other I shall, like Pygmalion, take her for my own" [3, 4, 211]). The result is that none of the women at the Urbino court can recognize herself, unless she does so passively, in the iconic image of femininity that the Magnifico produces and codifies for himself and for the Gonzaga court. Like Galatea, the court woman pieced together by our Renaissance Pygmalion stands as another symbolic representation of femininity, a woman-fetish allowed to think and speak only as long as she thinks and speaks according to her creator's expectations. Formed without history and without desires, this ventriloquial woman does not threaten the Magnifico's social identity or his own eros. In fact, our speaker goes even further in this reconstructive program. To counteract any anxiety a different woman might cause (a woman already punished by Canossa through his association of femininity with a mask), he immediately demystifies her by explaining or, in Castiglione's words, instituting her. In the Magnifico's discourse, *repetitio adjuvat*.

Having been made dismemberable by Canossa, rememberable by Gonzaga, distributable by Alexander, summable by Zeuxis, and prefabricatable by Pygmalion, this woman has only to show a certain pleasing affability in order to be loved by everybody. Again, faced with an idealized self, the court lady as a real woman has no choice other than to associate herself with the meta-discourse that interprets her, since she needs to erase the psychic discomfort created by exposure to courtly judgment. As a result, she sees her own body as a sign, is seduced by the image presented, and accepts once again becoming the object of the courtiers' eroticizing gaze, a gaze that institutionalizes her as order because of the need to exorcize her as disorder. And the cycle begins anew.

Even when properly enclosed and with her eros properly domesticated, even when physically inside the home, with her hands gloved, her legs stockinged, and her mouth shut, even then, however, woman stands exposed to male desire and more than ever constitutes a source of anxiety and a threat of castration. To control her, the courtiers need to shackle her at the cultural level and deny her desires at the psychological one. Pallavicino's discourse on the dangers of female sexuality is here not so much misogynist (a position the reader would naturally expect), as revelatory of male fear of castration vis-à-vis a sexual woman. Women, Pallavicino laments, "procurano quanto più possono d'aver gran numero d'innamorati e tutti, se possibil fosse, vorriano che ardessero e, fatti cenere, dopo morte tornassero vivi per morir un'altra volta" ("strive as hard as they can to win a great number of lovers, and if they could they would burn them all to ashes, only to bring them back from death to die a second time" [3, 74, 278]). Here, woman is not only insatiable but vampiresque.

The dissimilarity between points of view in the text regarding the construction of woman is thus minimal. The difference is simply between Pallavicino's position, which advocates sexual suppression, and the Magnifico's posture, which prescribes sexual repression, both in the verbal construction of the court lady and in the mythical and ahistorical collection of stories that he offers her as a model for feminine behavior. We can conclude that if sexuality is positioned, as usual, within the female body, sexuality itself does not belong to woman but rather to the person reading her body, a reading that naturally varies according to the private or institutional purposes pursued.

What does woman want, then? "Was will das Weib?" Freud kept asking himself. He eventually declared that he was unable to classify femininity as other than enigma. His hypothesis was— and the role of woman in the formation of the patriarchal unconscious rests on it—that woman wanted to be both a man (desiring what she lacked) and a woman (for the specificity of her orgasm, for example, or because through a son she could symbolically possess what anatomically she did not have) ("Femininity"). The instituters at the Urbino court posed the same question four centuries earlier and came up with the same answers. They declare that women are rebuses. It is difficult to guess what they want, they continue, because women "spesso desideran cose tanto strane, che non è omo che le imaginasse, e talor esse medesime non sanno ciò che si desiderino" ("often want such strange things that no man can think what they are, and indeed they often don't know themselves" [3, 61, 268]). According to Pallavicino, were women free to choose, they would rather be men, since "grande argumento della perfezion dell'omo e della imperfezion della donna è che universalmente ogni donna desidera esser omo, per un certo instinto di natura, che le insegna desiderar la sua perfezione" ("another convincing argument for the perfection of man and the imperfection of woman is that without exception every woman wants to be a man, by reason of a certain instinct that teaches her to desire her own perfection" [3, 15, 222]). Sexuality constitutes a continuous danger for women because their sex is frail ("per la imbecillità del sesso," 3, 39, 245). How lucky that female nature "naturally" leans toward maternity, "perchè il mondo non ha utilità dalle donne, se non per lo generare dei figlioli" ("for women bring no benefit to the world, save the bearing of children" [3, 39, 245]).

The theme of female excellence is developed at great length in the *Cortegiano*. The theses against women's worth are rebutted promptly and minutely with theses in women's favor; the reasoning, in fact, soon becomes empty and repetitive, because the debate does not propose to change opinions or to subvert cultural constructs. Neither the Magnifico nor Pallavicino, despite their different positions, questions the principle on which all courtiers agree: it makes little difference whether woman is a perfect or imperfect animal, a useful or useless being, since her position on the social ladder is not independently held but comes to her through a man. As woman, she is naturally, incontrovertibly, and legally inferior.

In his first, long tirade against women, Pallavicino sets out the theoretical apparatus surrounding the rationale for female exclusion. His discourse is prolix and misogynist, yet it shows quite clearly women's position in the discursive framework. "Voi," Pallavicino tells Fregoso, "per confirmare il parer vostro con ragione m'allegate opere di donne, le quali per lo più son fuori d'ogni ragione" ("to find reasons for your opinion you are citing what is done by women, who are quite unreasonable" [2, 35, 142]). Pallavicino affirms that a female discourse based on rationality is self-contradictory. He is hardly alone in this thinking; from Aristotle on, human capacity for conceptualization, and eventually for participation in conversation, has consistently been articulated as contrary to matter and to nature, and thus contrary to woman, who is metaphorically associated with these. Woman can imitate or, more specifically, reflect an opinion; she can also make this opinion her own by falling in love with it. Essentially non-active (Nietzsche will link woman to sleep), she cannot have access to the *logos*. Rationality itself does not belong to her.

Pallavicino denounces not only the credibility but the very possibility of a rational female enunciation, because, he states, women tend to follow their leaders like sheep ("come le pecore," 2, 35, 142), whether for good or bad motives. Outside male discourse, then, women can be dangerous, because they can be self-absorbed in their narcissism, tell their story, control their image, actualize a chain of desires, or shatter assumptions about themselves. Their words, therefore, need to be stopped, or at least decentered, before they are enunciated. Women are declared irrational from a philosophical point of view, because produced by chance ("animal produtto a sorte e per caso," 3, 11, 218), uncondonable from a social standpoint ("di poca o niuna dignità a rispetto degli omini"; "of little or no dignity compared with men" [2, 91, 198]), and finally unacceptable from a political perspective ("meravigliomi pur . . . che non vogliate ancor che esse governino le città e faccian le leggi e conducano gli eserciti, e gli omini si stiano in cucina o a filare"; "I am quite surprised . . . that . . . you do not want them to govern cities as well, and to make laws and lead armies, while the men stay home to cook and spin" [3, 10, 217]).[13]

Where is woman in this text? A sign of male desire because she is real (see Aretino's observation on the duchess) and of male codification because she can be seen as ideal (a court woman to put together), created by a Renaissance Pygmalion who wants her as myth so that she can better embody his frozen model, woman is presented as a fetishistic construction and is thus historically absent. Between the iconic image of femininity as the representation of others' desires (woman as object of visual pleasure) and the metaphorical image of femininity as mirror of the other (the court woman as replication of the courtier with the adjustments required by the difference in gender), she—as woman—does not exist. In other words, woman is either the object of a scopophilic look (by definition masculine) or a commodity to govern and exchange, to manage and guide away from wrong choices. Positioned between Freud and Lévi-Strauss, or rather, between the two master philosophers of our text, Aristotle and Plato (the latter coming center stage in Book 4), woman is, as usual, everywhere and nowhere.

In Book 3 the Magnifico Juliano states in full, and with an air of benevolent paternalism, the program that constructs femininity at court. This instituter cares deeply for his pedagogical task and proposes a large curriculum for his ideal court lady, one that covers all possible gratifications and all indispensable duties. Apart from some specific male or female tasks (weapons and certain sports, for example, are not proposed for women), the courtier and the court lady are described as having much in common. For each of them the same emphasis is placed on culture, the visual arts, music, polite conversation, and competency in organizing social life. Both, the Magnifico advises, should keep within the limits of the harmonious, the moderate and the pleasant.[14]

Two features are indispensable to any proper court lady: first, she must be conscious of her biological role and devote herself to sexual reproduction and to maintaining the institution of the family; second, she must be conscious of her social function and attend to reproducing communication and preserving order at court. Thus, the ideal woman should love someone whom she could marry, the Magnifico asserts, because "quando questo amore non po terminare in matrimonio, è forza che la donna n'abbia sempre quel remorso e stimulo che s'ha delle cose illicite, e si metta a periculo di macular quella fama d'onestà che tanto l'importa" ("when this love cannot end in marriage, the woman is always bound to suffer the pain and remorse caused by illicit things and runs the risk of staining the reputation for chastity that is so important to her" [3, 56, 263]). The worst thing one can do to a woman, and implicitly to the man responsible for her, is to impugn her sexual morality, because not only is she then ridiculed but also the institution of the family and the authority of the paterfamilias on which she juridically depends are questioned. The Magnifico shrewdly makes the desire for chastity an implicitly feminine one ("l'importa") rather than simply a social requirement: chastity is not just what woman needs in order to be respected by men (a patriarchal requirement) but also what she finds more congenial as a state of being (a personal choice). Federico Fregoso's hypothesis, immediately embraced by Roberto da Bari, that adultery should be condoned in the higher classes since love rarely comes spontaneously when marriage is imposed, is promptly rejected by the group because it runs contrary to the implicit normalizing program pursued throughout.

Together with Cesare Gonzaga, the Magnifico recycles the notorious patriarchal axiom anchoring women's value to the body, so that before, during, and after marriage, female continence is the foundation of the honor of fathers, brothers, husbands, and children. This ideological requirement is repeated in the majority of the examples advanced to defend women's worth. Chastity also serves as the attribute of femininity on which both defenders and detractors of women can agree. The woman presented for imitation at court is, then, a summa of cultural obsessions. As chaste maiden, honest wife, and cultivated matron, she displays the behavior appropriate to a person who has internalized since infancy the laws governing propriety, property, and kinship. As Catherine Belsey laments, "The role of ideology is to present the position of the subject as fixed and unchangeable, an element in a given system of differences which is human nature and the world of human experience, and to show possible action as an endless repetition of 'normal,' familiar action" (*Critical Practice*, 90).

Pallavicino is left objecting to female education. What can man do, he asks, if woman uses her skills subversively? In other words, what if a well-taught court lady one day pushes aside her Pygmalion, overturns sexual roles, exceeds the precise rules that have designated her as indispensable, and rebels against the society that wants her to behave according to others' guidelines? Not only does Pallavicino clearly see the disparity between what is proposed and what is feasible, but, afraid that the status quo may not last forever, he rushes to praise the women who conform. Moreover, conscious that female acquiescence itself has buttressed male superiority throughout the centuries, he hopes that women are not able, as yet, to accede to their own freedom.

Pallavicino claims that women have no problem in loving the "truth" the courtiers invent for them, "ancora che non sia tanto in suo favore, che le laudi false; nè hanno a male, che altri dica che gli omini siano di maggior dignità, e confesseranno che voi avete detto gran miraculi ed attribuito alla donna di palazzo alcune impossibilità ridicule e tante virtù, che Socrate e Catone e tutti i filosofi del mondo vi sono per niente" ("even if it is not at all that much to their credit, more than false praises; nor are they aggrieved if anyone maintains that men are of greater dignity, and they will admit that you have made some fantastic claims and attributed to the Court lady ridiculous and impossible qualities and so many virtues that Socrates and Cato and all the philosophers in the world are as nothing in comparison" [3, 11, 217]). For their part, women would choose this truth because it appears natural to them to behave as they are asked to behave. To reinforce his view, Pallavicino speaks of impossibilities (juridical, political, social) for women, rather than possibilities; the first term works better in his discourse because it is set next to the adjective "ridicule." Put another way, women themselves would laugh at the supposition that men could discard the opinion of women held by the very philosophers who constructed what has turned out to be a lasting cultural image of femininity. Interestingly, it is when the Magnifico, advocating a liberal view, chastises men for having claimed the right of total authority over the other gender that Castiglione portrays Emilia Pio as puzzled at the demystifying project of the disquisition.[15] Unwittingly illustrating a lack of female ratiocinative capabilities, Pio here is made to interrupt the conversation and bring it back onto more tranquil grounds.

Not only are women restricted during the discourse concerning them, in the sense that sexual parameters and practical limits are prescribed for them, but they are also restricted within the exempla of femininity advanced in the text. Book 3 is built on stories in which a female persona is constructed and reconstructed through concise Bildungsroman, in the manner of Boccaccio's *De claris mulieribus*.[16] Imagined and transfixed in art, as we have seen, just as they are imagined at court, women find themselves already and *a priori* typecast in stories that function as corollaries to their institution. The specific purpose of these episodes, in fact, is to emphasize the moral of tales in which the main characters behave according to the models with which women are invited to identify at court. Ironically, the Magnifico needs to mystify the female figure in these pages not so much to reiterate male desire as to codify an image *ad foeminam*, so that the woman in the present recognizes herself in the woman of the past and convinces herself of the goodness of treading the same ground.

The stories that the Magnifico and Gonzaga present (Luisa Mulas counts 52 generalizing examples) confirm the sexual value of women in society and eroticize or standardize the various protagonists.[17] Woman is represented either as defined by her sexuality (usually in the role of maiden in danger) or in a social capacity (which inevitably proves restrictive), and often in a combination of the two instances. Whether the female protagonist has a positive or a negative function, there is a single reason for telling her story, a reason that, contra the Magnifico, is not neutral since the protagonist is praised or punished according to the ideological and moral requirements of the orderly discourse that frames the tale. Both the masochistic and the idealistic elements reconfirm in the end the female position in the narrative sphere: produced as exemplary, exhibited as icon, and marginalized as myth, woman is, as usual, dispossessed of a personality.

Given the premises that sexual control is a must for the reproduction of the race and that women need to be socialized to desire to perform the roles expected of them, it comes as no surprise that the majority of examples in the text focus on chastity. In this context, class differences have no bearing, since the farm girl who drowns herself after she is raped behaves not unlike the rich Camma who poisons herself to avoid rape (albeit this rape would have taken place within a legal contract). Sexual violence can even be represented as providential, as in the case of the Sabine women, if this representation furthers the purposes of the instituters and the prince.

In the end, all instances reiterate the emblematic value of the duchess, who sums up, with her presence, each individual woman in everyday courtly life and thus perfectly reflects the discourse on womanhood advanced by the courtiers. Throughout the *Cortegiano*, Elisabetta Gonzaga is identified with order and normalcy, poise and reverence. Because of her husband she is powerful, and as such she is desired, but only as long as she appears to be above desire. In other words, she can function as a signifier for any courtier tempted to fantasize about femininity, but she cannot serve as a desiring subject because her power would be perceived as castrating. And yet, precisely because she accepts without quarrel a continence imposed on her by a sexually inadequate companion, she can be a monument of female exemplariness, courtly worship, and literary praise.[18]

Ironically, the examples of female virtues are better known by men than by women. Margherita Gonzaga rightly notices this discrepancy in her first intervention: "Parmi che voi narriate troppo brevemente queste opere virtuose fatte da donne; chè se ben questi nostri nemici l'hanno udite e lette, mostrano non saperle e vorriano che se ne perdesse la memoria: ma se fate che noi altre le intendiamo, almen ce ne faremo onore" ("I think that you are describing these noble deeds of women too briefly; for although these enemies of ours have indeed heard and read about them, they pretend not to know them and would like them to be forgotten. But if you will allow us women to hear them, at least we shall take pride in them" [3, 23, 229]). Margherita asks for more details, so that the women finding themselves for the first time protagonists of exemplary lessons can recognize a connection between themselves (at the Urbino court) and other women (prominent in other states, in other times, and in other courts). The narcissistic component in women's desire to know and be known is obvious. Margherita also asks that the stories be narrated in order to recall, for men as well as for women, the existence of famous female ancestors whose memory men have conveniently obfuscated in their writing of history. In other words, she is aware that women's actions have not entered popular culture and that women themselves have not had occasion to hear of them and recognize themselves in their precursors. Here, social incentive entices women to know more.

By clamoring for further examples, however, Margherita shows that she accepts as normative the dialectic present within the various stories and that, fascinated by the representation of an ideal "I" with which to identify, even though this is an "I" remembered/ created by men, she masochistically feels pleased even by the tales in which women are sacrificed for no reason. She thus consumes the stories in the way that the men—the courtiers who have the power to produce them as models for her sex—would want her to consume them. It is precisely by hailing his interlocutors as subjects, in fact, that the Magnifico binds them to courtly ideology.[19] "Uditelo," he answers to a request for a new story, "e voi, madonna Margherita, mettete cura di tenerlo a memoria" ("Listen to what I say, and you, madonna Margherita, be sure to remember it" [3, 25, 231]).

Ironically, the Magnifico himself notices that male connivance is behind the marginalization of women, since men have always been sparing with praise of the other gender (3, 13, 220). In the

Furioso, Ariosto echoes the lament in a lengthy proem on women. He notices that despite the numberless cases of worthy women throughout history, barely one name is still mentioned; this is because writers have consistently been deceitful, envious, and mean ("bugiardi, invidi ed empi," 37, 6).

The first long story offered to this courtly audience is that of Alessandra, married to Alessandro, her name being the feminization of that of the person legally possessing her. Alessandra offers her husband's dead body to the mob so that his angry subjects can vent their hatred upon him rather than on his children or her. The message is clear: woman, as mother, has the social function of saving the children of patriarchy. Alessandra is praised in this case for subterfuge and Machiavellian virtues.

The second story, that of Leona, carries a social message: Leona agrees to have her tongue cut out for fear that she may talk and compromise the life of some conspirators with her revelations (3, 23, 229). Female loquacity, as we have seen, is largely represented in the text as disruptive, and in this case woman is sacrificed for more important political and manly reasons. The myth of Philomela comes immediately to mind, except that in Philomela's case the cutting was, to say the least, involuntary.

The third story defines woman in reference to her sexuality: Camma transforms her wedding banquet into a funeral repast in order not to yield to her parents, who have imposed a new husband on her. As will be the case for Drusilla in the *Furioso*, Camma can rebel, but only at the cost of her own death. The Magnifico is interested not in granting Camma a desire, no matter how masochistic, but in showing how a willed exclusion from societal laws necessarily leads woman to suicide. Camma understands that her father's position is both normative and final when he wills her remarriage and that obedience to him carries more weight than fidelity to her husband's memory. Unfortunately, she loses no matter what position she takes: to obey her father, she must go through a wedding ceremony that she does not want; to honor her commitment to her dead husband, she must eliminate herself from that very ceremony. The only choice Camma does not have is to do nothing, which would be, paradoxically, what she wants.

The majority of the case histories concern female continence;

as I have already pointed out, there is no substantial disagreement among the courtiers about the value of chastity. Thus, one of the most extensive narrations is devoted to the submission, not only of woman, but also of man, to the Law-of-the-Father. Having fallen in love with a young man who fervently reciprocates her feelings, an unnamed woman chooses not to show her beloved signs of her affection because she is conscious of the hopelessness of the relationship. Forced to marry another man although still in love with the first, she follows paternal orders and pays no attention to the original suitor. The result is her death within three years (3, 43, 248). The lesson of the tale is that order must be maintained at all costs and that desire needs to be tamed (this time woman is guaranteed a desire, as long as she keeps it unsatisfied). Not only does the woman refuse the possibility of rebellion, but she also proceeds from hoping for the possible to accepting the necessary, and from melancholy to death through inanition, her body steadily mirroring the violence already endured by her spirit. Only with her death can the tale conclude convincingly, because the narrative can neither give satisfaction to her nor allow her to disobey her father. Both choices are beyond her. Instead, once again, as was the case for Camma, to whom this story provides a retrospective gloss, it is impossible for woman to be both a sexual and an economic subject in the order of the discourse and to live happily ever after.

At other times, the exemplary tale can be so exemplary as to disappropriate woman of her own story. Argentina is a case in point. Although desperate at the news of her husband's capture, Argentina does nothing. The tale pushes her aside and shifts to the son, who embarks on a heroic journey to free his father. At the news of her husband's liberation, Argentina returns to the forefront, only to die suddenly when she sees him. The act of dying is not only anticlimactic—and Pallavicino does not fail to notice this point— but also superfluous and decidedly harmful: "Per essere troppo amorevole fece male a se stessa ed al marito ed ai figlioli, ai quali converse in amaritudine il piacere di quella pericolosa e desiderata liberazione" ("Because she was too much in love she harmed herself, and her husband, and her children, whose rejoicing over his perilous and longed-for liberation she turned into bitterness"

[3, 28, 234]). In the end, Argentina is not simply unimportant to
the continuation of her story; she is even mocked by the story that
tells of her useless sacrifice.

The importance of women visibly diminishes when the topic of
conversation treads higher ground in Book 4. Appropriately, this
is the book in which the duchess, rather than Emilia Pio, moves
the conversation along. By emphasizing the homosocial world
in which his politically minded, statesman-like courtier wants to
move, Ottaviano Fregoso erases the court lady and the society of
leisure over which she was allowed to reign in the previous books.
Bembo then removes her from his lengthy discourse on Neopla-
tonic love by simply transcending both her and her implicit, im-
portant position in the context of courtly love.[20] The Magnifico
complains about this procedure in clear terms, for in his mind
Ottaviano's courtier has been so improved that women find them-
selves with no role to play (4, 44, 322). Ironically, the problem may
be that the Magnifico disagrees more with the new position carved
out for the courtier vis-à-vis the prince than with that of the court
lady vis-à-vis the courtier; indeed, the task of sage counselor that
Fregoso gives his courtier may prove too personally dangerous in
everyday life.

Book 4 stages two discourses within a structure of arrival/re-
turn to the father. The first, Ottaviano's political and Aristotelian
discussion, leads the courtier toward his earthly father, the prince,
because only in him can he both find gratification for his social
needs and valorize his image. The second, Bembo's Neoplatonic
ladder of love, leads the courtier toward God as the final destina-
tion of a longed-for, upward journey toward the satisfaction of his
desires. Both Oedipal journeys predicate woman's exclusion.

In his reconstruction of the passage from earthly to other-
worldly love, from a mimetic and mediated Girardian desire to
a transcendental and Ficinian one, Bembo proceeds to eliminate
woman at succeeding levels. First, he affirms that the beloved's ab-
sence is advantageous to the lover because it marginalizes the most
impetuous aspects of his passion. Beauty does not reside exclu-
sively in the body, he argues; on the contrary, the body diminishes
one's perfection. To lovers, especially young ones suffering from

their beloved's absence, Bembo suggests the elimination of the body—the feminine body—as a way to solve the problem: "Bisogna che 'l cortegiano con l'aiuto della ragione revochi in tutto il desiderio dal corpo alla bellezza sola e, quanto più po, la contempli in se stessa simplice e pura e dentro nella immaginazione la formi astratta da ogni materia" ("With the help of reason the courtier should turn his desire completely away from the body to beauty alone. He should contemplate beauty as far as he is able in its own simplicity and purity, create it in his imagination as an abstraction distinct from any material form" [4, 66, 344]).

Through his imagination, the courtier can then supplement or increase woman's beauty, and in the passage from the aesthetic to the ethical, he can eliminate the conflation of woman with beauty. As he ascends the ladder of love, certain that there is only one love and that this love is divine, Bembo's courtier establishes himself firmly as a Christian believer and a moralist. He also confirms himself as a narcissist, since love is now a vector, an inextinguishable desire for immortality, as in Socrates's *Symposium*.[21] Interestingly enough, Castiglione has Emilia Pio pull Bembo back to earth at this point: "Guardate, messer Pietro, che con questi pensieri a voi ancora non si separi l'anima dal corpo" ("Take care, Pietro, that with these thoughts of yours you too do not cause your soul to leave your body" [3, 71, 349]). The gesture is ironic in the sense that it partly demystifies this otherworldly discourse, but it may be yet another demonstration that women are too intellectually unsophisticated to appreciate philosophical and theological arguments.

Thus we return to square one: if in her social representation woman is so much the *trait d'union* between two men that she becomes invisible, in the Neoplatonic discussion just put forward, she is the *trait d'union* between a man and his God, once again at the center of a theory—woman assimilated to the idea of beauty—that can lead only to her elimination. The discourse on love, with its liturgical overtones, is, as usual, a discourse that does not include her and does not concern her. The book ends predictably with the contemplation of dawn and with the passage from the mother's domain (the night, in which the conversation is directed by the duchess) to the father's territory (the day, in which the distinct hours are "spent in honorable and pleasing activities" ["divise in onorevoli e piacevoli esercizi," 1, 4, 35]), all benignly controlled by Duke Guidubaldo.

Yet, eliminated from the conversation in which her identity is verbally constructed, excluded from the philosophical arguments on love, radically projected as "other" or as the sum of others' desires, woman refuses to disappear as an object of conversation in the text. I am referring not to the court lady herself, because she rarely rebels against the injunction not to speak but to the woman that the men try to identify, illustrate, and understand among themselves and for themselves. In this sense, the Magnifico's comment that it is difficult to depict a woman because he has to do the job all by himself ("queste donne, che pur lo san fare, non m'aiutano ad acconciarla"; "these ladies, who well know how, do not assist me to attire her" [3, 2, 208]) has a whining tone to it; the women do not participate in this system of signification because they are asked not to. All four books of the *Cortegiano* close, interestingly, with a return to woman. In the first, interrupted by the Prefect's arrival, the topic is woman as the object of attention for voyeurs; in the second, there is a call to institute the lady of the palace; in the third, there is an appeal to stop talking about women; in the fourth comes an invitation to resume talking about them to settle the argument between Pallavicino and the Magnifico. Thus, one can assume that woman, whether praised or denigrated, will also serve as the object of conversation the next day, both inside and outside the text.

This proliferation of discourses is in the end less unusual than it may appear, for as long as woman does not speak of herself by herself, as long as the happiness and pleasure Castiglione mentions are generated only by her absence or by her phantasmatic presence, there will be, always and everywhere, a discourse on her. It is a discourse that can never be concluded, because a question that ventures into the inexpressible, the excessive, the ahistorical, or the absent can only and inevitably expand. It is a discourse, moreover, that can only lead to the exclusion of woman because it constructs her as enigma, attacks her as incoherent, and laments her non-representability (a position that nevertheless makes her representable, for instance, in mythical terms). Set aside as unequal to the courtier by the misogynist Pallavicino (woman as opposite to man) and perceived as destabilizing because excessive by Canossa, woman is no less linguistically and historically marginalized by the Magnifico, who constructs her discursively, not for what she is but for what he wants her to be, an inanimate and certainly silent Galatea, hierarchically placed within a discourse that can only appropriate her. The Magnifico's woman is simply a non-man.

The issue should perhaps be posited differently. What would happen if woman were to decline to participate in the game and refuse to be represented? What if she were not to allow others to count on her supporting her representation or to think that she would support, *a priori*, the views of her desiring instituters? What if she herself proposed a game and moved from being a sign herself to being a producer of signs? She could choose, for instance, to respond with a counter-discourse to Aretino's enigma on the meaning of the letter S on the duchess's diadem, which for him is another artificial veil made to deceive ("un artificioso velame per poter ingannare," 1, 9, 42), a sentence connecting woman once again to artifice and mask. What is there behind the female veil? In other words, "What does woman want?" As Freud was to confess to Marie Bonaparte, he had been unable to answer this question in thirty years of research. Perhaps it would be better to keep this desired woman hidden ("occulta," 3, 2, 208), the Magnifico proposes, since she refuses to let herself be spoken about in toto at the very moment that she seems benignly to accede to her own reconstruction. Because of this, she will forever be a locus of desire and fear, everywhere willingly but never definitely or satisfactorily instituted.

CHAPTER THREE

The Comic Bond: Castiglione on Jokes Via Freud

The possibility of lying is the proprium *of semiosis just as (for the Schoolmen) the possibility of laughing was the* proprium *of Man as* animal rationale.

—Umberto Eco, *A Theory of Semiosis*, 59

A jest's prosperity lies in the ear of him that hears it, never in the tongue of him that makes it.

—Shakespeare, *Love's Labor's Lost*, V, 2

M Y ARGUMENT IN the preceding two chapters has been that
power is asymmetric in *Il libro del cortegiano:* the male voice is
hegemonic throughout because it controls representation, whereas
the female voice, even when heard, is obfuscated because it is as-
similated to the authoritative and always male voice appointed to
create civilized, courtly masculine and feminine identities. This
process constructs woman as indispensable to the courtier's being
and well-being (Chapter 1); it also keeps her in her place through
both a linguistic tour de force of minimization and desexualization
and an aesthetic process of idolization and iconization (Chapter 2).
I have argued that since subjectivity is formed through language,
access to the economy of discourse allows man to fashion himself
actively, and lack of access dooms woman to a passive, blatantly
marginal position. As a result, the courtier can ground himself his-
torically, but the court lady finds herself transhistorically surveyed;
he can inscribe himself in the text with a combination of idealized
and practical characteristics, whereas she gets only a romanticized
facade.

In this chapter I look at the way women are presented in the
conclusion to Book 2, where the subject of conversation is jokes
(a loose Italian translation of *facezie*). This section has seemingly
nothing to do with the institutional discourse on the court lady in
Book 3. To be sure, there is the same combination of discourse and
history vis-à-vis femininity as in the following book, but here the
court lady is not implicated in an economy of pleasure. Rather, she
finds herself the butt of a number of jokes. What makes woman's
position idiosyncratic in these pages? What renders woman not
just the usual passive object of representation, but that ever more
negative character, the disavowed "I" waiting for laughter to re-

move her from the symbolic order? Laughter, Bergson wrote, is a form of social control used to embarrass and frighten those whose behavior is judged to be rebellious—a statement the Neoplatonists, who also cherished the *ridendo dicere verum* dictum, would have applauded.[1] How does woman transgress societal codes, sex roles, or princely rules and come to be seen as needing punishment through merriment?

The conclusion of Book 2 analyzes the typology of witty plots and the techniques of delivery and effectiveness. My aim is not to study jokes per se or forms of humor in which only men are involved; rather, I concentrate on the *Cortegiano*'s *facezie* about women, which are admittedly few. Through a paradigmatic study of the triangular structure of jokes, I hope to link the problems posed by representation with those concerning the formation of identity in the *Cortegiano* and the positioning of the subject/object construct in discourse. First, I concentrate on jokes in which women are the target and consider the pleasures and dangers for jokers and courtly audiences when a woman is involved. Then I search for answers to the puzzling question: Can a woman enjoy a joke about herself? Can she laugh at herself while being laughed at? In other words, can she both "get" and "take" a joke?[2]

Introduced within the joke-work, not as a teller and only once as a member of a group of receivers, the court lady finds herself occupying, all too often, the place of the laughed at. The look that causes laughter, however, is different from that which contextualizes woman in Book 3. Created there through the reassembling of scattered images of her psyche and of her body from mythical, fictional, pictorial, and sculptural ideas of womanhood, this ideal woman is first disciplined, beautified, and normativized, and then offered as a spectacle, an object fashioned by and for masculine desire and for that reason cherished at the institutional level. In this section on jokes, however, woman does not function as an erotic spectacle for the gratification of the denizens of the Urbino court. If such were the case, there would be no reason to laugh at her. The courtiers continue to investigate woman and woman's body here, but something in their reading causes merriment, some eccentricities make her the repository of antic remarks, some stains somehow exclude her from the libidinal economy. The gaze that fixes her is no longer one of admiration, but more often than not one of violation.

The jokes in Book 2 target woman as excessive, inadequate, overbearing, unstable, prideful, foolish. She is matter, a point of division, a sign for the illogical and the contradictory. She is a non-subject, a nonbeing, playing the masquerade of femininity. What she needs, the text implies, is a demystification, a timely redefinition, and a pertinent verbal disavowal. By reading pathology into her behavior and by seeing symptoms in the answers her body gives to the outside world, the joker disparages her, reconducts her to silence, and remarginalizes her. He also shakes off his anxiety through the liberating, bonding laugh that he shares with his listeners, making the joke a good joke.

Book 2 is no exception to the *Cortegiano*'s usual game of sexual politics. The court lady does the listening, and the courtier does the talking. Were woman a speaker, however, anthropological studies of humor show that not only would she tell and laugh at other jokes, but she would most probably not even engage in the same forms of witticism. In a recent book on humor, Mahadev Apte examines the reasons behind women's lack of interest in pranks, slapstick, and clowning and considers a number of inhibitory cultural and psychological constraints that work against the production of female humor.[3] Men control women's wit, Apte points out, through their reiteration that some supposedly natural feminine qualities, such as passivity and virtue, are non-conducive to boisterous humor. Moreover, because they fear female aggressiveness, men tend to control all verbal forms in which belligerence and hostility are displayed, jokes included. Restrictions are especially stringent for unmarried and younger women. Female humor is generally not aggressive, Apte writes; women like to mock, not to insult. They rarely engage in practical jokes, and their verbal puns are usually not hostile. No matter which form of humor we consider, no court lady in Book 2 tells a joke either within the mimesis or the diegesis of the text. Again, such a posture mirrors the outer structure of the *Cortegiano,* in which woman cannot enter ideologically into the discussion and remains in narration only by agreeing to accept the function of go-between.

The section on pleasantries and witticisms occupies fifty-three chapters. It is strategically nestled between the institution of the courtier in Book 1 and in the first part of Book 2 and that of the court lady in Book 3. It concludes with a lengthy reflection on antifeminist humor, which in turn engenders the prolific and argumentative discourse on women in the following book. Many critics find this cluster of jokes unduly long, overworked, frivolous, out of place, and out of fashion. Yet wit was a popular subject both in Renaissance texts—witness the *Novellino*—and in classical works. In this sense, it is not surprising that Cicero's metatheories and classic pleasantries in the *De oratore,* recycled and modernized, influence this section of the *Cortegiano.*[4] Castiglione must have cherished the topic of humor from the very start, given the number of jokes he included in the first draft. Whether he thought that jokes might be overly dangerous can only be an unconfirmable suspicion at this point. The fact is that the final (1528) edition contains fewer jokes than do earlier versions.[5]

A taxonomy of humor proves useful beyond the purpose of discussing a fashionable subject or of lightening the atmosphere at court for an evening. It also teaches the would-be perfect courtier a number of techniques. As a performer at a refined court and an aristocrat continuously vying for recognition and favor yet always watchful for unpredictable changes, the courtier must consistently test his limits. He needs to learn, for example, how to graciously win a reputation at court in both serious and playful matters, and how to excel in *sprezzatura,* the practice of making actions seem effortlessly performed. In this sense, humor provides him ample opportunity because it is possible to elicit laughter only when appearing sufficiently spontaneous and natural. Joke after joke demonstrates the rewards of timely repartees, the pitfalls to avoid vis-à-vis an unknown audience, or the artfulness that goes with levity. The ninety-seven examples provided in this section thus both showcase the value of wit at court and offer a repertory of jokes for the use of any urbane courtier needing to ingratiate himself with an audience.[6]

Wit is potentially subversive because it cuts across class and sexual boundaries, destabilizes social relations, questions power, and bypasses moral inhibitions. It is therefore not surprising that a text that propagandizes hierarchical behaviors and chastises breaches of etiquette controls humor so tightly. Thus, wit moves tactically and tactfully from top to bottom, from more to less influential men, from pope to cardinal, from prince to courtier. It also moves from man to woman, since both in the telling of the joke and in the illustration of the joke-work, women are excluded as subjects. Throughout the section, wit is delivered in ways that reflect courtly criteria and courtly ideology. Courtiers use no profanities apart from those allusive language can evoke, cherish no defilements if they require crude humour, and offer no vulgarities unless they have been previously nuanced. Unlike Boccaccio, who turned to laughter in the *Decameron* to respond both to the atmosphere of death enveloping his company and to the confusion that disease was bringing to the social order, here laughter bonds the group together and is gentle throughout. A sense of property, harmony, and grace punctiliously controls delivery; license is authorized because it is disciplined, and decorum is maintained even when decorum is abandoned within the story.[7]

Put another way, this section does not question the collective identity of the courtly company. If it seems to produce subversion, it is also true that it immediately contains it; indeed, we could say that subversion is produced in order to show how easy it is to recuperate it. This explains the silencing of the official court jester, even though he is the most qualified wit. The laughter that low humor generates can be too disruptive when not controlled or censured intrafamilially from those above.

The place of the Gonzaga prankster is taken instead by an amateurish coterie of influential, talkative courtiers. Bernardo Bibbiena, the theoretician and master *de ridiculis* in this section, and Ludovico da Canossa, the other resident court wisecracker, join Cesare Gonzaga, Pietro Bembo, and the Magnifico Juliano de' Medici in a pyrotechnics of wit. Time and again they offer their own banter, quote each other's past quips, rehash practical jokes or recall occasions on which they were victimized by pranks. The stratagem of involving everyone in either telling a joke or laughing at one serves to legitimize the transgressions that laughter textualizes. The participation of peers, moreover, creates that "discursive fellowship" of which Foucault speaks (*Archaeology of Knowledge*, 225–26), that sense of bonding that flourishes in a homogenous, privileged group speaking the same language, enjoying the same sociopolitical background, and consciously fashioning itself as a repository of taste. Everyone in the group feels the homosocial pleasure of being an integral part of a community that knows itself and likes what it knows, so much so that as a group it can laugh at its members' idiosyncrasies. This also explains why the preferred form of laughter comes not from obscenities but from double entendres, puns, or slight changes in word position or meaning; in short, from jokes using techniques that the members of the group understand because they share a common vocabulary, education, and status.

Anything goes in this section—pranks, puns, jests, anecdotes, quips, mockeries, banters, double entendres, pleasantries, wordplays, dirty jokes, one-liners, shaggy-dog stories, sarcastic rejoinders, nonsense humor, ironic ripostes, regional eccentricities, and antimarital or anticlerical responses.[8] All possible techniques of the joke-work are employed, from condensation to displacement of words, from all-out absurdities to the representation of opposing ideas. The narrative strategy is to have a courtier introduce a joke within a frame that explains its typology and then illustrate the topic with one or more examples.

The discussion on humor starts quite properly with a semantic problem. Man loves a good laugh, Bibbiena claims, because he is by definition an animal capable of laughing ("un animal risibile," 2, 45, 153). The statement harkens back to both its direct and its indirect source, Cicero and Aristotle.[9] Laughter de-dramatizes life, it allows man to set aside his psychic anxieties and the censure of his superego and to cope with everyday problems. In defining laughter, Bibbiena dodges description and opts for circumlocution. Laughter comes, he hypothesizes, out of "una certa deformità; perchè solamente si ride di quelle cose che hanno in sè disconvenienzia e par che stian male, senza però star male" ("the source of the ridiculous is to be found in a kind of deformity; for we laugh only at things that contain some elements of incongruity and seem disagreeable though they are not really so" [2, 46, 154]). Laughter can be dangerous, then, because it carries a built-in hostility and unpleasantness, and yet it may not be risky after all, since it can relieve inner tensions.

There is no more powerful context for studying jokes than Freud's *Jokes and Their Relation to the Unconscious* (1905). Freud distinguishes innocent from non-innocent, or trivial from tendentious, jokes. Tendentious jokes can be hostile (told for aggressive, defensive, or satirical purposes) or obscene (used for sexual exposure, as in the case of the smutty joke). Subcategories in Freud's classification include jokes that show aggressive tendencies and those that move toward the exhibitionistic or the skeptical.

For Freud, jest (*Scherz*) is the only innocent joke because it is purposeless.[10] It produces only pleasure, just as play pleases children. A jest is the result of a gratifying combination of words and sounds that acquire meaning only when voiced. As such, the jest requires two people: the teller and the listener. Freud establishes a clear link between joke-work and dream-work and even uses the same vocabulary to describe these two psychic processes (i.e., condensation with substitution, displacement, omission, faulty thinking, indirect or opposite representation, absurdity, contradiction).

Castiglione seems to anticipate Freud's concept of the jest when he writes that the main purpose of wit is "ingannar la opinione e rispondere altramente che quello che aspetta l'auditore . . . o dissimulare o beffare o riprendere o comparare" ("to cheat expectation and to respond in a way that is unexpected. And . . . it must be flavored with deceit, or dissimulation, or ridicule, or censure, or comparison" [2, 83, 188]). Wit, moreover, is spontaneous: "Le facezie e i motti sono più presto dono e grazia di natura che d'arte" ("Pleasantries and witticisms are the gift and favour of Nature rather than of art" [2, 42, 150]). This mirrors Freud's thesis that jokes, as well as dreams, have their basis in the unconscious. Yet, whereas a dream is essentially good for the dreamer, a psychic product that does not need to be comprehended or communicated, a joke is good for the teller only when he has deprivatized it and made it intelligible. Telling per se makes joking a rewarding, enjoyable activity. The listener is mystified by the strange combination of meanings in the joke-work, puts to rest for a moment his rational and critical faculties or refuses to censor the content of what he hears, finds meaning where he usually would see none, and rewards the teller with a good laugh.[11]

The tendentious joke (*der Witz*) is more complicated for Freud in that a good subject and delivery alone are not enough to arrive at the desired result, laughter. For a dirty joke to be thought good, the teller must have a reason for wanting to tell the joke, since wit must always have a purpose, whether it is to crush inhibitions or provisionally set aside rational faculties. The reason behind a dirty joke is clearly tied to sex and to inner feelings of aggression on the teller's part that need release. The punchline provides exactly that—an explosive, automatic, and infectious laughter.

According to Freud, an effective *Witz* must involve three characters: a teller, a listener, and the object (butt) of the joke—a person or simply an idea that is unpleasant or difficult to entertain. The success of the joke lies not in the narrator's delivery, properly speaking. Rather, in anticipation of pleasure, the listener agrees to listen and to respond to the punchline with a laugh if, and only if, the joke achieves its ludicrous effect. The teller is not supposed to laugh at his own telling, although he will enjoy it vicariously and will laugh, Freud writes, *"par ricochet."*

With the dirty joke (*die Zote*) something interesting occurs. Freud assumes that this joke has a woman as its butt. In this sense the dirty joke becomes a substitute for an attempted, but unrealized or impossible, seduction, a dislocated or displaced "act of sexual aggression" performed in words. The teller participates in it vicariously; the listener, caught in his desire to know more, is engaged as a spectator. The story that Freud characterizes as distinctive of the joke scenario is then, not surprisingly, the usual story of triangular desire so central to Western narrative. In its most typical plot, desire is forever in search of fulfillment and yet is voiced in order to relieve the anxiety and share the tension that its non-fulfillment creates.

In such a context, it is easy to understand how this desire (whose gender can be postulated only as masculine) works. In his theory of the dirty joke, Freud describes an interaction of the teller, the woman, and the listener. The intrusion of the other man into a primal scene—an attempt at seduction, which then fails as a result of this interruption and of the uncanny injection of a moral inhibition—allows the once-binary relationship of would-be seducer and would-be seduced to be expanded. The coming of the rival third party causes the woman—who may have been unavailable anyhow, and who for this reason may already have engendered aggressiveness on the seducer's part—to become permanently unavailable and starts a displacement of the teller's hostility from the woman (mainly sexual) to the man (only verbal).

In telling his joke, the teller textualizes what he cannot have sexually and so regains his power. He controls the woman by punishing her rebuff and unyieldingness through a joke that makes fun of her or plainly exposes her, and thus he is more easily able to deflect or renounce his desire for her. She may feel so humiliated, Freud insists, that she leaves the room, thus disappearing from the triangle. The teller also controls the listener by gratifying his own libido through a discursive illustration of sexual characteristics in the woman, which he alludes to in veiled terms and which correspond to what he has been unable to attain. Since he is not dialectically or psychologically implicated in the pair's relationship, the listener—whether he is sexually excited by the joke and/ or embarrassed—feels no anxiety and can explode into laughter. This assures a feeling of complicity between the two men and a subsequent sensation of relief on the part of the teller. Through devious means that necessitate exposure, he has been able to satisfy his desire and to expend his emotional energy.[12]

Eventually the listener turns out to be the only one in the triangle who enjoys the joke, because he is the only one sufficiently disengaged to allow himself some loss of control through a good laugh. In fact, whereas listening to a joke is a conscious choice, the laughter that ensues is not consciously controlled. Laughter, however, is spontaneous only up to a point: the listener, who knows a punchline is coming whose only purpose is to make him laugh, willingly accepts the veiling of the sexual content of the joke until its resolution. The pleasure or the annoyance he derives from the attention he must give the joke also makes him want to share the joke with somebody else, and thus he starts the circular, repetitive process that makes a teller out of any listener.

This tripartite process, as Samuel Weber, Jerry Aline Flieger, and Jeffrey Mehlman have noticed, is Oedipal in structure: a third person, with his arrival upon a scene of desire, turns from rival to ally and allows the teller's ego to recognize itself (and a self) by coming to terms with a specular other. The father's explanation of the mystery in the Oedipus triangle corresponds here to the explanation of the story in the joke by a characteristic, all-resolving punchline. It is triangularity, moreover, that engenders discourse. "The exercise of language needs the presence of three persons, not just two," Todorov writes. "As long as there is only 'I' and 'you,' discourse is not indispensable. It is when a third person appears that discourse becomes necessary" (36). For the joke to be understood, shared, and enjoyed, both teller and listener must have a common set of possible desires, values, and inhibitions. This is precisely the social situation in the *Cortegiano*.

Jokes at the expense of women in Castiglione's text inevitably slide toward the mordant and the sensual, from the pun on Emilia Pio, whose one-word disguise tells a different story ("signora Emilia impia" [2, 61, 167] is not a mere flippancy, but a sexually charged play on words), to the double meaning itself ("Dicesi ancor: 'Colei è una donna d'assai,' volendola laudar di prudenzia e bontà; il medesimo poria dir chi volesse biasimarla, accennando che fosse donna di molti"; "One also hears it said: 'She is a much-loved lady,' meaning to praise a woman for her prudence and virtue; but the same words might be used to censure her for bestowing her favours widely" [2, 47, 155]). Within the structure of a joke involving women, even without having read Freud's theorization of the female position in the joking process, one could hardly fail to notice that women are in a losing, or at least awkward, situation. Four examples will illustrate my point.

The first joke centers on the unreadability of a woman's face and on the subsequent reasons for a laugh to cancel the enigma she represents. The next two punish and parody woman's body for incorporating something excessive, something that disfigures her person and makes the onlooker avert his gaze. The last joke deals with female commodification and hints at woman's uneasiness in participating in the general laughter. All four jokes enshrine the paradigmatic triangular structure: a man tells a story about something peculiar in a woman to another man or to an audience of eager listeners, with the result that the woman in his narrative is ridiculed. For his part, the listener, a father/rival figure in the Freudian scenario or the Law of the Name-of-the-Father in the Lacanian figuration, recontains woman's difference through a final, ponderous laugh.

The first joke of Book 2 is a full-fledged example of the politics of reading: a woman's seemingly empty gaze becomes the text for her inner thoughts. The *motto da ridere* is this: a beggar whining and pleading for alms, Bibbiena tells us, repeatedly importunes a lady hearing mass. She neither responds nor dismisses him and simply keeps doing whatever she is doing as if he were not there (2, 47, 155–56). For this she is ridiculed. At first the structure does not seem to be triangular, since we have five persons involved: the lover, whose love is classically unrequited, two of his friends, the beggar, and the beloved. The four men can be reduced to two actually, for there is a subtle game of doubling going on. The lover, for example, doubles for the friend who speaks first, because they share an identical fascination with sadomasochistic readings, and for the beggar, given their position vis-à-vis woman. The two friends mirror each other, first, by offering two contradictory aspects of the same reading and, second, by being Oedipal intruders in the dual relationship of lover/beloved. In the last case they also mirror the beggar, himself a voyeur.

As the story makes plain, the problem with this woman is that she refuses to look, to see, to make a choice, or, in a more general sense, to desire. She refuses to meet any of the men's eyes fastened on her face and, thus, by not returning their look, does not mirror their desires. No matter what she does, she is consistently at the center of the men's combined gaze, with all of them looking at her not-looking. Each man provides a reading of her behavior. Her lover assimilates her stance toward the beggar to the one she holds toward him. She is cruel, he says, because she neither acknowledges nor refuses his love. The two other men take opposite approaches: one defends her by reading her behavior pedagogically (excessive pleading, he warns the lover, gets you nowhere); the other chastises her through a tendentious remark (she likes the begging part of the game for its own sake, he suggests, even if, given her status, her assent to the request is out of the question). Finally, for the beggar, who does not talk, she is just heartless.

Here we have a useful example of the fantasy construct of woman as unreadable and enigmatic. In representation, be it written, oral, or visual, the identities articulated in the discourse seem to be consistently divided along sexual lines as active or passive, subject or object.[13] "One is always in representation," Cixous notices, "and when a woman is asked to take place in this representation, she is, of course, asked to represent man's desire" (quoted in Heath, "Difference," 96). In other words, woman is present in representation not because she represents her specificity (woman as woman), but because she is part of a system of oneness (woman as object of a supposedly ungendered discourse). Reconducted to male subjectivity, she becomes complementary to man, a metaphor for what he wants her to be, as long as she is linguistically disposable. Representation is never neutral; like discourse, it is backed by an ideology and a structure of power.

The lady of our joke—her lack of actions continually on display—is, as usual, excluded from the enunciation. Yet her unreadability tells a story, or in fact, three stories. Each fills her total, stubborn silence with partial truths, but she is never asked to provide her own reasons, even though she is the only one who could answer for her behavior. Her mute interrogators, however, experience anxiety at her taciturnity and discharge it by a laugh. This accomplishes two aims: it displaces the erotic rivalry among the men and de-eroticizes the woman. For the three friends, the noblewoman's failure to choose not only establishes her appeal but also engenders the fear that she may be hiding something, that she may have a different story to tell. She is thus regrounded as enigma and riddle and deciphered in a chain of readings meant to make her behavior acceptable. As a result, she is a true paradox: in order for the desire that she creates to remain alive, she must remain silent. Yet this is exactly what makes her laughable. Were she to respond to man's desire, she would lose her halo and be just as laughable for having changed the terms upon which her image needed to be constructed. Desire and power go together, Foucault reminds us. Only the person in control of discourse can express his subjectivity and his desire and thus establish the terms of representation.

The woman laughed at in the second joke, is exposed in a different way. In Freud's terms, this joke could be called hostile because it is aggressive and satirical. Bibbiena is its teller in the actual triangular joke-work and its reteller in the text. While he upbraids a woman in the street for her excessive makeup, Canossa, his friend and the third party, unexpectedly arrives on the scene and offers his own reading of the incident. He tells Bibbiena that his reproach of the woman is not admonishment per se but a self-reading through a proxy. In the woman, Bibbiena is scrutinizing not a person of the other sex but a degraded "I," and this uncanny feeling is creating in his own self a sensation of uneasiness. As Bibbiena retells it, "In quel volto, quando era acconcio, così vedeva me stesso come nello specchio; e però, per esser brutto, non arei voluto vedermi" ("When her face was made up I could see myself as in the mirror, and, being very ugly, I would rather not" [2, 62, 170]).

The story is a complex one, because the listener retorts with an explanation that, rather than questioning the content of the joke, deviously adds to the joker's pleasure. The movement from the sexual to the verbal through laughter reconfirms the usual outcome: for A to laugh with C and experience narcissistic gratification, B (the woman) must be dislodged. The result is that Bibbiena reestablishes his homosocial bond with Canossa through comic self-derision in his retelling; the woman, however, derided both for her makeup and for the ugliness and the grotesqueness that her makeup covers and emphasizes according to the men is displaced.

The moral of the story is that a woman can be praised if she incarnates the aesthetic ideals the onlooker narcissistically searches for in her; she can be chided, however, if she is perceived as excessive and transgressive. The "scandal" is eliminated if she slides, more or less consciously, toward an identification with the masculine look—or an acceptance of the masculine point of view. In other words, woman has to present herself as she is asked to be, a stand-in for man's desire, a mirror of whatever he wants her to mirror, and a symbol of possible erotic gratification.

Paradoxically, what is faulted in this woman is not that she disguises herself, but that she does not disguise herself in accepted ways. The mask that she has to wear as a woman to hide her lack and better reflect male desire does not coincide with the one she creates with cosmetics. She is parodied as excessive and duplicitous because she counterfeits her nature. Her goodness, on the other hand, Bibbiena implies, would make her both presentable and representable. Thus, the woman as artifice needs to be exorcised because she takes too seriously her exhibitionistic role in patriarchal culture, a role that constructs her as "feminine" and provides her with whatever attributes the word suggests. It is one thing for woman to offer her body to man's scopophilic gaze, but quite another to oversignify male desire by covering her nature and her sexual being with a masquerade of femininity.[14]

Reduced to a "thing," woman finds that even her "thingness" signifies; although she does not talk, her face speaks. Makeup alone provides all the clues Bibbiena needs to judge her. Upon seeing the woman, he informs us, he can only deflect his look. Rather than finding a beauty who gratifies his scopophilia, Bibbiena discovers a being whose facial disorder destabilizes his expectations.

The ludicrous becomes ridiculous. Fearing the unexpected self-confrontation and finding that he cannot recontain the woman through a fetishistic construction, he opts for a sadistic reading and disparages her.

The anxious laugh shared with Canossa allows Bibbiena to reestablish control and simultaneously to affirm and to deny that he is scrutinizing a problematic side of his selfhood, his own woman-ishness. This makes it possible for him to refashion woman according to male standards. Ornamentation is discursively punished as artifice—and thus as deviance—not on social grounds (or perhaps partly on social grounds, given the extensive sumptuary laws enacted at the time) but for what it psychologically reveals about a woman to the man engaged in reading her: the possibility of seduction, the fear of female flesh, the association with lust and mischief, the scandalous possibility that she is not unnatural but self-sufficient, not adulterated but whole, not concupiscent but sensitive, at one and at ease, body and flesh.[15] Psychoanalytically, such a woman enhances the male fear of castration; socially, her twist of independence undermines the written and unwritten laws of male hegemony over her sex. To deny her existence is to deny the possibility of male desire, yet to seek the danger of her excessive presence is literally self-treacherous. Thus, to cancel desire, man has to uncover her physical or psychological peculiarities; to turn away from her seductive front, he has to confront her Medusa-like image and refuse to flirt with death.

Puns on dressing/undressing, veiling/unveiling, essence/appearance are central to the third joke, in which woman is parodied as an example of the worst kind of affectation.[16] Affectations invite ridicule because they are exaggerated, Bibbiena tells us (2, 54, 163). With this statement he confirms an opinion already fully expressed, for example, by Plato, who in a dialogue between Socrates and Protarchus in *Philebus* contended that ludicrousness born out of conceit should be met with laughter. Asked why she was so bored, looked so out of place, and seemed so worried during a party, a noblewoman answered that her fear was ontological, as we would say today. She could not cope with the idea that she would appear naked in front of Christ on Judgment Day: "Io non posso tollerar l'affanno che sento, pensando che il mio ancor abbia ad esser veduto ignudo" ("I cannot tell you the distress I feel at the thought that my body will have to appear naked as well" [2, 54, 163]). The contemptuous telling of the joke makes the audience laugh. What for the woman is a feeling of abjection magnified by an overriding anxiety about her bodily defects becomes for the teller a pretentious and grotesque behavior; what in her is a hypochondriacal bent is for the narrator a hysterical penchant. Her listeners (our third party), as well as the courtly group lending their ears to Bibbiena's retelling, read stupidity in her melodramatic account, sneer at the nonsensical flow and at the prurience of her rationalizations, and promptly dismiss her as extravagant. She may indeed be a prude.

Yet where is the merriment in the laugh? Can the audience remain innocent? Let me briefly examine the problems generated by the lady's unwillingness to show herself naked at the moment of truth. As a text of her being or nonbeing, this woman's body inscribes a story, the story of a body that becomes a narrative subject of interest only because it may be unclothed. In a more general context, the joke allows us to study the difference between naked femininity and nude femininity.[17] All visual arts, from painting to cinema, have celebrated the beauty of the nude female body, an object to see and, through seeing, to appropriate erotically. Venus, for example, consistently appears as a nude in Renaissance art, and yet her nudity is, more often than not, veiled. Woman's voluptuousness needs to be iconologically evoked and enhanced by a cover that covers little in terms of area but much in terms of seeing. In Freudian terms, woman needs a veil to cover what she lacks so that the veil can both affirm and deny that she lacks anything and thus charm men into desiring her all the more. Female nudity, therefore, especially if the body is not totally exposed, functions as a powerful erotic spectacle for the gratification of the "I" and the eye of the onlooker, as, for example, in Alcina's apparition to Ruggiero in *Orlando furioso*. This spectacle, properly aestheticized, generates a scopophilic pleasure either in its voyeuristic or fetishistic form.

On this occasion, however, the sight of a naked woman causes anxiety rather than libidinal investment. The gaze that should idealize her is feared as problematizing her. The woman's penchant for un-loving herself is perceived as symptomatic of a certain inadequacy; her naked self, rather than being aestheticized as feminine body, is downgraded to female flesh. This noblewoman describes her ornamented self as lost; the moment of truth literalizes the fact that by nature woman cannot be associated with truth (in Nietzsche's words, "She does not want truth—what is truth to woman? From the beginning, nothing has been more alien, repugnant, and hostile to woman than truth" [163]). Naked, she is unrecognized and unrecognizable, a nonbeing devalued to herself and to others. She is a spectacle that meets no eye, a castrated other engendering apprehension, a commodity no one cares to price. Moreover, she not only finds herself unreadable, but fears God's reading as well, because his glance of judgment may prove even more unsettling than the searching, objectifying, wanton male gaze she is accustomed to receiving. Has she sinned so much in life that her guilt can be read on her body's surface when the time of judgment comes? Is the body the site of her undoing? Or is the response to the sight of her body so desexualized that she cannot recognize herself in what is being seen? What body does she confront? Whose identity does she fear to see reflected in God's eyes?

The scenario recalls Masaccio's famous painting, *Expulsion from Eden*, in which Eve's nudity and shame of nudity in front of God's eyes play a central part.[18] Constructed culturally as feminine and conditioned by that image, woman fears a loss of identity when despoiled of her clothes. When this noblewoman has to unmask herself in order to remove the guise she has assumed to hide her nonindividuality, she does not recognize what she sees reflected. The moment of revelation finds her fearful of being revealed bodily, fearful that she has nothing left under her clothes, that she never possessed an "I," or that her "I" was an endorsement of others' view of her "I." Properly attired, on the other hand, she feels at ease because she can somehow conflate her femaleness with the current image of femininity and better reflect the construction of woman as object of male desires and fantasies, an image whose willing captive she has become.

In the fourth example, Bibbiena claims that the presence of women changes the perception of a joke and makes it appear cruel, for what is clever for an all-male audience can be offensive, indecent, and unseemly for a mixed audience (2, 68, 176). In this joke, the political controversy between Florence and Siena is played out in phallic language, with women objectified by the rivalry. To a man from Siena boasting of his city's new ties with the imperial faction—ties reached, he points out, by marrying Siena to the emperor, with the city of Florence as a convenient dowry—a Florentine answers with an obscene rejoinder: "Siena sarà la prima cavalcata (alla franzese, ma disse il vocabulo italiano); poi la dote si litigherà a bell'aggio" ("Siena will first be ridden—meaning this in the French sense, though he used the Italian word—then the dowry will be settled at leisure" [2, 68, 176]). According to Freudian categories, this joke is both tendentious, because it is sexually hostile toward women and complicitous toward men, and cynical, because it attacks the institution of marriage (implies that political settlements are no better than one-night stands). Above all, it is obscene, no matter how veiled the word that supposedly brings on the final laugh through a euphemism accessible only to the listener and to the courtly company to which it is addressed. The joke both reduces a political alliance to a husband/wife transaction and displaces a city with the metaphor of a female body, first submitted to man and then disposed.

For Bibbiena the joke becomes obnoxious, however, not because it complacently hints at the joys of male traffic in women, but because it lacks tact. It is indelicate, he states, to embarrass the women in the audience by making female bodies objects of ridicule. He does not say that what "makes" the joke is the feeling of phallic complicity that surfaces both between the teller and the listener and between Bibbiena and the male audience at the very moment that the women in the company become conspicuous for their feeling of shame. Again, the pleasure of the joker is easily surpassed by that of the listener; the pair's hostility, which is well marked ("un fiorentino ed un Sanese . . . per lo più, come sapete, sono nemici"; "a Florentine and a Sienese . . . are usually at odds with each other"), is displaced by the final laughter of camaraderie. As Todorov would have it, along with Lacan and Girard, the issue in a triangular situation is not "Cherchez la femme," but "Cherchez un tiers" (37).

What makes women in general so prudish? Why should they leave the room, as Freud hints they would do, when the joke aims at attacking them? After all, one of the understood requirements of courtly life, according to the Magnifico, is that the *donna di palazzo* restrain herself from appearing overly squeamish and avoid parting company when the conversation takes a slight turn toward the lascivious. Pallavicino ponders the problem in Book 2 and chooses this occasion to requalify for his role of debunker of womanhood. He starts by pointing out that, contrary to common belief, women like obscene jokes, more so in fact if there is little in them to make one think that they would enjoy lewdness. "Sonomi trovato ad arrossirmi di vergogna," he claims, "per parole dettemi da donne, molto più spesso che da omini" ("As for me, I have found myself blushing for shame far more because of words said by women than by men" [2, 69, 176]). Bibbiena urbanely dismisses the banter by saying that he is talking of virtuous women, the kind of women who usually run away from situations in which their honor is at stake. Later, he warns that it is necessary to be careful in using or including women in explicitly sexual jokes because the procedure is socially dangerous: "Essendo il parlar dell'onestà delle donne tanto pericolosa cosa d'offenderle gravemente, dico che dovemo morderle in altro ed astenerci da questo" ("Since even to mention a woman's honour carries the risk of doing grave harm, I say that we should refrain from this and get at them in some other way" [2, 90, 198]). A joke, thus, needs some sort of veiling to be effective, both because the punchline works better under those conditions and because social pressures predicate a toning down of the vocabulary. This court, moreover, wants to avoid maliciousness and obscenity at all costs and project itself as being above the fray.

And yet, if a joke needs by definition to carry a sense of the incongruous, laughing at women is always out of the question, for it is at female sexual characteristics that one usually laughs. Pallavicino asks that men not be objects of women's mirth either, "in quello che a noi così è vergogna, come alle donne la incontinenzia" ("with regard to something as shameful in us as unchastity is in women" [2, 92, 199]). What can make man a laughingstock is the issue of honor, although the term has different connotations when applied to different genders. As Pallavicino knows well, man's honor gives honor to a woman (in both cases honor is understood as social), but his honor is always in danger of being lost if the woman does not safeguard her own sexual honor for both his and her sake. Yet women are, in Ottaviano Fregoso's caustic words, very imperfect creatures ("animali imperfettissimi," 2, 91, 198), and for this reason it is imperative to impose a certain continence on them. The issue of female pleasure is, as usual, tied to that of male power, animality being for Pallavicino a philosophical given for women (which translates into a call for their social restriction) and an unproblematic issue for men (which translates into nothing, since men have no fear of social reprimand as a result of their normal sexual behavior).[19]

What is interesting in this brief discussion is that woman becomes the culprit of unending reproaches both because there are gender differences and because such controversies better serve male needs. As the Magnifico points out, Pallavicino makes such cutting remarks because he wants to be taken into the graces of a superior man, Ottaviano Fregoso, who has just expressed some harsh opinions on the female sex, "perchè spesso si dà fede a coloro che hanno molta autorità se ben non dicono così compitamente il vero" ("since trust is often placed in those who have great authority, even if they do not speak the whole truth" [2, 98, 203]). Again, the function of woman is to further the bond between two men cast in a hierarchical, autocratic relationship (one of power, for example, or of age). The usual (false) triangular, heterosexual relationship involving two men and a woman reveals in the end the (true) binary relationship of one man with another man. This is the very paradigm that Freud analyzed and atomized in his theory of the dirty joke. Although woman is ostensibly the main character in the joke-work, her position there is to advance, by means of her presence, the homosocial strategy of those telling tales about her. This inevitably leads to her being expurgated from the text, unless of course, desexualized and normativized, she is willing to accept the role of intermediator.[20]

Talking of sexual matters is thus dangerous for women no matter the circumstances. But laughing at female sexuality carries even a larger stigma, for it is unsettling not only for women but also for the whole group when it consists of people of the same social class. Two jokes in particular illustrate this point. Alonso Carillo is a Spanish nobleman involved twice in Book 2, both times with Signora Boadiglia, a court lady. The first time we are treated to a cynical joke (for Freud a joke that gives "the pleasure of lifting inhibitions by bringing into prominence sexual facts and relations by speech" [*Jokes*, 97]); the second, to an obscene joke.[21] Laughed at by a number of lords and ladies after his release from prison, Carillo makes a sarcastic rejoinder to Signora Boadiglia's quip about her earlier fear that this time he might have lost his head. Feeling linguistically emasculated and perhaps psychologically castrated, Carillo snaps back: "'Signora,' disse, 'io ancor ebbi gran paura di questo; pur aveva speranza che voi mi dimandaste per marito'" ("Madam, I was also very afraid of that, but then I formed the hope that you would ask to marry me" [2, 76, 182]). Bibbiena explains the retort as a local custom: in Spain, a man on his way to the gallows can have his life spared if a common whore asks to marry him (2, 76, 182). To counteract Signora Boadiglia's power (she does the looking, the talking, and the teasing here), Carillo chooses to disparage her sexually, even though there was nothing explicitly sexual in her query. Thus, he cures his sense of personal vulnerability, satisfies his libido obliquely, and provokes the audience to side with him.

Bibbiena does not chastise this behavior excessively but rejects Carillo's posture in a follow-up joke that once again casts the Spanish nobleman as Boadiglia's nemesis. The first time Carillo was able to punish the lady's investigating gaze and manipulative ways with swift verbal aggression; now her absence from the scene of the joke induces him to show his superiority through a more cutting remark. Walking with a lady and other members of the court in the street where Boadiglia lives, Carillo points to horned animals adorning her door and facetiously interprets them as symbols of her sexual profligacy. This time, in exposing cuckoldry for its own sake, Carillo also exposes his concern that he himself may be emasculated. He also indirectly expresses his fear of again losing his position in the joking triangle, of becoming once the butt of a joke rather than the teller. Having been laughed at and as a result having felt exposed and objectified, he earlier unwillingly occupied the position of the silenced woman in the Freudian jokework. By laughing first this time, he hopes to recontain his rival once and for all.

Bibbiena faults this joke as scurrilous and useless. Carillo's exposure of Boadiglia, he notices, is retaliatory and does not answer provocations on her part. The witticism lacks spontaneity; it is ludicrous, and therefore it is dismissed as unusable (2, 93, 200). A bad joke is clearly one that turns castration anxiety into evident and unveiled verbal aggression. It is also one that does not bring comic relief—this joke provokes no laughter. In fact, the refusal by its immediate receiver—interestingly, and for the only time in the text, a woman who remains unnamed throughout—to enjoy Carillo's repartee and to match his overeager outburst, allows a second look at masculine neuroses. "A person who laughs at smut that he hears is laughing as though he were the spectator of an act of sexual aggression," Freud writes (*Jokes*, 97). This is exactly what the female listener refuses to do.

When can woman laugh at herself? Can the court lady enjoy or appreciate a self that is being ridiculed? I argue that this is possible if she is allowed to tell a joke involving herself (or another woman), a joke whose outcome is not particularly negative. It is also possible for her to participate in the laughter engendered by a practical joke, even if she is the victim of the mockery, as long as the content is not sexual.

As for the first point, in no joke in the *Cortegiano* is woman either the joke teller in the audience or the joker within the story. These positions are simply not open to her. Yet they were open to other women, in other texts, and Castiglione refers to them. In the *Decameron*, Boccaccio allows women to trick, treat, and tell: to be originators of the laughter, winners of the ruse, and active joke tellers. Apart from those of Calandrino, most of the stories from the *Decameron* recalled in the *Cortegiano* as examples of pranks center on stratagems and deceptions that wives play on their husbands to gratify their sexual desires or escape personal violence. The first recontextualized story narrates the trick that Ricciardo Minutolo plays on Filippello's wife to secure sexual access to her body. The result of his ruse is that, once awakened sexually, the woman recognizes her own desires and decides to continue with her new relationship, *pace* Filippello (III, 6). The second story taken from the *Decameron* relates the fraud played by Beatrice on her husband Egano in order to pursue her own pleasure (VII, 7). The third recounts the hoax Monna Sismonda plays on her husband to save herself after he discovers her adultery (VII, 8). Boccaccio not only has women actively engaged in the ruses but also makes other women narrate them: Filomela tells Beatrice's trick; Neifile, Monna Sismonda's; and Fiammetta that of Filippello's wife. He also seems to imply that practical jokes can be played by either women or men. But in his anthropological study on humor, Apte finds that it is rare for women to play pranks on other women or on men.[22] The *Cortegiano* contains no such cases, perhaps because, unlike Boccaccio, Castiglione is not specifically interested in examining the issue of sexual deception that is at the heart of laughter in the earlier work.

Bibbiena ends the conversation on jokes in the *Decameron* by dismissing Boccaccio as misogynist: "Giovan Boccaccio era, come sete ancor voi, a gran torto nemico delle donne" ("Like you, Giovanni Boccaccio was a wicked enemy of women" [2, 95, 202]). And yet, was he? Another taxonomy would emerge were Boccaccio's examples read as a text of what happens when women appropriate personal desires in the face of social conventions. Can desire be proper when its pursuit questions the laws of propriety and makes female behavior improper? Can women desire? Or can women of the lower class desire, whereas those of the upper class have to remain tied to their prescribed roles? In the *Decameron*, the issue is posited in a number of often-contradictory ways. The question of whether Boccaccio can be read as a feminist writer is intriguing, but I would recommend caution. It is true, for example, that Boccaccio recognizes the need for sexual gratification in women as well as in men. Yet, in the story of Ricciardo Minutolo, in which a woman eagerly pursues sexual pleasure after she has been unwillingly awakened to it through a trick, can we not say that Boccaccio, rather than taking the position of a progressive writer, is here offering once again the worn-out image of female nature as animal-like? Isn't this another case of the call of the flesh proving irresistible to woman after she possesses sexual knowledge?

In Castiglione's text, since the feminine audience consists exclusively of women of the upper class, granting the court lady the right to a sexual desire is deemed socially disreputable and legally inadmissible: "Noi stessi avemo fatta una legge, che in noi non sia vicio ne mancamento nè infamia alcuna la vita dissoluta e nelle donne sia tanto estremo obbrobrio e vergogna" ("We ourselves, as men, have made it a rule that a dissolute way of life is not to be thought evil or blameworthy or disgraceful, whereas in women

it leads to such complete opprobrium and shame" [2, 90, 198]).
The Urbino world is already domesticated, a world of "disciplined
spontaneity," to use Rosalie Colie's expression (33), and one in
which unbridled pleasure is, by definition, aberrant.

As for women's participation in jokes that seemingly victimize
them, it is within the context of a prank that the court ladies enjoy
a good laugh in the *Cortegiano*, a prank that, for once, does not
employ obscene smut. Castiglione revised this section on practi-
cal jokes extensively, for he knew that it could be dangerous for
a courtier, and for himself as a courtier, to introduce *burle* and
beffe. He ran the risk of arousing the fury and retaliation of the
higher-ups or of lowering his style, an equally undesirable out-
come. Thus, he ensures that the content does not overflow into the
context. It is good to laugh, his spokesman Bibbiena repeats, but
some sense of propriety needs to be maintained in the telling of the
tale (2, 85, 190). If pranks can suspend rules of conduct and sub-
vert hierarchical positions, if they can manipulate laws and violate
codes, then it is important to de-dramatize them by telling only
manageable ones.

Two ladies of high status, whom Bibbiena twice refuses to
name (their identities have been reconstructed as Elisabetta Gon-
zaga and Emilia Pio), become in the text butts of a practical joke in
which the problems of naming, talking, and decoding are crucial.
An uncouth, talkative farmer from Bergamo is introduced to the
two ladies as a Spanish nobleman (2, 85, 191). The male audience
experiences the doubly gratifying pleasure of first, ridiculing pre-
sumptions by laughing at a man from a lower social class undoing
himself by his absurd verbal incongruities and boastful "linguis-
tic" abilities and, second, of ridiculing women, especially women
of the higher class, for their misreading of signs, because they be-
lieve that nobody would play a practical joke on them, given their
social status. The laughter is an assertion of superiority.

As usual, the *beffa* destabilizes order by seemingly disordering
everybody's position. The farmer gets ridiculed for his pretensions
and stupidity and is expunged from the text; the two ladies are
ridiculed for their credulity and lose their authority; and the court
itself, traditionally a place for obsequious behavior and solemn
events, becomes the center stage for non-serious matters. True
pleasure comes not from laughing at the farmer, however, but

from laughing at two noble women caught off guard. The prank effectively manages to separate the duchess as a historical subject, one worthy of praise and naturally praised, from the woman in the duchess, a gendered subject who has difficulty understanding everyday situations.

Still, neither of the two ladies seems to mind the retelling of their gullibility. What allows them to participate in the merriment? In the last chapter of *Jokes and Their Relation to the Unconscious*, Freud briefly theorizes on the comic and the humorous, mainly to underline their difference from the joke itself. Later, he returns to the subject in a short essay entitled "Humor." Freud casts humor midway between the comic and the joke and elaborates on one of its features, the naive. Naiveté on the part of the person being ridiculed, he writes, allows the teller and the audience at large (the third party in the joke-work) to relieve inhibitions with laughter, especially if the ingenuousness or naiveté is found in speech.[23] In this case, the country bumpkin can be ridiculed because he so thoroughly misuses words; he cannot, however, laugh at himself, because he is personally unaware of his absurdities. The audience, women included, can laugh at the retelling of this prank because of the sense of power each feels in teasing a person considered stupid.

Even when they are ridiculed, the court ladies are in a more powerful position than the farmer, a naturally comic target not only for his lower social status but, more interestingly, for his pretensions about his ability to bridge a cultural gap through linguistic means. Confusion in rank is what these courtiers can afford the least. One can speak like them, but not as well or as effortlessly. This is the rule of thumb for courtly discourse: the courtiers' self-identity and self-promotion rest precisely on this dogma. Moreover, the two unnamed women can join in the drollery and laugh at the farmer's lack of sophistication and his nonsense because the verbal repetition of the prank gives them pleasure, just as Freud's repetition of play does for children (*Spiellust*). Again, what we have here is a power deployment with women as the usual targets; lower-class men can occasionally substitute for them in this scheme and provide the upper-class ladies with a moment of relief, but the principle of male hegemony itself is never challenged.

Can women laugh at themselves? Can they assume the position of subjects? Freud says that they cannot within the triangular structure of a joke, but that they can within a comic or humorous framework. The comic situation has two characters rather than three: the teller and the person embodying the ridiculous traits, that is, the "I" and the object-person, each relating emphatically to the other (A identifies with B or compares him- or herself to B, in order to laugh at B; as a result, A feels better than B). Humor, by contrast, requires neither a tripartite structure (as in the dirty joke) nor a binary structure (as in the comic) and can be enjoyed by a single person. Power is neither in the teller, as in the comic, nor in the listener, as in the joke. Thus, whereas in the joke women are condemned to remain objects of the story and to cause laughter, in the comic and humorous position they can also be principal characters, because neither state is tied to a specific sex.

My contention is that although the outcome of sexual jokes is always negative for women, comic and humorous situations allow women, as characters, to remain in the text and to participate in the general drollery. According to circumstances, they can shift between the comic (pleasurable because powerful) and the humorous (pleasurable and yet brimming with unexpressed, unexpressible anger) and back again. The two unnamed ladies can laugh at themselves when they see their personae not as characters in the prank (a situation in which they are helpless) but as listeners to its retelling (a situation in which they can make their higher social position work for them). They may read the scene as comic and not mind its being told, because in the comic mode anybody can be derided and anybody would have acted as they did ("Non si disconvien talor usare le burle ancor coi gran signori"; the duchess offers, "ed io già ho udito molte esserne state fatte al duca Federico, al re Alfonso d'Aragona, alla reina donna Isabella di Spagna ed a molti altri gran principi"; "It is not improper sometimes to play practical jokes even on great lords; indeed, I have heard that many were played on Duke Federico, on King Alfonso of Aragon, on Queen Isabella of Spain and on many other great rulers" [2, 85, 190]). The ladies may also choose to read the context as humorous, feel that they deserve pity as victims, and laugh, even though they remember the situation as painful, uncomfortable, or embarrassing. Rather than becoming furious, they become flexible and release (or displace) their frustation and anger with a cauterizing chuckle.[24] Humor in this case is enjoyed by a single person plus a literal alter ego (the duchess and her *locotenente*).

If the duchess can allow the representation of her gullibility, what kinds of reaction are open to the court ladies in the audience when one of their sex is being ridiculed? As I stated in Chapter 2, within a representation that she does not control discursively but in which she finds herself desired and spectated, woman has two choices. First, she can narcissistically enjoy the image of herself being presented. Lacking subjectivity, she accedes to the other's fantasies, makes them her own, and masquerades as the embodiment and representation of what is desired in her. This desire, which is objectified, is eventually read as her very own, and she feels desired more than ever, because she perfectly embodies the desire that her observer wants her to personify.

Second, she can align her consciousness with that of the desiring subject and see herself not as a self but as an object outside herself. She believes this self to be desirable because she has masculinized her viewpoint in order to help actively, although half-consciously, in the circulation of male desire and to yearn for what the male subject of discourse desires.

The issue becomes more complex when woman in representation is an image not of desire but of mirth. She has no reason to associate her ego libido with the image of femininity being represented, because it is evident that the image is being rejected through widespread merriment. Reacting in anger would not help, because woman would then find herself laughed at for being unable to "take" a joke. Thus, she is left with a final possibility, that of masculinizing her attitude and of laughing, as a man among men, at what the audience (the third party) finds so humorous. She can also laugh as a woman, by judging the situation comic ("It can happen to anyone!") or humorous ("It may be painful, but it is also so ridiculous!"). Complications arise if she is involved in the joke through sexual associations. In that case the laugh, if any, can only be one of masochistic release.

Freud insisted that jokes are subversive and disruptive of social order, and yet he imbedded them within a structure that celebrates the participants' homosocial bonding and defuses the unsettling impact the content of the joke is bound to have. In *Il libro del cortegiano*, jokes invariably end by ratifying the status quo. Each laugh reconfirms the rule of order, the sense that everything can be reintegrated and explained because the worldview envisioned and enforced by this coterie of rank-conscious, well-bred courtiers is structurally sound, socially privileged, and culturally homogeneous.[25]

What would happen, then, if women were to read the ludicrous content of jokes differently? What if they were to participate more actively in this *serio ludere* and integrate themselves by becoming tellers? Emilia Pio shows more than once, for example, how witty she is by nature. What if women were to use this mood of festive license to challenge the terms of their representation? If a text such as the *Cortegiano* were to offer the possibility of a break from a traditional, linear, Oedipal flow, what better background, in fact, than this section on jokes, one sufficiently pliable and eccentric to accommodate different readings?

It is a gesture, however, whose coming we await in vain. Breaking with tradition, and with the ideology supporting this tradition, is what *Il libro del cortegiano* is least meant to accomplish. The Law-of-the-Father, even an absent father, is powerful enough to subdue any iconoclastic tendency on the part of these parlor instituters. In the final analysis, the courtiers' identity depends too much on courtly connivance with autocratic rules and roles to be successfully, or even liminally, questioned. Laughter becomes, paradoxically, another institutionalizing tool.

Ariosto

CHAPTER FOUR

The Narcissistic Woman: Angelica and the Mystique of Femininity

That I did love the Moor, to live with him,
My downright violence, and scorn of fortunes,
May trumpet to the world: my heart's subdued
Even to the utmost pleasure of my lord.
—Shakespeare, *Othello*, I.iii.248–51

That she belov'd knows naught that knows not this:
Men prize the thing ungain'd more than it is.
That she was never yet that ever knew
Love got so sweet as when desire did sue.
—Shakespeare, *Troilus and Cressida*, I.ii.291–96

THE FIGURE OF Angelica in *Orlando furioso* has paradoxically been almost ignored in the current resurgence of critical interest in Ludovico Ariosto, his characters, and his interlaced plots. One reason may be that Angelica's personality is easy to stereotype. Everyone agrees that she is the obscure object of male desire in the text, the elusive center of attention and obsession forever residing, beautiful and proud, in fantasyland. Whereas studies of other female characters such as Bradamante and Marfisa have recently proliferated, Angelica seems to have been lost both by her errant pursuers and by literary commentators, both in the story that sings of her marvels and in the history of criticism, which seems to prefer women with clear-cut characteristics.[1]

There are many reasons for the lack of critical interest in this fictional character. Ariosto gives Angelica no compelling moral cause, such as the search for an adult identity, nor does he cast her in an all-consuming dynastic plot like the one he provides Bradamante. For D. S. Carne-Ross, Angelica is not even "a character; she is rather a poetic image or, more exactly, she is the *sequence of images* through which she is presented" (1976: 205). Emblem of mutable fortune, she could easily have been named, Peter Marinelli suggests, "Transitella, Ephemerina, Evanessa" ("Shaping the Ore," 36). Cast as a desirable sexual mate as long as she does not mate, punished by her pursuers as well as by her creator for mating inappropriately, Angelica is chastised by critics for both her actions and her lack thereof, held accountable for acceding to the fetishized image constructed around her and faulted for refusing to do exactly that.

Enrico Musacchio, for instance, refers to Angelica as the epitome of the cold and cruel female of the erotic lyric, a woman whose beauty hides a fundamental inhumanity ("fondamentale inumanità") that makes it impossible for her to recognize the worth of knights risking their lives to improve themselves and thus gain her as a reward (*Amore*, 17). For Musacchio, Angelica's fault—and the reason for men's disavowal of her—lies in disordering the cosmic order ("in dissonanza con l'ordine cosmico"). She does not seem to appreciate what is understood as normal: that women should see themselves as objects of male advances, the recompense for knights progressing toward their manhood. Such a characterization has unfortunately remained uncriticized for too long.

Angelica is read often as logically continuing the adventures initiated by her namesake in Boiardo's *Orlando innamorato*. Therefore, although no one seems tempted to regard Astolfo as the same man in the later as in the earlier epic or Ariosto's Orlando as essentially identical to his previous incarnation, Angelica keeps being seen at one with her earlier fictional form.[2] Marcello Turchi, for example, refers to her as a foolish and restless beauty preoccupied only by her looks (133–34). She keeps lovers at bay, he writes, out of coquetry ("trascendentale civetteria," 133) and for the pleasure of being chased. Where did Turchi find this Angelica in the Ariostan epic? When is she foolish there? Where does she appear pleased to be pursued? The first audible sound in the *Furioso*, after all, is made by a frightened Angelica running away from an erotic chase for fear of what being caught might mean to a woman ("Quanto potea più forte, ne veniva / gridando la donzella ispaventata"; "The damsel, screaming with terror, came galloping in headlong flight" [1, 15]). The image is repeated at her reappearance in Canto 2, when she frantically gallops away from Rinaldo's rapacious desire ("rapina," 2, 11), only to fall into the hands of a lecherous priest, who will devise more than one way to ravish her. In her last scene she flees once more to escape rape and possible murder, this time by a bestial Orlando turned madman.

Which games, and whose games should Angelica play? As a character in a courtly love text, she can inspire but hardly accept sexual advances. The genre itself rests on woman's unavailability, a position desired for women by men and created for men's purposes (recall the sword Tristan placed between himself and Iseult). As a character in a romance narrative, generator of the quests of all the main heroes, she is the indispensable object of mimetic desire, the other who keeps the plot unfolding through digressions and false starts.[3] Her accession to any of the positions created by the desires she engenders, however, would make her disposable. As a Renaissance lady, she could be posited as defiant and rebellious; in fact, Machiavelli, Aretino, and others did create an array of profligate women. In the same period, however, woman was also made to be the bearer of moral values, values exemplified by her virginity before marriage and her irreproachable chastity after.[4] In this context, a sexually liberated, exotic princess jumping, for a more or less sweet assault ("dolce assalto"), from one married man's bed to another (both Orlando and Ruggiero are married, although Ariosto mentions their status only after they have liberated themselves from their obsession with Angelica), could be proposed only as long as she could be dismissed as a temporary, replaceable fantasy.

As embodiment of desire, Angelica is the ideal subject of representation. Endlessly fantasized and mystified, an "objet a," to use a Lacanian term, she is the textual archetype of an obscure, inaccessible, longed-for, and yet seemingly easy to obtain Madonna. Too earthly to be Beatrice and too dangerously alive to be Laura, she is beyond man and beyond all men pursuing her, whether they want to rape her or make her comply with their desires. Radically different, she is inevitably posited in the dualistic context of man/woman as other than man and thus on the other side of power. Running away in fright from erotic and erratic pursuits is, after all, Angelica's most recurrent activity. Disempowered within discourse and not empowered to accede authoritatively to discourse, she finds herself surrounded and diminished by discourses that unceasingly present her as a prisoner of biological laws. Associated with nature, she is represented as closer to myth than to history and thus eventually unnecessary to the text. Presented as a simulated, ornamental image, she functions as a *summum pulchritudinis* on which her interlocutors inscribe their whims and wishes. The possibility that she could be self-confident and self-reliant is unimaginable within the libidinal economy that permeates her presence in the text.

Throughout the *Furioso* there is no mistake about the value of Angelica, no second thought as to where it lies. After all, no one is proposing marriage to this prototypical *bella donna*. True, neither Dante nor Petrarch bothered to marry their idolized objects of love, but Beatrice and Laura were already married and soon dead, both forever lost, and therefore never really lost as desirable objects. Alive and unmarried, Angelica is pursued for her rose—a trope of her maidenhood and her genitals—to which all her worth is tied, as long as the rose remains intact. Such is indeed the purport of Sacripante's famous Catullan hymn (42, 39–47) to the unpicked rose, a *virtuoso* poetic performance that is at times required reading in Italian high schools and at others consciously expunged from scholastic editions: "La verginella è simile alla rosa, / ch'in bel giardin su la nativa spina / mentre sola e sicura si riposa, / nè gregge nè pastor se le avicina; . . . // Ma non sì tosto dal materno stelo / rimossa viene e dal suo ceppo verde, / che quanto avea dagli uomini e dal cielo / favor, grazia e bellezza, tutto perde" ("A virgin is like a rose: while she remains on the thorn whence she sprang, alone and safe in a lovely garden, no flock, no shepherd approaches. . . . But no sooner is she plucked from her mother-stalk, severed from her green stem, than she loses all, all the favour, grace, and beauty wherewith heaven and men endowed her" [1, 42–43]).

In her function as object of desire, Angelica causes havoc: fights, disobedience to the law of the Father-King, insubordination. As a subject of desire, however, even within the limited time she is allowed to be one after her meeting with Medoro, she fares no better and causes worse havoc: mental disorder, ecological disaster, political uncertainty. It is almost axiomatic that whenever Angelica appears, male failure follows. The field around her is literally strewn with sexual fiascoes: knights lose their horses (Rinaldo, Sacripante), fall under dead horses (Sacripante), or are unable to "horse around" (the hermit); they forfeit control of their horses (Orlando, Ruggiero with the hippogryph), ride their horses to death (Orlando), or simply cannot exchange one mount for another (Orlando, Ruggiero).[5] This repeated male failure vis-à-vis Angelica is more than sexual and reaches the highest political levels. As his men leave for their amorous quest ("amorosa inchiesta"), the retrieval of Angelica, the emperor Charlemagne risks losing his empire, to say nothing of his authority, since, because of this woman, the war is far from ending. From Rinaldo to Orlando and from Ruggiero to Sacripante, Angelica consistently causes forgetfulness of proper civic and military duties. What can Ariosto do with a character that from the start he portrays as refusing to play by the rules? What can he do later with a "dis-angelicata" Angelica when the topos provides no alternative destiny for a sexually assertive woman?

In the following pages I examine some key points concerning the representation of Angelica throughout the *Furioso*. I begin with the commonly held belief that her function is that of an erotic love object with no fixed identity of her own, in order to analyze what makes Angelica so utterly and obsessively desirable. I argue that it is her narcissism that renders this princess both tempting and elusive to her pursuers.

Next I concern myself with the ways in which Ariosto remasters Angelica at the psychological level. Having created her as sign of male desire, the author has Angelica axiomatically chased throughout the text. Yet because as a woman she stands for difference and otherness, Angelica also represents danger; her image— precisely because it is haunting—generates castration anxieties in her pursuers. The desire she fosters therefore becomes necessarily ungratifiable and repetitive. To stop the chase, Ariosto has to rein in his creation. He controls her, I argue, through a complicated fetishistic process that at times invests her whole body and at other times centers on bodily parts or metonymic inanimate objects.

Finally, I look at the ways Ariosto restrains his character at the plot level. Since Angelica is a figure of disturbance, Ariosto needs eventually to normatize or disavow her through narrative developments. In other words, either he channels Angelica's femininity toward social goals proper to women, or, if he keeps her unrepentant, he needs sooner or later to cast her out of the text, for "ch'ove femine son, son liti e risse" ("where you have women you have quarrels and strife" [43, 120]). I argue that the author actively pursues the second alternative. Angelica is worked out of the *Furioso* at exactly its midpoint in order to facilitate the narrative movement toward the providentially dynastic, and therefore normal and normative, plot woven around the emblematic figures of Bradamante and Ruggiero. For Carne-Ross, Angelica's exit and Orlando's madness determine the shift in emphasis in the poem from quest to epic and the staging of a new, conventional world, which he laments (1976: 205). I argue that Angelica is the most significant victim of this shift from open-ended romance to closure-oriented epic, since what she stands for must be dismissed for the eventual, but unavoidable, recovery of Orlando and Rinaldo to the world of warriors that defines the *Furioso*.[6]

In this sense, Canto 23, the middle canto of the *Furioso*, offers a major reassessment of masculine and feminine goals. It is not only the canto in which Angelica is effectively taken out of the plot but also the canto in which Ruggiero ends his delays, Orlando goes mad, and Pinabello is murdered (accomplished in the preceding canto but significantly opening the narrative of this one). Just as the killing of Pinabello is the first of the climactic deaths that from this point punctuate the *Furioso*, Ruggiero's rejection of his magic shield marks in the mind of many critics a decisive step in his growth and thus a movement toward closure. On the feminine side, not only is Angelica no longer pursued, but Bradamante stops pursuing Ruggiero and returns home. All these changes mean that Ariosto is tightening the reins on women's yearnings and goals. By taming desire and directing it toward its proper resolution of marriage, as in the case of Bradamante and Olimpia (the latter episode placed much earlier in the text but written later), Ariosto is left with an Angelica, the personification of desire itself, who no longer has a place in the narrative. Unwilling to tame her, he discards her; as I point out later, however, there is a surprising coda even to this choice.

Turchi refers to Angelica as "fiera," a beast of prey. Like Petrarch's Laura in some sonnets, Angelica seems to have much in common with wild animals: a certain natural nonchalance, for example, and an apparent lack of interest in her surroundings. In his study "On Narcissism" (1914), Freud similarly compares beasts of prey to narcissistic women. During their growth from adolescence to maturity and sexual subjectivity, Freud writes, human beings displace their original narcissism with a love object. Upon completion of the process, men tend to overvalue their chosen object. Women, however, follow a more complicated detour.

Freud first isolates a number of feminine types, one of which is for him "probably the purest and truest one" (88): the narcissistic woman. This woman, he writes, experiences at puberty an increase, rather than a decrease, in narcissism and finds herself, as a result, unable to make a proper object choice. He speculates that narcissistic women are extraordinarily beautiful, thus already at the center of attention, and that often they are egotistic because they have somehow to compensate "for the social restrictions that are imposed upon them in their choice of object" (89). These women, he writes, seem able to love only themselves and prefer to be loved rather than to love. Their self-love, in turn, makes them self-sufficient, enigmatic, and inaccessible. Men are greatly attracted by these apparently selfish women, not just because their beauty generates fantasies but also because they have retained their self-centeredness instead of transferring it to a love object. These women, Freud writes, lure others the same way self-absorbed cats, children, beasts of prey, criminals, and humorists seem to do.

Posited this way, the narcissistic woman is dangerous. As Sarah Kofman argues, if this woman is so self-sufficient as to seem indifferent and so taken with herself as not to suffer from hysteria or envy—two characteristics of "normal" femininity for Freud—she is a woman not properly socialized. Most important, the narcissistic woman can disrupt sexual dichotomies because the self-enclosed nature of her desire enables her to do without man and his desire. It is no wonder that at the end of his study Freud turns away from this insight and, as Kofman points out, drags "women with him in his retreat: he leads them along the path of salvation, the path that, despite their basic narcissism, can lead them to fully realized object love—the path of pregnancy" (*The Enigma of Woman*, 57). Reconfined to her normal and normative role, the narcissistic woman-turned-mother becomes the most typical Freudian creation: the neurotic, hysterical, castrated, and thoroughly heterosexual female. In other words, she becomes a "real" woman. In the exchange, however, she loses both her independence and the power that comes with it. As a narcissist, the woman Freud delineates knows and yet refuses to tell; but as a neurotic, she needs a man to unravel the riddle of her sex, to explain and make plain to her her own lack. Her independence is gone, her danger erased. Man is back at the center of her world.

A little more preoccupied than Freud with the dangers that the narcissistic woman embodies, René Girard turns the self-sufficient, self-centered Freudian woman into a coquette, an object essential to mimetic desire. "The coquette seeks to be desired," he argues, "because she needs masculine desires, directed at her, to feed her coquetry and enable her to play her role as a coquette" (*Things Hidden*, 370). This woman is so taken with herself as to be not simply inaccessible but the epitome of insolent inaccessibility, the very view that Turchi reflects in his characterization of Angelica. Girard faults Freud for his unwillingness to recognize that all desires, both man's objectal desire and woman's narcissistic desire, are one identical imitative desire. Kofman in turn faults Girard for misunderstanding the specific Freud of this text, a Freud who, for once, did not construct woman as a castrated man (*The Enigma of Woman*, 62).

Paradoxically, the narcissistic woman is easily represented. For example, she speaks little. Is she chastised for that? Yes, since her silence may hide dangerous thoughts. And yet even her non-collaboration with discourse can become part of her appeal, for it frees her interlocutors to create for themselves their own unencumbered image of her. Through her narcissism, they can mirror their former, self-sufficient egos; through her beauty, they can assure themselves of their own worth in pursuing her; finally, through her silence they can create her according to their wishes. Thus, the narcissistic woman can easily be positioned as central to male desire in culture and happily made to carry that burden in narrative.

Angelica seems to fit the woman delineated by Freud better than the one created by Girard. Indifferent, impenetrable, beautiful, spoiled, and presumably self-sufficient when she recovers her magic ring of invisibility, she seems the very incarnation of the Freudian narcissistic type. It would be hard, in any case, to classify her as a coquette, *pace* Turchi and Girard. Angelica's intention in the *Furioso*, as Ariosto defines it, is not to play one man against another for her own sake. She knows, for example, that she is the cause of Orlando and Ferraù's fight in Canto 12, but the outcome of the quarrel makes little difference to her personally or to her cause. The duel is not to her advantage. Rather, being a woman and an object of man's interest for homosocial reasons, she occupies the woman's usual place in a triangle: that of observer. To be sure, the fight begins over the two knights' self-appointed rights to possess her physically, but it continues as a disagreement over helmets—other objects of desire, objects probably capable of engendering new pursuits, but only by men. Angelica illustrates woman's invisibility in triangular situations so well in this instance that she is literally made to opt for invisibility by means of her ring.

Angelica may be aware that desire feeds on desire, as Girard would insist, but she hardly seems to care. She wants none of the men pursuing her, and when one is absolutely needed to ensure her physical safety, she chooses the least significant of them, Sacripante, because he is the easiest to dismiss. Ironically, Sacripante is also the rival least feared by the men pursuing Angelica. Orlando would be perceived as much more powerful by his male competitors and thus as more dangerous, were he granted the princess's love. Moreover, although Angelica knows that she is an object of desire, she seems to know little of desire's imitative nature.

In the end, it makes no difference. Ariosto must obliterate Angelica's fictional self-sufficiency, understood either via Freud or via Girard. A Freudian Ariosto would relegate Angelica to the nursery; a Girardian one would portray continuous disruptions in the battlefield of desire, with Angelica as the coveted prize.[7] The goal is identical in any case, for both Freud and Girard aim to deny the narcissistic, independent penchant in woman by systematically capturing, explaining, and reconfining her. If she refuses a proper feminine role, she is expunged as problematic. If she accepts, she gets a husband. In other words, if Ariosto keeps Bradamante, the logic of the narrative requires that Angelica leave. Since texts are, however, not necessarily constrained in the same way that social life is, other female characters in the *Furioso* are allowed a wider range of possibilities. Marfisa, for example, seems to control all events around her; Gabrina's wickedness goes unpunished for a long time; and Fiammetta is rewarded for having confirmed misogynistic opinions about her sex. These "victories" are, however, Pyrrhic; in the program of normalization that Ariosto pursues, social conventions and power from above slowly but steadily delimit, contain, or eliminate the transgressive element. In this context, the disruptive character, such as Angelica or Olimpia, is important precisely because it demonstrates that it is preferable for women to be within the norm. In the end, disorder serves the purposes of those in positions of authority, for it reconfirms the order they codified in the first place.

Ariosto introduces his self-centered Angelica early in Canto 1, immediately after Sacripante laments that he might have arrived too late to be the first to enjoy Angelica's body. In this instance Angelica is narcissistically positioned next to a reflecting stream: "Ecco non lungi un bel cespuglio vede / di prun fioriti e di vermiglie rose, / che de le liquide onde al specchio siede. . . . / La bella donna in mezzo a quel si mette" ("Close by she noticed a beautiful thicket of flowering hawthorn and red roses mirrored in the limpid rippling water. . . . The lovely damsel stepped into the bower" [1, 37, 38]). Immediately aware of the advantages a sorrowful lover like Sacripante might offer a frightened woman running away from conquest and possible rape, Angelica asks for help. She feels no pity for his pain, however, Ariosto explains, and chooses to keep her heart safely clear of the whole business: "Dura e fredda più d'una colonna, / ad averne pietà non però scende, / come colei c'ha tutto il mondo a sdegno, / e non le par ch'alcun sia di lei degno" ("Hard, though, and cold as a stone pillar, she would not stoop to pity: it would seem she disdained all human kind, and believed that no man was worthy of her" [1, 49]). On another occasion, in Canto 12, Angelica again decides to use Sacripante for her own purposes by literally embodying his fantasies about her (12, 28).

What Ariosto offers in these scenes is the self-absorbed, inaccessible, and indifferent narcissistic woman described above. Knowing that an array of knights desires her, Angelica herself desires no man's desire. Indeed, she desires nothing but escape from the desire that creates a place for her in representation. Even the project of returning to Cathay, for example, takes some time to become a personal desire, as if the realization that she is entrapped in a collective fantasy had removed from Angelica the very possibility of desiring something for herself. What all men desire is plain in the *Furioso*. Sacripante calls it rose ("rosa"); Orlando, flower ("fiore"); Rinaldo, delicacy ("primizie")—metonymic substitutes for the pudendum. Ironically, such a desire can be sustained only as long as the organ that engenders it is not used. Knowing full well the value of her maidenhead, Angelica responds to Sacripante's lament as he would like her to, with a plain reference to her sexual status: "Ella gli rende conto pienamente / . . . / che 'l fior virginal così avea salvo, / come se lo portò del materno alvo" ("She told him . . . how her virginal flower was still as intact as the day she had borne it from her mother's womb" [1, 55]).

Attitudes toward a woman's "rosa," and concurrently toward a woman's virginity, are fundamentally different in men and women. Sacripante, Orlando, Rinaldo, and Ferraù want Angelica because she is desired by others and yet still a maiden. The possession of her body *in primis* would allow the possessor to think of himself as better than his male peers, with whom he naturally competes. Since this woman is also extremely beautiful, her conquest would increase his stature among his male friends. In his inscription in the cave, for example, Medoro not only writes of his lovemaking and names himself but also gives the name, rank, and status of the woman he has conquered for all to see and envy him for: "La bella Angelica che nacque / di Galafron, da molti invano amata, / spesso ne le mie braccia nuda giacque" ("Fair Angelica, born of Galafron, and loved in vain by many, often lay naked in my arms" [23, 108]). If in the *Furioso* what makes the pursuit of Angelica interesting is that she appears to say "no" to offers of seduction, what makes it compelling is that she seems to say that she is so taken with herself as to be indifferent to what goes on around her. Such a narcissistic show of elusiveness and assuredness needs redressing. The proprietorship of a woman who seemingly does not care to impress any man, not even men already so impressed by her as to forget their duties toward their kings, has decidedly higher stakes. It allows the winner to feel not only that he has tamed her independence and cured her waywardness but also that he has denied the logic that she is self-sufficient and needs no man's supervision. In the process, he has differentiated himself from his rivals in love, has bettered them, and has scored a point for them by grasping woman's very difference. The possibility of this multiple victory makes the pursuit worthwhile and again purely male-oriented.

Angelica, however, sees her virginity as an integral part of her body, a measure that she is complete, that she is wholly herself, and therefore that she can dispose of the others' desire. In this sense, her attitude is gender-indifferent since it works to reinforce her selfhood. It is precisely such a feeling of narcissistic omnipotence and self-reliance, however, that must again be denied by her pursuers.

Angelica's magic ring in the *Furioso* fully illustrates the dan-

gers inherent in feminine self-sufficiency.[8] The ring, the author
narrates, assures invisibility when its owners put it between their
teeth. It is only in Canto 12, however, that Angelica understands
that thanks to the power of the ring she can escape unwelcome
attention and perilous situations. In the past she allowed men to
desire her in order to assure her own survival, but with the ring
back in her hand, she realizes that she can dispose of both men's
desire and men's help: "In tanto fasto, in tanto orgoglio crebbe, /
ch'esser parea di tutto 'l mondo schiva. / Se ne va sola, e non si
degnerebbe / compagno aver qual più famoso viva" ("[She] grew
so haughty and supercilious she seemed to shun the whole of
humanity. She kept her own company and would have disdained
the companionship of the most renowned man alive" [19, 18]). The
ring allows Angelica to be herself, to narcissistically desire her own
desire, which for the moment is paradoxically that of escaping the
desire of others.

It is interesting that to fulfill this desire not to be obsessively
desired, Angelica needs to make herself literally invisible, a non-
being. Incorporeality guarantees Angelica's survival as narrative
matter, in the sense that it protects her against unwelcome sexual
attacks, which, by eliminating her value as "verginella," would
precipitate her exit from the text. Yet, as I pointed out earlier,
it is this very incorporeality that requires her eventual demise,
since an Angelica freed from the necessity of fleeing ravishment is,
narratively speaking, a dead Angelica.

The issue of seeing/non-seeing is central to Angelica's charac-
terization. As a narcissistic woman, the subject of her own desire,
she is supposed to see only herself. As object of desire, she is never
really seen, since she needs to function as a tabula rasa on which
each of her pursuers can inscribe his desire and then read him-
self in his creation. As the object of a triangular desire, moreover,
Angelica cannot properly be seen because her "I" is not central
to the rivalries and the struggles for power that mimetic desire
requires.[9] There is no reason for Angelica to be seen as a person
in any case, for it is her body, or the knights' perception of the
marvels of her body, that attracts men to her. Yet in a number of
instances in this romance epic Angelica's ability to see properly
and men's concurrent inability to see become an issue. The ring of
invisibility allows Angelica to see the knights' blindness, their at-

tempt to catch (when imprisoned within the castle of Atlante, for instance) what is by definition unseeable and ungraspable—desire.

Man's "unseeing," Ariosto points out, comes from his being caught in a dialectic of desire: "Quel che l'uom vede, Amor gli fa invisible, / e l'invisibil fa vedere Amore" ("What a man sees, Love can make invisible—and what is invisible, that can Love make him see" [1, 56]). But seeing too clearly is dangerous in the *Furioso*. By seeing Angelica's bracelet, Orlando finally understands what he has denied to himself all along—his beloved's infidelity to his self-made program—a conclusion that, ironically, he had correctly foreseen in a previous sleepless night. Suddenly dazzled, he turns into a madman.[10] Unfortunately, Angelica is psychologically invisible both when she is physically visible and when she is physically invisible. The sight of Ruggiero embracing air, while hoping to embrace a vanished Angelica on the island of Ebuda, well illustrates the problematics of male desire vis-à-vis the characterization of Angelica as the ungraspable object of that desire.

Orlando is able to really see Angelica only once in the narrative and, ironically, only in the place where she should be least visible, in Atlante's palace of illusions. Since she is an illusion herself, only in this place is Angelica "real," a true embodiment of longings for the men who cannot grasp her reality in the world. Interestingly, since she desires nothing illusory, she is the only person who can enter and exit the building at will and lead the men out of their voluntary imprisonment. She is no sooner in the open, however, than she finds herself re-embodying her status of desideratum, a status that again requires her invisibility. The result of this seeing/not-seeing structure is that Angelica functions as a libidinal object when seen by others; she herself contributes in many ways to the phallocentric economy of desire permeating the text by also seeing herself in such a fashion. When invisible, however, she discovers that she has an "I" and that this "I" does not need to be subjugated to male authority and male fantasies. It goes without saying that such a show of independence on her part ("tant'arroganza," 19, 19) needs to be restrained.

How can the ring of invisibility work as ring of reason, as Ariosto calls it (8, 2)? Critics usually cut such an association to pieces, for Angelica seems to them to demonstrate little reason even after she recovers the ring.[11] And yet, given the fact that Angelica's purpose in the narrative is to run away from a desire that is mostly a desire to rape her, one might ask how she could be more reasonable. After all, she uses her ring exclusively for her own safety and survival. The first time she resorts to employing its magic is to escape an almost inevitable rape by Ruggiero, a choice that seems quite reasonable. The second time, she utilizes it to enter the castle of Atlante, where she will liberate Orlando, Ferraù, and Sacripante from their illusions. True, this is not her original purpose, but the results speak for themselves. She then employs it again to escape them, since three knights in hot pursuit are not easy for a woman to confront, regardless of the irony that Ariosto introduces in telling the story. She also takes advantage of the ring, intermittently, to travel incognito throughout the countryside, since for a woman to travel as a woman is, as she knows, out of the question. Finally, she resorts to using the ring to escape a less-than-human Orlando, who would not have limited himself to rape had he caught her. Whether this is a ring of reason or not, Angelica seems to understand its importance for her safety so well that she chooses never to separate herself from it.

A narcissistic woman, Freud writes, usually possesses extraordinary beauty. Angelica could definitely epitomize the truthfulness of this statement, for it is her "bellezza rara" (1, 8) that engenders men's obsession with her. She herself, however, has doubts about the advantages of her physique and expresses them in a moment of utter helplessness: "Mi nuoce, ahimè! ch'io son giovane, e sono / tenuta bella, o sia vero o bugia. / Già non ringrazio il ciel di questo dono; / che di qui nasce ogni ruina mia" ("I suffer for being young, alas, and for being accounted, whether rightly or wrongly, beautiful. I cannot thank Heaven for this gift, as it is the source of all my sorrows" [8, 42]). We know that Angelica comes from China, although her long blond hair is unmistakably Caucasian. Naked and tied down on the island of Ebuda at the time Ruggiero attempts to rescue her in Canto 10, she is haunting in her physical grandeur. Yet the manner in which Ariosto sculpts her body with his pen is so euphemistic that the reader can decipher little from the associations he makes, for everything seems unnameable. Shying away from identifying breast and limbs, the author congeals his woman into a static pose and names "i bianchi gigli e le vermiglie rose" ("the lily-white, the rose-red" [10, 95]), the "fresche rose e candidi ligustri" ("her rose-fresh, lily-white cheeks" [10, 95]), concluding with a quasi Pre-Raphaelite touch, "crudette pome" ("unripe apple-breasts" [10, 96]). This fetishistic description conveys the same representational codes that Ovid lit-eralized in his *Metamorphoses* (4, vv. 672–81). There, his Andromeda rescued by Perseus had hair teased by the wind, tears streaming down her face, a bashful expression, and hands worthy to be tied, like Angelica's, by other chains. Ariosto here not only outdoes Ovid but also reshuffles an array of medieval texts.[12]

Giovanni Pozzi finds the rendering of Angelica's body in the poem in the Petrarchan tradition of the short bodily canon ("ca-none breve"). This characterization by way of stereotypes usually includes face, breast, and hands; it avoids other facial parts, such as nose, chin, and ears, and stops at the waist. Since Alcina and Olimpia are described in the long bodily canon ("canone lungo"), which is more typical of Boccaccio (e.g., in the *Commedia delle ninfe*), the change in the characterization of Angelica is made, ac-cording to Pozzi, to establish her superiority (19). Although aware that Angelica shares little with Petrarch's Laura, Ariosto knows that, short of silence, he has no choice but to elaborate on the cur-rent iconography and taxonomy. The proliferation of synecdoches, in any case, tells little about Angelica; it does show, however, that Ariosto has no idea of how a Chinese woman looks or, alter-natively, puts no stock in physiognomic characteristics of either Western or Oriental women. Perhaps he is right. When a woman functions merely as a mask of beauty, distinct racial features are of no importance.

Ariosto does not fail to eroticize and aestheticize each detail in his description. With no veil to cover her, as he coyly reminds his readers, Angelica becomes a spectacle; her body—carefully constructed by combining parts—is described as nude rather than naked, and thus open to possession and ready to claim.[13] And yet the description stops short of suggesting overt transgression in Angelica's countenance, for, as psychoanalysis teaches, the repre-sentation of a woman with striking features needs to be highly controlled, her body needs to be sufficiently fetishized in order to assuage in the onlooker the anxiety that her presence generates. Thus, although portrayed as available because of her nakedness,

Angelica must also be made distant, iconic.[14] To be manageable, she has to function as an eminently passive projection, a possessable object. This objectification requires that she be described piece by piece, a procedure that also works to render her remote and inanimate, a statue ("Creduto avria che fosse statua finta / o d'alabastro o d'altri marmi illustri"; "[You] would have taken her for a statue fashioned in alabaster or some lambent marble" [10, 96]). Looking at beauty, especially the static, enigmatic beauty that Ariosto puts together, also gratifies narcissistic identifications on the part of the onlooker.

For Ruggiero, the act of seeing is at first an act of remembering, for he immediately recalls Bradamante and feels sympathy for this unknown woman. But seeing is also inevitably phallic in the *Furioso*. After looking at Angelica in Canto 1, for example, Rinaldo raises his face ("drizzò lo sguardo"), Sacripante lifts his eyes ("levò gli occhi"), and Ferraù, opting for rapacity, peers at her ("la guata"). "What is seen is possessed," Sartre argues, "to see is to deflower. If we examine the comparisons ordinarily used to express the relation between the known and the unknown, we see that many of them are represented as being a kind of violation by sight" (709). When he looks into Angelica's eyes ("ne' begli occhi gli occhi affisse" [10, 97]), Ruggiero has an epidermal reaction. What he sees is not a woman, but Woman, a synthesis of myths and fantasies. Angelica's body becomes important not for itself but because, being naked and tied, it tells a story: the story of a beautiful woman who, like the mythical Andromeda, is in utter distress because of something connected to her physical shape.[15] By linking her body to a fantasy about it, Ruggiero masters what at first appears to be a distant, unapproachable, unknowable other.

There is no question that the gaze is masculine here. Angelica feels violated, lowers her face, and blushes all over. Her gestures, or rather her inability to make gestures, speak for her: "E coperto con man s'avrebbe il volto, / se non eran legate al duro sasso" ("She would have covered her face with her hands were they not tied to the hard rock" [10, 99]). Not only does she avoid returning Ruggiero's look, but she even attempts to cover herself, ineffectually, as it turns out, and prevent herself from being looked upon. With that motion, however, she confirms in him the idea that she is but a body and that he can control and appraise what he sees.

Feeling like a surveyed and passive receiver of a scopophilic look, Angelica keeps silent. When asked why she is tied, she answers with tears rather than words. When she finally starts to talk (whatever she says, if anything, is not reported), the Orca's arrival immediately silences her. It is important to remember that the only time in the *Furioso* that Angelica controls discourse is, unfortunately, when no one can hear her, on the shores of the Island of Tears, where she lands as a result of the black magic of a lecherous priest.[16] Even then, however, her speech serves only to reaffirm her passivity and her sense of loss, for it contains a catalogue of self-deprecatory postures. When she tries, with a Dantesque appeal, to communicate her fears and feelings to a fatherly priest ("Miserere, / padre, di me"; "Mercy, good father" [8, 46]), she finds not comforting Virgilian help but a quite unpriestly attempt to rape her.

Neither Angelica's voice nor her explanations carry authority or purport; there is no discrepancy between a seen Angelica and a silenced Angelica. Both are necessary to maintain the construction of woman as male fantasy and to reassert the illusion of male selfhood. In this context, woman becomes indispensable to the constitution of man's "I," because by seeing woman reflecting what he desires and appreciates, man thinks that woman mirrors his desire and thereby his self. Seeing, Lacan remarks, is a thoroughly autoerotic act. In the final analysis, although, as Freud suggests, extraordinary beauty is a characteristic quality of the narcissistic woman, both female beauty and female narcissism can be made to serve, ironically, male needs.

The narcissistic Freudian woman is enticing, then, because of her psychological difference from other women and her seeming indifference to men's games of wooing and conquest. Her impenetrability guarantees her lack of concern with men's desires and, paradoxically, the continuation ad infinitum of desire. But fantasies have short lives; desires must eventually be satisfied or discarded. In this section I concentrate on Ariosto's psychological strategies to solve the enigma of woman. If woman means castration, how can man cancel the danger generated by her presence and keep both an active libido and an "I"? How does one possess Angelica? On the other hand, since Angelica's fascination resides in her inaccessibility, how can desire be kept alive if she must remain unconquered? Finally, how can man rid himself of such an obsession? In the next few pages I try to answer these questions by examining four knights in the *Furioso* with a stake in capturing Angelica the ungrateful ("questa ingrata," 19, 32).

In her influential work on the position of women in classic cinema, a work drawing heavily on Freudian and Lacanian insights, Laura Mulvey posits two solutions to castration anxieties caused by a beautiful and desired woman: man can disavow his anxiety through a compensatory, fetishistic cover, or he can avow it, as long as he accompanies this avowal with a debasement of woman. The first option requires him to construct a fetish; the second implies a problematization of woman through punitive illnesses or crimes. Pleasure comes through renarrating the castration anxiety and restaging what is repressed (21–22).[17] In the following, I test these insights as they apply to the Angelica story by analyzing the choices, or non-choices, of each of the main knights in the *Furioso*: Ruggiero and Sacripante, whose positions are eminently voyeuristic, and Orlando and Rinaldo, whose responses are more complex. As for Ferraù, Angelica is only one of the many things he desires. He makes little psychological investment in her and can easily replace his desire for her by a desire for something else (for example, a headpiece). He then pursues this new desire with equal dedication and equal compulsion, no matter how far it causes him to stray from the political and heroic goals that brought him to France.

Ruggiero's desire is eminently libidinal: he wants Angelica as soon as possible. His desire would be easier to satisfy than that of her other pursuers because Ruggiero is not competing with them. He sees Angelica and wants her, just as Rodomonte, upon seeing Isabella, immediately plots to rape her. And yet Angelica's femaleness poses a psychological threat. She is not only amazingly beautiful but also absolutely naked: "Un velo non ha pure, in che richiuda . . . / . . . quelle parti ignude, / ch'ancor che belle sian, vergogna chiude" ("Not even a veil did she have to cover . . . those parts of her exposed to view which, for all their beauty, modesty would conceal" [10, 95 and 98]). Ruggiero, however, can manage this threat. By asking Angelica the cause of her distress ("Chi è quel crudel che con voler perverso / d'importuno livor stringendo segna / di queste belle man l'avorio terso?"; "Who is the miscreant so perverted as to blemish the smooth ivory of your delicate hands with unwelcome bruising?" [10, 98]) and by gallantly offering help, Ruggiero knows that reward is forthcoming: if he saves her, he qualifies as worthy of her possession. This is, after all, what life, literature, and myth have consistently promised man. In performing a similar rescue, for example, Perseus, fresh from having slain the Medusa, is able to save, and subsequently have, Andromeda.[18]

Thus, the retelling of the myth that *a priori* guarantees the male overcoming of the female threat and the retelling of the reasons that woman needs to be helped, a position that allows man to act and feel manly, together allow Ruggiero to control the anxiety he experiences at the sight of an unknown but stunningly beautiful woman. Moreover, the description of Angelica as an icon of marble freezes her image and makes her much less threatening than, for instance, the metaphorical Medusa whom Rinaldo later encounters. As a result, Ruggiero can demystify the princess as an erotic/aesthetic object to such an extent that he can attempt to rape her. Ariosto recapitulates his mood by moving from a euphemistic to a commodifying vocabulary: "Pazzo è se questa ancor non prezza e stima" ("He would still be a fool not to make the most of the maiden present" [11, 2]).[19]

Angelica's disappearance by means of the magic ring infuriates Ruggiero. He tells her that she had no need to steal the ring from him since he had intended to give it to her. The emphasis on his spontaneous gift over her self-assured appropriation is textually important. Ruggiero is saying that he has the phallic signifier and can give it to Angelica willingly, in fact that he is pleased to give it to her, as long, of course, as she gives her body to him in return. It is by granting it himself, in short, that he can remain in power. Angelica's bypassing of his offer is threatening.

Sacripante chooses a slightly different route. To control Angelica, who occupies much of his time and distracts him from important knightly duties, he opts for genital logic. By taking her virginity, to him her only valuable asset (a point that the "Verginella" song makes clear), and by thereby devaluing her through physical possession, he knows that he can both debase her in the eyes of her pursuers and establish control over her. Power, for a person like Sacripante who has little of it in the eyes of the other knights, can be established only through possession. In order to empower himself, Sacripante has simply to read Angelica's "no" as "yes," since a woman's denial comes simply, he fantasizes, from not knowing what is in store: "So ben ch'a donna non si può far cosa / che più soave e più piacevol sia, / ancor che se ne mostri disdegnosa, / e talor mesta e flebil se ne stia" ("Full well I know that there is nothing that a woman finds so delectable and pleasing, even when she pretends to resent it and will sometimes burst into tears" [1, 58]).

Thus, whereas Ruggiero must demystify Angelica in order to proceed with libidinal violence, Sacripante must disavow her self. His strategy is to emphasize in his mind woman's beauty and femininity in order to render the object of his desire radically non-male, give woman the phallus, and thereby obliterate or assuage the fear of castration that her presence enhances. If narcissistic women attract men because they remain the way men themselves would like to have remained (i.e., as they were before their object choice), then narcissistic women, more than anyone else, can become the phallus.[20] Sacripante, moreover, knows much about fetishes. He is, after all, the greatest worshiper of Angelica's rose in the text, a fetish that both disavows castration and asserts it, since it marks the very site of woman's lack while also metaphorically displacing it.[21] As Ariosto makes clear, the rose as an erotogenic image can function only under the fiction that no sexual defilement has occurred. The statement that in representation woman stands for what she lacks is literally true for Angelica.[22]

In Canto 1, Sacripante sneers at Orlando for having willingly, and perhaps even stupidly, deferred consummation of his sexual desire even though he had safe access to Angelica's body. In hindsight, Orlando himself is the first to regret this indecisiveness: "E il fior ch'in ciel potea pormi fra i dei, / il fior ch'intatto io mi venia serbando / per non turbarti, ohimè! l'animo casto, / ohimè! per forza avranno colto e guasto. / Oh infelice! oh misero! che voglio / se non morir, se 'l mio bel fior colto hanno?" ("And your flower, which could set me among the heavenly gods, the flower which I preserved for you intact, so as not to sadden your chaste heart, will they, alas, have plucked and despoiled it? / O, woe upon me, what would I but to die if they have plucked my pretty flower!" [8, 78–79]). What is the source of the impediment, and why does this anxiety-ridden knight think that sexual knowledge would defile and pollute his object of love? Although married, Orlando is in no way encumbered by a wife. Rather, he seems to know that an object of desire must be elusive, that only through deferral can a subject continue believing he is able to transcend and complete himself. In this sense, the amorous quest in which he so earnestly engages after leaving Charlemagne's camp is eminently a quest for the self. This requires that he project woman, the object of desire, as different from himself, a non-self. By the same token, Orlando needs to repress in Angelica what ironically makes her so important to him, her femaleness.

One thing is certain: Orlando wants Angelica, and he wants to be the first to have her. Unlike the other knights, however, he does not want her immediately and puts all his energies into defending her from sexual assaults. Such an overriding desire to have Angelica, and such a suppressed desire not to have her together confirm that Orlando's problem is tied to the threat of castration that women, especially narcissistic women, pose to men's unconscious. For Lacan, man's need to put woman on a pedestal, as evident in courtly love literature, reflects his own lack. "For the man, whose lady was entirely, in the most servile sense of the term, his female subject," he writes, "courtly love is the only way of coming off elegantly from the absence of sexual relation" ("God and the *Juissance*," 141). To control this threat, Orlando makes an icon of Angelica. Overvaluation of woman is, after all, in the Freudian scenario, what man does in regard to his chosen object when he overcomes his own adolescent narcissism ("On Narcissism," 94). Beauty so satisfies Orlando that he is content to have Angelica fetishistically, by transforming her whole body, the signifier of his desire, into a fetish. In doing so he can entertain feelings of godly omnipotence without fear of failure.[23]

Orlando's desire is mimetic because it feeds actively on his peers' desire for Angelica. But it is also a desire for Edenic bliss, a craving, as Peter Wiggins suggests, for "a prelapsarian world where faith can be replaced by certain knowledge and all instability is eliminated" (*Figures*, 111). The world Ariosto describes, as every reader realizes after a cursory look, is one of mutability and change. Orlando, however, has his own reasons for wanting stable possession. His obsession with a phantasmatic Angelica has feminized him too much.[24] The point comes across clearly in the text. Although as a knight Ariosto makes Orlando superior to the other knights, as a man in love he compares him not to men, but, surprisingly, to women, especially to Virgil's Dido. The same haunting thoughts that keep Dido awake (*Aeneid*, Book 4) keep Orlando tossing around on his cot until he resolves to begin his quest for Angelica. In Orlando " 'l male è penetrato infin all'osso" ("the disease has eaten . . . to the bone"), Ariosto writes; again the expression comes from Virgil, who applies it in similar circumstances to Dido (Book 4, 101).[25]

Orlando's favorite hallucination of Angelica as a damsel-in-distress crying for help, or to use his metaphor, as a lamb pursued by wolves, speaks volumes about his anxieties. The cry with which Angelica enters the narrative, for instance, mirrors the cry that Orlando hears in his dream the night he decides to embark on his quest for her, a foreboding scream of distress he hopes to transform into one of coital joy.[26] Alas, even in the dream this emblematic Petrarchan *jouissance* is chased away by another, nightmarish scream ("orribil grido," 8, 83), Orlando's own this time, although it seems to come from nowhere.[27] Interestingly, it is only in Orlando's fantasy that Angelica is helpless. In the text, she has alternative sources of aid to escape rape: a woman in male dress, for instance (Bradamante in Canto 1), or her own self, when she recovers her magic ring. To overcome the threat of castration, Orlando projects his own fear onto woman and imagines himself indispensable to her. Saving virgins in distress is, after all, what knights of courtly love literature are supposed to do.

As a Petrarchan lover, Orlando faces a real problem. Like Petrarch, he can feed his desires by never satisfying them. Unlike Petrarch, however, he is unable to rule or restrict the woman born of his obsessions because he fantasizes such a woman as being real. Real, of course, not in the sense that she exists in reality (for he would be unable to recognize her), but real in that he believes his mental image of her to be real, and his psychic representation of her to be not a representation but the embodiment of her original self. Such an un-Petrarchan approach proves deadly to him. As Ariosto suggests, Orlando should know that images are false when "per tema o per disio si sogna" ("fear or hope projects in the dreaming mind" [8, 84]). In the end, he conquers neither Angelica nor his desire for her. The Petrarchan scheme of mastering a poetic creation by dismembering it and reconstituting it according to a lover's personal and poetic need—the scheme Ariosto offers on the Island of Ebuda—does not work for Orlando. Angelica is always a lost lamb in his mind, always in need of protection (8, 76). Unfortunately, the more he desires her, the more she refuses him. This "coupling of monomania and schizophrenia," as Chesney puts it (188), can only prove self-destructive.

In the end Angelica unmans Orlando. On her account he forgoes his intellect and, symbolically, his manhood; later, when he miraculously retrieves his mental powers, he finds himself less important than Ruggiero. His frenzied undressing at the onset of his madness echoes at the narrative level his decision, following another sleepless night, to kill himself if Angelica's flower has been picked. When he finally understands that what he fears has in fact happened, he can only commit psychological suicide.

Orlando anticipates his mental dissolution when he hangs his helmet—a metonym for his rational faculties—on a branch during a duel with Ferraù (12, 46). His subsequent loss of the headpiece, through no fault of his own, foreshadows the "losing" of his head (which ironically comes about as a result of what he first reads on trees), and harkens back to the image of helmets as empowering or disempowering objects of male desire (Ferraù in Canto 1). Zerbino discovers the wreckage Orlando has caused in his frenzy and piously reconstitutes a simulacrum of his beloved friend by tying his armor and arms around a pine tree. He is able to reassemble, however, only an impotent, or metaphorically castrated, Orlando.[28] Later, Mandricardo removes from the pile what he phallically desires the most and what he is sure will make him more than a man—Orlando's sword, Durindana. A few cantos later, he makes even more poignant the association between loss of sword and loss of phallic power by claiming that Orlando inflicted his own castration, the way beavers do: "E dicea ch'imitato avea il castore, / il qual si strappa i genitali sui, / vedendosi alle spalle il cacciatore" ("The count had imitated the beaver, he explained, who rips off his genitals if he sees the huntsman closing in" [27, 57]).

For Orlando, Angelica belongs to him because he has spent so much time assuring her possession. In this sense, Medoro's crime in taking "his" princess is, for Orlando, a theft of personal property. In his mind, Angelica carries a concrete sign of his ownership of her—a bracelet. The episode culminating in the knight's giving the bracelet to his queen ("alla regina sua," 19, 38) belongs to the urtext of the *Furioso*, for Ariosto appropriates a narrative motif invented by Boiardo—*sans* bracelet (*Innamorato* 2, 12 and 13)—and charges it with new meanings. As he reminds his readers, Orlando won the bracelet with honor and prowess in the Isole Lontane, where he freed Ziliante from the fairy Morgana. We discover, although only much later, as if Ariosto had forgotten, repressed, or purposely deferred putting the meaning of this object in context, that Angelica is able to retain it and wear it even when otherwise naked in Ebuda.

We may guess that Orlando's gift psychologically assures him of Angelica's prelapsarian status. In "Fetishism," Freud writes that a fetish functions only for the fetishist, who gives value to seemingly unimportant objects: "The meaning of the fetish is not known to other people, so the fetish is not withheld from him: it is easily accessible" (154). In this sense, the bracelet gratifies Orlando's narcissistic bent since it makes of his beloved, at least in his mind, someone he owns and about whom he can fantasize at will; it makes her someone, moreover, through whom he can be present even when absent. Freud defines the fetishist as a man unable to accept sexual difference in woman, for he continues desiring her lack and denying her castration. This indecision allows him to cast aside his own fear of castration.[29] The fetishist gives woman a substitute for what she does not have and is thus able to cancel her dissymmetry. For Freud, the substitute can be an inanimate object like a shoe, an ornament like a veil, or a part (and sometimes the whole) of the female body. In Orlando's case, the bracelet represents the reasons a fetish is built; that is, because there is both a desire and a need to repress that desire.

The construction of a fetish is always circuitous. In this instance, if Orlando accepts Angelica as other, he has also to accept the evidence of her castration. Castration, however, is exactly what a fetishist needs to deny. The strategy of having the fetish cover and metaphorically substitute for woman's lack makes it impossible to disallow the lack being covered. It also makes it impossible to accept it, and thus ironically both constitute the reason the fetish exists: to testify, as well as to disprove, that there has been castration.

We can infer that Angelica refuses to burden the gift with meaning: a bracelet is just a bracelet. She wears it because it gratifies her narcissistically and has an appealing decorative value: "non per amor del paladino, quanto / perch'era ricco e d'artificio egregio" ("not out of love for the paladin but simply because it was costly and finely wrought" [19, 39]). Thus, for Orlando, the bracelet speaks of virginity and stands for the unpicked rose of Sacripante's song; for Angelica, its rich stones speak of status: this is an appropriate gift for a princess.[30] Orlando wore the bracelet for a time, Ariosto writes, although he was conscious that it feminized him, as it had feminized Ziliante earlier (19, 38). Often what feminizes is what castrates. The decorative fetish must then be returned to the other sex: from Morgana it must go back to Angelica, two women sharing in Boiardo and Ariosto the same evanescent attitude toward Orlando. Significantly, Orlando loses his mind when he sees the bracelet transferred from Angelica's wrist to the shepherd's hands.

Given Orlando's obsession with Angelica's flower, this bracelet functions as a metonymic substitute for what he thinks should be ringed and self-enclosed in his object of desire. As a displaced sign, it works to disavow his fear of castration; a bound wrist is like a bound foot, a fetish in Chinese society whose value Freud fully describes in his essay on fetishism. The bracelet also recalls other rings: a wedding ring, a charmed ring of invisibility, even the knots encircling the names of Angelica and Medoro on the trees. Subliminally, the bracelet may be a phantasmic chastity belt and thus mediate, in Orlando's eyes, the social and the personal, as well as desire and desired non-consummation. As such, it is antithetical to whatever Angelica stands for: it suggests closure, whereas Angelica is typically unbound; it stands for restraint, Angelica for flight; it speaks of order, Angelica of disorder. Linked with the rose, the bracelet simultaneously points to desire and denies its consummation; it manifests what this desire is and immediately represses it.

In the end, the bracelet serves to reiterate, at the level of plot, the process that predicates Angelica's exclusion, a process that the narrative adumbrates throughout but makes visible only now. The bracelet's absence from its proper place suggests that what it denies has been gratified and spells narrative death for Angelica. The climax of the Angelica-Orlando story is signified then by an absence

that contains more information than anything Orlando has seen
or read in the previous hours. The story of the ring and the story
of the bracelet eventually complement each other. If the bracelet
functions as a sign of Angelica's non-possession of herself, the ring
has the opposite meaning. The first is disposable; the second, a
passport to freedom.

The rhetoric of the text demands that Orlando eventually re-
coup his knighthood and straighten out his allegiances. Thus, if
like a Virgilian Silenus (*Sixth Eclogue*, 24), he looks forward to his
untying when he reconquers his wits ("Solvite me," 39, 60), he also
knows, as an Erasmian Silenus, that reality is double, the positive
always having a negative side: "What at first sight is beautiful may
really be ugly . . . the disgraceful, glorious; the learned, ignorant;
the robust, feeble; the noble, base; the joyous, sad; the favorable,
adverse; what is friendly, an enemy; and what is wholesome, poi-
sonous" (Erasmus, 36).[31] Yet the same strategy that again makes
Orlando glorious, learned, noble, wholesome, and a paragon of
wisdom and manliness ("più che mai saggio e virile," 39, 61) dia-
lectically serves to turn woman into the irreconcilably different,
the radical alterity, the disposable non-self: "Sì che colei, che sì
bella e gentile / gli parve dianzi, e ch'avea tanto amato, / non stima
più se non per cosa vile" ("The damsel who had seemed hitherto
so beautiful and good in his eyes, and whom he had so adored, he
now dismissed as utterly worthless" [39, 61]).

Orlando's funeral oration for Brandimarte brings the narra-
tive full circle, for even as he tearfully and publicly expresses his
sorrow, an undying, gratifying, and true male bonding surfaces:
"O forte, o caro, o mio fedel compagno, / che qui sei morto, e so
che vivi in cielo, / . . . perdonami, se ben vedi ch'io piagno; / per-
chè d'esser rimaso mi querelo, / e ch'a tanta letizia io non son teco"
("Dear, loyal comrade, Brandimart the strong: here you are, dead.
I know you are alive in paradise. . . . Forgive me if you see me
weeping: it is because I have remained here and am not with you in
so great a joy" [43, 170]). Compared to female inaccessibility and
enigma, the gratifications born of brotherhood seem comforting
and understandable.

Like his cousin Orlando, Rinaldo too is destined to be saved
and cured of his purposeless passion for Angelica, for Ariosto
scrupulously extricates all Christian knights from their amorous

obsessions. The rivalry between Orlando and Rinaldo for Angelica is well marked in the text. One almost killed the other twice, San Giovanni claims, and all because Orlando had been blinded by his incestuous love ("incesto amore," 34, 64) for a pagan woman. "Incesto" is usually translated as "impure" or, as in the Innamorati edition of the *Furioso*, interpreted as incestuous in the sense that Angelica and Orlando practice different religions (869*n*). But I would claim that this word has a deeper contextual meaning and refers literally to the two cousins' incestuous feelings toward their common object of desire.

Unlike Orlando, Rinaldo plans to pursue Angelica into Asia and even more persistently than in the past once he is informed that a Saracen has picked her flower. Actually, Rinaldo cannot believe that Angelica, who had all the worthiest knights of Christendom at her feet, has fallen for such a lowly man: "Ha sempre in mente, e mai non se ne parte, / come esser puote ch'un povero fante / abbia del cor di lei spinto da parte / merito e amor d'ogni altro primo amante" ("What he could never escape was the thought of how a poor simple soldier could have displaced in her breast the entire merits, the full ardour of all the previous suitors" [42, 45]). Like Orlando, Rinaldo begins his search with a regret. He reasons that although in the past (that is, in Boiardo's poem) he could have had Angelica a thousand times, he has consistently refused to follow through on his desires, even though he has never been hesitant in sexual matters.[32] The logic of this behavior is clearly lost in the *Furioso*, for now, rather than avoiding Angelica, he pursues her. Alas, in one of those coincidences that provide bountiful narrative motifs, Angelica starts to hate him. No matter how much he desires her, she will have nothing to do with him.

But possessing Angelica can prove dangerous. Rinaldo unguardedly expresses this thought in Canto 42. For a day with her, even a short one, he vows, he would not mind dying: "Ed ora eleggerebbe un giorno corto / averne solo, e rimaner poi morto" ("Now he would accept to die could he enjoy but one brief day of it" [42, 44]). The lines do not suggest that Rinaldo equates death metaphorically with coital bliss; rather, that he would not mind dying as a result of engaging in sex with the woman of his desires. In this sense, he could not have better expressed the psychic fear of castration and the threat of nothingness that constitute the ultimate

signs of entrapping female sexuality. Being too close to Angelica—
the Angelica-cum-Medoro standing for unbridled female sexu-
ality—may prove just as deadly to Rinaldo as to Orlando. If the
pre-Medoro Angelica could be happily pursued as an unobtainable
object of desire, now, as a postlapsarian woman, Angelica carries
different perils. After all, she has just chosen a young lover. By
declaring that he wants her more than ever, Rinaldo shows that he
is unable to grasp the senselessness of his behavior. But help is on
the way.

Enter the Medusa. During the first stage of his quest for An-
gelica, while passing through a secluded forest, Rinaldo notices a
strange monster in the shape of a woman ("un strano mostro in
feminil figura," 42, 46) coming out of a dark cave. The monster
has a great tangle of snakes instead of hair ("in loco de crin serpi a
gran torma," 42, 47). Rinaldo's reaction is one of sheer disgust.[33]
"In mythology," John Freccero points out, "the Medusa was said
to be powerless against women, for it was her feminine *beauty* that
constituted the mortal threat to her admirers. From the ancient
Physiologus through the mythographers to Boccaccio, the Medusa
represented a sensual fascination, a *pulchritudo* so excessive that it
turned men to stone" ("Medusa," 7–8). The connection between
Angelica and the Medusa is not as gratuitous as it may appear. Both
are incredibly beautiful, for example, and Angelica's rare beauty is
specifically held responsible for Rinaldo's behavior.

How does one overcome, then, the terror and the fascination
that the sight of the Medusa clearly evokes in man? In "Medusa's
Head," Freud equates the Medusa with fetishization and castration.
Ariosto's narrative strategy is to empower Rinaldo the way Ovid
empowered Perseus—by giving him the tools to replace his admi-
ration for Angelica with repugnance. This is accomplished through
the textual repetition of the fear of the viscid animal / viscid sexu-
ality motif. This time, however, there is a significant reversal of
subject. Earlier on, Angelica displayed revulsion ("schivo") toward
Rinaldo as if he were a snake ("serpe"); now Rinaldo experiences
the same feeling toward the entwining aggressor while attempt-
ing to escape the Medusan embrace: "non ch'altrimente il serpe
lo moleste; / ma tanto orror ne sente e tanto schivo, / che stride
e geme, e duolsi ch'egli è vivo" ("not so much lest the serpent
molest him further as because it inspired in him such horror and

revulsion. He cried out, he groaned, he wished he were dead" [42, 51]). As Angelica's feelings for Rinaldo move from infatuation in the *Innamorato* to horror in the *Furioso*, so the image Rinaldo now holds of his princess *en abîme*, through the Medusa, repeats—by displacing it—the same sensation of horror.

Rinaldo's next step is to pass from aversion to salvation. He moves away from the monster and regains his eyesight through the help of an allegorical father, a leader and guide ("guida e duca," 42, 58), who, in the manner of Virgil in the *Commedia*, leads him away from the woods of darkness ("luoghi oscuri e bui," 42, 57–58). Like Dante the pilgrim, but with no transcendental reason attached to his action, Rinaldo drinks in due time at the "right" source of water and delivers himself from a life of error and blindness ("cecitade," 42, 66).[34]

By way of Angelica (the desired and yet feared woman), who is freed from the sea monster thanks to Ruggiero's use of a shield identical to the one Perseus used in his slaying of the Medusa and in his liberation of Andromeda, we can tie this episode in Canto 42 to a similar one in Canto 10. Ruggiero has seen a Medusa of sorts in the ugly face of a now elderly Alcina, and an Andromeda of sorts in Angelica. In this canto Rinaldo-Perseus uses a sword against a Medusa who, like the sea monster, represents sexuality and illustrates the castration threat that he consistently tries to disavow. Since Orlando, not Ruggiero, kills the sea monster, and since Perseus sees Andromeda only after slaying the Medusa, in fact while still shaking her head, we can see how intertwined are the Perseus myth and the main story of the *Furioso*.

The connection goes even deeper. Ovid writes that Medusa, a maiden with golden hair, was raped by Poseidon and then, as punishment, turned into an image of horror by Athena (*Metamorphoses* 4, 5). Although innocent, Medusa is punished first for what may have been incestuous rape and next for having been raped in the wrong place, the temple of a goddess. In the *Furioso*, the strange custom of feeding a woman a day to Proteus's sea monster on the island of Ebuda has the same equivocal origin. Here, Proteus, a sea god, rapes the daughter of a king. The father subsequently kills the daughter as punishment for submitting to rape. Enraged, Proteus invades the island. As a result, each day a woman is sacrificed to the Orca until Proteus can find the one who looks like the daughter.

As the story makes clear, woman is punished for sins she did not commit and punished again for being the victim of sins she was unable to avoid.[35] Through Ruggiero's providential help, Angelica escapes the sea monster, but she is still punished and eliminated from the epic for having allowed the plucking of her "rosa" and thus for having displaced a narrative motif indispensable to her presence.

In both episodes, man conquers the forces of evil / female sexuality (i.e., the dark cave that the monster inhabits). As Orlando *in bono*, Ruggiero attempts to kill the Orca with the same instrument Perseus used to overcome the Medusa. He succeeds only in stunning the female monster. The feat of killing a femaleness so visibly threatening belongs not to Ruggiero, who has quite a different route to follow in the epic, but to the two married and mature cousins: Orlando, who kills the sea monster (gendered in Italian in the feminine), and Rinaldo, who overcomes the serpentine beast (usually considered female in myth). Both animals have an active oral appetite: the sea monster eats maidens; the serpents entwine themselves around Rinaldo and they also eat themselves. "The orality of monsters," Munich writes, "is often a female equivalent, its open mouth a symbolic counterpart to fantasies of devouring female genitals" (32). Orlando kills with a phallic instrument, an anchor attached to a rope he places in the monster's mouth; Rinaldo kills with the help of a patriarchal father, Indignation, wielding another phallic instrument, a flaming torch. The viscid, slimy snake ("biscia") that Orlando fights is an apt counterpart to the serpents around Rinaldo. Rinaldo is eventually able to get rid of the coiling twisting mass ("massa che s'aggiri e torca," 10, 101) around his torso, just as Orlando is able to confront the monster by immersing himself into her large mouth ("tanta boca"). His swimming out of a mixture of blood and whitish seawater signals a rebirth; likewise, Rinaldo's immersion in the stream of oblivion prefigures a new life.[36]

In the end, through narrative repetitions of the myth of a castrating but always conquered female, our paladins rid themselves of the danger that Angelica represents. As Mulvey suggests, such a process is voyeuristic and sadistic for both Orlando, who moves from worshiping his woman to wanting to destroy her, and Rinaldo, who reaches back to the myth itself and reenacts it in his process of remastering. Subsequently, the two men partake in a ritual baptism into Christian order, and ask for God's forgiveness. San Giovanni says that Orlando shares in the same destiny as Nebuchadnezzar, and his cousin Rinaldo in that of the blind Tobias.[37] Through the image of Tobias, who like Oedipus has lost his eyesight, Rinaldo is connected to the same incestuous love that San Giovanni chastises in Orlando.[38]

If it is the possession, or, more accurately, the non-possession, of a seemingly possessable object of desire that keeps male rivalry and the male competition for political power alive, narrative closure can come only after such an object loses its value. Since the vying for Angelica is rooted in physical possession, one would imagine that the plucking of her rose would solve the problem at the level of the plot. In this section I argue that such is hardly the case, for regular knights will not do for Angelica. Ariosto could easily refashion her worth as object of desire before she "knows" sex into her worth as object of desire after she "knows" sex. He would simply need to change aims and rivalries. In the Girardian plot, for example, Angelica would be all the more valuable to the other knights following the loss of her maidenhead, since a future rival in love could improve his own standing by challenging and defeating any of the possessors of her body—Orlando, Rinaldo, Sacripante, Ferraù, or other knights. Her possession would guarantee the paladin his own stability as subject and his own worth within his male-oriented world. Given the homosocial logic that Eve Sedgwick has recently explored in heterosexual interrelations, the reasoning informing the Girardian triangular relationship, and even the plot Freud outlines in his essay on jokes, woman becomes more valuable when a third man, or a group of men acting as a third party, challenge the original lover.[39] If this were the case, Angelica would remain in the narrative.

A woman who has transgressed, moreover, can transgress again. The competition among men, then, would no longer be a competition to possess her body first or to take her away from a peer who has already possessed her but to possess her last and finally. The procedure is problematic. Stealing the desired woman would indeed prove a knight's worth to his peers, but it would put him in the position of having to worry about remaining on top. Such a course of action would be as disruptive and damaging to authority as a still-unpossessed Angelica. The solution must be found elsewhere.

Having any of the knights possess a woman like Angelica would mean that she is worthy of the competition. Angelica, however, is too different to belong fully, too beautiful or too spoken about for the rights to her as property to remain forever safe. Moreover, she is ethnically too foreign and follows a faith too dissonant from that embraced by the poem. Assimilating her into the Christian world would be complicated. But in fact, it is unnecessary, since another woman in the narrative is Ariosto's exemplar of correct femininity. Bradamante is central both to the *gesta* the author invents and to those he hints at, in which a predestined female warrior will give birth to the first male Este.[40] Bradamante thus has a place within both the story Ariosto narrates and the history that he, as a good courtier, refashions for his princes. Like Angelica, she is allowed to experience sexuality (in her case, in the afterplot of the *Furioso*), but unlike Angelica, the expression of that sexuality is approved because it leads to a generation of dynasts.

Given that the story of a woman as object of desire is inescapably sexual, Ariosto needs a man to rid the text of Angelica, a man who will not be perceived as a competitor by her knightly pursuers, but who, for this reason, can effectively put her out of the game. Enter Medoro. As a foot soldier, Medoro is no social match for the other characters. Indeed, he stands completely outside the system for which the knights fight, in terms of ethics, politics, and class.[41] Judging from his description, Medoro is not even much of a man: "Medoro avea la guancia colorita / e bianca e grata ne la età novella; / e fra la gente a quella impresa uscita / non era faccia più gioconda e bella: / occhi avea neri, e chioma crespa d'oro: / angel parea di quei del sommo coro" ("Medoro was born with lovely fair skin and pink cheeks: among all the host assembled on the expedition there was not a comelier or more pleasing face. He had dark eyes and a golden head of curls—he might have been an angel, indeed a seraph" [18, 166]). He is so handsome, his curly blond hair so enticing, that in a surge of homoerotic desire Zerbino is unable to kill him (19, 12).

And Medoro is certainly not a match for Angelica. Even the shepherd in whose hut the love story of this new couple develops marvels at the downfall of such a princess: "E sanza aver rispetto ch'ella fusse / figlia del maggior re ch'abbia il Levante, / da troppo amor costretta si condusse / a farsi moglie d'un povero fante" ("And, forgetting that she was daughter of the greatest monarch of the East, driven by excessive passion, she chose to become wife to a poor simple soldier" [23, 120]). In the class-conscious Renaissance world and Ariostan mind, a princess marrying a foot soldier does more than simply fall below her status. She is engaging in a dangerous, improper, and disorderly act. By putting herself in the hands of a barbarian ("d'un vilissimo barbaro ai servigi," 42, 39), Angelica thoroughly defeats the social order that women are asked to guarantee in semiology through their proper exchange in marriage. Again, she proves too unconventional and culturally different from "normal," Christian society. Moreover, if the prize for a manly warrior is a woman, then Angelica's choice of an androgynous pagan youth over a Christian of unquestionable military might such as Orlando can only undercut cherished male assumptions about masculinity and manhood.

Interestingly, this is the only time in the narrative that Angelica, the epic's eternal feminine, is given a desire and a purpose, and thus a less narcissistic and enigmatic characterization. Unfortunately, Orlando cannot acknowledge that his princess may nurture desires of her own and denies their possibility, only to find each and every mark of her passion. First astonished, then infuriated, he proceeds to eradicate all possible proofs of her passion before finally surrendering to evidence: "Veder l'ingiuria sua scritta nel monte / l'accese sì, ch'in lui non restò dramma / che non fosse odio, rabbia, ira e furore" ("To see his calamity written there in the hillside so inflamed him that he was drained of every drop that was not pure hate, fury, wrath, and violence" [23, 129]). This is a complete reversal of that other famous Dantesque reason for lack of "dramma di sangue" (*Purg.* 30, 46–47) when the pilgrim Dante finally meets Beatrice, and it serves as an ironic reminder that some revelations are better left veiled when the subject has a penchant for blindness. After that, Ariosto delegates the task of continuing to refashion his heroine's story to other poets ("miglior plettri"). As might be expected, Angelica suffers further narrative crimes at their hands. Both Ludovico Dolce in *Il primo libro di Sacripante* (1536) and Vincenzo Brusantini in *L'Angelica innamorata* (1550) make her a prostitute.

As has been pointed out, Angelica's exit from the text is igno-

minious, since she escapes from Orlando's sight and homicidal
fury by using her magic ring. But, timing her exit badly, she falls
from her horse in total disarray. Why such an undignified, carniva-
lesque ending? Granted that Angelica has to escape from Orlando's
desire, now more bestial than human ("Gli corre dietro, e tien
quella maniera / che terria il cane a seguitar la fera"; "He ran after
her the way a hound pursues game" [29, 61]), still why is it neces-
sary that in the process her femininity has to become laughable? I
submit that although it is necessary for Angelica to marry a person
of a much lower status to be expurgated from the text, it is also
necessary that she be deprived of the last laugh. By siding with his
audience in its disapproval of Angelica's recent actions (Orlando
is for the moment beyond understanding), Ariosto reconducts his
heroine to the order of his world and takes care narratively to
isolate and condemn her independence from codes and rules.[42]

Critics essentially agree that Ariosto's end for Angelica is puni-
tive; the problem, I think, lies in the attribution of the guilt. Julius
Molinaro sees a moral structure of sin/punishment at work in the
epic and argues that Angelica deserved chastisement. Since she
"had treated her many and willing suitors as puppets . . . it was
thus not unexpected that Love would refuse to endure Angelica's
arrogance any longer. . . . [Her] marriage to a Moor of an obscure
family was an obvious punishment" ("Sin," 40). As Shakespeare's
Desdemona illustrates, marriage to a Moor is always deadly to
women; no matter the circumstances, the choice of a man outside
the system is permanently scarring. Angelica's punishment seems
to me inevitable from the beginning, since her characterization
bars her survival as an independent being. Angelica can exist only
in the erotic dark jungle of man's imagination ("selva oscura,"
1, 22; 2, 68), inside the winding paths and thick vegetation of
romance narratives, thoroughly entrapped in the myth of woman
as dark continent. The same world that requires woman's inacces-
sibility postulates her expendability. Emblematically different, she
was never created to fit in.

Does this mean that Angelica will finally be able, in her faraway
country, to live by a different standard? Hardly so. Cathay may
be enormously distant and the journey home long and dangerous,
but the Law-of-the-Father knows no boundaries. Angelica's story
of loss does, in fact, have a coda. Through a final narrative twist,

Ariosto admits an option he seemed to have discarded earlier, that of channeling his princess's femininity toward standard feminine goals. In the final lines and before losing interest in her ("di seguir più questa non mi cale"; "I do not care to pursue her adventures any further" [30, 17]), he suddenly normalizes her behavior by making her act in a wifely manner. Upon her arrival home, he tells us, Angelica gives her crown to her husband. Can a child-heir be far behind? By playing by the rules at last and becoming a wife, this narcissistic woman will perhaps find a proper object choice in "His Majesty the Baby," as Freud puts it ("On Narcissism," 91), a child whose coming would guarantee, and finally legitimize, her husband's dynastic right. Child or no child, once again the logic of familyism vis-à-vis woman is being reasserted.

In this context, I disagree with Mario Santoro's conclusion (*L'anello*, 81) that Angelica's return home is a return to innocence, to the world of memory and utopia. Santoro considers but rejects the possibility that going home may bring no freedom to Angelica. It seems to me, however, that there is no place for Angelica, no home outside society and societal conventions. Her return to Cathay simply signifies a return to sameness: the same rules, the same views, the same judgments, as in the Christian world. Similarly, I both agree and disagree with Giorgio Barberi-Squarotti's conclusion (111–12) that Angelica chooses a pastoral ending with Medoro in order to stop running away. For Squarotti, Angelica restores order and peace by renouncing her condition of princess and heroine. What I question is not this statement per se, which is quite correct, but Squarotti's reading of these choices as good ones, as if it were better, or praiseworthy, for a woman to be a shepherdess rather than a princess. Would Ariosto have preferred such a course of action for any of his noble male warriors? In my opinion, it is wrong to praise Angelica for what in the final analysis amounts to a deliberate renunciation of her selfhood and her status. Rather, such an outcome follows the logic of epic narratives, since there is no substitute role, except narrative suicide, for a transgressive woman unwilling to regulate her sexuality.

Angelica finds herself out of the game, then, not because she has been sexual and not because she has not been sufficiently sexual toward her unsatisfied pursuers, but because she is in the text to enrich other plots, to guarantee other identities. The paradox of her position is unresolvable within the epic. Had she been like Bradamante, she would have been given a feasible story and a worthy man to marry (although of course Bradamante performs other functions for men). Had she been like Marfisa (I am comparing her to women who remain alive at the end of the epic), she could have been granted a moral plot, perhaps a search for revenge for the deaths of her brother and father. Even if she had been imagined to be like Doralice, an object of mimetic desire between Rodomonte and Mandricardo, her choices or non-choices would still have mattered. The comparison with Doralice is pertinent because her pursuers fight a duel to possess her, a duel that Orlando and Rinaldo would perhaps have fought had Angelica not run away. In the text, Ariosto allows Doralice to choose along sexual lines. She prefers Mandricardo, he makes plain, because she has known him many times ("più fiate e più di piatto," 27, 106). Whom would Angelica have chosen? Is a choice available to her? After all, although neither Rodomonte nor Mandricardo is married, both Orlando and Rinaldo are. I mention marriage not because I want to enforce a moral outlook but because Ariosto asks his readers to do so by emphasizing the love match of his other, exemplary pair, Ruggiero and Bradamante.

My point is that, as long as Orlando or any one of Angelica's pursuers or even the narrator as lover of a woman like Angelica is unwilling to acknowledge the other's desire and prefers simply to desire the other, there is no room for Angelica in the fiction of *Orlando furioso*. As long as she can be posited as both spectated and spectral, as hallucination as well as illusive emblem of womanhood, and as long as her representation is so neutral that she can wear many different personalities, so abstracted that she can be unceasingly portrayed as a figure of desire (a different figure of desire for each man desiring her), Angelica cannot have a positive role. Always scrutinized but never seen, she is condemned to remain invisible because there are too many versions of her. In the end, Angelica remains a fantasy both when she is present and when she is not, either with or without a ring.

CHAPTER FIVE

Ego Games / Body Games: The Representation of Olimpia

That wench is stark mad or wonderful froward.
—Shakespeare, *The Taming of the Shrew*, I.i.69

My father was betrayed, I left both kingdom and country. My reward? I am at liberty to live whatever life of exile I like.
—Medea, Ovid's *Heroides*, 12: 109–10

CRITICS DISAGREE over the representation of Olimpia in *Orlando furioso*. For some, Olimpia is an example of undying virtue and selfless love; for others, she is a vengeful, spoiled, immoderate princess, pathologically unable to know when to say when. These different responses begin in Olimpia's characterization in the epic, which D. S. Carne-Ross defines as "undoubtedly disappointing" (1976: 154). Indeed, Olimpia seems to be both a positive and a negative representation of womanhood, both a subject and an object of desire, lovely and lovable as well as loveless and lovelorn.

In the previous chapter, I examined the representation of woman as object of desire; here, I examine her representation as desiring subject. Unlike Angelica, Olimpia is given an assertive personality and a powerful narrative: she is happily in love and willing to go to any lengths to fulfill her desire. What gives a twist to her characterization is that there are actually two Olimpias, one assertive and the other passive, and essentially two stories, one in Canto 9 and the other, quite different, in Cantos 10 and 11. What is wrong with the first ending? What has Olimpia done that requires amending? I argue that Ariosto's reopening in the latter cantos of a seemingly concluded narrative is necessary in order to give the Olimpia story a more suitable "feminine" conclusion. That he accomplishes this rectification by grafting it onto another scene written almost two decades earlier, that of Angelica's liberation from bondage in Ebuda, testifies to his careful attention to problems of closure for each of the narrative strands in his burgeoning romance epic. The recasting works to place woman on the side of law and order through a slow but continuous normalization of feminine behavior. The willful Olimpia of Canto 9 becomes the

acquiescent Olimpia of Canto 11; the Angelica escaping sexual en-
trapment in Canto 11 through the use of her magic ring (thereby
creating further havoc in the Christian camp) gets refashioned into
a domesticated counterpart, a shy Olimpia now happy with a wed-
ding ring. This dichotomized image of woman is the subject of
the present chapter: woman as autonomous self, or as body to be
admired; woman as defiantly rebellious, or as meekly accommo-
dating; woman as a realistically rendered person, or Woman as
an idealized image. Ariosto eventually privileges Woman, but the
glimpse he gives of the first Olimpia before he produces a properly
feminized second version suggests perhaps that all is not well on
the domestic front.

The story of Olimpia was a significant addition to the 1532 edi-
tion of the *Furioso*. It is distributed across four interrelated cantos
(9, 8–94; 10, 1–34; 11, 21–80; and 12, 1–4) and is often seen as cen-
tral to the main epic because of Orlando's role in it. Cesare Segre
sees Ariosto's decision to add the Olimpia story as reestablishing
an equilibrium of heroic functions between Orlando and Rug-
giero and as counterbalancing the Ruggiero-Bradamante-Leone
triangle, also added in the last edition. Without the adventures
in Holland and in Ebuda in Cantos 9 and 11, Segre argues (31–
32), examples of Orlando's might before the onset of his madness
would have been almost nonexistent, and, in spite of the title,
Ruggiero would have become in effect the principal hero of the
Furioso. With the addition, Orlando becomes a more heroic, just,
and stalwart knight. Along the same lines, Walter Moretti (49)
sees in the Orlando of this episode a Messiah of order redressing a
world marked by greed, injustice, and betrayal.[1]

Olimpia enters *Orlando furioso* by introducing herself to Or-
lando, summoned to her aid by an old man, as the daughter of
the Count of Holland: "Io voglio che sappiate che figliuola / fui
del conte d'Olanda" ("I would have you know that I was the
daughter of the Count of Holland" [9, 22]), thereby inscribing her-
self immediately within the Law-of-the-Father.[2] As is always the
case for important characters in Ariosto, whether male or female,
Olimpia's name is withheld for the moment.[3] Her mournful ap-
pearance, her seeming carelessness about her looks, and her evident
physical distress soon create a classic narrative of persecution and
punishment. Olimpia tells Orlando how some time earlier she had

fallen in love with Bireno, Duke of Selandia, who had tempo-
rarily landed in her father's territory. He reciprocated her love and
soon the two were ready to crown their story with a lawful union:
"Che 'l matrimonio con solenne / rito al ritorno suo saria tra nui, /
mi promise egli ed io 'l promisi a lui" ("We exchanged vows that
on his return we would be married with solemn ritual" [9, 24]).
Olimpia herself broke the news to her father, who accepted the
arrangement. Problems arose, she explains, when Cimosco, the
nearby king of Frisia, proposed his son Arbante for her hand in
order to establish a future legal claim on her land. Unwilling to
be considered an item of barter for a political end, she refused the
match with her father's assent, for he was always willing to enter-
tain her desires ("al qual sol piace quanto / a me piacea"; "whose
only pleasure was my pleasure" [9, 27]).

This refusal soon brought tragedy, Olimpia laments: when
Cimosco invaded Holland in retaliation, she lost her two brothers
and her father (as usual, there is no mention of a mother). Soon
after, she also lost her land, for her subjects found her obstinacy
in the name of love too costly and chose to betray her. Having
become Cimosco's prisoner, she decided to play his game tempo-
rarily and to postpone vengeance. She accepted the same offer of
marriage refused earlier but secretly arranged for Arbante to be
killed on their wedding night. In fact, she herself struck a blow
against him. In the meantime, Cimosco imprisoned Bireno, come
to rescue Olimpia, and ruled that she must exchange places with
him to secure his release.

The year set as the outside limit for the exchange is now coming
to an end, Olimpia adds in concluding her heart-wrenching story,
and she has unsuccessfully spent all her remaining money in
attempting to bribe neighboring states into fomenting revolts
against her irascible father-in-law. She asks Orlando not to protect
her but to make sure that Cimosco frees Bireno once she delivers
herself to him. Orlando, of course, reads the desire of the other as
his own and redresses every injury: he successfully fights Cimosco,
reunites the two lovers, and makes sure there is no lingering im-
pediment to their future happiness.

Unexpectedly, Olimpia reappears in the following cantos. In
Canto 10, the author, who is now in charge of narrating, informs
the reader that Bireno has suddenly fallen in love with Cimosco's

teenage daughter and has abandoned his wife on the shores of
Ebuda on their way to Selandia. In Canto 11, taken prisoner by
the men scouting the area daily for sacrificial maidens, the naked
Olimpia, tied to a tree, is about to be swallowed by the same
sea monster that earlier threatened Angelica. Thinking that the
chained woman is "his" Angelica, Orlando runs to her rescue, kills
the monster, and frees her. Again the Christian paladin redresses
all wrongs and manages to marry Olimpia to Oberto, the young
king of Ibernia, who has independently (and quite conveniently)
arrived that day to liberate the Ebudans from the insatiable resident
monster.[4]

The narrative movement that characterizes the Olimpia story is
straightforward: given a damsel in distress and a knight willing to
perform noble acts, we know that the damsel will be saved and that
the worthy knight will either marry her or marry her off. Since
Orlando cannot marry her without committing bigamy, only the
second option is available. This in turn opens up two further pos-
sibilities: either to have Olimpia marry the object of her love or to
have her marry another worthy knight. The first outcome consti-
tutes the narrative of Canto 9, the second that of Canto 11 (ignor-
ing for the moment the issue of Olimpia's brief, unwanted, and
unconsummated marriage to Arbante). Ariosto achieves narrative
closure in both cases through woman's containment in marriage.
There is a significant difference in the second rendering, how-
ever. Olimpia's first marriage is to the man she herself chooses and
for whom she fights ferociously. As it turns out, closure proves
temporary: this choice is sadly wrong. The second time, Olimpia
marries the man chosen for her (Bireno has been killed), and here,
as in fairy tales, marriage not only opens up access to a higher rank
but also secures vengeance for herself and her family and allows
her to acquire land in the bargain: "Olimpia Oberto si pigliò per
moglie, / e di contessa la fè gran regina" ("Hubert made Olimpia
his wife, and raised her from countess to mighty queen" [11, 80]).
The destiny a woman manages to weave is paraded as one of loss;
rewritten by man, it becomes one of gain.

Even a brief glance at Canto 9 reveals that Ariosto portrays a
willful, at times imperious, but extremely articulate and ratioci-
native Olimpia. No one would mistake this maiden for a passive
character. Although her goals are eminently feminine—marriage

to a man already approved by her father—Olimpia is not shy. On the contrary, she seems empowered to seek assertively, perhaps even excessively, the satisfaction of her desires. But Olimpia's gestures, decisions, and speech are eminently inappropriate in a woman. Unlike Isabella, who can communicate only in the language of love and passivity, and unlike Angelica, who prefers invisibility to sexual confrontation, Olimpia screams and schemes. Her sentimental attachment to Bireno and her total faith in him, moreover, ironically make her act in a way more mannish than feminine. Faith is, of course, a key term in the *Furioso* for men, women, and even horses (as in the case of Rinaldo's Baiardo), but too much faith, Ariosto suggests, not only jeopardizes growth but also stunts efforts at compromise.[5]

It thus becomes clear why in Canto 10 the author moves to regulate Olimpia's independence and to chastise her excessiveness. In punishing her sexual assertiveness and overinvestment in feelings, he uses not only a philandering man, as we will see, but also another woman, one sufficiently unlike Olimpia as to be unable or unwilling to rebel against her own objectification. Canto 11 offers, then, a third stage in the representation, one that presents a surprisingly different, helpless, and withdrawn Olimpia. No longer represented as having mental agility, Olimpia is shown now as possessing primarily bodily graces. Thanks to them, she finds the very happiness that eluded her in her previous, more assertive, stance. From here it is easy to co-opt her into law and tradition through a marriage to a young and kind king. This marriage also affirms a founding patriarchal bond, that of a father (Orlando) and a son (Oberto) celebrating a heroic code through the transfer of woman, whom the first saves and the second makes rich.

Olimpia's desire becomes "correct" only when it becomes a desire for the phallus. Therefore even the father who in his shortsightedness puts no restraints on the satisfaction of a daughter's desire has to be punished: he will lose his children, his heirs, his kingdom, and his life. Significantly, Olimpia's father is killed by a bullet piercing his eyes, a literalization of his own blindness. As Ariosto makes plain, allowing a woman to desire is not wrong, but allowing a woman to satisfy her desires with too strong a sense of direction and purpose is intrinsically dangerous, even when these desires are pursued for legal ends, for women are capricious.

To redress the problem and establish order, the narrative needs to offer a reversal of the earlier image of excessive female libido and defuse the threat woman represents. This task is accomplished by portraying Olimpia's love as monstrous. Ariosto is hardly alone in opting for such a sadistic narrative twist, for as Teresa De Lauretis argues, it is in the logic of Oedipal desire that women "*either* consent *or* be seduced into consenting to femininity. . . . Women's consent may not be gotten easily but is finally gotten, and has been for a long time, as much by rape and economic coercion as by the more subtle and lasting effects of ideology, representation, and identification" (*Alice Doesn't*, 134).

It has lately become fashionable to attack Olimpia. What is questioned specifically is the Olimpia portrayed in Canto 9, who is reproached for her willfulness, no matter the cost, and for her lack of political sense, no matter her personal losses. Even the truthfulness of her love for Bireno is challenged, not to mention her understanding of his feelings toward her. Emilio Zanette (83) concentrates on what he defines as Olimpia's overindulgent lugubriousness and mental exaltation, Alfredo Bonadeo (49) argues for her blindness, and Barbara Pavlock (162) cites her lack of responsibility for the events unfolding in front of her and her unwillingness to engage in realpolitik.[6] But to say that Olimpia fails to understand the degree of Bireno's commitment amounts once again to making woman responsible for man's fickleness. If Bireno were not in love, one could ask, why did he come back to help Olimpia? Moreover, he had one year to save his own life by betraying her. Why did he not do so? My impression is that Bireno, young and inexperienced like Olimpia, reciprocated her love but was satiated as soon as she became sexually accessible. Then, blinded by his newly acquired power, he looked for more and for better.

The other consensus among critics of the *Furioso* is that the Olimpia of Canto 9 is too faithful and should have given herself to Cimosco once her losses multiplied; ironically this view leads to approval of her Dutch subjects' giving away her own land. Enrico Musacchio ("L'Olimpia," 108) even accuses Olimpia of desiring Bireno's betrayal out of a masochistic love of self-punishment.[7] Fortunately for this woman, there is a remedy, Musacchio argues: a therapeutic exposure, naked, to a sea monster bent on swallowing her and to two paladins with different agendas in regard to women. A physical threat, a good dose of objectification, and a willing surrender of their own self, this critic seems to suggest, can do wonders for the health of unassimilable females. That this "woman's cure" works only in the context of male representations of sick, disruptive females is an issue that goes unexamined.

My point is that without a love plot there is no Olimpia in the epic, but with one Olimpia is asked to accede to essentially the same agreement she refused earlier. Even if she had been able to perceive herself as a commodity to be bartered, however, she would still have had no choice after the war that follows her refusal to marry. Whether she agrees to Cimosco's request to put herself under his "protection" and equate her body with the body politic or refuses one more time, Olimpia knows that she is bound to lose both her reign and her life. Her agreement to Cimosco's demand would simply legalize his usurpation of her father's land, the murder of her family, and a prison-like marriage to Arbante. No present or past critic/criminologist, however, faults the second Olimpia. It is as if only when powerless and devoid of anger can Olimpia be worthy of love; only when bound and waiting for a man to save her can she become proper and commendable.

Discussing the inner dangers that individuals often perceive when confronted with different cultures and behaviors, Roland Barthes writes in *Mythologies* that the Other threatening the bourgeois or the status quo was excluded in the past "because the Other is a scandal which threatens his essence" (151). However, in contemporary society, Barthes adds, every outsider can find a niche inside (150). In the following discussion, I take two of Barthes's insights—identification and inoculation—a bit further, in a historically retroactive way, and apply them to the representation of Olimpia.[8] I argue that Olimpia is first involved in a narrative that excludes her as irreducible Other (she embodies wrong femininity at this stage, although she has correct beauty and class). This is done by teaching her a lesson. Then she is recuperated through a strategy of identification by which she loses her disruptive characteristics in the process of being projected as radically different, a spectacle (she embodies correct femininity now, which the author surveys voyeuristically). Finally, through inoculation—that is, through inclusion in the controlled system in which she should have remained, given her birthright—she is brought back to the reality of virginal, aristocratic female characters, a reality that spells a dynastically correct and corrective marriage. As usual, the progress from disorder to order has to posit disorder as undesirable to show the desirability of an ordered course of action.

In Canto 10, when her misadventures are no longer told in her voice, Olimpia loses her subjectivity and even her story. Giuseppe Dalla Palma (*Le strutture*, 61) attributes the shift from a narrating to a narrated Olimpia to the fact that the second part of her story is no longer exemplary. As I see it, however, the shift is necessary precisely in order to make her story exemplary. The restraining of Olimpia goes through three stages: first, she is phallicized by being made a murderer; then she is dephallicized by having another woman choose to associate herself, in opposition to Olimpia, with the phallus; finally, she is described as phallus-substitute herself, shot into art as a fetishized figure of desire.[9] On the mythic level, she moves from an assertive but eventually abandoned Ariadne to a restrained but eventually saved Andromeda (Barthes's identification strategy) and finally to a reconstructed and perfectly fetishized, and thus properly acceptable, Zeuxian beauty (Barthes's inoculation move).

The process of Olimpia's exclusion is quite subtle. Although the story of her desire is presented sympathetically (her father, after all, approves of her love for Bireno), Olimpia's will is from the very beginning contained within a series of masochistic scenarios that inhibit the reader's identification with her and dampen any pity for her distress. First, her characterization is surcharged with black images. When Orlando appears, Olimpia is dressed in black, and every object in her house, every wall is covered with black drapes. To be sure, Orlando is also in mourning after Angelica's "abandonment," and his black vest reflects his mood. Unlike Orlando, however, who leaves king and country behind, Olimpia spends her days paralyzed in her house, waiting for a solution she can no longer buy and a male savior able, she hopes, to enforce it.

The rendering of Olimpia as a shaken, perhaps hysterical, but thoroughly committed lover works to engage the reader's sympathy, although there are hints throughout the canto that she may be overdramatizing. Yet sympathy suddenly turns into horror when, in recounting her distress, Olimpia reveals that she is a murderer.[10]

Her killing of Arbante on their wedding night is, moreover, unnecessary, and thus more shocking, since it results sheerly from vengeance and not from self-defense; she jumps on him only after he has been dispatched by her hired men: "Quel mio fedele . . . / alzò un'accetta, e con sì valoroso / braccio dietro nel capo lo percosse, / che gli levò la vita e la parola: / io saltai presta, e gli segai la gola" ("My trusty servant . . . lifted an axe and brought it down on the back of his head with such a mighty blow that he dispatched him before he could utter a word. I leapt at him and slit his throat" [9, 41]). Homicide in the name of love or in order to avoid death might be justifiable, but it is difficult to condone a crime that accomplishes nothing: Olimpia's blow is not meant to save her virginity but to vent her hatred of this man and what he stands for.[11] This gesture only displays a sadistic, and heretofore unseen, penchant of the murderer. Such a decapitation / castration, moreover, recalls Judith's decapitation of Holofernes in which, once again, the upper part of the body substitutes for the lower one.[12] Ariosto makes Olimpia responsible for this murder but also takes care of circumscribing man's fear of castration; the man Olimpia kills, he tells us, is already dead and therefore no longer castratable.

The recounting of the murder is thus a turning point in the story because it gives a radically different characterization of Olimpia and allows the author to deflect pity from her.[13] It also facilitates closure because it necessitates narrative punishment. If Olimpia can be shown not just as deranged but as murderous, if she can be perceived not simply as romantically maddened by love but as morally repugnant, then more than ever she needs man's help.

That Olimpia's assertiveness and anger are wrong is also evident in another narrative twist. The woman for whom Bireno abandons Olimpia is a mirror image of his wife: both have had their fathers and their families killed by an enemy. But whereas Olimpia rebels against her destiny and is abandoned in return, Cimosco's unnamed daughter accepts both a marriage she cannot desire with Bireno's brother and an affair with Bireno himself. Unlike Olimpia, she understands that in order to survive, an unprotected woman needs to create her own protection, which often means that she has to voluntarily play the role of sex object for the conqueror. No wonder Bireno prefers her: she has no sense of her own subjectivity.

The staging of this female doubling for corrective purposes works to eliminate the possibility that woman's unruliness may extend without punishment to other areas, that Olimpia may be, for instance, as sexually active as she is verbally strong and be praised for it. In an earlier scene, half-awakened in the tent in Ebuda in which her marriage bed had been set, Olimpia is described as searching for her husband's body in a move of sexual assertiveness and post-coital abandon: "Nè desta nè dormendo, ella la mano / per Bireno abbracciar stese" ("Neither waking or asleep, Olimpia reached out to embrace Bireno" [10, 20]).[14] In contrast, Cimosco's fifteen-year-old daughter passively accepts the lascivious touch of a man she should hate: "E se accarezza l'altra (che non puote / far che non l'accarezzi più del dritto), / non è chi questo in mala parte note; / anzi a pietade, anzi a bontà gli è ascritto" ("And if he made much of the little maid, who could not prevent him from paying her undue attentions, nobody ascribed this to evil motives but to compassion, to goodness of heart" [10, 14]). The assertive woman is punished through abandonment; the passive one is rewarded with a kingdom (although only temporarily, since Bireno is later killed). This plot shows not only that women have to play up to man's desire but also that any woman is necessarily an enemy to other women in male Oedipal narratives, for the advancement of the one means the retrenchment of the other.[15] The danger woman represents is methodically displaced onto her own sex, and once again she is chastised for having active rather than passive desires.

Rather than being a victim of misplaced faith, Olimpia has willfully and with premeditation done something criminal. At this point Ariosto has the male hero, Orlando, assume the task of saving this woman. In the process, he makes man encompass, nullify, and set aside her threat. First, he has Orlando rescue her from the Orca in a repetition of Angelica's similar sadistic encounter in Canto 10. Then he circumvents her menace through the use of structures of voyeurism and fetishism that confirm man's power to see and to judge, and thus his possession of the phallus. These points and the myths that they recall are the focus of the remainder of this chapter.

Olimpia's abandonment by Bireno recalls Theseus's abandonment of Ariadne on Naxos.[16] Like Ariadne, Olimpia is extreme:

disheveled, deeply grieving, masochistically bent, desolate. She feels like an outcast, degraded as the ruler's daughter, bereft of any sense of self-worth, ashamed for having helped a man unworthy of her, a man with no *fides*. Worse still, Bireno—unlike Aeneas when he abandoned Dido—has deserted her not to pursue some heroic deed or promise but to eliminate the odd person in a newly formed triangle. Neither Olimpia nor Ariadne has a family. Olimpia lost her brothers and father for the sake of the very man abandoning her now; she has, moreover, no country, having been deprived of the one she was born into and having given away the other that Orlando earned for her by defeating Cimosco. Her inability to define herself in terms of relatedness—she is no longer a wife, a daughter, a sister, a countess—mirrors her inability to act now that she is alone. Once outside her own society, Olimpia finds that her new place has no laws. Like Ariadne, there seems to be no choice for her other than jumping into the sea.

But she is rescued. Given her nature, one would expect that Olimpia's fury would not disappear once she is saved and that she, like Clytemnestra, would pursue revenge for having been abandoned. Or, as in a second version of the Ariadne myth, that she would take that revenge upon herself and commit a Dido-like suicide (in this version Ariadne hangs herself with her thread). Or even, as in a third version chosen by Ovid in *Heroides* and by Boccaccio in *Elegia di Madonna Fiammetta*, that she would be unable to forget her beloved, notwithstanding his cruelty. But Ariosto opts for a different reading, one that corresponds to a fourth version of the Ariadne myth, one particularly cherished in the Renaissance. In Titian's famous painting *Ariadne and Bacchus*, Ariadne is rescued by Bacchus, who marries her and gives her a crown made of stars and a ring.[17] Likewise, Ariosto has Oberto give Olimpia a ring and a crown. The unvindicated Olimpia forgives and forgets, as if she had truly learned her lesson. After all, as Ariosto warns in a conclusion that echoes the *Cortegiano*, women should not fall in love with young men, for they are fickle. Olimpia's tone is dry when she recounts her abandonment, and rather than exploding in outward anger, she, like Job in the Bible (3.3), reproaches herself: " 'o maladetto / giorno ch'al mondo generata fui' " ("Oh cursed the day I was born!" [10, 27]).[18]

The comic resolution of the Olimpia story echoes another myth of rescue, that of the dejected, despondent, handcuffed Andromeda saved from a marine monster by the arrival of winged Perseus. Here Orlando rescues Olimpia from the sea orc terrorizing Ebuda. The sea monster embodies threatening femininity and, like the Medusa, can be overcome only by a magic shield (the one used by Perseus and Ruggiero) or killed by a phallic anchor penetrating its vagina-like mouth (the solution enacted by Hercules and Orlando).[19] Its killing is a victory for reason and virtue over passion and naked fury, but it is also, in many ways, a rebirth. The entire scene repeats a typical male fantasy of rescuing the beloved female from water, a fantasy Freud links to strange erotic choices in certain men and to maternal fixations.[20]

Perseus's slaying of the Medusa marks the Greek hero's entry into manhood, his becoming a good citizen/king and founder of a lawful generation. In the *Furioso*, men fail to heed the lesson of Perseus. Ruggiero tries to rape Angelica after the rescue, and Orlando resents the time he has to spend with Olimpia because he would rather rejoin his obsessive object of desire. In the case of Olimpia, however, the retelling does more than narratively repeat a myth of distress, female powerlessness, and male prowess. It provides closure. Unlike Angelica, who physically disappears, and thus remains very much psychologically present in the mind of her pursuers, Olimpia exchanges the chains that bound her to the tree for the chains of marriage (Oberto is introduced at this point). This narrative choice guarantees a satisfying end to a story of affliction and closely resembles the most common conclusion of the myth. "By slaying the Medusa and freeing Andromeda," Adrienne Munich writes, "the hero tames the chaotic female, the very sign of nature, simultaneously choosing and constructing the socially defined and acceptable feminine behavior. He thus assures himself of licensed rather than unlicensed sexuality, legitimate progeny, and protection of his household name" (32).

To rescue a woman, then, means to reconduct her to the patriarchal order by canceling her narcissistic self-sufficiency and by forcing her to see an other more powerful than her self. In the myth, Andromeda is chained to a rock as a punishment for her mother's boast that she is more beautiful than Poseidon's daughters, the Nereids. What the myth teaches is that beauty can work against women unless it is inscribed in a plot controlled by men.

According to a common version of this story, Andromeda's beauty attracts Perseus; he falls in love as a result and restores her to society through marriage.

The Olimpia episode tells us that a woman in distress through faults of her own, one who will not become a new Halcyone and commit suicide after her husband's inexplicable abandonment and death,[21] still has a good chance of being rescued by a man who will solve her quandary and make her happy. But at a cost. In shackles, in distress, blushing, and unable either to look or to speak, Olimpia epitomizes the submissive and grateful female that her culture has often celebrated: valuable because she is beautiful, ruled because she asks to be, and praised because she is modestly in her place. Her reintegration into society cures her despondency while alienating her from her own self.

After the rescue, Orlando recognizes Olimpia and asks why she is in Ebuda. In tears, Olimpia concisely recounts her ordeal. As she moves, the poet writes, she brings to mind the goddess Diana in yet another myth, that of Diana and Actaeon: "E mentre ella parlava, rivolgendo / s'andava in quella guisa che scolpita / o dipinta è Diana ne la fonte, / che getta l'acqua ad Ateone in fronte" ("As she spoke, she turned away in the same pose in which Diana is captured in sculptures and paintings when she is bathing in the spring and throws water in Acteon's face" [11, 58]). The story of Actaeon (Ovid's *Metamorphoses* 3, vv. 139–97) also appears in one of Petrarch's best-known compositions, Canzone 23.[22] As Nancy Vickers ("Diana Described") has shown, within the dichotomy poet/woman, seer/seen, subject/object that structures Petrarchan poetry, the threat for man of dismemberment/castration at the sight of woman is always present. The potential splashing of water into Actaeon-Orlando's face by Ariosto's Diana-Olimpia can thus be read as threatening in that it stands for woman's response to the menace of sexual violence.

In Orlando's case the threat is necessarily limited, for the paladin's interest in Olimpia is almost nonexistent: her rescue is a considerable embarrassment for him. Throughout most of the *Furioso*, Orlando is a man who has yet to prove what it means to be a man, although he is obviously manly in his knightly pursuits. As I argued in Chapter 4, his desire rests on absence and on continuous, willed deferral. Beside the lady of his desires, he can only hesitate.

In short, Orlando's fear of woman's sexuality is well ingrained, and he circumvents it by idealizing the desired, but necessarily unpossessable, object. The case is obviously different for Oberto, who arrives at this point and starts playing the part of Actaeon minus his mythical end.

In Canzone 23, Diana punishes Actaeon's voyeuristic look with literal dismemberment just as the poet-persona punishes his unavailable woman by scattering her body across his scattered rhymes. Ariosto creates the same effect for Olimpia by freezing the action and parceling out her body through description. He first establishes that Olimpia is punished because she has done something wrong ("Orlando domandò ch'iniqua sorte / l'avesse fatta all'isola venire"; "Orlando asked her what wicked fate had brought her to this island" [11, 56]), and then moves to a strategy of Barthesian identification by turning woman into a spectacle, so that she herself no longer desires but desires to be desired. This move diminishes the threat woman represents because nakedness displays woman's lack/castration, and thus by way of a controlling, reifying look it reiterates man's identification of femaleness with lack. The subsequent fetishization of that naked body displaces woman's lack so that man can deny that she lacks anything and reassure himself in turn that he lacks nothing.[23]

To counteract the fear of dismemberment enacted by the Actaeon myth, the author first freezes woman in time to make her passive and second reifies her by subjecting her to an omnipotent and controlling gaze, no matter how admiring this gaze is made to be. Remember that before beheading the Medusa by using his mirrored shield to trap her petrifying look, Perseus stole the eye shared by Phorcys's two daughters, Stheno and Euryale (Ovid's *Metamorphoses* 4, vv. 774–78). The desire to see more is intended to deny the possibility that one does not see enough, or worse, that one is not in control (as Freud points out, "Anxiety about one's eyes, the fear of going blind, is often enough a substitute for the dread of being castrated"; "The Uncanny," 231).

The myth of the Medusa is thus as much an apotropaic myth for controlling female sexuality (and here the description of Olimpia as a marble statue serves that purpose) as it is one for appropriating the power of the gaze, the power to see, constrain, subsume, and petrify whatever is dangerous. It is important to point out that

Olimpia's ability to see properly is questioned throughout; she often looks around but seems to see nothing ("va guardando . . . / se veder cosa, fuor che 'l lito, puote; / nè fuor che 'l lito, vede cosa alcuna"; "[she] strained her eyes . . . to see whether anything could be made out beyond the shore—but she could see nothing, only the shore" [10, 22]), and she even hallucinates, as when she perceives wild animals coming to devour her (10, 29).

In the narrative rendering of her nudity, Olimpia is represented as shy and withdrawn, her ineffectual attempt to cover herself inscribed as another instance of her passivity. But there is a more specific reason for Olimpia's desire to screen her nakedness. According to Freud, although woman stands for castration, the site of her castration is not usually visualized, for the male onlooker needs to deny his own castration. Ariosto illustrates this point by having the chains binding the unclothed Olimpia sufficiently loose as to allow her to move sideways and cover what should not be seen, although, he states, covering her front means uncovering her back: "Quanto può, nasconde il petto e 'l ventre, / più liberal dei fianchi e de le rene" ("She concealed her breast and belly as best she could, / being more liberal with her sides and back" [11, 59]). Shyness and passivity make Olimpia safe now, for she does not flaunt her nakedness and cannot properly be faulted for her state.

Oberto will later rush to clothe Olimpia, but he is unable, Ariosto tells us, to fetishize her body properly because he cannot find appropriately fine material. Ironically, no sooner does he dress her than he uncovers her in his mind: "E fè vestir Olimpia, e ben gli increbbe / non la poter vestir come vorrebbe. // Ma nè sì bella seta o sì fin'oro / mai Fiorentini industri tesser fenno; / . . . degno di coprir sì belle membre, / che forza è ad or ad or se ne rimembre" ("Hubert had the damsel clothed—and much did he regret not being able to dress her the way he would have liked: / never, though, have Florentine weavers turned out silk or cloth of gold . . . worthy to clothe limbs so splendid—which perforce he kept recalling vividly to mind" [11, 74–75]).[24]

In Renaissance painting, the tradition of bodily representation tends toward decarnalization, aestheticization, and universalization of schemes. Brunelleschi's and Alberti's discovery of perspective and the relation of perspective to visual images (be it the linear Albertian or the revised, synthetic Da Vincean) revolutionized the way the artist of the Early Modern period represented reality. The universe was no longer perceived as geocentric; rather, as Victor Burgin writes, it became "homocentric and egocentric." The human being was placed at the center of the space and "by degrees the sovereign gaze [was] transferred from God to Man" ("Geometry," 13). As in the camera obscura, perspective rests on monocular vision fixed immediately, artificially, and intellectually on an image. It changes the terms of visual rendering in that it places the gazing subject in control of the representation.[25] Perspective follows what Norman Bryson calls the logic of the Gaze rather than the logic of the Glance in the sense that it tends to fragment, distance, and reify the subject represented under the gaze of the other, even when the representation has an erotic message. This trend is well illustrated in the technique of freezing the body in a specific moment in time and in a gesture a real person could hold only fleetingly.[26] This posture effectively, although paradoxically, dematerializes the body. The technique of mythologizing the representation, moreover, makes the body even less real and more available to the onlooker at the level of fantasy.

Representation is, of course, closely linked to ideology, for visual images of women both constitute femininity and define it for others. The Renaissance female nude works somewhat like today's fashion photographs, contemporary film images of unclad starlets, or even pornographic pictures. They, too, articulate and circulate specific ideologies and points of view about their subject. Since looking is a form of control, looking at a passive, nude woman on display reinforces structures of authority and gender-related codes of behavior. During the Renaissance, with the exception of Caravaggio and occasionally Titian, the one-way look from the spectator to the spectated object was predominant. A distant, beautiful, and desexualized naked female on display was never allowed to look back and establish complicity with the spectator.[27] The represented subject, moreover, was no longer provided with a story to contextualize the representation and give it a historical, religious, or social connotation. The fetishization and commodification of the image typical of such portraits can also be linked to new capitalistic enterprises and to the expanded marketability of works of art.

By reconstructing Olimpia as innocent, Ariosto makes her an

example of *nuditas virtualis*, the state of nakedness that for medieval theologians was associated with female non-contamination. Furthermore, by investing her body with tropes of perfection, by invoking myths and ancient pictorial representations, and by making her an iconic, perfect female figure, the author achieves the aesthetic distance his two male characters, Oberto and Orlando, need in order to see woman as safe, unthreatening. In short, the gaze constructed by Ariosto is masculine, and the object on which this gaze is fixed is necessarily that of an exhibited, fetishized female.[28] The entire rendering also shows that although Olimpia must have done something wrong to deserve such a harsh punishment, she is not inordinately transgressive, judging from the desire that her body engenders.

In order better to describe Olimpia as spectacle, Ariosto, not unlike Castiglione (1, 53, 98), recurs to visual artists famous for the fetishization of their female constructs, Fidia and Zeuxis. The latter would have needed Olimpia as his only model, the poet claims, had he known her, rather than having had to rely on five women to reify the seductive image of the perfect one: "per una farne in perfezione, / da chi una parte e da chi un'altra tolse: / non avea da torre altra che costei; / che tutte le bellezze erano in lei" ("[he] assembled such a number of lovely nude women, meaning to borrow from each one a different part in order to compose one beauty to perfection, [but] he would have not needed to look beyond Olimpia, for in every part of her sheer perfection resided" [11, 71]). Ariosto also refers to the woman most closely connected with spectacle in antiquity, Helen, for whose beauty, the legend goes, a ten-year war was fought. Had Paris seen Olimpia, the poet suggests, he would have forsaken Helen. Olimpia's beauties are here true to her Olympian namesake.[29] And yet there is a twist even to this praise. Ariosto writes that if Olimpia had ever shown herself naked to Bireno, he would not have left her: "Io non credo che mai Bireno, nudo / vedesse quel bel corpo; ch'io son certo / che stato non saria mai così crudo, / che l'avesse lasciata in quel deserto" ("I do not believe Bireno ever saw that exquisite body naked, for I am convinced that otherwise he would have never behaved so cruelly or abandoned her in that desert place" [11, 72]). Again, woman's worth is in her body.

The representation of Olimpia's naked body as a nude body is extremely visual.[30] Even more than Castiglione, who defined his work "come un ritratto di pittura della corte d'Urbino non di man di Rafaello o Michel Angelo, ma di pittore ignobile" ("as a portrait of the Court of Urbino, not indeed by the hand of Raphael or Michelangelo but by a worthless painter" [1, 1, 25]), Ariosto closely approximates painterly techniques in his writing. Painters of the time were even advised to look at his mimetic descriptions when conceptualizing female beauty.[31] Ariosto's rendering of Olimpia could compete with Titian's famous *poesie*, mythological paintings in which eroticism is a key factor.[32] Cesare Segre (32) judged the nude to be one of the best female portraits in Ariosto. So perfect, I would add, that it is full of stereotypes, for Olimpia's body is denied any individualized or particularized characteristic, and even any blemish, in order to make it stand for the idea of perfect femaleness.

First, Ariosto describes Olimpia's face, which he compares to spring water, and then her tears (also mentioned in Ovid's rendering of Andromeda and in the Angelica episode) and her eyes, which are dangerous because they wound man's heart. At this point the description becomes more specific and each body part is associated with some natural phenomenon so that woman is equated to nature. Moving from top to bottom, as if in the act of unveiling her, Ariosto quickly mentions Olimpia's forehead, eyes, cheeks, hair, mouth, nose, shoulders, and throat until he gets to her breasts. They are singled out for a lengthy twelve-line comparison to snow, ivory, milk, hills, and valleys (11, 67–68). The author then moves down and lingers on her well-contoured hips, handsome sides, flat stomach, and white thighs, until a blank ends it all: "Di quelle parti debbovi dir anche, che pur celare ella bramava invano?" ("Am I to describe to you those parts, too, which she was so vainly hoping to conceal?" [11, 69]). As usual, Olimpia's sex is unrepresentable, but has to be noted.[33]

There are three fully described female nudes in the *Furioso*: Olimpia, Angelica, and Alcina. Olimpia's *laudes membrorum* differ radically from those of the other two, although the vocabulary used in the three descriptions does not vary significantly, whether the woman is Christian or pagan. As Giorgio Padoan (" 'Ut Pictura Poesis,' " 360–61) notices, Olimpia's rendering is less euphemistic, body parts are named directly, and allusions to nudity abound.

Fredi Chiappelli (341) considers the representation of Olimpia as less statuesque and less perfect than that of the other two women; for him this reflects Ariosto's growing interest by 1532 in portraying what happened within the character and what reactions the character inspired as opposed to his earlier interest in describing unsurpassable beauty per se. The sense of mystery, the feeling of slight uneasiness that Ariosto creates, continues Chiappelli, anticipate Tasso and Baroque poetics. Yet the description of a woman's breast in topographical terms is hardly realistic: "Spazio fra lor tal discendea, qual fatte / esser veggian fra picciolini colli / l'ombrose valli, in sua stagione amene, / che 'l verno abbia di nieve allora piene" ("They were so set apart, they resembled two little hillocks and between them a pleasant shady dell in the season when winter snow still lies in the hollows" [11, 68]). Rather, I read the depiction as another instance of the long-standing assimilation of woman to nature.

Of the three women described, only Alcina is partially dressed, but her veil hides nothing: "Come Ruggiero abbracciò lei, gli cesse / il manto: e restò il vel suttile e rado, / che non copria dinanzi nè di dietro, / più che le rose o i gigli un chiaro vetro" ("The mantle she abandoned to Ruggiero as he embraced her; this left only the unsubstantial gossamer-gown which, before and behind, concealed no more than would a pane of glass placed before a spray of roses or lilies" [7, 28]). Ascoli (*Ariosto's Bitter Harmony*, 162) sees the veil as a screen between what Alcina is and what she appears to be. When the veil is removed, the deceptiveness of Alcina's posture and the decaying of female flesh come to the fore. Thus it could be argued that the total exposure of Angelica and Olimpia means that there is nothing to hide in them, that their nakedness functions as an expression of their complete availability and possessability. Indeed, unlike Alcina, who knows how to hide allegorically what she is (and for this reason will be sadistically punished), Angelica and Olimpia have literally nothing to uncover. This makes them non-threatening; if the unveiling of a veiled woman reveals her horrifying, Medusan side, a woman with no veil can offer no surprise, for she can have no self other than the one read upon her by her eager readers.

The point is not that these descriptions of nakedness have little sexual importance or that nakedness stands for a higher form of love. Female nakedness is never meant to signify innocence (although occasionally it could—Titian's *Sacred and Profane Love* represents perhaps such an exception, since in it the naked woman stands for virtuous love and the clothed one for the profane, although there is still critical disagreement on the issue). Concepts of sexuality or sin were never used, in any case, in representing male nakedness. As Margaret Miles ("Nudity") argues, a nude male body stood for male subjectivity in that the body was seen as a mirror of the soul: a strong exterior testified to a strong interior. Michelangelo's *David* is an excellent example of this reading of male nakedness, as are the many representations of Christ's body in the period. Female nakedness in this canto means that woman needs to be offered as unavailable in order to keep male desire alive and as surface in order to embody only the desires of her creator/viewer. He in turn obtains a measure of self-worth and plenitude through his idolatrous sense of her imagined perfection.

The difference in representation between the aestheticized nudity of Olimpia and the shameful nakedness of Ullania later in the *Furioso* is instructive because it shows what happens when lack of clothing is not meant to activate visual pleasure and when the mechanisms of fetishization are purposely blocked. Marganorre punishes women in his city of terror by cutting off their skirts at the waist precisely in order to expose their sex (37, 27). Rather than desexualizing women by refusing to notice the organ that specifically makes them female, Marganorre wants others to note this hideous side of femaleness, for his punishment uncovers the site that makes women appear both castrated and improper. In order to cover their exposed lower half, a crying Ullania and her ladies-in-waiting have to squat on the grass: "E per non saper meglio elle celarsi, / sedeano in terra, e non ardian levarsi" ("Not knowing how better to conceal themselves, they were sitting on the ground and dared not rise" [37, 26]).

To explain their posture, Ariosto recurs to the myth of Erich-thonius, "the babe no mother bore" as Ovid writes (*Metamorphoses* 2, vv. 757–60), who used a chariot to hide his serpentine legs (37, 27). The connection with serpents extends to the earlier part of the Erichthonius story. Athena gives Erichthonius to the three Cecrops sisters with the understanding that the basket in which she has secretly hidden the baby is to be left unopened. When Aglauros disobeys, she finds a snake beside the baby (*Metamorphoses* 2, vv. 551–65). The basket is then changed to stone, and the crow that reported the event to Athena is punished. The reference to snakes and to petrification is typical of the Medusa complex: castration is the result of improper seeing.

In his short essay "Medusa's Head," Freud sees the act of perceiving the female genitals and the horror the sight creates in man as having a circuitous effect: "It may be recalled that displaying the genitals is familiar in other connections as an apotropaic act. What arouses horror in oneself will produce the same effect upon the enemy against whom one is seeking to defend oneself. We read in Rabelais of how the Devil took to flight when the woman showed him her vulva" (274). Marganorre's purpose in requiring women's exposure is to generate in other men the same horror he feels toward women; in his mind, seeing should make men run away in disgust. It eventually takes two women, Bradamante and Marfisa, followed by a willing Ruggiero, not to feel horror at "the terrifying genitals of the Mother" ("Medusa's Head," 274), but to see as women and redress the opprobrium. The narrative rightly concludes with Ullania throwing Marganorre from his tower in a literal transposition of his now-accomplished social and psychic castration.

As for Olimpia, once her body is eroticized and sanitized through description, she has no choice but to depend on men to make her destiny "right." Earlier, she could plot for her own sake; now she is even unable to see because her eyes are full of tears: "I begli occhi sereni / de la donna di lagrime eran pieni" ("The damsel's serene and beautiful eyes brimmed with tears" [11, 64]). One could ask why Ariosto chooses the adjective "serene" for an occasion that must at the very least have been bewildering for the one living it. But the Olimpia who looks and sees nothing while appearing calm (previously, after Bireno's abandonment, she saw nothing but at least was bereaved) is definitely a spectacle and thus safe for men. Her returning look would destroy the illusion of utter passivity and possessability needed for male identification with the author and male disavowal of the female sexual threat.[34]

The progress from Olimpia's mistaken first desire through trials that required a loss of self and a literal death warrant thus leads to woman's recovery of an identity that men find suitable for her gender, that of a wife.[35] Once again, as orthodoxy conceals disruption, the domestication and strict regulation of sexuality becomes a fait accompli. The reason for the different versions of the Olimpia story, then, is that the first Olimpia is essentially unrepresentable. Even Pio Rajna, who has found sources for everything else in the *Furioso*, is unable to produce a good one for the early Olimpia, although he conjures a number of myths for her later, domesticated embodiment. Finally, the reason critics find plenty to reproach in the first Olimpia and little in the second points perhaps to a larger truth: that a woman like the Olimpia of Canto 9 has gone largely unrepresented in narrative. Her fettered double, on the other hand, has been sketched so many times as to be easily recognized and hailed as a commendable, perfectly produced example of femininity. There is no doubt that a properly "emasculated" Olimpia—to use Barthes's terminology—can stand as the exemplar of Renaissance womanhood delineated by Leon Battista Alberti and intently fostered by Renaissance thinkers: "Women . . . are almost all timid by nature, soft, slow, and therefore most useful when they sit still and watch over our things. . . . The woman as she remains locked up at home should watch over things by staying at her post, by diligent care and watchfulness" (207–8).

CHAPTER SIX

(Dis)Orderly Death, or How to Be In by Being Out: The Case of Isabella

I will kill thee,
And love thee after.
—Shakespeare, *Othello*, 5.i.18–19

Thy wretched wife mistook the matter so,
To slay herself, that should have slain her foe.
—Shakespeare, *The Rape of Lucrece*, vv. 1826–27

Funny, every man I meet wants to protect me;
I can't figure out what from.
—Mae West

IN *Orlando furioso*, Ariosto reserves the highest praise and the longest eulogy for Isabella. Not coincidentally, she is the only major female character to die. Isabella stages her own death in Canto 29 when she asks the Saracen hero Rodomonte to strike at her neck in order to test her newly invented herbal salve. As a result, she masochistically delivers herself from a threatened rape and circumvents her beloved Zerbino's deathbed injunction not to commit suicide for his sake. Like Ariosto, critics have praised this character and have compared her favorably to other more fickle, less faithful, or simply more sexual, women in the text.

It is my intention to scuttle these bourgeois pieties and to emphasize—both at the mimetic and at the diegetic level—the reasons for the (male) canonization of Isabella's self-willed homicide. By focusing in the first part of this chapter on the connections between power and sex, pleasure and violence, and rape as pollution (for women) and as assertion of mastery (for men), I show how a politics of rape postulates the death of woman as subject. Ariosto canonizes Isabella, I argue, precisely because she chooses death over rape; self-erasure is the road that virtuous women often take in narrative. Had she survived her rape, Isabella could have stayed in the *Furioso*, but only as a defiled, diminished princess. In opting for death to remain faithful to a dead beloved and for self-victimization over survival, Isabella confirms the workings of both a gender ideology that idealizes disembodied women as proper objects of love and a Christian ideology that canonizes what the dominant culture finds praiseworthy. Paradoxically, as the critics' responses make clear, this very gesture of self-denial guarantees her literary survival as encomiastic matter.

The second aim of this chapter is to link the manner of Isabella's death—decapitation—to man's fear of female sexuality and eventually to the myth that most commonly embodies it, that of the Medusa. Rodomonte rationalizes his murder by transforming woman into a fantasy. This idealization allows him to overcome the sense of inadequacy and discomfiture that female unavailability has fostered in him in the past and to deny that he has committed a crime. Such a peculiar program of pleasure protects him from sexual defeat, for it centers not on sex but on a repetitive mourning for a perfect, forever unpossessable, and thus forever desirable woman. Given his arrogant nature, however, it is not sufficient that Rodomonte mourn by himself. He needs an audience of other knights to join him in his idolatry, both to emphasize the worthiness of his choice of an unreachable beloved and to obliterate his responsibility for the mourning process.

This cycle of domination by intimidation carries its own ironies, for it gives Rodomonte a psychological victory, even if a Pyrrhic one. By making every knight, of any religion, worship a person that he has chosen to invest with meaning, Rodomonte eventually becomes the true knight of courtly romances: not simply a fearsome, unbeatable warlord but a compassionate, caring hero. The fact that in order to derive a sense of self he has to bury this seraphic woman three times, first inside a casket, then within a church, and finally deep in a mausoleum, speaks volumes about the depth of his fear of the other sex. His conception of this process of mourning in phallic terms (he defends in a combat of lances the memory of a woman dead for the sake of her chastity) is evident in his later abandonment of the project when his masculinity is questioned anew and his pseudo-piety finally smashed by a re-empowered woman, Bradamante.

The narration of Isabella's ordeal is one of the fourteen diversions that punctuate the *Furioso*.[1] As in the episode of Olimpia, the action is divided into two distinct parts for the sake of *entrelacement*. In the first, Isabella tells Orlando a woeful story of typical feminine problems: love, pain, and virginity. True to the codes of romance, the paladin saves her and reunites her with the man of her choice. Some cantos later, the reader unexpectedly finds that Orlando's solution was temporary. This time, again as with Olimpia, the author relates the new developments. Orlando is no longer present, however, and Isabella's life ends in a tragic way.

Isabella—the offspring of a Spanish Saracen king of the House of Aragon (she is, as usual, motherless)—first meets Orlando in a cave where she has been imprisoned for nine months. She is fifteen and a paragon of beauty: "Era bella sì, che facea il loco / salvatico parere un paradiso" ("Such was her beauty, she made this inhospitable place look like a paradise" [12, 91]). Like Olimpia, Isabella tearfully tells Orlando a story of incredible misfortune. In tones that often echo those of Francesca in Dante's *Inferno* V, she introduces herself as the daughter of the king of Galizia and reminisces on her former, happy state: "Già mi vivea di mia sorte felice, / gentil, giovane, ricca, onesta e bella" ("Mine used to be a happy life. I was well-born, young and beautiful, rich and esteemed" [13, 5]). Having fallen in love with the Scottish prince Zerbino, a participant in jousts organized by her father, she soon realized that, given their different religions, only elopement would permit their union. Since Zerbino was busy waging war, she accepted his solution of waiting in her father's garden one night for some men, including Zerbino's most trusted friend, Odorico da Biscaglia, to take her to him by boat. In the *Furioso*, Fortuna plays with destinies, and journeys by sea are usually unreliable. The boat capsizes, but Isabella survives. She is no sooner ashore than Odorico tries to rape her, and only the sudden arrival of pirates provides a providential rescue. They in turn leave her in her virginal state, not out of pity, but because they plan to sell her to a rich procurer from the East. The story ends as it usually does when Orlando is at hand: the paladin gives Isabella a new life by destroying her enemies with understated gusto, and he even manages to reunite her with an incredibly happy Zerbino, fortuitously in the area. This is the narrative of Cantos 12 and 13.

The story of Isabella continues in Cantos 28 and 29. In the meantime, Orlando goes mad (Canto 23), and Zerbino is killed by Mandricardo while defending Orlando's sword (Canto 24). Just before dying, Zerbino asks a desperate Isabella to promise to go on living. She is still crying over his corpse when a monk passes by. He consoles her, converts her to Christianity, and offers to lead her to a convent to retire for the rest of her days. Soon they encounter Rodomonte, who has just been rejected by Doralice in favor of Mandricardo. Disturbed by the monk's arguments about the need to respect Isabella and her new faith, the Saracen kills him first and then plays the part of the Petrarchan lover in the hope of piercing the princess's heart. What he has in mind is hardly love, of course. Aware of the danger of rape, Isabella resorts to a ruse: she claims that she can make a salve that bestows immortality and offers to prove its virtues on her body first. Being a paragon of narcissism, Rodomonte accepts, deferring the rape. Isabella spreads the concoction on her neck and urges him to strike her there, conscious throughout of what she wants to accomplish. Her head rolls down. Overcome by what he has unwillingly caused and more puzzled than ever, Rodomonte decides to cast aside his hatred of women, forget his sexual urge, and worship Isabella as an exemplar of chastity. He feverishly builds a mausoleum for her and a lookout tower for himself, with a narrow bridge connecting the main road to this sanctuary. There he vows to joust with any passing knight for the sake of Isabella's honor, which he alone, it seems, can understand and protect. Only the arrival of Bradamante in canto 35 puts an end to this show of piety. Utterly ashamed at being bested by a woman, Rodomonte retires to a cave until his climactic return in the last canto for a final, deadly combat with Ruggiero.

In this chapter I concentrate on the second part of the Isabella story. My aim is not only to cast some light on the construction of Isabella's femininity but also to examine Rodomonte's masculinity. The knight most identified as virile in the *Furioso*, Rodomonte is surprisingly characterized as having problems with his masculinity. From his never-finished tower to the broken sword that dooms him in his final joust, from his record of failures with women to his whining attitude when things do not go his way, Rodomonte seems metonymically associated with "broken" manhood. He may appear manly, but he is not necessarily so.

A second, more significant reason for my concentration on a man is that death is essentially unrepresentable: a dead Isabella has little value in representation. Yet, precisely because she is dead and because her death has been beautified through the construction of a proper burial ground, Isabella becomes pure representation. Her corpse safely stored away, she can be cast as the object best authorizing Rodomonte's new courtly incarnation, because her shadow (as a corpse and as a memory) makes it possible to read her life and her death purely in relation to him. As was already clear in Petrarch's case, a woman's death can be the starting point for the reinscription of a man's poetics of contrition, self-discovery, and self-celebration. A story of violence and rape can then slowly recede into the background in order to make room for a story of the survival (by forgetting the violence) and the empowerment (by remembering courtly ideals) of a hero whose overblown sense of self makes him sadly unable to read the meaning of his own actions.

Paradoxically, the celebration of Isabella's death takes place not only in the mimesis of the text, with the ritual combats that Rodomonte fights in her honor, but also in the diegesis, with the author's lengthy narrative mourning. Ariosto's program is no less subtle than Rodomonte's jousts, which are plainly invented for his own aggrandizement and subsequent recasting as a man of piety. By aestheticizing Isabella's murder, Ariosto too is able to transform an outrageous death into a charming one. "Alma, ch'avesti più la fede cara," the poet offers in his valediction, "e 'l nome quasi ignoto e peregrino / al tempo nostro, de la castitade, / che la tua vita e la tua verde etade, / / vattene in pace, alma beata e bella! / . . . / Vattene in pace alla superna sede, / e lascia all'altre esempio di tua fede" ("Depart in peace, then, beautiful, blessed spirit, who preferred fidelity and a name for chastity [virtually alien and unknown in our day] to your life, your green years! . . . Go in peace to the supernatural seat, and leave to other women an example of your faith" [29, 26–27]). This mourning becomes the pretext for the celebration of another, much more powerful Isabella, the author's as well as Boiardo's patron, Isabella d'Este. Once again the narrative appropriates a woman's death in order both to reassert an ideology of chaste womanhood and to reinscribe the desirability of chastity in an influential woman, who as a result becomes an exemplar for real women. This process is similar to that found in Castiglione, where the duchess stands as a paragon of chastity, no matter the reasons that require her to embody this virtue, and thus can be endlessly offered for imitation to all ladies of manners.

Reflecting on the difficulty of achieving closure in a text offering seemingly endless repetitions of "errore/errare," Patricia Parker argues that Ariosto brings his work to a satisfying conclusion through a series of deaths, of which Isabella's is the most unexpected. "We are shocked by Isabella's death when it occurs," Parker writes, "its finality stands in such sharp contrast to the deathlessness of the poem's enchanted knights that it jolts us, momentarily, back into the world of waking reality" (*Inescapable Romance*, 37). The celebration of Isabella's sacrifice undoubtedly engenders some of the most touching verses in the *Furioso*; as Edgar Allan Poe fondly wrote, the death of a beautiful woman "is, unquestionably, the most poetical topic in the world" (265). Chaucer highly praised five out of nine women in his *Legend of Good Women* because they committed suicide; Castiglione, like Boccaccio in *De claris mulieribus*, has also hailed some ancient women for choosing self-destruction for the sake of love and honor. Throughout the centuries, famous suicides like those of Dido, Lucretia, Ophelia, Emma Bovary, and Anna Karenina have unfailingly aroused readers' sympathy and engendered vicarious identification.

Like Lucretia, Isabella is a paragon of masochism for the sake of faithfulness and of audacity for the sake of self-respect. Whatever the historical truth behind the legend of Lucretia, this Roman matron's martyrdom has enjoyed enduring literary fame. The classic rendering of her ordeal—rape followed by public suicide for the sake of husband and father—can be found in Ovid, but offerings come from, among others, Livy, Plutarch, and Coluccio Salutati. Like Lucretia, Isabella chooses suicide to avoid defilement and, in so doing, shifts the boundaries of victor/victim and victimizer/victimized.[2] Saint Jerome praised women's decision to commit suicide when their chastity is at risk: "In persecutions it is not lawful to commit suicide except when one's chastity is jeopardized" (1129). Saint Augustine, however, condemns the suicide of true Christian women in any circumstance, including women seeking to erase their now-contaminated body for the sake of husbands and relatives. "If she was adulterous," he asks about Lucretia, "why is she praised? If chaste, why was she put to death?" (80)

What makes female suicide so compelling? Or, to put the question as Nancy Miller does, "What is the appeal of the feminine death: if it is a literary strategy, what is its objective; if it is a code, what message does it transmit?" ("Exquisite Cadavers," 37) Miller shows that woman's death, which is usually connected to spurned love or sexuality, often turns into man's celebration of himself and the world of men. Dying for chastity may render women powerful, but this power is defined by men, since they are willing to bestow it on women as long as they remain the way men desire. Of course, this power is not so much actual political/social power, but the power of a role model to affect others' lives or to be used in that way. Thus, a chaste woman may posthumously be given power because a dead role model is even more likely to influence female behavior along desired lines. No power given to chaste women, however, compares to that enjoyed by chaste men, since men claim that their choice of chastity is a thoroughly difficult achievement, given their natural urgings. Women's chastity, on the contrary, as the *Cortegiano*'s courtiers have made clear, has been traditionally cast as easy to attain: in Western ideology good women have an inborn dislike for promiscuity. In the case of Isabella, although her virginal status is debatable, her standing as a figure of chastity is not. Described as a monument of chastity, she is equated in the end to a literal monument, a mausoleum built in her honor to stand for the everlasting celebration of chastity in women. In this process of incorporation, the real female body is made expendable by having the woman request her own narrative disposal. Technically speaking, Isabella does not commit suicide; rather, she stages her own murder. Her action is in keeping with Nicole Loraux's argument that in Greek tragedy wives usually kill themselves, but virgins are customarily killed (31).

Critics show no hesitation in their choice of adjectives to best describe Isabella. Attilio Momigliano calls her a beautiful and heroic virgin ("vergine bella e eroica," 152), and Marcello Turchi refers to her as a martyr of faith ("fantastica martire della fedeltà," 133). Together with Fiordiligi, Isabella is the only woman in the *Furioso* consistently and endlessly eulogized. She also shares with Fiordiligi the same macabre destiny. Since neither woman can opt for suicide after her beloved's death (one for religious reasons and the other for the sake of a promise), each circuitously chooses to be forever near him. Isabella prompts her homicide; Fiordiligi practically buries herself alive in a chamber next to her dead husband, Brandimarte. Both enjoy oratorical praise, for rhetorical flourishes are often easy to come by for women already dead or ready to die for the sake of their men. Their death is celebrated because it ennobles man by magnifying his standing among his peers, due to the sense of self-worth that woman's fidelity to him generates; it also ennobles woman when one of her sex is memorialized as exemplary, usually for social reasons (as with the praise of female chastity). Even more than Lucretia's, the story of Isabella stands as a hymn to women's *pudicitia*, since Isabella chooses suicide in the *Furioso* not simply to keep faith with the memory of a living beloved, but—in a twist that Ariosto uses to full effect—with that of a dead one.

Throughout *Orlando furioso*, Isabella is powerless: men take command of her life but are unable to provide any security; in fact, their very presence as protectors threatens her safety. From the moment she leaves home, Isabella's fate is grief. She herself recognizes the losses generated by her choice to live outside parental jurisdiction and disavows her right to be considered a good daughter: "Isabella sono io, che figlia fui / del re mal fortunato di Gallizia. // Ben dissi fui; ch'or non son più di lui, / ma di dolor, d'affanno e di mestizia" ("I am Isabel. I used to be the daughter of the luckless king of Galicia. I say I used to be—for now I am no longer his: I am daughter to grief, misery and sadness" [13, 4]). Isabella ceases to be the victim of a baffling destiny only when she starts preparing her self-directed death; her body is a burden she no longer wants to carry. Having absorbed Christian doctrine, she looks to heaven for a proper reward for her pain and her love. Her self-immolation is bathed in liturgical, baptismal overtones.[3]

Had Ariosto not created an elegiac reason for Isabella to disappear, there would hardly be a plausible role in the text for her after Zerbino's death and Rodomonte's rape. A polluted Isabella cannot go back home, for she has already strayed from her father's law and the social order. Even Olimpia did not defy her father, and Doralice chose a man different from the one willed on her only because circumstances had changed so radically in the meantime. But Isabella has not simply disobeyed her father; she has also opted for a political and religious enemy, thereby symbolically mutilating paternal authority. There is no turning back for her. Yet Isabella could hardly survive without parental protection; unlike Bradamante and Olimpia, she is completely unable to defend herself against man's violence. Like Angelica, she exists only as an image of undefended womanhood, the maiden-to-be-raped. Utterly unassimilable, she is eventually given the freedom to choose not the manner of her life but that of her death.

Rodomonte stands as Isabella's virtual opposite. A powerful, proud, heroic Saracen knight, he is described principally through his cruelty. As pure energy and darkness personified, as snake (17, 11), demon (16, 86), and Satan (16, 87), he represents masculinity equated with physical power.[4] In Boiardo's work, Rodomonte's ancestor is Nimrod, the giant who defied God to do battle with him (2, 14, 34), and his boorish and capricious nature is properly highlighted in the English term *rodomontade*. Not only is Rodomonte constructed in an exaggerated fashion, he also narcissistically loves to boast of his physical attributes. He enters the war, for instance, sure of being the best in either camp and fulfills his desire for superiority with the sight of the carnage and fright that his sudden appearance customarily creates. Throughout the epic, Rodomonte is constructed as the unassimilable Other, the scapegoat necessary to the completion of the "right" hero's (Ruggiero's) process of self-fashioning.[5] In this sense, Aldo Scaglione ("Cinquecento Mannerism," 125) is correct in judging Rodomonte to be "the most intriguing, the most puzzling, the most 'human'" character in the *Furioso*.

A man consistently in need of magnifying his valor must have a scant sense of self-worth. Rodomonte proves himself pathologically unstable. He consistently accuses others of his own faults and, what is worse, makes them pay for his faulty rationalizations. He chastises women for inconstancy, for example, although his own claims to constancy are flimsy. Later, he finds himself so accustomed to what he believes is women's constitutive characteristic, fickleness, that he cannot understand its opposite, fidelity, when Isabella comes his way and pays dearly for his blindness. He accuses Ruggiero of betraying Agramante but could justifiably be reproached himself for that very sin, and he fights a duel for this reason that strategically can end only with his death. In short, this hero is unable to learn from any lesson.

Rodomonte's problems begin when a bride is offered to him. He boasts that his prowess is sufficient to obtain the love of any woman, for in his mind women are objects of exchange to be given to the worthiest men in battle. After winning his battles, however, he finds that he cannot get women as a result. His masculinity is challenged, a crisis that is evident each time he tries to marginalize the wounds to his ego inflicted by the other sex. Following Doralice's choice of Mandricardo, for example, he decides to cast away his fealty to king and country and leave the world of men. Full of unabashed Achillean pride, he feels rejected because of both his promised bride's determination to bypass him and his companions' decision not to side with him following her choice. He comes across as reflecting not only unhealthy pride but also whining femininity ("Di cocenti sospir l'aria accendea / dovunque andava il Saracin dolente"; "Wherever he went the grieving Saracen scorched the air with burning sighs" [27, 117]).

Later, Rodomonte decides to float aimlessly down a river and take lodging in a chapel, thus moving from the world of fathers to that of mothers. Again, he is perceived as having emasculated himself. When Isabella commits suicide because she prefers a dead man to his prized sexual prowess, he chooses to stay beside her burial ground rather than rejoin his fellow men in war and hence comes across as having feminized himself anew. Later, his desire to drown any knight not paying respect to his idealized woman allows him to mentally erase his own drowning in alcohol the night she died, a drunkenness he recognizes as a secondary cause of the reckless murder. As Luce Irigaray points out, however, fluids are associated with the feminine world (*This Sex*, 116), and so once again Rodomonte casts himself on the side of femininity. Finally, his confinement to a cave for a year, a month, and a day after Bradamante's victory over him symbolizes a metaphoric return to the maternal womb. In this context, his last fight in the epic, the brutal one with Ruggiero, can be read not only as a struggle to live in the world of men but also as a struggle to deny any femininity within himself.

Rodomonte's masculinity may be in crisis, but his masculinism is very much in place. In fact, Rodomonte uses the ideology that supports masculinism to bolster his shaky masculinity. Such an attitude can only doom Isabella by making her the hinge upon which man's power is exercized and gender inequalities come to be predicated. As a cultural construct, masculinity—like femininity—has had various meanings in different historical and social situations. But masculinism, as an ideological construct, is firmly in place in society. As Andrew Britton writes in *Masculinity and Power*, "Masculinism is the ideology that justifies and naturalizes male domination. As such, it is the ideology of patriarchy. Masculinism takes for granted that there is a fundamental difference between men and women, it assumes that heterosexuality is normal, it accepts without question the sexual division of labour, and it sanctions the political and dominant role of men in the public and private sphere" (4). In the *Furioso*, Rodomonte's expressions of masculinity are violent, and his understanding of masculinism reflects the social customs of his day among both Christians and Saracens.[6]

Rodomonte's aggressiveness, both at the linguistic and at the physical level, is well marked in the text. Lacan links aggressiveness with narcissistic traits in the individual. "Aggressivity is the correlative tendency of a mode of identification that we call narcissistic," he writes, "and which determines the formal structure of man's ego and of the register of entities characteristic of his world" (*Ecrits*, 16). I have already pointed out that Rodomonte's repetitive boasting and showing off of his bravery accurately reflect his narcissism. His verbal aggressiveness toward women results directly from the threat he associates with them, since his martial side has served him better in the past than his amorous one. In Freudian psychoanalysis, man's contempt for woman is linked to fear of castration, for the boy's reaction at the first sight of female castration is, in Freud's words, one of "horror of the mutilated creature or triumphant contempt for her" ("Some Psychical Consequences," 252). Not only do women make Rodomonte appear ridiculous and feminized, but they also induce men to question his abilities and judgment and to laugh at him for being duped and dumped by the women. Most of all, Rodomonte is enraged by the fact that women, who are not even his equal, shamelessly dare to choose what they want.

Such an attitude also explains why Doralice's choice of Mandricardo is traumatic for Rodomonte. Doralice has chosen a knight so similar to him in strength, nobility, personality, and even religion, that the difference between them, if any (and Doralice must have found some), can be located only in a different perception of their sexuality. For Ariosto, woman is not simply different from man; she helps differentiate one man from another ("la donna da cui viene lor differenza," 27, 103). As the Angelica story fully illustrates, the possession of a prized woman helps the winner assert his mastery over an equally qualified man of the same rank. It makes him feel powerful, and it aggrandizes his ego. A rebuff, on the other hand, creates crises of manhood and self-worth.

The need to contain Doralice's show of independence goes without saying. Not only does Doralice lose Mandricardo, but her final characterization in the *Furioso* is a devalued one: she becomes a coquette. At her lover's death, she goes through the obligatory motions of mourning while casting an eye at Mandricardo's possible successor, the victorious Ruggiero. This unflattering (and unjustifiable) picture of Doralice has led a number of critics to embrace Rodomonte's view that all women are fickle and that Doralice exemplifies female moodiness. I would claim instead that Doralice was practical, rather than wanton, in choosing to transform Mandricardo's inevitable rape of her into a seduction and that she showed self-respect in refusing Rodomonte's claim to her person as a prize.[7] In any case, like Isabella without Zerbino, there is no meaningful place for Doralice without Mandricardo in this romance epic, and she is conveniently forgotten.

Women's fickleness, the *Furioso* tells us, drives men mad. Orlando, who believes Angelica is inconstant, is only the first example. Rodomonte fares no better. One might then imagine that woman's faithfulness is the crucial element for men, and the story of Bradamante's unwavering love for Ruggiero could demonstrate the point. But what is Olimpia's reward for her faithfulness? Men as well as women betray in the *Furioso*, it seems; if it appears that women change their minds more often, it is because, being objects of desire, their selves are articulated from the point of view of the other.[8]

Rodomonte pits woman's inconstancy against his own constancy. But his feelings for first Doralice and then Isabella have nothing to do with either constancy or love. They simply reflect his instability and his view of manliness. Rodomonte wants Doralice because she has been described as beautiful and has been desired by somebody else; he continues to joust for her because his honor is at stake once others know that she is his promised bride. Rodomonte's love for Doralice neatly fits Girard's logic of mimetic desire. In the *Innamorato*, Ferraù states that he stopped loving Doralice, for whom he came to France in disguise, once he saw Angelica. Yet, piqued by Rodomonte, he decides to fall back in love with her: "Amai colei; lo amore ebbe a passare: / Per tuo dispetto voglio ancora amare" ("I loved her; love passed away: because I despise you, I want to love again" [2, 15, 37]). As a result, Rodomonte jousts with even more fervor for Doralice, since his fame as a warrior is at stake. When the Rodomonte-Doralice-Mandricardo triangle is formed, once again the logic is that of mimetic desire. Mandricardo's interest in Doralice is stimulated by the knowledge that she is affianced to Rodomonte (14, 40), and Rodomonte's interest in Doralice deepens when he sees Mandricardo desire her to the point of challenging his authority over her. Rodomonte puts more emphasis on being slighted by a fellow man than on acting out of love.

The Saracen knight's desire for Isabella is not mimetic in the sense that other knights are present as alternative male desiring subjects. Rodomonte simply sees Isabella and decides to have her. Like the lovers evoked by Andreas Capellanus, he is seduced through the eyes, for love is "a certain inbred suffering caused by sight of and excessive meditation upon the beauty of the opposite sex, causing desire for embrace" (28). But unlike Capellanus's courtly lovers, Rodomonte forgets to meditate on what he sees. Contrary to Orlando, for whom desire is associated with deferment, he believes in instant gratification, since delays in the past caused him to lose both Doralice and his reputation among men. Thus, Rodomonte decides to stand with Ovid and brushes aside the inscrutability with which Isabella has wrapped herself.[9] He is sure that visceral instincts and flattery will inevitably seduce any woman, since for him female chastity is hardly a credible virtue. Isabella's intention to live in a convent heightens, rather than lessens, his desire for possession through transgression.

Of the two attempts at Isabella's chastity, the first is the most difficult to understand, for it is made by a Christian described as an honorable and faithful man. His abduction of Isabella is foiled only by the timely arrival of other abductors, who abstain from raping their victim not in the name of morality but in the name of money ("Se mi serban, come io sono, / vergine, speran vendermi più molto"; "By keeping me a virgin they hoped to sell me for a far better price" [13, 31]). Odorico justifies his attempted rape as a form of libidinal release: alone with a beautiful woman, he is unable to control himself or to remember social and cultural conventions ("Io mi sforzai guardarla; ma al fin vinto / da intolerando assalto, ne fui spinto"; "I made every effort to guard the

fortress . . . but in the end I was defeated by the irresistible on-
slaught and was driven out" [24, 32]). Odorico admits no loss of
honor for attempting to rape the maiden he was asked to protect.
He would have behaved honorably indeed, he explains, if he had
been assigned a manly task, such as defending a city. Zerbino does
not question his explanation, since he too seems to think that the
call of the flesh can bestialize man's nature.

The second attempt at rape, by Rodomonte, is not rationalized;
it is understood, in the gender system defining feminine and mas-
culine roles, sex can be used to affirm male superiority, and a
woman can be conquered in the same way as a country. Rodo-
monte clearly states this in a later combat with Bradamante. He
will give her the phallic symbols she requests—his horse and arms
for her to put on Isabella's tomb—if she defeats him. But if he de-
feats her—and he has no doubt about this outcome—he wants to
possess her body: "Ma s'a te tocca star di sotto, come / più si con-
viene, e certo so che fia, / non vò che lasci l'arme, nè il tuo nome, /
come di vinta, sottoscritto sia: / . . . / . . . basti / che ti disponga
amarmi, ove m'odiasti" ("But if you are the one to succumb—
which is more plausible and is bound to happen—I would not
have you surrender your arms or leave your name to be inscribed
among the vanquished. . . . It is enough if you dispose yourself to
love me where before you hated me" [35, 46]).[10] As he boasts, "Io
son di tal valor, son di tal nerbo, / ch'aver non dei d'andar di sotto
a sdegno" ("Such is my valour, such my strength, that you should
feel no disgrace at being beneath me" [35, 47 (modified)]).

Rodomonte is first attracted to Isabella by a strange combination
of factors: sorrow, eroticizing mysteriousness, and pervasive pas-
sivity give this woman an enigmatic allure. But such a hold over a
restless man proves dangerous to Isabella, for Rodomonte has no
intention of repeating his previous mistake with Doralice. In his
mind, if a lonely and beautiful maiden appears available because
she has no guardian, any man can possess her with or without
her consent.[11] Since he views women as commodities, Rodomonte
claims ownership when no one is around to object. As Marx was
to write, commodities need guardians to guarantee the rightness
of an exchange: "Commodities cannot themselves go to market
and perform exchanges in their own right. We must, therefore,
have recourse to their guardians, who are the possessors of com-

modities. Commodities are things, and therefore lack the power to resist man. If they are unwilling, he can use force; in other words, he can take possession of them" (I, 178). Rodomonte judges Isabella according to masculinist stereotypes and ends up with a loss he did not know he could feel.

A second reason for the rape of Isabella is that Rodomonte can vindicate himself through her body for what he perceives as Doralice's sexual profligacy. By punishing a woman who seems to have nothing to do with promiscuity, he can externalize his rage at having been discarded by another, more powerful one and at having subsequently suffered the scorn of other men. His attitude runs counter to that of courtly knights, since it is their duty to help, defend, and protect damsels in distress.

A third reason for the rape is that it reinforces in Rodomonte an image of himself as invincible in and out of bed, an image in reality so tenuous that it consistently needs to be confirmed. Through rape, he can use the body of a person he sees in reified terms to enhance the feelings of self-assurance that previous events have shaken in him. By humiliating a particular woman, he can deny that he has ever been humiliated by women and thus heal his narcissistic wound. Rape does not constitute a crime in this version; rather, it is a part of the spoils of war, a political act meant to take possession of an inferior.[12]

A fourth reason for Isabella's rape is more paradoxical, since Rodomonte may unconsciously be motivated to defile an indecipherable Isabella precisely in order to cancel any admiration he feels for her, an admiration at cross-purposes with his earlier misogynous tirade. In other words, Rodomonte needs to rape Isabella not only because she is potentially unchaste (as are Doralice, Angelica, and Fiordispina), but also because she is chaste, and this may tempt him to fall in love with her. However, the prospect of reappearing on the stage of love as madness, or of being lured into woman's net in the name of incommunicability and unknowability, is too dangerous to entertain anew. Isabella's mysteriousness has to be demystified. By conquering a woman, moreover, Rodomonte can conquer his own perceived femininity.

Yet even rape can be delayed when immortality is promised. Because of his vainglory, Rodomonte accepts Isabella's reasoning that the wonders of her herbal concoction should first be

tried on her: "Chi si bagna d'esso / tre volte il corpo, in tal modo
l'indura / che dal ferro e dal fuoco l'assicura. / / Io dico, se tre volte
se n'immolla, / un mese invulnerabile si trova / . . . / Io voglio a far
il saggio esser la prima" ("Whoever bathes himself with this juice
three times so hardens his body that he becomes proof against fire
and steel. / Truly, whoever applies the liquid three times is invul-
nerable for a month. . . . I want to be the first to try [it]" [29,
15–16, 24]). He will live to regret his consent, for the "little death"
usually associated with sexual climax now becomes a literal one.
I strongly disagree in this context with Giuseppe Resta's psycho-
analytic reading of the episode leading to the murder of Isabella.
Resta writes that Rodomonte differs from Orlando in his reaction
to a woman's refusal of him only in that he acts more aggres-
sively. Rodomonte kills Isabella, the critic argues, in order to avoid
falling victim once again to feminine seduction and beguilement.
Isabella's unconscious complicity in her seduction is evident for
Resta in her preparation of herbs, in her subsequent invitation to
Rodomonte to strike her, and in her willing exposure of her neck.
What is bewildering in this reading is the critic's absolute desire to
put women on trial and declare them complicitous with their rapist
because of their inability to defend themselves. Continuing this
rational displacement of responsibilities, Resta finds Rodomonte's
behavior after Isabella dies full of affection and delicate sentiments
("delicatezza dei sentimenti," 70).

Being close to the head and connected to lower body members,
the neck links ratiocinative (head/thinking), sensitive (heart/cour-
age), and nutritive (abdomen/pleasure) elements. In *De partibus
animalium*, Aristotle organizes these parts hierarchically, with what
is closer to the brain as more important. In Greek tragedy, necks
are by custom the most vulnerable female part, Loraux writes,
since "it is by that part that one hangs, and by that part also that
death comes to young girls chosen for sacrifice. . . . It is as though,
quite apart from ritual practice and its requirements, the throats of
women invited death" (50–51).

Man wounding woman's neck can substitute for man raping
woman as, for instance, in Francesco Berni's remake of Boiardo's
Innamorato, where Malagigi is bent on wounding Angelica in the
neck, then changes his mind, opts for rape, and drops his sword

(I, 1, 45). In the *Furioso*, Marganorre slits women's throats on the tombs of his sons, as if they were sacrificial victims, precisely in order to punish them for their femaleness. Loraux (61) points out that in Greek gynecology women have two necks, the upper and the lower (the cervix), as well as the notorious two mouths.[13] In Freud's "Fragments of an Analysis of a Case of Hysteria," the most frequent of Dora's symptoms is a cough, which Freud reads as a displacement upward, the throat having become an erogenous zone.

When Isabella offers herself to Rodomonte's gaze, she offers him her neck: "lieta porse / all'incauto pagano il collo ignudo" ("[she] joyfully offered her bare neck to the unwary pagan" [29, 25]). He beheads her: "Quel uom bestial le prestò fede, e scorse / sì con la mano e sì col ferro crudo, / che del bel capo, già d'Amore albergo, / fè tronco rimanere il petto e il tergo. // Quel fè tre balzi" ("The brute believed her and used his hand and his cruel sword to such effect that he lopped her fair head, once the abode of love, clean from her shoulders. / Her head bounced thrice" [29, 25–26]). Since Perseus, too, killed Medusa through her neck, we have a seemingly unlikely myth to connect with the Isabella story—that of Medusa.

We know that Perseus slays Medusa, the only mortal among the three Gorgon sisters, as a wedding present to Polydectes, king of the island where Perseus and his mother, Danaë, live.[14] Although Polydectes publicly declares that he will marry Hippodamia, his private strategy is to have Danaë instead. Danaë has been described throughout the story as an asexual, virginal figure, a woman whom even Zeus did not touch with his body when he impregnated her, for he appeared as a shower of gold. Indeed, Danaë has been compared to the Virgin Mary.[15] On his return home after slaying Medusa and rescuing Andromeda, Perseus kills Polydectes by turning him into stone through the display of Medusa's head, for during Perseus's absence, the king has become a menace to Danaë and wants to force marriage on her. "The aim of the myth," William Tyrrell writes, "is the suppression of the negative side of the mother, which it defines as her physical sexuality. . . . On the narrative level this is worked out by slaying Medusa, preventing Danaë from using her sexuality, and eliminating sexual males. . . . The Perseus myth endeavors to remove sexuality from the mother in order to make her solely a virginal nurse. In the ways of myths Medusa is done away with and Danaë turned into a virtual virgin" (107, 110).

The killing of Isabella, Perseus-style, testifies to the fact that Rodomonte can have women only by sublimating their sexuality. It is important to remember that Ariosto has already literalized in Isabella the disfigurement associated with sexual threat by linking her almost oxymoronically with rape. The connection with bodily violation extends to Danaë and Medusa. Famous for their beauty, these two mythical women have also been raped by gods and then punished for being raped. One can theorize that if women's allure entices men to rape, this allure must be eliminated after the violence because it reminds the rapists of their loss of control.[16] The best way to punish such women is to make other women responsible for the punishment. Thus Athena, rather than Poseidon, retaliates against Medusa for having allowed rape in Athena's sacred place by turning her hair into a writhing serpentine mass.

In the myth of Perseus, the movement of the hero is from mother (Danaë) to wife (Andromeda). In order to become a man and grow from the status of son to that of father/king, Perseus has to conquer his fear of femaleness by killing the Medusa. What is missing in the Rodomonte story is the myth's final stage, the hero's rescue of an Andromeda-like, passive heroine representing proper femininity. Perseus's achievement affirms the correct, reproductive side of male sexuality and the value of conjugality, a point that the Andromeda story confirms because it promotes the corollaries of matrimony, societal acceptance, and kingly rule.[17] In other words, the myth tells us that sexuality needs to be regulated for social purposes in both women and men. But Rodomonte is unable to overcome his narcissism, rein in his sexuality, and take his place in society. Such an inability to govern his instincts is evident in his fight against Ruggiero, the champion of faith, honor, and law in the *Furioso*. The fact that Ruggiero tries to wound Rodomonte on the head and finally succeeds whereas Rodomonte aims at the groin explains the two men's different natures and destinies. In the final analysis, rationality, and not simply faithfulness to king and God, is what differentiates Ruggiero not only from Rodomonte but from Orlando as well.

Another aspect of the myth of Medusa is relevant. As Tyrrell writes, since Medusa represents the physical aspect of the mother, she "must be slain because the purpose of the myth is the denial of birth from a female" (108). Rodomonte, too, cannot accept that he was born through woman. "Perchè fatto non ha l'alma Natura, / che senza te potesse nascer l'uomo, / come s'inesta per umana cura / l'un sopra l'altro il pero, / il corbo e 'l pomo?" he laments after leaving Agramante's camp. "Non siate però tumide e fastose, / donne, per dir che l'uom sia vostro figlio; / che de le spine ancor nascon le rose, / e d'una fetida erba nasce il giglio" ("Why has not fair Nature arranged for men to be born without you, just as human skill can graft one pear or sorb or apple-tree onto another? . . . Do not preen and puff yourself up, women, with asserting that men are your children: roses are born on briars; the lily springs from a fetid weed" [27, 120–21]). Rodomonte regrets that men are unable to be generated by men or born parthenogenetically, autogenetically, or even autochthonously, that is, without the sexual encounter, the mediation of the female element, and straight from the earth.

Isabella finds herself playing both the part of Medusa (female sexuality as threatening, as in the case of Doralice) and the part of Danaë (female sexuality as nonexistent). Eventually, since a sexual woman is mysterious (and Medusa's mysteriousness is one reason Perseus wants to dominate / overcome her), Rodomonte prefers a second woman, one he can idealize and fetishize. This choice in turn allows him to dispose of his recurring fear of rejection. In the myth, Perseus overcomes Medusa's threat of petrification by killing her. Rodomonte responds to this threat first by expelling Isabella's physicality and then by literalizing her petrification by building a stone monument memorializing the only aspect of her he chooses to remember, her faithfulness to a dead man.

Decapitation of woman illustrates man's fear of castration. To assuage this threat, iconographic renditions of the Medusa multiply the number of phallic signifiers in the shape of snakes, meant to deny castration (Isabella, like Medusa, is shaggy-haired). Petrification is also a denial of castration in that it stands for erection.[18] Rodomonte calms his fear through a staged externalized penance; by way of ritualized jousts, he proclaims anew with each victory that he is not castrated. He also erects a tower for himself, another apotropaic emblem meant both to deny woman's threat and to symbolize his own phallic power.

This identification of Isabella with Danaë allows Rodomonte to renew an Oedipal fantasy in which the other as all-fulfilling entity becomes inscribed as loss. This loss in turn makes it possible for desire to be sublimated. To adore such an absent woman, to use an unrequited passion for an ideal other to protect the worshiper from his own sexual dread, makes man become like the person he reveres; he, too, is superior to other people. By identifying with Isabella and no longer with men or father figures (after all, he feels derided by his peers and king), Rodomonte further avoids castration anxiety. Isabella as Eternal Feminine now becomes his god, his ego-ideal, and the goal of his desire. But this god exists only to satisfy the need that required the creation of such a non-threatening icon in the first place.

Rodomonte displays no less misogyny now when he mystifies Isabella than earlier when he reviled womankind; both responses are founded on the denial of woman's value as subject. Since the core of a misogynist discourse is the rejection of woman and her desire, idealization is as pernicious as vituperation; both require the body of a universal, abstracted—and thus necessarily dead—Woman: a corpse. Idolatry (the myth of the Medusa is also linked with it) properly reflects Rodomonte's excessive nature, since it requires martyrdom and subsequent reification.[19] In this context, Isabella's salve—which she claims would render its user unassailable and unpierceable—does indeed work, postmortem. Although it kills her, it functions in the same way as the Medusa's head on Athena's shield, an emblem that renders the goddess unassailable, beyond desire and beyond sexual pollution, and for this reason worthy of worship.[20]

Isabella's death inaugurates in Rodomonte a period of ritual purging of inner excesses, a period of neurosis, self-abjection, and melancholia. "To take one's life," Margaret Higonnet writes, "is to force others to read one's death" (68). This is not true in Rodomonte's case, for rather than displaying shame and a bad conscience, he chooses to anesthetize his sense of guilt with a perverse narcissistic solution. By commemorating Isabella rather than once more vituperating her, by in a sense giving birth to a new woman, formed in his own image, to replace the woman he has just killed ("poi ch'a morte il corpo le percosse, / desse almen vita alla memoria d'ella"; "though he had slain her body, at least he could

give life to her memory" [29, 31]), Rodomonte manages to fash-
ion himself into a man with a mission and to change a story of
imposed self-sacrifice into one more acceptable to his solipsistic
nature, a story of homage and retribution.

Rodomonte fancies that he cannot be faulted for beheading Isa-
bella because this was hardly his intention and that he cannot re-
proach himself for once again failing to possess a desired woman
since the present one is unavailable to everybody and has chosen
death over submission. He refuses to read Isabella's death as a
response to a series of utterly victimizing moments he himself gen-
erated. He equally refuses to read her gesture of escape through
self-annihilation as a form of masochism or the opposite, as a
moment of self-empowerment, albeit through utter negation. In-
stead, he takes her death as the expression of a desire for chastity.
In short, Rodomonte sees Isabella as Lucretia. Just as Lucretia's
suicide made it possible for the Romans to further their political
agenda, so Isabella's bloodied body makes it possible for Rodo-
monte to reconstruct his identity. Just as Shakespeare's Collatinus
was unable to see that he was endangering Lucretia by boasting
of her virtues, Rodomonte must forget that in order to preserve
what he plans to memorialize Isabella had to die.

Unlike Orlando, who desires a woman thoroughly elusive but
at least alive and thus available in principle, Rodomonte truly de-
sires Isabella only after she is dead. His earlier desire had been
simply sexual; once it had been satisfied, Isabella would have be-
come discardable. But satisfaction would have thrown Rodomonte
back into the world of uncertainty in which Doralice had placed
him. Sublimation instead enables him not only to renounce his
sexual appetite (or simply displace it) but to use the loss of an
object as a way of creating himself as a subject.[21]

What better way to implement this program of self-empower-
ment than by constructing a public display of a knight's contri-
tion? Built in memory of what Isabella would not give up, the
mausoleum both reflects Rodomonte's sizable ego and testifies to
the construction of woman according to man's desire.[22] This con-
struction requires, first, that the woman be silent, so as not to
impinge on the story that Rodomonte chooses to narrate to him-
self and everybody crossing his path. A reborn Pygmalion, he
makes this phantasmatic woman stand for what the other woman

he wanted, Doralice, declined to stand for. The message is that Rodomonte is worthy of woman after all. When the other knights ridiculed him, he had simply fallen in love with the wrong one; had he known Isabella, he would not have been the object of their scorn. In this version, Isabella still represents sexuality but, once again, in the perverse form of being beyond it.

By reading Isabella as the maiden who prefers chastity to life, Rodomonte can finally cast himself in the role of the perfect courtly lover, a role that allows him to enforce the universal cult of such a paragon of faithfulness. This new agenda of hagiology permits him to rephallicize himself, for now he can invest Isabella with signifiers that are important to him and are easily understood by other men.[23] Moreover, by exhibiting Isabella's corpse as the commodity that gives him a pretext for engaging in combat, he can prove his mastery to passing champions and finally undertake the jousts that he was never metaphorically able to fight with women. The knights take his argument at face value, inquire not at all about his need to tyrannize over them, and rush into combat in the name of male honor: "alcuni la via dritta vi condusse, / . . . / altri l'ardire, e, più che vita caro, / l'onore" ("Some arrived in the course of their journey. . . . Others were attracted hither by adventure and by honour (dearer than life itself) to try their mettle" [29, 38]). In accepting Rodomonte's challenge because they want to emulate one another rather than because they are morally engaged, they end up fighting, as usual, not for the sake of a wronged, real woman (Isabella) or an exemplary, ideal one (the body in the mausoleum), but for the sake of being homosocially recognized as worthy by their peers.[24]

Once again the discourse of demonology and angelology vis-à-vis woman is a discourse by men, to men, and for men. Rodomonte's requirement that combat take place only between knights, a distinction based entirely on gender and class requirements, confirms this. When he meets Orlando—naked, dirty, and unrecognizable—he angrily explains that the pact applies only to those of higher status: "Indiscreto villan, ferma le piante, / temerario, importuno ed arrogante! / / Sol per signori e cavalieri è fatto / il ponte, non per te, bestia balorda" ("Stop, you rash, reckless peasant, you impudent, meddlesome oaf: / this bridge is for lords and knights, not for the likes of you!" [29, 41–42]). In other words, Rodomonte plays a game his opponents thoroughly understand. And the game is so rewarding, the emulation so ingrained in chivalric ideals, that when he is offered the hand of Agramante's cousin in return for rejoining the Saracen camp, he finds it preferable to remain where he is.

That this service to the lady is not only self-justifying and self-ennobling, moreover, but also self-empowering is evident in another, all-consuming activity that Rodomonte now begins: collection. He requires that after losing the joust with him on the bridge, each and every passing knight deposit on the walls of Isabella's mausoleum his arms, armor, and armorial bearings. He also makes Christian knights prisoners. The reasons behind collecting are psychologically complex; accumulation both boosts the collector's ego by displaying his strength and uniqueness and allows him to control compulsive desires by regulating repetition.[25] With this requirement, Isabella's death guarantees Rodomonte his masculinity, since the arms decorating her mausoleum testify that he is as omnipotent as his ancestor Nimrod. The value of the arms as fetishes depends on others' willingness to risk their lives for their possession. By taking them away from men, Rodomonte is metaphorically castrating his male enemies (he requires both the knights' armor and the inscription of their names); by displaying his masculinity through a personal arsenal of phallic signifiers, he can assure himself that he indeed possesses the phallus.[26]

Woman has become both subject and object of the representation, both the catalyst engendering a story and the content of a story of loss that is being refashioned into one of male one-upmanship. From object of Rodomonte's desire, a position that brings her death when she finds herself unprotected by other men, Isabella becomes a collective object of desire for the men called on to test the laws of chivalry that her "lover" has newly redefined. Killed because her sexuality lured men, Isabella finds herself killed in representation as well, a derealized body important only for the political choices of passing courtly knights and for the psychological need of her murderer to reinforce his sense of self-worth.

It takes a woman to disrupt such a game and offer a posture of moral indignation. Bradamante, on her arrival on the bridge for a joust that she is undertaking for the sake of another woman, Fior-diligi, tells Rodomonte that she will fight for Isabella rather than for his right to have others, through defeat, accept his right to determine whom and why they should worship. As Isabella's alter ego, Bradamante rightly understands that to vindicate her and re-store the social order, Rodomonte himself needs to be defeated and his narrative of mastery revealed: "Perchè vuoi tu, bestial, che gli innocenti / facciano penitenza del tuo fallo? / Del sangue tuo placar costei convienti: / tu l'uccidesti, e tutto 'l mondo sallo" ("Why do you make the innocent do penance for your crime, you brute? It is with your own blood that you should placate her: you killed her and the whole world knows it" [35, 42]). She also tells him that her victory as a woman will better satisfy Isabella. In short, Brada-mante knows that the mausoleum should not replace a woman, dead or alive, but should represent a woman's right to choose a life of her own, even if this right masochistically requires her death. Bradamante makes clear that the power of the phallus can be detached from that of the penis.

Rodomonte's compulsion to challenge any knight indicates that he is in mourning, and that he needs to be libidinally attached to the lost object in order to disavow, or at least postpone, the inevi-table pain and sense of guilt he must feel as the cause of that loss. In another sense, however, Rodomonte has not yet even begun to mourn—mourning being a finite mode of understanding what has been lost and of coming to terms with that loss—but instead has remained fixed in the state of melancholia. The melancholic ego chooses to identify with the lost object, often eroticizes it, and re-fuses to let it go.[27] In "Mourning and Melancholia," Freud couples melancholia with incorporation and idealization of the lost object and thus with the subject's inability to regain the mother's love or to separate from her world. In short, the melancholic individual cannot accept castration. Unable to cut himself off from the lost other whom he perceives as powerful, he chooses to retain the loss within himself through imitation and identification ("In mourning it is the world which has become poor and empty, in melancholia it is the ego itself," 246). Since it is impossible for him to accept and forget and in the process to constitute his self, the melancholic prefers to hide his bereavement, indeed to entomb it. Successful mourning, instead, postulates the subject's recovery from his sense of loss and the subsequent creation of a self. It is easy to see in this sequence how for Freud melancholia comes to be associated with narcissistic drives: "The narcissistic identification with the object then becomes a substitute for the erotic cathexis. . . . The ego wants to incorporate this object into itself and in accordance with the oral or cannibalistic phase of libidinal development in which it is, it wants to do so by devouring it" ("Mourning," 249–50). In other words, a melancholic individual feels as powerful as a narcissistic child.

Rodomonte, who has exorcized Isabella's sexuality and transformed his sexual desire for her into one for a lost object that he retroactively invests with meaning, narcissistically feels pleasure in the imaginary plenitude of the identification with his ideal. This identification, however, is one of misrecognition. Like the child caught in a dyadic relation to his mother in Lacan's description of the mirror-phase, Rodomonte needs to identify with an other perceived as whole. However, such a perception only reconfirms his incompleteness and his distance from that whole other, which conversely fosters the very desire that makes him seek identification. The fact that Rodomonte cannot let Isabella go not only hides his fear of dissolution but also empowers him, because it fosters closeness to a person he clearly perceives in transcendental terms. Only then, by projecting nurturing and maternal qualities onto her, can he protect himself from the danger of being engulfed in female sexuality.

Although Freud saw melancholia and mourning as two distinct processes initially, he corrected himself in a later essay. In "The Ego and the Super-Ego (Ego-Ideal)," he writes that not only the melancholic individual but also the mourner needs to identify with the lost object for the process of healing to be successful.[28] The melancholic is at times aggressive, since in mourning a loss to the self (and also a loss to his sense of self-worth) he ends up hating what he chooses to idealize and idolize. Such is Rodomonte's case during his misogynist rampage after Doralice rejects him. Later, his compulsive request for a joust with each and every knight in the hope of throwing them off his bridge has definite sadistic connotations. Rodomonte has become a pathological mourner with no sense of shame ("Feelings of shame . . . are lacking in the melancholic," Freud writes ["Mourning," 247]).

For Julia Kristeva, melancholia is tainted less by aggression than by a hurt ego, for sorrow would contribute "the most archaic expression of a narcissistic wound, unable to be symbolized or named, too precocious for any exterior agent (subject or object) to be correlated to it. For this type of narcissistic depressive, sorrow is in reality his only object; more exactly, it constitutes a substitute object to which he clings, cultivating and cherishing it, for lack of any other" (107). This sort of depression and moroseness leads the individual to cut his ties with the outside world and to regress into his own universe, a withdrawal that points to a symbolic death. In his rereading of Freud's *Beyond the Pleasure Principle*, Samuel Weber links the death drive to narcissism and thus to the desire for mastery. As the compulsion to repeat leads to narcissism, so the death drive "might be just another form of the narcissistic language of the ego" (*Legend of Freud*, 129). Lacan sees repetitions tied to *moi* fixations, and therefore once again to the death drive. Rodomonte heals the wounds to his ego caused by previous sexual failures precisely through moroseness, as when he decides to return to Africa after Doralice's rejection. His death-in-life stance is later symbolized by his decision to effect a distance from others following Isabella's death and, more specifically, by his self-willed burial in a cave following Bradamante's victory.

As has progressively become clear in this essay, the Isabella story has slowly become the Rodomonte story, for even when the signified (Isabella's corpse) is refashioned into an outside signifier (the mausoleum) and made to stand for the body, representation can take place only by progressing further and leaving death behind. What comes to be represented, then, is neither Isabella's life nor her sacrifice, but Isabella as projection of male desires. Petrified and penned down, she is slowly turned into the silent Laura of Petrarch's sonnets *in mortem*, the void around which male identity can be predicated, the simulacrum and guarantor of a melancholic man's shaken sense of self-worth. Petrarch could not have written of this loss, and of his own subsequent birth as a poet, with more poignancy: "E viva colei ch'altrui par morta / e di sue belle spoglie / seco sorride et sol di te sospira, / et sua fama, che spira / in molte parti ancor per la tua lingua, / prega che non estingua, / anzi la voce al suo nome rischiari" ("She is alive who seems dead, and she smiles to herself at her beautiful remains and sighs only for you; and she begs you not to extinguish her fame, which sounds in many places still by your tongue, but rather to make bright your voice with her name" [*Rime sparse* 268, vv. 70–76]).

CHAPTER SEVEN

Transvestite Love: Gender Troubles in the Fiordispina Story

When you meet a human being, the first distinction you make is "male or female"? and you are accustomed to make the distinction with unhesitating certainty.
—Freud, "Femininity," 113

A woman is a changeable thing by nature.
—Petrarch, *Rime sparse*, 183

⊶⊷ ⊶⊷

THE STORY OF the Fiordispina-Bradamante-Ricciardetto trio in Canto 25 of *Orlando furioso* is a whirlwind of surprises. Characters show themselves as radically different from what they seemed at first sight; gender differences become unreadable on the surface and bewildering when assumed through magic spells; and clothes, which usually illustrate and enforce sexual divisions, here complicate rather than facilitate matters. A knight in arms, for example, is a woman but prefers to dress like a man. A woman roams the woods and behaves in masculine ways in her erotic pursuits, only to reveal herself as thoroughly feminine. Finally, a man dresses like a knight in order to pass himself off as a woman so that, he can don feminine garb and seduce a woman, once he convinces her that he is a man.

The young knight Ricciardetto tells the story of this imbroglio to his rescuer, Ruggiero. His twin sister, Bradamante, was sleeping in full armor one afternoon next to a stream. Her helmet was off, and her hair had been closely cropped to cure a serious head wound. Fiordispina, the daughter of the Spanish king Marsilio, happened to be hunting in the area. She saw the woman warrior, thought her a male knight, and immediately fell in love with him/her. But when she tried to be more forward toward the stranger, she found to her bewilderment that she was wrong in her assumptions: the warrior was a woman and had no interest in her advances. Still, she courteously invited the visitor to the family castle at dusk and dressed her in becoming feminine clothes for presentation at court. Later that night, as was the custom, the two women shared the same bed. Bradamante fell asleep immediately, but Fiordispina was too troubled to follow suit. From time to time throughout the night, she would extend her arm toward her bedmate to check if a miracle had changed her sex. Wearied by the disturbance her presence at court had created, Bradamante rushed out of the castle early the next morning. Once home, she told her family about the incident.

Among those who listened attentively was Ricciardetto, still living with his mother and younger siblings. He read his twin's adventure in his own way and decided to use the occasion to his advantage. He stole her clothes and horse, both gifts from Fiordispina, and rushed to the princess's castle. Fiordispina joyfully received him, believing that Bradamante had come back, and dressed him in the same clothes his sister had worn. The evening at court unfolded as had the preceding one: same gathering, same dinner, same bed at night. But as soon as the servants left, Ricciardetto told Fiordispina the tale of a surprising transformation of sex: his own timely, magic change from woman to man, thanks to a feat of prestidigitation on the part of a benevolent water nymph. Then, to make sure that Fiordispina had not missed the meaning of his story, he asked her to look at and touch his new equipment. The couple lived happily for a while until the king discovered the ruse and punished both his daughter and her seducer. Ruggiero received a call for help from one of Fiordispina's servants and managed to save Ricciardetto from the stake. Surprised at the resemblance between the young knight and his beloved Bradamante, whom he had tried in vain to locate for the last few hours, Ruggiero asked Ricciardetto to tell the story of his distress.

What Ricciardetto relates is a fantasy of male bravado that touches on the imbrication of desire and law in the process of retracing an Oedipal journey from mother to father, through woman and sex. My purpose in this chapter is to follow the process by which Ariosto constructs, by way of apparent transgressions, socially correct gender identities. As I understand it, this is a story of neither male nor female desire, neither a parable of lesbian relations nor an allegory aimed at refiguring gender roles. It is instead an eloquent tale about the enshrining of male identity and sexuality. By examining, through a Freudian/Lacanian lens, a series of moments of fluidity of gender, I aim to show how superficial the violations of gender codes in this canto are; in the end, everything is subsumed to male norms. This investigation of cross-dressing, female impersonation, penis envy, and castration aims to add another dimension to my overall concern throughout this book: the construction of women's subjectivity and femininity.

The literary antecedents of the encounter between Fiordispina and Bradamante can be found, once again, in Boiardo. In *Orlando innamorato*, the scene between the two women is the last in the final, interrupted book. Fiordispina herself, however, is introduced as early as Book 1, 4 when she request's Ferraù's help in her father's war. Boiardo also originated the episode of Bradamante's haircut, the result of a wound inflicted on her unhelmeted head (3, 8, 61). Cured by a monk, Bradamante later kills her attacker, Martasino, in an incident also mentioned in the *Furioso* (14, 17). In Boiardo, there is no mention of Ricciardetto's ruse. The author simply relates the encounter between Fiordispina and Bradamante in the woods, describes Fiordispina's sexual arousal, and refers to Bradamante's ambiguous reaction to the Spanish princess's advances ("il corpo insieme e l'anima vi dono"; "I give you both my body and my soul" [3, 9, 12]). Despite her words, Bradamante is, of course, unable to give what she seems so ready to promise, a point that is not lost on the author, who writes of woman's lack, but refuses to name it: "L'una de l'altra accesa è nel disio, / quel che li manca ben saprè dir io" ("Each is burning for the other / what they are missing I could very well name" [3, 9, 25]).

Years later, in his *Quarto libro* (1506), Niccolò degli Agostini undertook to provide a rational closure to Boiardo's unfinished epic. Faced with this puzzling ending, he has Ruggiero arrive at the scene of the unfolding seduction. The change reconstitutes the founding couple Bradamante/Ruggiero and displaces Fiordispina and the transgression attached to her presence. As she comes to recognize that Bradamante is in love with a man, Fiordispina accepts the heterosexual ending and bows out "sconsolata, / quasi piangendo" ("disconsolate, almost in tears" [4, 34]).[1] Surprisingly, Ariosto does not begin the *Furioso* with this bawdy episode. When he does take it up, he separates its beginning in Canto 22, when Ruggiero gets a request for help, from its ending in Canto 25, when he provides it.

Ariosto's Bradamante differs considerably from Boiardo's in this episode. Boiardo's heroine is bold and assertive and refuses to deny her non-maleness; Ariosto's creation immediately speaks to reaffirm her biological sex. Boiardo's character, moreover, is self-

confident; Ariosto's is apologetic and lies to explain her deceptive
outlook: "Gloria, qual già Ippolita e Camilla, / cerca ne l'arme; e
in Africa era nata / in lito al mar ne la città d'Arzilla / a scudo e
a lancia da fanciulla usata" ("She was in quest of glory at arms,
like Hippolita and Camilla of old. Born in Africa, in the seaside
city of Arzilla, she was accustomed from childhood to the use of
lance and shield" [25, 32]). Boiardo hints at room in Bradamante
for experimentation; Ariosto dismisses Fiordispina's misreading of
Bradamante's cross-dressing and enforces the boundaries delimit-
ing heterosexual desire.

The issue around which the sexual intrigue of Canto 25 re-
volves is cross-dressing and the related problem of masquerade.
Cross-dressing is subversive by definition. The use of nonregula-
tion outfit to suggest a different or opposite personality, and often
a different gender and a different social class, fosters pleasure and
comic relief, but it also challenges institutional power. At the very
least, it shifts the boundaries of self and other and rewrites assumed
gender differences. Often it implies vice and unbridled libido, as
would perhaps be true in the case of Ricciardetto, were not his
actions culturally approved. At other times it provides a means for
destabilizing social and cultural expectations, as when Bradamante
dresses as a man.[2]

Dressing in the other's clothing often marks a rite of pas-
sage, a temporary access to a different identity before embracing
adulthood. As Jean-Pierre Vernant (24) writes, many such trans-
formations took place in Greek rituals and myths, usually before
marriage or before individuals were marked as fully grown.
Throughout the centuries, women have loved to appear as men and
assume the power and freedom that could symbolically accompany
the clothing of the other sex, even if only for the limited space
of an evening. Such cross-dressing was also lawful in the Renais-
sance as long as it occurred during specific carnivals.[3] Everyday life
was, of course, another matter: women's cross-dressing stood for
sexual license. Since sumptuary laws closely regulated size, shape,
and material of both male and female clothing, dressing differently
meant not only that sexual differences could be obscured but that,
just as threateningly, social distinctions could be erased. Thus, as
Jordan (*Renaissance Feminism*, 303) points out, writers of treatises
endlessly argued against women's transgression of dress codes be-

cause cross-dressing allowed women to cancel rank for the simple pleasure of a temporary equality with men.

Dressing in female garb and indulging in unruly acts were surprisingly even fashionable on certain occasions among men in the Renaissance. In suggesting the right garb for a courtier, Castiglione opts for black as a serious, professional color (2, 27, 133–34), but he sees nothing wrong in subversive outfits in public shows and masquerades because they enliven the atmosphere ("portan seco una certa vivezza ed alacrità," 2, 27, 133).[4] The masquerade, moreover, allows the courtier some freedom and license ("lo essere travestito porta seco una certa libertà e licenzia," 2, 11, 115–16) to assume the roles he wants and show indifference ("sprezzatura") toward those he does not plan to replicate.

As a result of cross-dressing, men better understood, one can assume, what it meant to be men. This playing out of sexual anxieties may have also helped them understand what it meant to be women, which may have led them to sympathize with women's lot. Of course, it may also have not engendered any desire to know femininity and, in fact, may have awakened the fear of difference, along with a related unconscious need to explain and domesticate that difference through the assimilation of the other to the same, of woman to man. In this case cross-dressing can be understood not simply as an aberrant desire for laughter but as a perversion, and thus another occasion for reinforcing gender differences, another reason for regrounding woman as the enigma necessary for the shaping of male subjectivity. Reasons for cross-dressing indeed differ by the sex of the individual involved.

In the Fiordispina-Bradamante-Ricciardetto story, clothes both make and unmake the persons wearing them, since they are not reliable indicators of gender differences. Men turn up as women, and women are discovered to be men. It is even possible to dress as a man in order to be considered a woman, as when Ricciardetto puts on his sister's knightly clothes in order to be taken for her. Nor do physical traits foster clearer distinctions: Bradamante and Ricciardetto look so similar that even their own siblings on occasion fail to distinguish them. There is, however, even in these circumstances one means of gender differentiation immediately available to the characters in the story, as Lacan would have it: language. On his arrival at the scene of the rescue, unable to differentiate his beloved from the stranger in front of him, Ruggiero hears something odd in the inflection of the other's voice: "Veggo (dicea Ruggier) la faccia bella / e le belle fattezze e 'l bel sembiante, / ma la suavità de la favella / non odo già de la mia Bradamante" (" 'I am looking at the comely face and beautiful figure of my Bradamant,' Ruggiero mused, 'but I do not hear the dulcet tones of her voice' " [25, 20]).

Of the many instances of cross-dressing in the text, Bradamante's open assumption of male identity is paradoxically the least threatening. Masculine clothes hardly masculinize this female warrior. Rather, they allow her to fight in a holy war as if she were a man and to search for her own beloved, Ruggiero, unencumbered by the dangers associated with being a woman in a man's world. Unlike Angelica, who can escape the limitations imposed on her sex only by traveling invisibly, Bradamante finds that her disguise facilitates her circulation in society and in the woods. Whereas Angelica's every appearance occasions a desire to rape her on man's part, the knowledge that Bradamante is a woman in armor has no effect on others. Everyone treats her sex as unimportant.

This difference in characterization foreshadows the two women's different fates. Destined to marry the progenitor of the Este family, a family for whose descendent Ariosto is writing, Bradamante, unlike Angelica, can hardly be characterized as sexual. No one but her beloved seems to desire her, and the author allows her to desire him in return because from the start she wants only a lawful husband, one whom even heaven conspires to give her. The sexual ambiguity created by Bradamante's choice of masculine apparel can thus be discounted because Bradamante's sexuality is not in question. She is an appropriately feminine character from beginning to end, and her military phase early in her youth constitutes only a temporary activity before her public espousal of the joys of domesticity. In her case, rather than being transgressive or virilizing, cross-dressing neither questions identities nor problematizes issues of sexual difference. No matter what she does or what clothes she wears, Bradamante is positioned in the epic as a virginal, unimpeachable female subject.

Fiordispina's case is different. Although there is no cross-dressing on her part, Fiordispina does change substantially during the course of the story. At the start, for example, she appears stereotypically mannish: she hunts and joyfully takes the initiative in courting the object of her desire. Soon, however, she turns into a very feminine and passive type, lamenting her harsh destiny, of course, but essentially accepting it. Her new behavior, I would suggest, underscores her assumption of what has been called the female masquerade, the disguise and role-playing that a woman sometimes willingly sets in motion in order to comply more fully with the cultural constructions of femininity that society weaves around her. In a famous psychoanalytical study, Joan Rivière discusses the case of a female patient who chose to renounce her recognized power and outer assertiveness for the sake of acceptance in the world of men. She earnestly embraced a male notion of what woman should be like and disguised her true nature with a constructed, more acceptable, womanly one. "Womanliness therefore could be assumed and worn as a mask," Rivière writes, "both to hide the possession of masculinity and to avert the reprisals expected if she was found to possess it. . . . Womanliness and masquerade . . . are the same thing" (38).

The female masquerade is, then, an overt and overdone display of femininity to hide masculinity in women. In other words, there is no essential femininity; femininity is invented and worn. Like Luce Irigaray, who wrote on the subject later (*This Sex*), Rivière shows that the women's desire to masquerade makes masculinity the standard point of reference, as Freud said all along. This is also Lacan's point when he takes up Rivière's reasoning and associates masquerade with femininity in his discussion of the phallus: "It is in order to be the phallus, that is to say, the signifier of the desire of the Other, that the woman will reject an essential part of her femininity, notably all its attributes through masquerade. It is for what she is not that she expects to be desired as well as loved" ("Meaning of the Phallus," 84).[5]

Masked or not, Fiordispina is perceived as transgressive whether she longs for a woman or for a man. In the end, there is no room for her in the text. Unlike Angelica, who is at least sent home when of no further narrative interest, Fiordispina is literally abandoned by the author in her father's dungeon, crossed out of the story without even a stroke of the pen.

As for Ricciardetto, his histrionic cross-dressing is downright dangerous, for his purpose is to seduce and deceive, to appropriate for himself what is not his to have, a maiden of different religion and superior social status. Ricciardetto uses cross-dressing to play on Fiordispina's naivetè and master her, for he has no personal doubt about his own masculinity and steps out of his gender only to reaffirm the values of masculinism.[6] Cross-dressing provides him with an unexpected reward. By temporarily dressing as a woman, he at last becomes a man, a knight. In this sense Canto 25 is both the canto in which Bradamante fully assumes her feminine identity through a return home and the canto in which Ricciardetto stops being a youth living in his parents' house and starts to engage in warfare beside other mighty warriors. Ironically, Ruggiero continues to mistake him for a woman, although he knows that he has come to rescue a young knight ("ma se pur questa è Bradamante"; "if she really is Bradamant" [25, 20]).[7]

Even at first reading, there is no doubt that "quel nodo," the male organ, is a major issue of Canto 25. Given a narrative in which sexual and gender differences are questionable because of the ready availability of deceptive costumes, the confirmation of an individual's sex can come, as we would expect, only through the obvious possession or non-possession of the male organ.[8] Not only, then, does woman in representation stand as a sign of castration, but also, as we will see in this particular representation, woman's acknowledged castration can constitute the turning point of the story.

Why is the desire for a penis so central to the structure of longing and satisfaction in this narrative? Why this extra valorization of what is not there ("quel che li manca," as Boiardo puts it [3, 9, 25])? Why indeed does Fiordispina show to such an extent what Freud considers essential to female development—penis envy (*penisneid*)? In Freudian psychoanalysis, penis envy is a peculiarly feminine phenomenon that comes from woman's discovery, early in her growth, of her own castration. Rather than accepting reality, Freud writes in "Some Psychical Consequences of the Anatomical Distinction Between the Sexes," the girl desires what she so visibly lacks. She does so because she recognizes the power that is invested in the male organ, even after she knows that her lack is absolutely unrecoverable.[9]

Sarah Kofman argues that a theorization of penis envy serves only Freud's and man's needs since it works "to make the woman an accomplice in man's crime, make her disparage her own sex and valorize man's, make her establish life's rejection of femininity as a general law" (*The Enigma of Woman*, 182). Irigaray concurs; women are made to desire what men define as important because their desire for something different would be perceived as dangerous and "would call into question the unity, the uniqueness, the simplicity of the mirror charged with sending man's image back to him, albeit inverted" (*Speculum*, 51). Closure is achieved in this canto only when the most visible signifier of sexual difference has been located—and located where, in terms of the narrative, it always should have been, in man. The recovery of the penile referent thus provides the much-anticipated cathartic moment and heterosexual celebration.

At masculinism's starkest level, woman, her sex defined by her orifices, is the one missing a body part. The desire she is given, then, is a desire to recover that part. But whose desire is this? Is it woman who is lacking, or is it man who has to identify her with castration in order to project his own original lack onto her? For Lacan, male (or female) subjectivity is based on symbolic castration. The young boy can enter into the symbolic order only after he acknowledges his own lack: "What might be called a man, the male speaking being, strictly disappears as an effect of discourse . . . by being inscribed within it solely as castration" ("Seminar XVIII," quoted in Mitchell and Rose, 44). But he can also deny his lack because he is in possession of an external organ that seems to represent fullness, his penis. Soon he comes to identify possession of the penis with possession of the phallus and with the wealth of psychological privileges this identification entails. As a result, woman is made both to stand for castration (her own) and to bear man's denied castration, since her "visible" castration works to disavow his.

To be sure, Lacan does not identify penis with phallus, the former a male member endowed by culture with phallic meaning and the latter simply a signifier. Yet he chooses the term *phallus* because it "stands out as most easily seized upon in the real of sexual copulation, and also as the most symbolic in the literal (typographical) sense of the term" ("Meaning of the Phallus," 82).[10] According to Lacan, having the phallus, the signifier of lack, allows representation, since representation depends on the absence of something desired. Boys and girls would, of course, have a different access to representation, with girls experiencing problems since they have to lose what, in point of fact, they have already lost.[11] Or, to paraphrase Parveen Adams ("Representation," 67–68), if the phallus represents lack for both boys and girls, then what girls lack is not a penis, but the possibility of representing lack through the usual association/assimilation of penis and phallus.

On the surface, Bradamante seems to suffer from penis envy since she dresses like a man, behaves like a man, and claims that she is a man even when everybody is convinced otherwise, as in the Rocca di Tristano episode. But Bradamante's self-masculinization is only superficial, for she is psychically described as feminine in her feelings and physically represented as doubly castrated. Bradamante not only is, as a woman, already castrated but is regrounded in femininity just before the encounter with Fiordispina through two closely related incidents that represent castration. First, she receives a head wound from a Saracen knight, an action that occurs when she is not wearing a helmet, precisely because she is behaving like a woman by showing her face to her beloved Ruggiero. The wound, then, reasserts what she is by making her gender visible. But this wound demands another one, the cutting off of her tresses to better cure the original injury.[12] The haircut in turn creates an almost totally androgynous look and causes her to enter a territory usually reserved for men, a point exemplified by Ricciardetto's identifying his short haircut specifically with the male gender ("questo crin raccorcio e sparto / ch'io porto, come gli altri uomini fanno"; "I wore my hair short and loose in the male fashion" [25, 23]).

Thus, even though she masquerades as a man, Bradamante carries within her body the story of the original, indelible scar that marks her as a woman. She is, as she immediately tells Fiordispina, a "femina gentile" ("a member of the gentler sex" [25, 30]). At the same time, precisely because she seems androgynous, she engenders a greater fear of castration in men, for she appears as both woman and man and signifies both lack and absence of lack. As Francette Pacteau writes, "In a symbolic order in which the woman's body stands for signifier of lack, the androgyne figure invariably evokes castration: 'I see somebody as a woman'—its affirmation—'and as a man'—its negation" (70). Since a subject enters into the symbolic only after the resolution of the Oedipus complex and the recognition of sexual difference, an androgynous figure like Bradamante paradoxically disavows gender identity and fosters fantasy. Interestingly, Ariosto allows a woman, but not a man, to fantasize about Bradamante, as if it were overly subversive to have men fall in love with a seemingly too manly other.

But even in the case of Fiordispina, I would submit, her penis envy, which she seems to display so literally, is illusory. There is no question that Fiordispina continues to desire against all logic for the recuperation of the missing organ in the story, but she does not desire a penis for herself. Rather, she desires it for the woman she would prefer was a man. In other words, Fiordispina knows that she herself is castrated. Kofman writes that woman's stubbornness in wishing for a penis can "derive only from blindness, the feminine counterpart to the boy's fetishism" (203). Interestingly, Fiordispina is shown throughout as having faulty vision; had she been able to see well she would have had different desires. Ricciardetto, on the other hand, has no problems with vision. He tells Ruggiero that he had previously seen Fiordispina in two different countries, Spain and France, and that both times he had correctly realized that she was unattainable. As a result, he had judiciously chosen to abandon the enterprise: "ma non lasciai fermarvisi il disio, / che l'amar senze speme è sogno e ciancia" ("but had not let my thoughts dwell upon her: to love without hope is idle dreaming" [25, 49]).[13] Now circumstances have changed radically in his favor, and he goes resolutely ahead to show who has the standard ("stendardo," 25, 68) after all.

On acceptance of her castrated status, Freud writes, woman sublimates her penis envy, accepts a proper love object, and desires a husband who possesses what she envies him for or at least can give her a baby boy as a substitute. (The only proper woman for Freud is the mother.) Enter Ricciardetto. Not only does Ricciardetto satisfy all Fiordispina's desires, but he also makes sure that she desires exclusively what he can provide. But does Fiordispina desire woman, or would she have desired woman, had she known the sex of the knight? Or is it rather that she is made to desire what woman does not have in order once again to place center stage whatever is central to male desire?

It would certainly be hard to qualify Fiordispina's love as "vi-

cious," for if at the center of a homosexual economy is the de-
nial of difference and the narcissistic desire for the same desire
that the other mirrors, Fiordispina's desire is not monstrous, but
plainly heterosexual. She has no interest in a woman, as her re-
peated checking during the night for what Bradamante lacks makes
clear.[14] According to Freud, female homosexuality is based on
disavowal of castration. Fiordispina, however, does not disavow
castration. It is because she accepts woman's castration that she
looks for the male organ, not in herself but in the androgynous
other. Moreover, homosexual desire hardly recuperates or dupli-
cates heterosexual practices; for a lesbian couple the lack of a penis
is the sine qua non only in heterosexual rationalizations.

Fiordispina's response to inhibited/prohibited sexuality takes
the form of a masochistic fantasy. Masochism is not extreme in her,
however, for as Kaja Silverman writes, "Woman's position within
the symbolic order is already so subordinate that further degrada-
tion changes nothing" ("Masochism," 62). Lamenting her destiny,
Fiordispina identifies with a number of mythical women who have
suffered for their unorthodox choices, women who have invariably
been characterized as hysteric, paranoid, or murderously inclined.
She evokes Semiramis, who desired her son; Mirrha, who desired
her father; and Pasiphae, who desired a bull. The only difference
between their desire and hers is that they desired males and she
alone, alas, desires females. Incestuous longings and bestial copu-
lations fare better in these octaves than homosexuality, which she
considers perverse.

The fact that the absent penis has to be the narrative center in-
scribes, I believe, a specific male desire for positioning this organ
as central not only to masculinity but to femininity as well, in both
natural and inverted modes.[15] In this context I disagree with Giulio
Ferroni's statement that Ariosto fosters the concept of a homo-
sexual passion in the ruse ("Da Bradamante," 148) and with John
McLucas's similar emphasis on Fiordispina's "homosexual desires"
("Ariosto," 128). Similarly, I disagree with Eugenio Donato's de-
tachment of desire from sex, for it seems to me that the two go
together in this story.[16] True, Fiordispina acknowledges certain de-
sires as unnatural, but she stops there. She does not desire the
woman in the story, nor does she wish to substitute a woman for
a man or even to deny sexual differences by making one stand

for the other. She wants a man, and she is satisfied when it turns out that the woman is a man. In other words, she wants to fulfill her desire according to her understanding of the laws of nature, which makes her wish heterosexual and normative. And although her desire is infinite, her mourning is limited to the expression of her despair. Fiordispina's unruliness belongs to the mind, not to the body.

To illustrate how little subversion there is in Fiordispina, I would like to dwell for a moment on the episode of her enamorment. Fiordispina sees a sleeping knight, takes pleasure at the sight, and falls immediately in love. As in Petrarch, love comes at first sight and through the eyes. In this scene, male and female roles seem surprisingly inverted. Dressed as a woman, Fiordispina goes hunting in the woods the way men do; dressed as a man, Bradamante is asleep on the grass like a woman.[17] Fiordispina invites the knight to hunt with her, leads him to a secluded space, attempts seduction with words and acts ("con atti e con parole"), and finally steals a kiss. Her courtship could not be more open. Bradamante, the supposed man, is immediately forced into playing the role of the woman and denying any desire whatsoever by revealing a feminine self behind her masquerade ("venne a dir come donzella fusse"; "had her know that she was a maiden" [25, 31]). Yet the scenario hardly seems transgressive, for the attempt at seduction follows a precise heterosexual structure. To a sleeping, femininized Bradamante corresponds a masculinized Fiordispina, attracted to her both aesthetically and erotically. Whatever subversion this arrangement could possibly provoke is recuperated by the act of showing that when clothes stand for signifiers of difference, an acceptable heterosexual couple is portrayed.

What I find interesting in the scene is that a woman's active look seems to conflict with the usual representation of woman as the person who is looked at. Here the woman is described as gazing at a knight on display, a spectacle offered to the other's sight as if he were a woman. From Fiordispina's position, the person she sees is a man and one whom she desires. Thus, we see man as an erotic object. Does Fiordispina's active looking rewrite gender laws by assigning a woman the gaze—and therefore desire and subjectivity—and by making a man a sexual object of fascination? Not really, although it is interesting that once again Ariosto is questioning gender norms. Unlike Fiordispina, the reader knows that the object of her visual pleasure is not a man but a sleeping beauty awaiting the prince's kiss. The knight is spectated, then, because he is really a she, and as usual in classic representation, woman, not man, is under the control of the gaze.

The desire to cover up (female) lack so as to disavow it finds its expression in the ensuing change of clothing from male to female that Fiordispina imposes first on Bradamante and then on Ricciardetto. Fetishism is considered a male problem, and Mary Ann Doane ("Film and the Masquerade") points out that it is hard for woman to fetishize and acquire the necessary distance from the other.[18] At the source of male fetishism, Freud ("Fetishism," 153) insists, is an anxiety over castration born of man's visual verification of sexual difference in the woman found lacking a body part. Faced with a choice between accepting castration (displaced onto the body of the female) and having to face feminization, the boy accepts the first option and enters the domain of the law. In the unlikely case that he refused to take a position, he would become a problem, because a non-specifically gendered (androgynous) or bigendered figure is difficult to classify.[19]

Bradamante can illustrate this difficulty. She is first portrayed as ambiguously sexualized. Her claim that she is a woman, although she appears otherwise, understandably puzzles Fiordispina. Words enforce an identity that vision disqualifies. In fact, not only does Fiordispina think that the knight is a man, but she has specifically fallen in love with his manly build ("viril fattezze," 25, 28), another demonstration that femininity and masculinity are cultural constructs, often predicated, as in this case, on dress codes. Thus, whereas the letting down of her hair at the Rocca di Tristano in a later canto marks Bradamante's realignment with femininity, here her looks leave Fiordispina unconvinced that the other belongs to the sex she claims is hers, a posture that ambiguously, although perhaps unwillingly, fosters Fiordispina's desire. When she reads Bradamante according to cultural stereotypes, Fiordispina comes up with a man and wants the woman to be in actuality what she seems to be in appearance. When she listens to her, however, she discovers an androgynous female, and for this person she has no desire.

To control her libido, Fiordispina overplays gender roles

through the enforcement of a specific identity: she first reassumes femininity for herself by behaving like a proper princess once back in her castle and then bestows it on Bradamante by making her change clothes. Her decision to realign Bradamante with her gender has both a psychological origin—Fiordispina hopes to tame her own desire once the other person is no longer in knightly gear—and a social one because, dressed as a man, Bradamante would uselessly ruin her reputation: "Però che conoscendo che nessuno / util traeva da quel virile aspetto, / non le parve anco di voler ch'alcuno / biasmo di sè per questo fosse detto" ("Realizing how little benefit she derived from Bradamant's apparent masculinity, Fiordispina did not want any blame to attach to herself on her guest's account" [25, 41]).

For her presentation at court, Bradamante wears an outfit charged with signifiers of femininity, being both white and elaborately embroidered. Yet, if the fetishization of Bradamante's body assures completeness and self-sufficiency, as all fetishes do, it also unconsciously reminds the onlooker of what the dress covers and of what is missing. Thus, the new clothes are unable to do for Fiordispina (who assumes the position of the male fetishist) what she thought they would do, that is, convince her that the person she desires is not a man but a woman. Puzzled and acting against all reason, she keeps checking Bradamante's body throughout the night. As she knows, it is in the body that truth is ultimately located.

Adorned with feminine clothing or, rather, masqueraded in it, since Fiordispina's conscious desire is to make a masculine-looking Bradamante appear as a woman by overdressing her, Bradamante represents lack—that is, woman. Her masquerade "serves to show what she does not have, a penis, by showing—the adornment, the putting-on" as Heath writes in describing Rivière's phallicized woman ("Joan Rivière," 52). What feminine clothes cover is not female lack, which is a given, but the impossibility of positing male lack as seriously inhabiting male bodies dressed in male clothing. Feminine clothes, then, do not hide female castration; rather, they disavow male castration.

This is precisely why Ricciardetto surcharges his story of cross-dressing with a number of phallic referents, all designed to deny that he is castrated. Having accepted masquerading as a woman for

presentation at court, he has to do his best to disprove that clothes
reflect the status of the wearer. Whereas, as we saw, a female body
dressed in feminine clothing needs to function as a fetish to deny
castration, a male body dressed in feminine clothing cannot have
this use, for there is nothing missing to cover up in men, no rea-
son for a fetish. Thus, dressed as a woman, Ricciardetto is more
conscious of his sexual identity than ever, and makes continuous
references to the fact that he is parodying femininity, that there is
something sturdy and robust ("valido e gagliardo," 25, 56) under
his unconventional outfit. In this sense, Ricciardetto acts as a true
transvestite, for "the transvestite needs his penis as an insignia of
maleness," Robert Stoller insists. "One cannot be a male trans-
vestite without knowing, loving, and magnificently expanding the
importance of one's own phallus" (1: 188).[20]

The body of the female once again becomes the site on which
males test their identity and their subjectivity. Men can at times
inhabit this body for the sake of facilitating their games and their
schemes, as long, of course, as there is no hint that the value of
masculinity is at stake, no occasion on which being male does not
also mean being in command. By covering what man fears, by
disavowing that fear through its projection onto a different body,
the fetish guarantees intactness to the male subject. If earlier the
emphasis was on penis envy in regard to Fiordispina, now, with
Ricciardetto, it can only be on castration. Both concepts are im-
portant elements in men's rationalizations to counter any threat to
their own narcissism. Both prioritize male sexuality. In Kofman's
words, "because it signals woman's loss of omnipotence, woman's
penis envy increases man's power and allows him to overcome
the inhibiting horror: as if 'penis envy' restored woman's value
as sexual object by exhibiting—negatively as it were—man's still
intact and complete sexuality" (*The Enigma of Woman*, 85).

By insisting that only the presence of a penis provides sexual
pleasure for both sexes and that only the recovery of the missing
referent can guarantee closure, Ricciardetto denies the possibility
of any form of sexuality specific to the other sex, such as a form
of sexuality that would be inaccessible to man and would thus
keep woman as other. This strategy again can only serve male
needs; as Luce Irigaray points out, it has always been in man's
interest to deny the multiplicity of locations of sexual pleasure

in women, even though "the geography of [woman's] pleasure is much more diversified, multiple in its difference, complex, subtle, than is imagined" (*This Sex*, 28).[21]

How can Ricciardetto identify with the female sex, a sex that, to paraphrase a famous essay by Irigaray, is not one? If "seeing" a lack engenders castration anxieties, in what sense can Ricciardetto personify that lack and still remain whole? After all, the men living with the Mankilling women in Laiazzo in Cantos 19 and 20 are made to demonstrate their personal and social demotion precisely through the enforced wearing of female clothing. Ricciardetto can stage this female impersonation, I submit, because stable identifications and stable gender positions are problematic for him, given the close presence throughout his lifetime of his double and alter ego, Bradamante. For others, even his parents, Ricciardetto's gender is apparently unclear unless marked by clothes and by a specific haircut. But these two signifiers can at times be discarded or give way to further ambiguity; after Bradamante's haircut the brother/sister gender difference once again, as was the case in early childhood, is not marked by any external signifier and thus has to be relocated in the genitals.

Freud focuses repeatedly on the continuous psychic shifting of the individual between masculine and feminine identifications. In "Three Essays on the Theory of Sexuality," "A Child Is Being Beaten," and "Analysis Terminable and Interminable," he elaborates on the theory of bisexuality, a theory that is extremely important in clarifying the issues of sexual identity and subject positions.[22] According to Freud, the non-positions regarding libido of the pre-Oedipal, objectless bisexual are overcome when the individual successfully passes through the Oedipus triangle. Later, as a result of mastering the Oedipus complex, the child of either sex accepts separation and becomes fixed into a specific sexual identity. In the Freudian schema, the boy opts for a parent of the opposite sex as a love object and sees the other parent, with whom he will identify, as a rival object (positive Oedipus complex). The same happens for the girl, although her detour is more complicated since she is not only renouncing her mother, like the boy, but also renouncing someone belonging to her sex (negative Oedipus complex).

To his credit, Freud uses terms such as activity/passivity rather than masculinity/femininity, and in this sense he closely relates sexuality to subjectivity: "In human beings pure masculinity or femininity is not to be found either in a psychological or a biological sense. Every individual on the contrary displays a mixture of the character-traits belonging to his own and to the opposite sex; and he shows a combination of activity and passivity whether or not these last character-traits tally with his biological ones" ("Three Essays," 220). Freud affirms that all human beings are capable of making a homosexual object-choice. This unconscious homosexual, "perverse" choice is then repressed in the process of socialization and construction of a gendered identity. In other words, sexual instincts are not necessarily fixed; one desires what one fantasizes as desirable because ideology and culture foster such a representation of desirability.[23] Lacan points out that sexual allegiances cannot unquestionably be traced in mental processes, for "in the psyche, there is nothing by which the subject may situate himself as a male or female being" (*Four Fundamental Concepts*, 204). Both authors agree that through the process of socialization, certain fantasies are repressed and certain latent desires become tainted as individual beings construct a sexual identity for themselves and make a "proper" heterosexual object choice. This still makes homosexuality central to heterosexuality, although in a sublimated way.

The problem with Ariosto's twins is that gender positions are reversed, or so it seems at the start. A woman dresses as a man and fights in a war, while her twin, the man, stays home with his mother and younger siblings. Traditionally, the boy leaves home and goes out into the world in search of adventure, in search, indeed, of an identity. But here a woman wanders in the woods and comes back with the tale of an unlawful, if not perverted, love. Moreover, Ricciardetto not only is identified all too often with his sister and the feminine world, but even socially is marginalized as the younger brother of a mighty hero, Rinaldo. No wonder he is anxious to prove his masculinity.

In order to be manly, Ricciardetto does not need to deny that he is homosexual, transsexual, or too dangerously androgynous. He simply has to eliminate anyone's perception of latent femininity in him. In other words, he has to remind his listeners of his mas-

culinity whenever any show of femininity implies a correspond-
ing degree of feminization in him.[24] Similarly, he has to assert
his manhood when his actions speak of his social impotence—his
symbolic castration—which means that his impersonation of the
female must stop at the transvestite garb. In short, Ricciardetto is
not refusing gender but constructing his fortune through accept-
able gendering. As his example testifies, cross-dressed or not, man
is always a man because he fully possesses the only thing desired;
on the other hand, cross-dressed or not, woman is just a non-man.

Although Ricciardetto can enter Fiordispina's bedroom only by
masquerading as a woman, ultimately he must possess her as a
man to reconfirm his "I." What better way to underline this move-
ment into adulthood than through a militaristic vocabulary: "Non
rumor di tamburi o suon di trombe / furon principio all'amoroso
assalto, / ma baci ch'imitavan le colombe, / davan segno or di gire,
or di fare alto. / Usammo altr'arme che saette o frombe. / Io senza
scale in su la rocca salto / e lo stendardo piantovi di botto, / e la
nimica mia mi caccio sotto" ("There was no roll of drums, no peal
of trumpets to herald the amorous assault: but caresses like those
of billing doves gave the signal to advance or to stand firm. We
used arms other than arrows and slingstones; and I, without a lad-
der, leapt onto the battlements and planted my standard there at
one jab, and thrust my enemy beneath me" [25, 68]). The compari-
son of women with enemies to be conquered is an acknowledged
literary topos, as is the comparison of women's sex to a "rocca"
difficult to win, which Castiglione also uses (3, 46, 252). In this
case, the presence of warlike, manly metaphors allows Ricciar-
detto to claim a double victory: he can assert not only that he has
conquered a woman but also that he has conquered the woman
in himself, the feminine side that it was his purpose to deny all
along. In the war between the sexes—which only man can re-
count since he is the one usually engaged or associated with war—
woman is naturally the antagonist. Castration anxiety still looms
on the horizon.

Stories similar to that of Ricciardetto's sexual transformation
are easy to find, as we would expect, in Ovid. In the *Metamorphoses*
(4, vv. 285–388), for instance, Ovid recounts the tale of Herma-
phroditus, a young man desired by the water nymph Salmacis,
whom he refuses. While he bathes naked in a pool, she dives in

and intertwines herself with him. As a result, he acquires feminine sexual attributes.[25] Desperate, Hermaphroditus curses his destiny and pleads with his mother and father, Hermes and Aphrodite, never to allow any man bathing in the pool to emerge as a man. Hermaphroditus experiences his transformation into the other sex as a diminishment (no matter the change, he thinks of himself as a man, and of course he is not a woman), and rejects both the disfiguration that sexual desire in the other generates in him and the possibility that he himself can act as a desiring subject. In short, he rejects his own sexuality and subjectivity.

Ricciardetto's sexual transformation, however, is given as total, from woman to man, and not as hermaphroditic and aberrant. As Ricciardetto tells it, a water nymph (a mother figure in her connection with water, but without the phallic/castrating connotations of Salmacis) sprinkles his face as thanks for his saving her life from a faun bent on devouring her. Rather than threatening or emasculating, Ricciardetto's transformation reenacts a *Fort/Da!* game, a disavowal of dismemberment and castration. Unlike Hermaphroditus, Ricciardetto does not have to give up desire or his active position as desiring subject. On the contrary, he establishes the domain of the phallus by placing it center stage, for he reads his sex change not as a monstrous transformation that leaves him in limbo but as a way of showing his ingenuity and thus his mastery. In this sense, Hermaphroditus's pool stands for that of Narcissus: seeing leads to self-empowerment.

A second parallel Ovidian story (*Metamorphoses* 9, vv. 670–797) is that of Iphis, a woman dressed as a man and given a nongendered name. Her mother chooses the ruse to keep the baby alive in spite of her father's desire to kill the newborn if it is a girl. When Iphis is promised to Ianthe, the goddess Isis transforms her into a man to solve the problem caused by the same-sex relationship. In the tale of Hermaphroditus, man felt emasculated by sexual intercourse; here woman is literally empowered by it. Although renounced in the first story, desire is the driving force for the transformation in the second.[26] In both cases, however, the individual's phallicization is described as necessary to satisfy female desire, which is essentially the story Ricciardetto tells Ruggiero. The difference once again is that whereas for Hermaphroditus the merging stands for castration ("and so at last [she] entwined him, like a snake" [*Metamorphoses* 4, v. 363]), and for Iphis no sexual act can take place before her transformation, Ricciardetto is already in possession of the truth ("veritade espressa") that will inscribe his empowerment directly onto woman's body. Rather than pain, his embrace brings *jouissance*: "Non con più nodi i flessuosi acanti / le colonne circondano e le travi, / di quelli con che noi legammo stretti / e colli e fianchi e braccia e gambe e petti" ("Never did twisting acanthus entwine pillars and beams with more knots than those which bound us together, our necks and sides, our arms, legs, and breasts in a close embrace" [25, 69]).

A third Ovidian analogue can be found in Actaeon's transformation into a stag following his voyeuristic survey of naked Diana bathing in a pool (*Metamorphoses* 3, vv. 131–260). Actaeon sees what should be left unseen, the forbidden beauty of a virgin goddess, and is punished by dismemberment. Ricciardetto, however, sees and is rewarded with literal re-memberment in his made-up story. Having prevented an act of cannibalization on the nymph with his timely arrival, he is not turned into the inferior being of the stag but into the superior one of the man, indeed he blooms through prestidigitation: "L'acqua incantata: / . . . non prima al viso mi s'accosta, / ch'io (non so come) son tutta mutata. / Io 'l veggio, io 'l sento, e a pena vero parmi: / sento in maschio, di femina, mutarmi" ("The enchanted water . . . the moment it touched my face I was quite transformed, I know not how. I could see, I could feel—though I could scarcely believe my senses—that I was changing from woman to man" [25, 64]). Coyly Ricciardetto refers to himself with a word gendered as feminine, "mutata," as when he earlier described his status in the feminine, "dispogliate" (25, 58) when undressed in bed with Fiordispina. In Petrarch's Canzone 23, Actaeon/Petrarch responds to Diana's scattered water with scattered rhymes that scatter woman's body across two hundred poems. For the poet to regain power, it is necessary to displace the possibility of man's castration onto woman (Diana's sprinkle) with a description that presents her as castrated and fetishized and therefore as easy to control.[27] This is exactly Ariosto's procedure.

Ricciardetto claims that it is easy to identify with women and, in fact, seems to do it almost nonchalantly. Yet, at what cost to his masculinity, if any, can he do this? He can switch gender effortlessly, I suggest, because Ariosto devises a number of stratagems that smooth his task and muffle dangerous questions about his sexuality. First, he takes control of the act of narrating; the story of a desiring woman is thus conveniently circumscribed within the narcissistic story of the fulfillment of a man's desire through a woman's desiring exactly what he, and only he, can give her. In this sense, the narrative slowly shifts from Fiordispina to Ricciardetto. The displacement is essential for the conclusion of the ruse, since Fiordispina's desire carries no practical solution and is addressed to the wrong sex. Ricciardetto's desire, however—being normal in the sense that it is active and heterosexual—can not only incorporate and cancel out the other but also provide the unity and the pleasure necessary to a satisfying ending.

Second, by controlling the gaze, Ricciardetto is always in charge of what is seen; he is never placed in the feminine position. The ability of a voyeuristic look to feminize a man is evident at the start of the canto when Fiordispina's eyes lovingly survey Bradamante's manly features (25, 28) and Bradamante immediately declares that she is a woman, not a knight. Ricciardetto too, when dressed in women's clothes, becomes the object of the gaze (a lascivious one, as he points out), but he immediately disavows this objectification by reminding both himself and his listener, Ruggiero, that he is taking the position of the looked-at simply because nobody knows of his hidden weapon.

Ricciardetto has two distinct forms of seeing: he sees as a man, whether in man's or in woman's clothes; and he sees himself seeing as a woman, when he must play that role. As Lacan would say, he is in the enviable position of seeing from the place of the other. Ricciardetto points out that he lowers his eyes like a woman when he is being prepared for the official dinner. He notices men's active looks when he is displayed to their voyeuristic gaze in the evening and jokes about it, as a man, rather than accepting it as normal as a woman, accustomed to it throughout her lifetime, would do. Most important, he wants all the lights on when explaining to Fiordispina his newly found manhood ("Coi torchi accesi che parea di giorno"; "The flaming sconces left the room as bright as day" [25, 58]). Then he rhapsodizes on the pleasure of seeing himself being seen as powerful and complete, wholeness personified: "Così la donna, poi che tocca e vede / quel di ch'avuto avea tanto desire, / agli occhi, al tatto, a se stessa non crede" ("She saw and touched the object she had so craved for, but she could not believe her eyes or her fingers or herself" [25, 67]).

Ricciardetto insists that his organ be seen, since the possession of the penis confirms to him, by seeing Fiordispina seeing him, that he has the phallus. Only when the absent turns out to be present does the need to cover woman's lack disappear and the fetish can be thrown away. This is indeed the last time that Ricciardetto is described as wearing female clothing. The scene of his conquest duplicates not only a similar moment in bed between Fiordispina and Bradamante two nights earlier but also a previous one on the grass at the very beginning of Canto 25, between the two women, one of whom thought the other was a man. Only now, when the knight reveals himself to be an impostor no longer but rather the possessor of the unsubstitutable signifier of manhood, can the earlier scene be concluded and the pre-coital, sensual mood that it evoked be replaced by the post-coital embrace of the new, "proper" couple.

A third control the narrative exerts through Ricciardetto is at the diegetic level. Ariosto has only men involved in telling this tale and in listening to it; woman finds herself always in the position of the object, the spoken one, in the triangle, whereas men can identify phallically with each other. Readers are also engaged through a masculine point of view: a man, after all, is telling the story of a woman's desire for a man, and a male writer is controlling and authorizing the story. Through Ricciardetto's telling, the reader is conscious, unlike Fiordispina, that the object of her desire is wrong and that there will be a reassignment so that woman will stop looking and desiring, man will possess her, and phallocentric logic will be reestablished. By choosing what to say, Ricciardetto also neutralizes the anxiety over his own masculinity generated by a tale of sexual transformations.

In the mimesis, then, we have a triangle consisting of two women and a man (Bradamante-Fiordispina-Ricciardetto); in the diegesis we have another triangle, of two men and a woman (Ricciardetto-Ruggiero-Fiordispina). Whether Ricciardetto mirrors Bradamante and Fiordispina as images of femininity or mirrors himself with Bradamante as a twin, thus reducing the triangle to a binary structure, nothing is better for the teller than to reveal to a third person, a man, the pleasure of male power and the final victory of masculinity. The bonding between men is achieved, as usual, with an illustration ad hominem of a male fantasy of potency and self-assurance, a fantasy centering on a woman's naive erotic desire, which only male logic can satisfy. This allows Ricciardetto to reestablish power, defeminize the contours of his cross-dressing, and reaffirm sexual differences. From this perspective, Fiordispina is led to err by her own naiveté but behaves correctly when properly directed and propped up by a man. The process is identical to the one examined earlier in Olimpia.

By showing how he can redirect an inappropriate and unnatural desire with the proper tools, Ricciardetto both fosters his ego and aligns with the law. Recuperated to patriarchy, he has no problem accepting his punishment, because he recognizes that the improper use of the body and the willful defiance of socially sanctioned gender identities intrinsically endanger the body politic. Man's masquerading as a woman, then, because of its connotative traits of dissimulation and demystification and its rejection of identities and gender differences, is not only—or not simply—a transgression of his essential nature. It is a crime against institutions and against hierarchical class divisions, a defiance of authority in the name of libido. Ricciardetto is aware that sexuality needs to be regulated, and that the discourse of the law/king often needs to be made through a public, voyeuristic punishment. Therefore, although he is infuriated with the king's subordinates, he never reproaches the king directly for his own exposure and retribution.[28]

His punishment, in fact, becomes a blessing in disguise. The king not only reestablishes order by recuperating (sexual) transgression but also, and more important, ratifies Ricciardetto's phallic self by publicly presenting him as a man, no matter how androgynous his appearance to that point. In this sense, he acts as a symbolic father guiding the son back to the law by reading youthfulness rather than degeneracy in his conduct. He also masculinizes Ricciardetto by restoring him to the society of knights after months of seemingly endless lust. As Ariosto shows in the episode of Alcina and Ruggiero, unbound lust does not simply feminize man; more dangerously, when placed above knightly duties, it unmans him. Once freed, Ricciardetto understands the correct, and also marginal, place that women and sexual gratifications should have in his life and engages only in manly adventures.

Although complicitous in committing the same crime, Fiordispina and Ricciardetto are shown as different sorts of criminals according to the Law-of-the-Father. What is condemned in Fiordispina is a typical feminine crime against propriety and morality. She is punished for having defied the father. Having chosen fornication, she has appropriated a sexual desire eminently improper and scandalous in women. What is condemned in Ricciardetto, however, is his abuse of power and his transgression of the law through a crime against property and class, the taking—deeply within the castle's gynaeceum—of what does not belong to him. In short, Ricciardetto dares to rob the father/king of value and to make a spectacle of his authority. Remember that in Canto 8 the king of Ebuda chooses to kill his own daughter when her rape diminishes both her value and his prestige as lawgiver.

The king's punishment is not, in any case, homophobic; Ricciardetto would have fared much worse had his cross-dressing evoked homosexuality. Rather, it is a correct social mortification, since it assures women's sexual inviolability for the purpose of enhancing both the virginal daughter's disposal through marriage and the married daughter's practice of chastity for the sake of offsprings' legitimacy. We may also guess that the king reconnects desire and law by visually reestablishing sexual polarities through clothing. When Ricciardetto is rescued, he is dressed as a man.

A tale of disorder thus points the way to order. Put in terms of Foucault's insights on nineteenth- and twentieth-century discourse on sexuality, power disciplines sexuality although apparently fearing it. The individual often does not object to submitting to the very authority that requires his confession because of the benefits to be gained. In Ricciardetto's case, for example, the narrative establishes once and for all that he is no longer a boy. In this light, Canto 25 is not the story of how Fiordispina actualizes her longings but the story of how Ricciardetto, through cross-dressing and because of cross-dressing, establishes sufficient distance from the female other (from his mother, from his twin sister) to move from the world of a male adolescent in search of a self to the world of a knight who knows his identity. In short, Ricciardetto manages to pass smoothly from the realm of romance to that of epic and to have fun in the process.

CHAPTER EIGHT

Un-dressing the Warrior / Re-dressing the Woman: The Education of Bradamante

Beauty in a woman must be judged not only by the charm and refinement of her face, but still more by the grace of her person and her aptitude for bearing and giving birth to many fine children.
— Alberti, *I libri della famiglia*, 115

Be that you are,
That is, a woman; if you be more, you're none.
— Shakespeare, *Measure for Measure*, II.iv.133–34

As a woman almost consistently dressed in knightly gear and as one of Charlemagne's most worthy paladins, Bradamante is a particularly apt character in *Orlando furioso* to illustrate a seeming breakdown of gender and sexual dichotomies. Whenever present, she seems to destabilize or subvert masculine identities (as, for instance, in the case of Sacripante, Rodomonte, Pinabello, and the three Northern kings) and to ground feminine ones in ambiguity and enigma (as in the Ricciardetto and Fiordispina story). Whether dressed in male or female clothing, Bradamante appears free of the limitations usually associated with her sex.

In Chapter 4, I dealt with Ariosto's motives for expurgating Angelica from his text; here I examine the reasons that Bradamante can remain and live happily. Since it is in the name of disorder that Angelica is made to leave, it must be in the name of order that Bradamante, her textual opposite, is allowed to stay. I first discuss the reasons behind Bradamante's lengthy education in femininity, then I show how Ariosto recuperates transgression—which Bradamante embodies almost oxymoronically through her cross-dressing—by presenting it as an expedient for reaching an approved, heterosexual ending. This point rests on two significant examples: Bradamante's encounters with Ruggiero (here I draw heavily on Boiardo's rendering of the scene of their first meeting in his *Innamorato*) and her sojourn at the Rocca di Tristano. Each centers on her helmet and questions her identity and subjectivity. Once again, as in the preceding chapter on Fiordispina, I concern myself with issues of cross-dressing, masquerade, and castration.

In her role of lady knight, Bradamante has a counterpart in Marfisa. Both are well-known warriors and earn the respect of their male colleagues. But Marfisa pays heavily for reveling in a male-related course of action, for she is characterized as unfeminine and placed only in comic or semi-comic situations.[1] Bradamante is approached differently. Like Marfisa, she cross-dresses, yet she assumes a man's role not to implement a transgressive choice—be it a refusal of her sex or a questionable identification with the other sex—but to strive for a woman's supposedly all-comprehensive goal: marriage. Thus, whereas Marfisa keeps behaving as if her sex were undecidable throughout most of the narrative, whether she dons a skirt or a suit of armor, Bradamante relinquishes, one by one, all her manly accoutrements, from her breastplate to her spear, from her helmet to her masculine postures. In time the empowered, phallic woman warrior entering the scene in Canto I with a lance, a pennant, and a horse turns into the swooning bride exiting the epic forty-six cantos later, aghast at the thought that her husband is locked in combat with a knight whom ironically she herself, as well as her mate, bested earlier. In the end, gender differences are reestablished, subject positions are secured, and Bradamante comes to be represented no longer as a *quasi* woman, like Marfisa, but as a motherly woman.

Still, it is as a quasi woman, an individual lacking (or hiding) some exterior feminine attributes, that Bradamante can enter the narrative with assertion and be treated as an equal. According to Burckhardt, the term *virago* had only positive connotations during the Renaissance, since "the highest praise which could then be given to the great Italian women was that they had the mind and the courage of men. We have only to observe the thoroughly manly bearing of most of the women in the heroic poems, especially those of Boiardo and Ariosto, to convince ourselves that we have before us the ideal of the time" (251–52). Contra Burckhardt, I argue that the women warriors in Ariosto are not praised because they are like men (although it is because they resemble men that they can be given interesting and intelligent plots). Rather, it seems to me that the ideological purpose of the epic is to show how necessary it is for women eventually to act as women, how important it is to their society that they understand their acceptable and praiseworthy role is that of being nurturing wives and mothers. Aptly, Bradamante last appears dressed as a bride sitting on the right side of the Emperor, embodiment of whatever is desired in woman (the Lacanian woman as phallus) and personification of the female masquerade encouraged, nurtured, and authorized by the Law-of-the-Father.

In this sense, the ideal woman praised throughout the *Furioso* is not like a man but like the woman men like: chaste before marriage, chaste after, and chaste throughout; chaste in mind, chaste in actions, and chaste in reactions. In order to become that woman—and she does it more than willingly—Bradamante needs to abandon whatever is unwomanly in her, specifically her place as a woman warrior in the social arena, her role as *Venus armata*. Since the narrative enforces different subject positions for male and female individuals, Bradamante cannot pursue with impunity both political and domestic aims. Rather, her course is that of an androgynous-looking woman who, having embarked on a quest dictated by a desire for a man that is characterized as both a sexual desire and a desire for fulfillment through the other, eventually understands her societal duty, stops playing the warrior, and embraces her womanliness.

Given her destiny, spelled out as early as Canto 3, of being progenitrix of the men of the Este dynasty (there is no mention of women for now),[2] we know that Bradamante must *a priori* be as compassionate, nurturing, virtuous, obedient, and meek, as well as beautiful and chaste, as we would expect an idealized female dynast to be—and as are, in fact, the idealized women of the Este family whom Ariosto celebrates: Isabella, Beatrice, and Eleonora. Apart from their beauty, they were famous, he writes, "di pietà, di gran cor, di gran prudenza, / di somma e incomparabil continenza" (for "mercy, courage, prudence, matchless continence" [13, 57]), the sine qua non of aristocratic wives in the treatises of the period on women. The same applies to Vittoria Colonna, the other woman praised in the text as an example of imitable womanhood: a chaste wife ("casta mogliere," 37, 20) famous for writing of her endless, and purely spiritual, love for a husband already dead.

As historians have pointed out, the rise of capitalism in the Renaissance redefined external social relationships, particularly changes in workplace relations between employers and workers, and internal ones within the conjugal family, such as relations between husbands and wives or parents and children. The discovery of childhood as a stage in human growth, the new emphasis on domesticity in the choice of marriage alliances, and the pristine authority that the husband/father rushed to seize within the household have been the subject of far-reaching inquiries. Philippe Aries uses iconography to bear on some of his conclusions, Richard Goldthwaite relies on building changes, and Kelly-Gadol foregrounds gender. What is unquestionable is that the Renaissance saw a reassessment of the roles of husband and wife within the nuclear or extended family and in society at large. Legislation concerning the family, for example, increased during the period: specific laws were enacted to regulate every facet of everyday life from homosexuality to orphan child care, and merchant families began keeping genealogical records.[3]

This new attitude toward family life brought sexual and gender differences into question, and as a result, for a short while, there was room for experimentation in sex roles. Catherine Belsey suggests that a "radical discontinuity in the meaning of the family, which is not in any sense an evolution, produces a gap in which definitions of other modes of being for women are momentarily visible. . . . The redefinition of marriage entails a redefinition of the feminine" ("Disrupting Sexual Difference," 178–79). Stephen Greenblatt argues that the fascination that the literature of the period displayed for cross-dressed female characters was closely bound up with the fascination with male self-identity. Women, Greenblatt writes, were represented as acquiring their own identity by first passing "through the state of being men" ("Fiction and Friction," 92). The statement reminds us once again how extensive was women's use in literature as stand-ins for men's problems; even their travesty, Greenblatt tells us, is represented because, paradoxically, it is important not to their self-definition but to that of men.[4]

With a gusto unknown in earlier days, the Renaissance literary world frequently deployed lady knights, transvestites, amazons, nymphs, and sirens; during this same period, moreover, Ovid's hermaphroditic stories reached the apex of their revival, and theaters bustled with comedies of twins, mistaken identities, and cross-dressed characters. Even homosexuality came to be less frowned upon, although anti-sodomy laws became tougher.[5] All these activities later either disappeared with the gradual acceptance of Counter-Reformation orthodox postures or were incorporated, with important modifications, into new genres (e.g., the pastoral).

Along with a specific emphasis on property and legitimacy, the Renaissance also lavished attention on the family as the proper place for sexual love within a legally and religiously sanctified union. The period saw the publication of celebratory epithalamic poetry, such as Pontano's *De amore coniugali*, and of treatises on the family aiming at normalizing women's domestication, such as Francesco Barbaro's *De re uxoria* and especially Alberti's *I libri della famiglia*.[6] In this sense, a warrior woman such as Bradamante, who roams the woods in search of her future predestined husband, epitomizes both Renaissance trends: the tendency toward the representation of the freak, brought about by shifting perceptions of gender roles; and that toward the representation of the chaste, brought about by the reorganization of the nuclear family. By desiring more strongly from the very beginning to be chaste rather than to be a freak, Bradamante aligns herself with the law and is rewarded with an enduring place in the *Furioso*. To emphasize her restoration to Christian order, she is eventually given in marriage by none other than Charlemagne himself, as if she were his own dutiful daughter: "Fansi le nozze splendide e reali, / . . . / Carlo ne piglia cura, e le fa quali / farebbe, maritando una sua figlia" ("The wedding was of suitably regal splendour, for it was the emperor himself who took charge of the preparations—for all the world as if he were marrying off his own daughter" [46, 73]).

In rewriting Boiardo's romance epic, Ariosto consciously adds the flux of history, the inevitability of death, and a moral overtone to what in the *Innamorato* was an endless, episodic, digressive, interlaced accrual of actions.[7] The curtailing of the quest motive for the sake of closure and the new importance that power, prestige, and authority slowly acquire in the overarching narrative are also evident in the shift between the first and the third version of the *Furioso*.[8] Closure brings normativeness, which in epic narratives usually translates into the true hero's triumph over a false one and in his being rewarded with a throne and a wife. The Ruggiero story is a typical one of a growing man leaving the security of his retreat in the mountains in order to prove his worth and find his place in the world. In the process of balancing desire and law, he discovers who he is and who his parents are and converts to the proper religion. His dual rewards are the wife he has wanted all along and the kingdom he never thought he could have. As in all Oedipal narratives, he is allowed repeated mistakes, changes of mind, and shifting loyalties, even when he seems to have clearly understood his lesson.

The Bradamante story travels a different path. As a woman, Bradamante seems to know her goal quite clearly, since she has imbedded in her, as Cesare Segre flatly puts it, the vocation of a mother ("una vocazione di madre di famiglia," 19). Unlike Ruggiero, Bradamante needs no education through false starts, no changes of mind, no lapses, and no inner growth to propel her toward marriage and maternity. She is never allowed to doubt her own commitment toward Ruggiero, even when Ruggiero forgets his own toward her. Marriage, in any case, whether desired or not, was women's only possible avenue at the time, apart from enforced spinsterhood; female militancy, although often entertained in literature, was an unlikely option in everyday life.[9]

Not only is Bradamante stable in her goals, but she is never on the verge of desiring anything or anybody not already desired, from the beginning of the *Furioso* or even in Boiardo's urtext. And what she desires is marriage. Ruggiero perpetually wants something different from what he is offered, which makes him fall back into the same situations or sins from which he has just been rescued, even with the ring of reason in his possession. Bradamante, however, wants nothing but Ruggiero, wants him only legally as her husband, and only after he has become a proper choice from a religious perspective. In this sense, Bradamante's quest may be judged unconventional but not transgressive. No matter what the circumstances, she is a paragon of faithfulness. And yet, because her role rewrites gender-defined rules of conduct pertaining to quests, Tasso found it absolutely inappropriate that a woman could be made to do what is typically a man's job, that is, to pursue a person of the other gender. Tasso was particularly incensed that from an apparently unmanly man such as Ruggiero, Ariosto would presume to create the august family of the Estes, the same one Tasso himself would celebrate two generations later.[10]

To be sure, Ariosto cannot be reproached for postponing re-addressing and redressing the quest movement of his couple. If at the beginning he lets a woman do the pursuing, as early as the middle of the book he sends the woman home to wait for her beloved's request of her hand from her father. Still, although narratively important, this particular reversal is hardly needed to reverse gender positions. True, at the start Bradamante is active whereas Ruggiero seems to lose himself in self-made illusions, but he, too, has an important goal of his own: the search for an identity. This quest requires, above all, faithfulness to the highest father, the king, and not to the companion he is destined to marry for the sake of future legitimate issue. And as with every predestined epic hero, the end of the quest entails Ruggiero's winning, among other prizes, his beloved, although he constitutes the single prize Bradamante aspires to obtain in her own quest.

In Boiardo's *Innamorato*, Bradamante faithfully answers Charlemagne's call to arms to defend Christianity. In the *Furioso*, however, she places the pursuit of a man ahead of her duties as a warrior, for no sooner is she introduced to a stunned Sacripante in Canto 1, than she is presented as a proper exemplar of womanhood, "una gentil donzella. / Ella è gagliarda ed è più bella molto" ("a gentle damsel. / She is brave, but, more than that, she is beautiful" [1, 69–70]). By the time a messenger reaches her in Canto 2 with a request for help from Marseille, her own fiefdom, readers are not surprised at her decision not to respond to the call until she has rescued Ruggiero. Ruggiero, on the other hand, keeps his duty to Agramante too much in the forefront and as a result forgets his promise to Bradamante. It is not because of Atlante, for example, that he does not get baptized, for after the destruction of his second castle Ruggiero is free to do as he pleases and still does not act. He thus finds himself in a number of awkward situations precisely because of his delays, as when he is chosen to joust with Bradamante's brother, Rinaldo, to solve the Christian-pagan conflict once and for all (38, 68–70).

Bradamante has none of Olimpia's problems with matrimonial goals. Not only is she in love with the right man, but it is even written in the stars that she should be in love with him. Lest she forget her future maternal duty, she is reminded of it (and so are the readers) so early in the narrative that no innuendo can ever be made about her honor. With such a genealogy, who would dare to question her reputation? Thus Bradamante can easily have supper with men, although the same is not possible for Angelica; she can keep company with knights in deep woods, and they will experience no temptation, although these settings are unsafe for Isabella and Doralice.

Bradamante never desires anybody but Ruggiero; growth by

sexual trial is not an avenue open to "good" women. For instance, she cannot demonstrate that she is continent because that would prove that a different sexual choice is available to her. In fact, to preserve her right to be in the story, she needs both to be chaste and to have a reputation for chastity, and this reputation must be inscribed in her outfit even when she dresses as a man. Thus, in Canto 1, she appears in white clothing and rides a white horse: "Candido come nieve è il suo vestire, / un bianco pennoncello ha per cimiero" ("His raiment was white as snow, and a white plume crested his helmet" [1, 60]).

Ruggiero is able to justify both his victories and his failures in the name of male honor, but Bradamante is not given a serious task as a warrior, no matter what her first appearance in the poem conveys. Her role does not allow her to prove herself in combat for combat's sake or to improve in the act of proving herself. Bradamante fights men and women, but we are soon told that most of her prowess comes from her magic spear and therefore that she is not as skilled as she appears.[11] This spear overcomes the (male) enemy but does not kill him, it stuns but does not pierce, and is therefore phallic rather than castrating, sufficiently empowering but not overtly dangerous. Unlike Ruggiero, who casts away Atlante's shield because he is ashamed to win with its supernatural advantages, Bradamante remains unaware of the power of her enchanted weapon, as if she were too narcissistic to notice or too sure of herself to acknowledge the comic results generated by its use. Being a woman, we know that the only lance Bradamante can have must necessarily be magic; moreover, being an image of phallic power, the lance can only be given to her, given indeed by the most critically admired representative of law and reason in the text, Astolfo.[12]

As a warrior, Bradamante's spoils of war are also scant. She kills few men: one in the *Furioso*, Pinabello; and two in the *Innamorato*, Martasino and Daniforte. Bradamante refuses to kill even when expressly advised to do so, as in the case of her first encounter with Pinabello. Not surprisingly, the only duel she loses is the one with her husband, since it is narratively and ideologically unthinkable that she could win it. Nor is Bradamante allowed any serious joust with a female knight: the encounter with Marfisa is treated comically.[13]

When dressed in full panoply, Bradamante is customarily addressed as an equal, that is, as a man, whether the other person is aware of her gender or not. No sooner, however, does she take off her helmet and show her hair than she is addressed as a woman, and her representation becomes thoroughly sexualized (as in the episode of her presentation at court in Fiordispina's castle, for instance, or following the discovery of her identity in the Rocca di Tristano episode). Moreover, the knights she defeats feel psychologically castrated when they realize who defeated them. Rodomonte hides in a cave after she makes him fall from his own bridge, Sacripante is so stunned that he cannot rape Angelica, and the three Northern kings refuse to wear armor or carry arms for the rest of their days in France.[14]

Bradamante's choice of masculine clothing suggests that she has seized the phallus for herself and that she knows what counts in the world of men: a certain boldness and boastfulness, a good horse, a reliable spear, shining armor, and, of course, the ability to treat others assertively, as if she were a man. With this accoutrement of phallic signifiers, she appears so manly that her encounter with Pinabello in Canto 2 is a parody of the knight / damsel-in-distress topos with a reversal of gender roles: a masculinized Bradamante does the rescuing and a feminized Pinabello does the crying. But since such a male-identified woman can have only a short life in narrative, the project of the epic, as I understand it, is to define the limits of her appropriation of paternal rights, and to show that her choice of unconventional clothing and of an unfeminine role is temporary and, paradoxically, made in the name of feminine and not masculine goals.

Bradamante's cross-dressing is in any case hardly an inversion or a perversion. As I briefly contended in the previous chapter, Bradamante assumes some of the trappings of masculinity but does not subvert them. If anything, Ariosto continuously reminds readers of her femininity, even when her clothes or her behavior would suggest its lack. This is not to say that the author refuses to use examples of sexual nonconformity in his romance epic, since he does so at least twice. The Mankilling women story in Cantos 19 and 20, in which Amazon-like women refuse men except for strictly reproductive purposes, for example, parallels that of Marganorre in Canto 37, in which one man's misogyny dictates social separation between the sexes.[15] Still, I would claim that even these extreme rejections of the other gender are hardly transgressive on their own, for they somehow recuperate a place for rebellion and unconventionality within an ordered society.

The reinscription of transgression offers in fact a clear indication of how ideology works. The Mankilling women and the men of Marganorre's city do not practice homosexuality, no matter how deeply they hate the opposite gender. They are essentially heterosexual, for power, rather than erotic choice, is the springboard for their unorthodox behavior. For the Mankilling women, homophobia is the outcome of their anxiety about their psychological and sexual identity; for Marganorre, misogyny is the result of paranoia. In the case of women, even in utopia Ariosto is unable to envision a gynocracy. Unlike Marganorre's, in fact, the reign of the women of Laiazzo is one that includes men and makes a king out of any man who defeats ten men in battle and satisfies ten women in bed ("del letto e del governo . . . consorti"; "[he is] invited . . . to share their beds and rule with them" [20, 31]). This is hardly a female fantasy. Marianne Shapiro writes that in this city men are "relentlessly exploited by the institutionalized lust and domination of women" (*Poetics of Ariosto*, 180). But I think that these women must have little lust if they content themselves with sharing a man with nine other female citizens. Caring little for sexual gratifications because they are fully aware of the problems that sex created for their ancestors, they limit copulation to strictly reproductive goals. Yet Ariosto describes their power as castrating. This point is illustrated once again, as it often is in the text, through a reversal of traditional clothing choices: the men in Laiazzo are required to don skirts. They have no phallus left.

The same process of normalization by recuperation works for Marfisa. She does indeed enter the narrative as a castrating Amazon, slicing up men with gusto (by age sixteen she has killed the king of India to avoid rape), but before long she gets rewritten into a much more acceptable feminine persona. First, Marfisa is made to embrace Christian faith and society through a climactic decision to abandon her pagan religion once she hears of her genealogy from the ghost-like voice of a father-identified Atlante. Then, since recuperation into the dominant order also requires an ideological recuperation into femininity—at least of sorts—she is given more of the overt characteristics of her gender. To be sure, she does not behave as a womanly woman, but at least she behaves like a sister, a role whose nurturing, caring characteristics do not get lost in her society.

In this context, Bradamante's movement from Amazon to wife becomes a commentary on the process of construction of her femininity. Page DuBois defines Amazons as preadolescent "female/ male beings." Their Amazonian years "represent a stage in the evolution of the individual human being before sexual differentiation" (*Centaurs and Amazons*, 69). For William Tyrrell, "The Amazon myth concerns the specter of daughters who refuse their destiny and fail to make the accepted transition through marriage to wife and motherhood. Amazons are daughters in limbo, neither men nor women nor nubile girls. . . . They are beautiful women who arouse men sexually, but their appeal cannot be civilized in marriage, its proper sphere, and so is loose, socially unproductive, and dangerous" (65–66). It is just such a looseness that a politically approved and religiously correct union, such as that between the two progenitors of the Estes, needs to destroy in the *Furioso* through the recovery of the marginal female into a structure of exchange and into the heterosexual imperative.[16] Monique Wittig and Sande Zeig (5) see the harmony of a world of self-sufficient Amazons destroyed by motherhood. The Amazons who join in the new society are called mothers, they write, whereas those who refuse to join are considered eternal children and are banished from the cities of the mother.

The Amazon myth, then, like the stories of the Amazon-like characters in this romance epic, is a myth about the position of males (and therefore of females) and about the necessity for normative social customs. In other words, it is a myth that predicates the conflation of what a subject is and what biology has determined the subject to be, of psyche and anatomy. It is understandable, then, that Virgil's Camilla, to whom Bradamante is often compared, loses her life, whereas Bradamante is allowed to crown hers with a literal crown. As Amazon, Camilla has no place in the new Latin society that Aeneas is creating. She is unassimilable, threatening and proud to be so.[17] None of this is true for Bradamante, who more resembles Lavinia, Aeneas's predestined wife and mother of future dynasts.[18]

Seen in this light, it is inaccurate to complain that Bradamante
is too conventional at the end of this romance epic, for her final
actions are consistent with her characterization throughout. Pio
Rajna (*Le fonti*, 54) laments Bradamante's final narrative transfor-
mation into a good daughter who lacks the courage to disobey
her mother.[19] But I believe that Bradamante cannot narratively dis-
obey parental judgment and choose a husband for herself when
her narrative destiny is that of being an obliging wife, a duty that
presupposes her being an obedient daughter and sister.[20] Rebellion
is hardly a word one associates with a maiden destined to fulfill
biological dreams and yearning to take her place in history.

The construction of Bradamante's femininity is a lengthy nar-
rative process. Here I follow it through the epic by concentrating
on a wound, a literal wound on the head that Boiardo describes at
length in the *Innamorato* and that keeps reappearing in the *Furioso*.
The first and only encounter between Bradamante and Ruggiero
in the *Innamorato* (3, 5, 45) is replete with changes and reversals.
Ruggiero comes upon a Saracen and a Christian locked in combat.
The former is Rodomonte and the latter is Bradamante, although
Ruggiero is unaware of either identity. He asks the Saracen to let
the knight depart in order to join the Christian troops retreating
to Paris after Charlemagne's rout at Montalbano. Rodomonte's re-
fusal incenses Ruggiero. Such lack of pity for the sake of a victory
in the field makes him challenge the Saracen directly. This oppor-
tunity allows the Christian knight to leave. Soon after, however,
she comes back, sorry for having permitted someone else to fight
in her stead and curious about the identity of the kind enemy. At
her return the combat has just concluded, and Ruggiero stands
magnanimously over a stunned Rodomonte.[21]

Ruggiero tells the knight, still dressed in full panoply, that he
will accompany him since there are pirates along the route. This is
an unexpected posture on his part. Bradamante accepts, and since
she burns with a desire to know his identity, she asks his name. As
if unconsciously aware that this meeting will have a momentous
outcome, Ruggiero does not limit himself to revealing his patro-
nymic, but relates his whole genealogy, as far back as his Trojan
ancestors, until he thinks he has bored his companion. Asked "his"
name, Bradamante surprises him by declaring a female identity and

no story of patriarchal succession from father to son as a way of situating herself. She then removes her helmet and asks him to do the same. Suddenly Saracen troops appear, and Martasino wounds her on the head. In the mayhem that follows, the two would-be lovers lose sight of each other, never to be reunited again in the *Innamorato*: Ruggiero is sent magically away from France (3, 8, 57), and Bradamante is next engaged in the adventure with Fiordispina (3, 8–9), with which the poem abruptly ends.

Bradamante's revelation of her sex through the removal of her helmet and the falling of her hair is a stock feature of medieval and Renaissance narratives.[22] Added here is the wound, a wound that comes at the critical moment of her meeting with her eventual spouse and constitutes the climax of the narrative, a reenactment, for a purpose, of an Oedipal crisis. Ariosto takes the episode verbatim from Boiardo and introduces it directly and emphatically into the first presentation of the couple in the *Furioso*. Recognizing Bradamante after she has freed him from the first Castle of Atlante in Canto 4, Ruggiero "le fè buona e gratissima accoglienza; // come a colei che più che gli occhi sui, / più che 'l suo cor, più che la propria vita / Ruggiero amò dal dì ch'essa per lui / si trasse l'elmo, onde ne fu ferita" ("gave her the heartiest welcome—/ the sort of welcome he would extend to one whom he loved more than his eyes, more than his heart, more than his very life ever since the day she had removed her helmet for his sake, with the result that she was wounded" [4, 40–41]). Bradamante's first encounter with Ruggiero in the text establishes her masquerade as a man although everybody knows that she is a woman. It also underlines reversed gender roles, for Bradamante wins as a man (that is, by courage, strength, and cunning) while a fatherly wizard, Atlante, keeps Ruggiero in a castle of pleasure in a more or less feminized status.

Not surprisingly, Ariosto uses the motif of the wound again during the couple's second encounter. In Canto 22, after the destruction of the second Castle of Atlante, a newly reunited Bradamante and Ruggiero meet a woman who asks them to save Ricciardetto. The Ricciardetto and Fiordispina episode is based on the fact that Bradamante has had to cut her hair because of her wound and is later taken to be a man by a woman who falls in love with her. As Ariosto restates it, Bradamante was "ferita da uno stuol

de Saracini / che senza l'elmo la trovar per via, / fu di scorciarsi as-
tretta i lunghi crini, / se sanar volse d'una piaga ria / ch'avea con
gran periglio ne la testa" ("wounded by a party of Saracens who
had come upon her without a helmet, so she had been obliged
to cut her long tresses if her dangerous headwound was to heal"
[25, 26]).

In the couple's third encounter, in Canto 36, the emphasis is
again on wounds, but this time they are displaced onto man and
are not real. Dejected because of Ruggiero's behavior, Bradamante
tries unsuccessfully to wound herself, then goes to look for him
because she would rather that he slay her. By the time she ar-
rives at the Saracen camp, however, she is so jealous of Marfisa,
whom she is sure is having a dalliance with her beloved, that once
again changing her mind, she decides to wound Ruggiero directly.
Bradamante is of course unable to injure or even to unseat the man
she loves: "La donna, ch'a ferirlo e a fargli offesa / venia con mente
di pietà rubella, / non potè sofferir, come fu appresso, / di porlo in
terra e fargli oltraggio espresso" ("The damsel, who was closing to
strike and injure him, her mind hardened against pity, could not
bring herself, once she was near, to throw him to the ground and
do him intended harm" [36, 37]). In fact, she will refuse to wound
Ruggiero even when expressly asked to do so for providential rea-
sons. In Canto 13, Melissa warns her that a figure resembling her
beloved will suddenly appear and ask for help, but that this double
is another of Atlante's tricks to save his putative son from his des-
tiny. Bradamante's safest action, Melissa emphasizes, is to undo
the magic by getting rid of Ruggiero's look-alike. At the moment
of truth, however, Bradamante chooses not to believe Melissa.

In their fourth encounter, Bradamante is bent on wounding
Ruggiero in earnest, thinking him to be another man, Leone, but
the task again proves impossible: "Brama ch'ella / entri nel ferro,
e sempre al vivo giunga, / anzi ogni colpo sì ben tagli e fore, / che
vada sempre a ritrovargli il core" (She "willed it [the sword] to
penetrate his armour and pierce his living flesh; she wanted each
cut and thrust to be so well delivered as to attain his heart" [45,
70]). Ruggiero will indeed be seriously wounded, but only by the
most manly characters in the text, his only true, religious enemies,
Mandricardo and Rodomonte.

The enactment of Bradamante's wound and haircut, repeated at key moments in the narrative and when she is close to Ruggiero, thus stands for something with which woman has to reckon consistently in representation: the retelling of her castration. Psychoanalysis teaches that by acknowledging castration the individual enters into the symbolic order. The first two references to this female warrior's wounds demonstrate that Bradamante is not a man, for she has literally inscribed on her body the symbolic castration that makes her a woman. The latter two come after she has entered a thoroughly feminine stage with her sojourn in her parents' house and show that a "normal" woman cannot wound (castrate) man. In other words, the pre-Oedipal and phallic woman warrior is shown as castrated to remind readers that she is a woman, and the post-Oedipal womanly woman is shown as non-castrating to point out that she is not dangerous.

There is a further reason for producing Bradamante as already castrated. Since dressing as a man phallicizes woman, cross-dressing should stand for woman's denial of castration. Such a construction could work for Marfisa but definitely should not for Bradamante, given her destiny. The narrative strategy, then, is to deny Bradamante any phallic empowerment by showing at each opportunity that she is only pretending to be a man. Thus, she wears armor, but the armor is a strange color—white; she has a lance, but the lance does not kill.

In Boiardo's work the removal of the headgear amounts to a literal revelation of one's sex and leads immediately to the punishment of being wounded.[23] This wound requires a haircut, which in Bradamante's case makes it impossible to place her specifically in either sex, a problem that Ricciardetto recalls in Canto 25 as being a recurrent feature of their childhood. The act of unveiling is typical of the Oedipus complex, for the establishment of sexual difference comes, according to Freud, through a momentous seeing, an uncovering. In the case of women, the lifting of the veil/ helmet should uncover nothing since there is nothing to see in them, from the male point of view. Freud writes that the discovery of sexual difference in women and the threat of castration that such a discovery engenders in men lead the male child to repress his desire for the mother and to associate with the father, who stands for authority. The girl has a longer route to follow. Upon seeing, she does not fear the castration that makes the boy opt for assimilation with the male/father, but acknowledges that she is already castrated. She then associates with her mother, chooses her father as a love object, and replaces her envy for the penis with the acknowledgment that she will be able to have a penis substitute in the son she will engender through a father figure ("Some Psychical Consequences" and "Female Sexuality"). This is Freud's normative path; it is also possible that a woman may disavow her castration or refuse this definition of femininity altogether. In fact, even after a woman has made a choice, Freud writes, there are some fluctuations in gender identifications and some possible, if temporary, returns to a phallic state ("Femininity," 131).

It is by seeing oneself in the eye of the other and by taking pleasure in seeing the other's pleasure, Lacan later emphasizes, that the onlooker constitutes himself as a subject. For Ruggiero, the act of seeing translates into his falling in love with what he sees.[24] Bradamante's vision, however, is limited because she is unable to see what she is looking for: Ruggiero does not take off his helmet. The refusal to specularize man while holding woman to the gaze of the other both posits castration in the female *a priori* and phallicizes the male. Since he is heard but not seen, he is placed in an authoritative position. Thus, whereas the removal of her helmet and her abandonment of her fight with Rodomonte feminize Bradamante and show that her masculinity is a public masquerade, Ruggiero's retention of all the emblems of a knight, from the headpiece to the sword with which he has just stunned the most ferocious of the pagans, emphasizes his possession of masculinity and his power to control what he does and what he sees.[25] Bradamante's sense of self, on the other hand, is soon given as less (or as no longer) autonomous, since from this very moment her quest for a phallic self (as a warrior) is forever undermined by her new quest for a feminine self (as a woman in love).

Disparity in the act of looking reflects cultural constructions of gender differences. As Susan Stewart writes, being invisible to the person to whom it belongs, a face "becomes a text, a space which must be 'read' and interpreted in order to exist. The body of a woman . . . is spoken by her face, by the articulation of another's reading. Apprehending the image becomes a mode of possession. . . . The face is what belongs to the other; it is unavailable to the woman herself" (125).[26] It is important that this unveiling of woman stop at the face. Showing more would either be understood as too assertive a posture on her part, and for this reason could arouse castration fear in the male, or would label woman as available, thus contributing to the loss of the sense of expectation and revelation necessary to keep desire alive.

It is because this wound and the subsequent haircut make woman enter traumatically into the regime of sexual difference ("la ferita che era grande e strana"; the wound was large and strange [*Innamorato*, 3, 8, 61]) that for Lacan the symbolic phallus becomes a metaphoric emblem of plenitude. That a woman's castration must be recalled at this point in the narrative, soon after an encounter with the man destined to marry her, shows that only when represented as castrated can woman become a safe object of adult male desire, and a tame one as well, since, Freud writes, her passage through the Oedipus complex means that "she develops, like a scar, a sense of inferiority" ("Some Psychical Consequences," 253). Only if this happens is she perceived as non-threatening, because man has already acknowledged her castration and disavowed his own castratability by making the phallus the privileged signifier of his desire. Thus, he enters the symbolic with the assurance that his desire is right and powerful. As Monique Plaza points out, sexual difference becomes hierarchized, since the person who has the phallus—man—is the one socially empowered to enforce this disparity.[27]

After her first return home, which mirrors her last visit before her marriage, Bradamante assumes her femininity in earnest, has bouts of tears, and neurotically waits for news of Ruggiero. This return is preceded by three episodes, all of which work to diminish her standing as a mighty warrior and emphasize her non-manly nature. First, she becomes betrothed to Ruggiero with her request that he get baptized and ask her father for her hand in marriage (an episode that definitely establishes her daughterly obedience and conservative values); second, she kills Pinabello in a rage at having to defer to Ruggiero's injunction to leave the fight to him since he is the man; and third, she accepts Astolfo's gift of a magic lance, which from this point on makes her jousts comic and her demonstrated valor useless. Since Ruggiero does not arrive, Bradamante decides to take the initiative and return to the

world of men. At this point Ariosto inserts a narrative explicitly
dealing with gender roles. The Rocca di Tristano episode in Can-
tos 32 and 33 constitutes an addition of about 130 octaves in the
1532 edition and demonstrates the seriousness with which Ariosto
and his period questioned, however playfully, assumptions about
gender identities.

The name Tristan's Rocca immediately evokes connections with
love and the castle of love of medieval and Renaissance allegoriza-
tions. The owner of the Rocca rigidly enforces a tradition one of
his ancestors, Clodione, unwillingly established one night when
he denied the famous lover Tristan accommodation next to his
wife.[28] Tristan read this refusal as contrary to any courtly sense of
honor and responsibility; he defeated the jealous husband, locked
him outside the house, and spent the night inside.

The custom presently enforced in the Rocca is gender based:
only one knight or one party of knights with their lady or ladies
is allowed inside each night. If a newcomer, or a group of new-
comers, arrives (the subject here is understood to be male), the
occupants have to defend their right to remain inside by winning a
joust. A contest between women is judged by standards applied to
their gender: only the most beautiful has the right to stay. Brada-
mante arrives in full armor, is told about the custom, and asks to
joust with the other knights already lodged there, in this case the
three Northern kings. She defeats them all and finds herself inside.
Everyone involved is sure that she is a man because she wins like
a man.

Later, when she removes her headgear to get ready for dinner,
her hair falls down: "Caderon sparsi / giù per le spalle, e la scopriro
a un tratto / e la feron conoscer per donzella, / non men che fiera in
arme, in viso bella" ("Her hair fell loosely over her shoulders, all
at once revealing her for a maiden no less beautiful than fierce in
battle" [32, 79]). Suddenly the game changes, and the owner of the
Rocca makes clear that Bradamante cannot stay unless she wins
the other contest, designed for women. Already inside the castle
is fair Ullania, ambassador of the Queen of Iceland. Bradamante
easily wins this contest as well, but feels pity for the other woman
and refuses to acknowledge the result of the competition on the
grounds that she has entered the castle as a man and plans to stay
there as such, no matter what her gender is determined to be.

The undressing of a female character is usually the occasion for an erotic and psychic representation. As in the Ricciardetto-Fiordispina episode, here identities shift and are at best unstable. What appears to be a man is a woman, and femininity can literally be worn to empower the individual (as in the case of Ricciardetto) or disempower him (as in the case of Bradamante). According to Freud, absolute gender differentiation does not exist, and a subject of either sex often changes his/her position in sexual fantasy. The threat of castration eventually establishes the difference by making men, much more willingly than women, "submit to the great exigencies of life" ("Some Psychical Consequences," 258). For Freud ("Three Essays," 144–46), the choice of an appropriate object-love is not easy, and the heterosexual result is not a given. The same sort of instability is basic to Lacanian theory ("Meaning of the Phallus").

Bradamante argues that her gender is whatever she claims it is at any particular moment. She affirms first of all that difference cannot be located in hair length, because there are men with long hair.[29] Nor can difference be discovered through clothing, since she is taken for a man when wearing armor. Difference is not to be seen in personal behavior either, for everyone considered her behavior manly until they saw her hair. Even technically she could not be called into the unequal contest, she argues, because she is perceived to be a man, and the rule states that men will fight men and women will prove themselves with women: "La legge vostra vuol che ne sian spinte / donne da donne, e non da guerrier vinte" ("Your law requires that women should be ousted by women, not by warriors" [32, 103]). Nor does she claim that she is androgynous, asexual, or bisexual for preferring to dress unconventionally. For Bradamante, difference is located in the body and can be ascertained only when the body is naked: "Ma chi dirà, se tutta non mi spoglio, / s'io sono o s'io non son quel che'è costei?" ("Who will say, unless I take off all my clothes, whether or not I am of the same sex as she?" [32, 102]). Since what is hidden is unknown, one should not reach conclusions of any sort, especially when they can be painful to others ("E quel che non si sa non si dè dire, / e tanto men, quando altri n'ha a patire"; "What is not known should be left unspoken, especially when someone would suffer from it" [32, 102]). Bradamante, in short, grounds gender difference in biology, which makes it too difficult to verify. Outside biology, she claims, gender is too unstable a category and cannot be precisely positioned or enforced in the individual, because it is constructed by social, aesthetic, and political discourses. Everything is relative because subject positions are not fixed. In other words, Bradamante—who wittily anticipates here both Foucault and Lacan—chooses to use gender ambivalence to her own advantage.

As I pointed out earlier, it is important in social relationships that one take a place in relation to the signifier phallus by assuming an appropriate subject position and by defining oneself as either male or female. But Bradamante claims that gender positions can shift and that in her present situation she possesses the phallus whether or not she is perceived as having it biologically. To underline the point, she concludes her argument for indeterminacy with a strong phallic statement: "E s'alcuno di dir che non sia buono / e *dritto* il mio giudizio sarà *ardito*, / sarò per *sostenergli* a suo piacere, che 'l mio sia vero, e falso il suo parere" ("And if anyone dares maintain that my judgment is not straight and hardy, I am ready to sustain it against him any time he chooses—mine is right, his is wrong!" [32, 106 (modified)]; my italics).

But if woman is incomplete because of a missing part, and if what is needed to make her whole is absent even as gender fluidity is invoked as an asset, then she needs to be put together. The way to create this collage is to emphasize those attributes that she usually displays within culture: beauty, femininity, powerlessness, emotionalism. That is, the narrative must construct a fully gendered character even though Bradamante herself refuses to take up a specific subject position in public. By gendering her, Ariosto makes her discourse of genderlessness comic rather than subversive and can therefore recuperate it as harmless.

One way of gendering Bradamante is to give her traditional feminine characteristics. Thus, the narrative of gender indeterminacy in the Rocca di Tristano is preceded and followed by episodes of female helplessness meant to frame Bradamante's femininity. Before engaging in the adventure that leads her to the Rocca, Bradamante hears of Ruggiero's rumored relationship with Marfisa and hysterically decides to commit suicide. She fails, however, because she forgets that she is fully armed and that her sword will not pierce her armor.[30] This episode trivializes her male-identified stance as a warrior and shows that she is ineffective and melodramatic, that her crying while wearing manly accoutrements is grotesque, and that the way she resolves sexual frustration is too masochistic. In short, by demonstrating that it is impossible for Bradamante to behave like a man, the text produces a correct feminine subject position. Later that night, while still in the Rocca, Bradamante is demasculinized a second time with a narrative follow-up: she is portrayed as desperately crying over Ruggiero. The scene confirms that she is just a hysteric, despite her earlier public bragging about her manly valor.

Another way Ariosto suggests a correct feminine position is by showing a fully feminized woman opposite Bradamante. Like the queen who sends her to France with a shield and the promise of her body to the mightiest warrior, Ullania defines womanhood as a commodity to be won and sees beauty as woman's most important asset. At the Rocca, she abides by the rule of the beauty contest between women and fears for her safety after Bradamante wins. Fortunately for her, Bradamante rushes to her defense, as she always does whenever women are involved.[31]

A third way of gendering Bradamante is by showing her as a properly feminized object for the onlooker. Immediately after she is perceived as being a woman, Bradamante in fact stops being portrayed as active. Her beauty becomes an issue, and she is no longer an equal other (a knight) but the other to be known (a woman). Judging her to be a commodity, the owner of the Rocca calls on his servants to assess her as such: "Chiama duo vecchi, e chiama alcune sue / donne di casa, a tal giudizio buone; / e le donzelle mira, e di lor due / chi la più bella sia, fa paragone" ("He summoned two old men and some of his maid servants as proper judges in the matter. He scrutinized the two damsels and compared them to see which one was the fairer" [32, 98]). With this gesture, the master of the house complies with the culturally produced image of femaleness as self-evident and judges the others' look as sufficient to put woman on the side of lack.

Bradamante's challenge of the laws governing hospitality in the Rocca di Tristano, laws dictated by a loss of faith between men and by strictly enforced gender differences, leads to a breakup of the established order. If it is impossible to tell man from woman, if male selves are in crisis and female selves refuse to be disempowered, then it is impossible to enforce roles and rules based on cultural assumptions. Bradamante also breaks the law of gender in her second joust with the three kings early the next day. Her victory shatters the rules of the contest, not so much because she wins and the kings are ridiculed as a result, but because she changes the terms of their engagement. The joust is created for men's aggrandizement and for men's goals. This means that their prize for victory is a commodified woman. When she overcomes them, she undercuts their philosophy about women's powerlessness, and they willingly give up in shame all symbols of masculinity: lance, sword, armor, and armorial bearings. As in the case of Rodomonte in Canto 29, Ariosto renders the three kings' feminization in a theatrical fashion.

Still, before we see woman as the destabilizer of social customs and identities, it pays to point out that the entire adventure in the Rocca is delimited by a lengthy discourse on power that effectively recuperates the threat that Bradamante creates through her reclamation of equal sexual empowerment. This discourse is written in a tapestry that so fascinates Bradamante and Ullania that the cook cannot serve the evening meal. The tapestry describes future historical events and constitutes the most sustained effort on Ariosto's part at historical analysis and comprehension of Italian politics.[32] In this tapestry, described in an ekphrasis of fifty-eight octaves, Merlino, its creator, magically envisions a world of men and arms, a world in which it is understood that power goes naturally to men and, conversely, that one does not get power by appropriating signifiers of masculinity. Earlier, in Canto 3, Merlino had visualized another future history of men for Bradamante, that of the House of Este, which she herself would begin with the procreation of her son. One reason for having women, rather than men, once again function as privileged onlookers to histories of men's valor is that they are outsiders and thus less likely to contest the representation. In other words, women are chosen to confirm male readings of dynastic genealogies because they have no recognized role in creating them.

In the 1532 edition of the *Furioso*, the description of the tapestry is preferred over an ekphrasis of Ullania's shield.[33] The discarded description of the shield is available today in an autograph fragment of fifteen octaves titled "Lo scudo della regina Elisa"

("Queen Elisa's Shield"). Santorre Debenedetti speculates that the fragment, which concludes the story of Ullania, was intended to be inserted at the end of the *Furioso*, after peace had been achieved and the dynastic couple had celebrated their wedding. In that version, Ullania brings to Charlemagne the shield that the beautiful virgin queen Elisa of Iceland wishes to offer to the French warrior best in valor and courtesy before offering herself. Charlemagne hesitates in accepting the gift because he is aware of the discord that the prize is bound to generate among his paladins. In the fragment, there is an allusion to the possible jealousy between Orlando and Rinaldo (XXI). The same allusion is present in the final edition of the *Furioso*; upon hearing the story, Bradamante correctly speculates that the shield is bound to bring disagreements in the Christian camp because it will make men fight over who is the best among them. There is no further mention of the shield. It is plausible to speculate that had the fragment been inserted, the closure achieved with marriage in the 1532 text would have proved temporary, since it is in the structure of mimetic desire to be endlessly repetitive. That Ariosto decided to act otherwise testifies to his close attention to the overall structure of the *Furioso*.[34]

In the unpublished fragment, Ullania recounts that the shield she carries is the only one remaining of twelve made by the Sybil, each covering a century. It describes the history of Italy from the Emperor Constantine to the Sack of Rome, and the Sybil is portrayed as dismayed at the consequences of Constantine's decision to move the imperial seat from Rome to Constantinople. Ullania explains the stories on the shield to distract Bradamante, who is on the verge of crying. What Ullania possesses is a version of history written by a woman, from a woman's point of view, and with a woman's criticism of history. It is no wonder that this history is displaced in the final edition by a patrilineal, prophetically empowering, and ideologically correct history of Italy inscribed by the most powerful father figure in the epic, Merlino himself.

This tapestry foreshadows another tapestry made by a woman that appears at the end of the *Furioso*. This second tapestry was embroidered by Cassandra and magically transported from the East to cover the bridal bed of Ruggiero and Bradamante. It, too, describes a story of future events, in this case events more closely related to the first of Ariosto's patrons, Ippolito d'Este, whose birth is hailed and whose military actions are praised. The tapestry also harkens back to another bridal bed in the narrative, that in which Olimpia is abandoned in the middle of the night by the faithless Bireno, in Canto 10. In this sense, the Olimpia story ties in with the specific rendering of the mythical story of Ariadne and Theseus in Naxos told by Catullus in his Poem 64. Catullus recounts the abandonment of Ariadne through an ekphrasis describing the tapestry over the mythical bed of Thetis and Peleus. The story within the story in Catullus can be read as an admonishment to his new couple not to behave like their mythical counterparts, Ariadne and Theseus, and not to cast aside the moral and social values enshrined in their approved, lawful union. In the *Furioso*, the tapestry tells Bradamante, who already knows her duty ("Sol Bradamante, da Melissa istrutta / gode tra sè; che sa l'istoria tutta"; "Alone Brada- mante rejoiced in secret: instructed by Melissa, she knew their full history" [46, 98]), not to behave in socially dangerous ways for the sake of a passion, as was the case, for instance, of Olimpia/ Ariadne.[35]

Bradamante is by now so well instructed on how to read that she keeps reading in one way and sees the greatness of her progeny rather than the destruction caused by the wars that her progeny will further. Therefore, whether she knows what she is reading, as in the Cassandra tapestry, or whether she does not, as in the Rocca di Tristano, Bradamante is represented as unable to read his- tory. Her vision brings no real clarification. Tapestries are for her either aesthetic artifacts that she admires with Ullania or prophetic artifacts that she accepts as willed from above.

As these two episodes make clear, the story of Bradamante, like the story of Fiordispina and Ricciardetto in which gender distinc- tions are also blurred, ends with a refixing of gender roles and of gender characteristics. In both cases, the woman thought to be a man, as well as the man thought to be a woman, is unclothed and defined. Ricciardetto shows his phallic power and moves to affirm it both biologically and culturally; Bradamante shows her female nature when taking off her helmet and then proceeds to embody her femininity by crying and assuming a melancholic, passive atti- tude in the aftermath of the Rocca di Tristano episode. In short, both characters are made to overemphasize the stereotypical attributes of their gender specifically because they have playfully claimed that there are no such secure differences.

It is indeed only after gender boundaries have been reaffirmed and precise positions embraced that closure can be achieved. Described as not too manly, Ricciardetto eventually associates himself with the phallus, embraces knighthood, and goes on to prove himself in the world of men. Described as not too feminine, Bradamante in time embraces domesticity and goes on to prove herself in the world of nurturing women. As state and sexual politics merge, she becomes the beacon of domestic fidelity, her body no longer the possibly transgressive body of the woman warrior but the appropriate one of the mother of the state. True to her characterization, she now offers a heterosexual reconciliation in which power and phallus are located in man, and woman is the signifier not of privilege but of the other. Only then is her process of education into femininity complete, and she can resemble the ideal court lady of Castiglione's text, a woman also produced as a properly feminine type by her instituters.

In contrast, the newly married Ruggiero, finally ready to assume his historical destiny, cherishes an active life and engages in earnest exploits in and out of bed. As Ariosto writes, complicitously coupling the sexual and the political, Ruggiero jousts, dances, and wrestles all the time; whatever the activity, he always remains honorably on top ("vince sempre, e giostra il dì e la notte; / e così in danza, in lotta ed in ogni opra / sempre con molto onor resta di sopra" [46, 100]). The epic has come full circle.

Afterword

ARIOSTO HAD a great admirer in Italo Calvino, who prefaced a witty edition of the *Furioso*, wrote an enjoyable parody of the Bradamante/Ruggiero story in *Il cavaliere inesistente*, and cast Bradamante as the prototypical woman warrior in yet another novel, *Il castello dei destini incrociati*. Calvino's last book, *Mr. Palomar*, which shows no apparent influence from Ariosto, will serve for a final reflection on the politics of looking and of representing femininity in literary works.

Walking alone one morning, Mr. Palomar sees a woman suntanning with the top of her bikini removed. Passing a first time, he decides to respect her privacy and chooses to appear not to see that she is partly naked. But on second thought, he decides this posture is incorrect because it means that he is conscious of the woman's nakedness while trying to ignore it. He strolls by a second time with the intention of acknowledging her uncovered breasts, as if they were a part of nature and essentially unimportant in the scheme of things. This attitude proves equally unsatisfactory, because it means that he is objectifying the suntanning woman by seeing her as indistinguishable from the landscape. He passes by a third time with the intention of acknowledging rather than ignoring her sexuality. But he does not like this posture either because it casts him in an old-fashioned role. Finally he walks by a fourth time with the desire to include everything—her person, her breasts, and her sexuality—for he feels "good will and gratitude for the whole" of nature (11). At this point the woman gets up and leaves the scene, thoroughly infuriated by his persistent staring.

Mr. Palomar laments the fact that it is impossible for him to look at woman with "enlightened intentions" (12), for the customary way of looking and the customary response to that look seem too ingrained in society to accommodate good readings on man's part. This modern rewriting of the Angelica and the Olimpia episodes on the island of Ebuda in Ariosto and of the Campaspe episode in Castiglione reveals once again that no look can ever be innocent. It also acknowledges that woman will no longer willingly submit to an inquisitive gaze or remain silent vis-à-vis a desiring one.

How, then, can man look at woman? How can he represent what he sees? Ways have still to be found to include woman in earnest, but at least we know that she will look back, as does Titian's Venus perhaps, or more unflinchingly and with impunity, as does Manet's Olympia. In the same vein, woman is more than likely to question any representation of her and to respond, both in her own stories and in those of others. For, as Marfisa in the *Furioso* argues with poignancy, the time has come to confront—and to defy—myths of femininity: "Io sua non son, nè d'altri son che mia: / dunque me tolga a me chi mi desia" ("I belong to nobody, only to myself: who wants me must first reckon with me" [26, 79]). Interestingly, her call to arms reappears later in the century in the first treatise in Italian written by a woman. As Corinna in Moderata Fonte's *Il merito delle donne* insists, she belongs only to herself, thus she anticipates that her progress toward fame will not be marred by men's biases ("Non servo alcun, nè d'altri son che mia, / . . . / Poichè fallacia d'uom non m'interrompe, / Fama e gloria n'attendo in vita, e in morte"; I serve nobody, and belong only to myself. Since no man's fallacy interrupts my progress, I expect fame and glory for myself in life as well as in death [18–19]). Corinna may indeed be too optimistic, but she is at least serious in her claim. The women gathered around her, unlike Castiglione's court ladies, moreover, know that they have no longer to sit still; at first tentatively, and then more assuredly as the day goes on, they bestow on themselves limitless chances to express their views and represent themselves realistically as women.

Reference Matter

Notes

For complete author's names, titles, and publication data for the works cited here in short form, see the Bibliography, pp. 301–23.

INTRODUCTION

1. See Mazzacurati, "Negazione delle origini" and "Baldassar Castiglione"; Vasoli; and the essays collected in the two-volume *La corte e il cortegiano* (ed. Ossola and Prosperi, respectively). The golden years of courtly influence fell between 1480 and 1520, precisely the years in which Castiglione and Ariosto's works were being written. On the power of printing presses to foster changes, see Eisenstein. For a study of the Estense court in Ferrara, which for decades dominated political and literary life in Italy, see the study by Papagno and Quondam. For a general introduction to the period, see the essays in Chittolini, especially his "Introduzione," 7–50.

2. Ariosto was ambassador for the Estes.

3. The reference to Ariosto in the early *Cortegiano* edition by Cian ("messer Lodovico Ariosto . . . in un solo ci dà Homero e Menandro," 378 *n*14) was deleted in the final edition.

4. On the success of the *Cortegiano*, see Guidi, "Reformulations." For an estimate of copies of the *Furioso* (25,000), see Marinelli, *Ariosto and Boiardo*, 215 *n*1; Lee, *Names*, 91–92 *n*37; Dionisotti, "La letteratura italiana," 194; Beer, 227–35; and, most recently, Javitch, *Proclaiming a Classic*, chap. 1. Both texts were so successful that writing treatises and romance epics became a popular undertaking in the following decades. To give a rare example of a woman writer, Moderata Fonte (pseudonym of Modesta Pozzo) wrote both a treatise modeled on Castiglione's *Cortegiano* (*Il merito delle donne*, written in 1593, published in 1600) and a romance epic modeled on Ariosto's *Furioso* (*I tredici canti del Floridoro*, 1581).

5. See Lythe and Orgel; and Vasoli. This is clearly true not only for Italy but for all of Europe. For a similar point regarding the English Renaissance, see Montrose, 332.

6. Castiglione experienced little pleasure at court, as his private letters to his mother show (Gorni, "Il rovescio del *Cortegiano*").

7. I read *ideology* in the Althusserian sense as not specifically meaning the enforcement of a master view of life upon a lower class by a class in power, but as a system of beliefs having a pervasive presence in society through discursive and cultural practices. See also Belsey, *Critical Practice*, chap. 3; and Geertz.

8. See especially De Sanctis, 451–52; and Croce, 7.

9. Ariosto's praise of the House of Este is often muted: his hyperboles are rare by sixteenth-century standards, and his tone in many references is hardly poetic. Apart from Ippolito and Alfonso d'Este, Ariosto praises Francis I and Charles V. Surprisingly, the most adulatory reference to Ippolito is not in Ariosto, but in Castiglione: "Look at Don Ippolito d'Este, Cardinal of Ferrara, whose fortunate birth has influenced his person, his appearance, his words and all his actions. . . . When conversing with men and women of every sort, when playing or laughing or joking, he has such charming ways and such a gracious manner, that anyone who speaks to, or merely sets eyes on, the Cardinal feels a lasting affection for him" (1, 14, 48). Ariosto was to find personally how different reality was from appearance. For studies of the society and of the intellectual world in which Ariosto moved in Ferrara, see Bertoni; Piromalli; and Gundersheimer. Piromalli emphasizes Ariosto's otherness in the context of courtly culture, his belonging to a popular rather than to an aristocratic milieu. Bacchelli instead sees Ariosto as very conscious of realpolitik, like Machiavelli and Guicciardini. More recently, Zatti (147) has emphasized Ariosto's awareness of the contemporary use of poetry as a means for courtly propaganda.

10. See also Quint, *Origin and Originality*, 106. Durling takes Ariosto's position ironically: "For to suppose that Ariosto meant to suggest that he was lying in praising his patrons is tantamount to thinking that he meant to suggest that the Evangelist lied about Christ" (149). Yet I would agree with McLucas's suggestion that Orlando's throwing the cannon (a symbol of the Estes' might) into the sea after his defeat of Cimosco can be read as a metaphorical castration of the authority of the ruling prince ("Ariosto," 20).

11. See Quondam, 19.

12. See Saccone, "Prospettive"; and Moretti, 34, for a reading of the new darkness in the third version of the *Furioso*, which is marked by profit, power, and an obsession with wealth. See also Debenedetti's introduction and Bologna's essay for a study of the additions, rewritings, and corrections preceding the 1532 edition.

13. The *Cinque canti* was first published in 1545 by the editor Manu-

zio from a manuscript copy provided by Ariosto's son, Virginio. It was published again in 1548 by Giolito. The critical consensus is that Ariosto started it around 1519 and worked on revisions concurrently with other revisions he later chose to include in the definitive edition of the *Furioso*. For a good introduction to the work, see Caretti's preface. Saccone sees in Ariosto's pessimistic vision a reflection of the crisis in self-identity brought by the upheavals of the period (*Il "soggetto" del "Furioso,"* 132–35). For a reading of the *Satire* as reflecting contemporary preoccupations, see Cavalluzzi.

14. For a different view and a defense of Burckhardt's sense of self-hood, see Kerrigan and Braden (specifically, in this context, the footnote on p. 223). Recently, Patterson ("On the Margin") has reclaimed subjectivity for the Middle Ages as well, and Mazzotta ("The *Canzoniere*") has shown how much Petrarch was able to play with the concept of a shifting self. On Marxist and new historicist positions, see Patterson, "Historical Criticism," in *Negotiating the Past*, 41–74; and Howard, "The New Historicism." On the new historicists' marginalization of gender issues in debating questions of subjectivity and strategies of silencing, see Neely; and Boose.

15. In his sixth satire, Ariosto attacks the humanists in unambiguous terms: "Few humanists are without that vice which did not so much persuade, as forced, God to render Gomorrah and her neighbor wretched! . . . The vulgar laugh when they hear of someone who possesses a vein of poetry, and then they say, 'It is a great peril to turn your back if you sleep next to him'" (trans. Wiggins, 153). In the discussion in the *Cortegiano* of the value of letters and arms, Bembo defends the humanist concern for the retrieval of poetry and for the importance of letters in general, but Canossa, the court intellectual, partly dismisses the humanists' pursuit of preserving works at any cost (1, 45–46, 88–89). See also Mazzacurati, "Il 'cortegiano' e lo 'scolare.'"

16. Padoan concurs: "It is often said that the humanist-Renaissance civilization has as a fundamental tenet man's centrality, that is, it resolutely places man at the center of his actions: *quisque faber fortunae suae.* And yet, if in the chivalric romance (as in the novel) chance is obviously a determinant element, in *Orlando furioso* Fortune really dominates everything and everybody. . . . Illusion, elusion, frustration. In the end, there is uncertainty about oneself and others in a manifold, varied, always moving, and always changing reality" ("L'*Orlando furioso,*" 293–94).

17. Burckhardt remarks on Ariosto's indifference toward creating complex characters (212). Ascoli argues along the same lines that "the very multiplicity of characters and the general predominance of narrative exigencies over autonomy of characterization militate against the emergence

in the *Furioso* of a 'fully represented self'" (*Ariosto's Bitter Harmony*, 49).

18. For an extended reading of the metaphor of play in early Italian literature, see Mazzotta's *World at Play*. Constance Jordan (pers. comm.) has suggested the importance of applying the model of play to the *Furioso* in order to construct a not-too-deterministic analysis of the motifs of order / disorder / reimposition of order as they run through the text. On the importance of role-playing, masking, and playfulness in the *Cortegiano*, see Rebhorn.

19. Frye writes: "The quest-romance is the search of the libido or desiring self for a fulfilment that will deliver it from the anxieties of reality but will still contain that reality" (193). Jameson ("Magical Narratives") takes Frye to task for not offering a more historical account of romances. On the dilation of romances, see Parker, *Inescapable Romance*; on romance as a shifting genre, see the essays in Brownlee and Brownlee, especially Quint's "Boat of Romance."

20. "We laymen have always been intensely curious to know," Freud writes, "—like the Cardinal who put a similar question to Ariosto—from what sources that strange being, the creative writer, draws his material, and how he manages to make such an impression on us with it" ("Creative Writers," 143). Studies that use psychoanalysis in discussing Renaissance works are proliferating. For an example in the context of the Italian epic, see Bellamy. Recently Greenblatt ("Psychoanalysis," 221) has argued against using psychoanalytical tools in studying periods predating Freud, since psychoanalytic studies must read their concerns back into the past and find them in authors who conceived the psyche in different ways. However, he sees this historicizing process already in place in Lacanian thought. For a critique of this position within Italian Renaissance studies, see Bellamy, "Introduction"; and Schiesari, 233–36.

21. See Belsey, *Subject of Tragedy*, 149.

22. For two good studies along these lines of the *Furioso* as the poem of a hero's (Ruggiero's) bumpy and problematic education, see Marinelli, *Ariosto and Boiardo*; and Ascoli, *Ariosto's Bitter Harmony*.

23. See Quint, "Epic and Empire," 27.

24. On the *querelle*, see Kelly-Gadol; Kelso; MacLean; and Jordan, "Feminism and the Humanists" and *Renaissance Feminism*. More often than Ariosto, Castiglione defends women against misogynist attacks. On this subject, see Zancan; and Chemello. Ariosto's attitude toward women is at times one of praise and at others one of condemnation. This varies even within the same canto. See especially some of his proems (Cantos 20, 22, 28, 29, 30, 37). For a reading of Ariosto's "pro and con" comments on women, see Durling. For studies of the specific relationship between the *querelle* and Ariosto, see Santoro, *Letture ariostesche*; and Shemek, "Of

Women, Knights." Kelly-Gadol finds Ariosto different from other writers since, together with Boccaccio, he does not "establish chastity as the female norm and restructure the relation of the sexes to one of female dependency and male domination" (21). My argument is that Ariosto experiments with these issues but comes to less liberal conclusions than Kelly-Gadol acknowledges.

25. For Castiglione's reference to Zeuxis, see Chapter 3 below; for Ariosto's, see Chapter 5.

26. Althusser (*For Marx*) would contrast what the author says and what the reader brings to the interpretation of the work by reading both the conscious and the unconscious of a text. Psychoanalysis is, of course, dependent on the interplay between conscious and unconscious elements in any text.

27. It is debatable how much power real (historical) women had in the period. The very number of treatises written on the issue shows that it was difficult to systematize women's position and worth within society. Misogynist discourses may have put boundaries on women intellectually, but everyday life may have been another matter. Studying patrician women's wills written in early Renaissance Venice, Chojnacki argues for female freedom and power, since women were able to make decisions about their dowries and other possessions. For a contrary view, see Kelly-Gadol. Kelly-Gadol, however, falls into the same trap as Burckhardt, for she uses rhetorical, literary images of women to draw conclusions about real women. For lower-class women, Herlihy shares Kelly-Gadol's opinion: they too suffered during the Renaissance as modes of production shifted. Kelso suggests that the very need for men to interact in the secular world required a stricter definition of women's role (for example, women had to show reserve in public and an attitude of general humility). Paul Grendler (*Critics*, chap. 1) argues that between 1530 and 1560, thus only a few years after Castiglione and Ariosto published their works, Italian society saw an opening that was not only surprising for the period but was also not to be repeated for a long time. Moreover, thanks to the gradual acceptance of the vernacular and the flourishing of publishing houses, especially in Venice, women suddenly started to be published in significant numbers (Grendler, *Schooling*, 93–102). Dionisotti ("La letteratura italiana") also notes the spurt in women's writing. For an overview of family life and the role of women in the family during the period, see Diefendorf.

28. See Ariès; Stone; Klapisch-Zuber; and Hamilton. Marx dated the beginning of capitalism to the sixteenth century, with intermittent traces of capitalistic ventures in previous centuries. The present-day view is that capitalism was born earlier, with the introduction of the wage system.

Kerrigan and Braden find the bourgeois-state tie anachronistic, for the bourgeois always chose to invest his new money as the nobleman did, they argue, on new land. Contrary to Marxist historians, they notice that "a bourgeois-state alliance has proved difficult to document, and it is not entirely clear that the Renaissance middle class had a class consciousness, or a class allegiance, sufficient to carry out such a program" (47). Engels (chap. 2) strongly emphasized that sexual division of labor and women's secondary position in society are not necessarily related. Barrett (181–85) argues that the normalization and domestication of women are not so much the direct result of the social inside/outside separation and capitalism, but the quite natural result of an ideology that assigns the feminine a place within the household and relegates female work to the family. For a study of the discrepancy in wages between men and women in Renaissance Florence, see Brown.

29. For the imbrication of myths of domesticity and gender strategies, see De Lauretis, "The Female Body," 260–61.

30. For a study of notions of female sexuality in the Renaissance, see MacLean; Jordan, *Renaissance Feminism*, 29–34; Boch and Nobili; and Greenblatt, "Fiction and Friction." For Foucault, sexuality as we define it today was born only in the early eighteenth century (although in vol. 2 of his *History of Sexuality*, he admits to a long prehistory). Chronological boundaries are debatable, and Foucault's sense of sexuality has been successfully applied to other periods as well, including the Renaissance. Ruggiero, for example, suggests that sexuality was invented and regulated in Venice by state intervention as early as the fourteenth century.

31. For a reading of female allegory in the *Furioso*, see Ascoli, *Ariosto's Bitter Harmony*; and Kennedy.

32. On this shift, see Quint, "The Figure of Atlante," 80; Parker, *Inescapable Romance* (with some qualifications), 37; and Ascoli, *Ariosto's Bitter Harmony*, 376. On closure, see Chapters 4 and 8 below, on Angelica and Bradamante, respectively.

33. For Bakhtin, it is through heteroglossia and carnivalization that a text can question, subvert, and expose the dominant ideology at its base (*The Dialogic Imagination*). My reading of jokes in Chapter 3 below shows that jokes have a disruptive potential and are used specifically for this reason, which explains why Castiglione, treading on thin ice, chooses to exert an even tighter control over his material in this section.

CHAPTER I

1. For courtly culture and Castiglione as a court intellectual, see Vasoli, 64–87; Dionisotti, "N. Liburnio"; and Quondam.

2. Castiglione defends himself against possible accusations of auto-
biography and of excessive independence or self-presumption through a
double strategy. First, he declares that the conversations he is transcribing
were narrated to him earlier by a participant and took place during one
of his absences from the court. Second, he complains that the text was
made public without his authorization, by an impertinent woman, Vit-
toria Colonna. See Ossola, *"Il libro del cortegiano"*; and Saccone, "Trattato."
The locus classicus for an absent narrator is in Plato; for example in the
Symposium, where Diotima of Mantinea's discourse, which Socrates re-
lates, is told by Aristodemus to Apollodorus, who was not present. The
precedent is also Ciceronian. In *De oratore* (III, 4, 16), C. Aurelio Cotta
relates conversations that took place in Tusculum in 91 B.C. On a more
contemporary note, Bembo, in *Prose della volgar lingua*, detaches himself
twice from the present. The Magnifico's arguments, which he transcribes,
Bembo claims, were recounted to him earlier by the Magnifico's brother,
who had personally heard them.

3. Uncovering the genesis of *Il libro del cortegiano* has not been an easy
task. See Ghinassi for a convincing reconstruction of the different elabo-
rations of the text, from the drafts in the Casa Castiglione to the three
manuscripts in the Biblioteca Vaticana (Vat. Lat. 8204, 8205, 8206) and to
the Codice Laurenziano-Ashburnhamiano 409. The *editio princeps*, which
appeared in Venice in April 1528, a few months before the author's death,
was printed by Aldo Romano and Andrea d'Asolo. For the success of the
Cortegiano, see Guidi, "Reformulations."

4. I use the nouns "institution" and "institute" to indicate a genre much
used in the Renaissance to portray, often in an idealized fashion, specific
individuals (e.g., a courtier, a court lady, a gentleman, a poet, a lover) or
a group in the society at large (a family). As Greene points out, the new
emphasis on self-fashioning led naturally to the period's rediscovery of the
institute: "The Renaissance was not a fertile age in the invention of new
genres, but it was immensely creative in recapturing and extending the
potentialities of those genres which it inherited. The Renaissance institute
was inspired by such works as Plato's *Republic*, Cicero's *De Oratore*, and
Quintilian's *Institutiones Oratoriae*, ideal portraits of a society or institution
or occupation" ("Flexibility," 250).

5. On the first point, see Saccaro Battisti; on the second, Ghinassi. Ghi-
nassi found a set of pages (sheets 76–79) in the first draft of the *Cortegiano*
that seem to be "a self-contained short work, a sort of *Defense of Women*
argued by Castiglione against an interlocutor called Frisia, who will be
Niccolò Frisio in the *Cortegiano*" (189). He thinks that these pages might
have been written before the *Cortegiano*. The "Lettera al Frisia in difesa
delle donne" appears in the "Appendice" of Ghinassi's article. Castiglione

also addresses a letter to an unspecified "Messer Paulo" early in the six-
teenth century. The letter requests information on names of women and
on authors who have written about them: "I would like to know about
women of old or modern times who have been great in whatever areas, in
letters, in arms, in chastity, in constancy, in some generous acts, women
from Greece, Rome, or other places. I would particularly like to know
about women of the last one-hundred, two-hundred or three-hundred
years, without leaving aside unknown women from Sparta. I would be
satisfied in knowing the names of the authors who wrote about them, so
you can content me without too much trouble" (*Lettere inedite*, 109–10).

6. During this period the theme of female "worth" was discussed from
a variety of perspectives. Among the most notable participants in the con-
troversy are Mario Equicola, *Libro de natura de amore*, 1525; Galeazzo Flavio
Capella, *Della eccellenza et dignità delle donne*, 1525; Cornelius Agrippa, *De
nobilitate*, 1529, although written in 1509 and probably in circulation since
that date; Alessandro Piccolomini, *La Raffaella, dialogo della bella creanza
delle donne*, 1539; Sperone Speroni, *Della dignità delle donne*, 1542; Giuseppe
Betussi, *Dialogo amoroso*, 1543; Ludovico Dolce, *Dialogo della institutione delle
donne*, 1545 (it was very similar to Vives's influential work *De l'istituzione
de la femina christiana, vergine, maritata e vedova*, published in Venice in 1546);
Vincenzo Maggi, *Un brieve trattato dell'eccellentia delle donne*, 1545; Lodovico
Domenichi, *Nobiltà delle donne*, 1549; and Cornelius Agrippa, *De la nobiltà
et precellentia del femminile sesso*, 1549. Fahy gives 41 titles in his Appendix.
See also Chemello; Jordan, *Renaissance Feminism*; Jones; M. Pozzi; and the
bibliography in Kelso.

7. Francesco Asolano, for example, dedicates the preface to an edition
of the *Cortegiano* published in 1533 in Venice (by the printer of the *editio
princeps*) to the "Gentili Donne" with the recommendation that they "keep
it in their breasts" because it is to women that the work belongs: "Take it,
then, most noble women, for whom alone this work was written." The
first English edition of the text was ready in 1556 but not published until
1561, precisely the years that saw the appearance in England of a good
number of works on women. William Seres, the editor of this translation,
emphasizes that Castiglione's text gives much space to women. Thomas
Hoby, the translator, declares in the preface that he originally intended to
translate only Book 3, the one on women.

8. Burckhardt's generalizations on this topic have been often revised.
See, e.g., Kelso; and Kelly-Gadol. For a general discussion of woman's
condition in Castiglione, see Guidi, "De l'amour"; and MacLean.

9. For a more detailed analysis of strategies three, four, and five, see
the following chapter.

10. In this sense, a subject is for Althusser always already subjected,

for ideology guarantees "that everything really is so, and that on condition that the subjects recognize what they are and behave accordingly, everything will be all right" ("Ideology," 181).

11. For Greene, who traces the origins of Renaissance games in the *cours d'amour* and in the Provençal *jocs partitz*, the proposals not chosen "all deal with the socially aberrant, with private passions and imbalances and blindnesses which could threaten the harmony of the group" ("*Il Cortegiano*," 3). See also Woodhouse, 71. For a study of the genre "dialogue" as conversation, see Stati, 12–17.

12. See Zancan, 26. Zancan has greatly influenced my thinking on Castiglione. See also Chemello; Saccaro Battisti; Kelly-Gadol; and Guidi, "De l'amour."

13. As Mulvey poignantly puts it, "Woman then stands in patriarchal culture as a signifier for the male other, bound by a symbolic order in which man can live out his fantasies and obsessions through linguistic command by imposing them on the silent image of woman still tied to her place as bearer, not maker, of meaning" (15).

14. To be fair, Sperone Speroni's treatise on woman, *Della dignità delle donne*, was brought to the attention of the Inquisition because of some assertions about marriage that the church found unacceptable (namely, that men created it to better disempower women). The treatise is reprinted in M. Pozzi, 1: 570–71. See also Daenens, 15.

15. As Jones writes in this context, " 'conversation,' like 'intercourse,' has two meanings: with men it is civil; with women it is sexual. Men are refined through the artful practice of speech; women are corrupted by it" (44).

16. Let us take as an example (and I could quote many similar ones) an unexceptionable sentence by Saccone that so brilliantly illustrates the purposes of conversation at court: "The speaker in the book is, one can very well say it, the court: by reflecting on itself in the first person, the court draws its own image and offers not so much an ideal portrait as the portrait of its own ideality" ("Trattato," 5). As Saccone underlines, the courtiers' discourse and courtly discourse are one, and everybody agrees on the point. But such a discourse is also deceitful because power and philosophy are seen as coextensive. As I hope to show, the discourse presented in the *Cortegiano* is consistently, necessarily gendered, and woman has access to it only in the sense that she accepts being spoken of. On the usual representation of the subject as male even when there is no reference to gender, see Heath, "Difference," 53; Owens, 58; and Braidotti.

17. On a "transvestite" identification of woman with the male authority figure, see Mulvey, chap. 4.

18. In *The Archaeology of Knowledge*, Foucault identifies a "fellowship

of discourse" that intends "to preserve or to reproduce discourse, but in order that it should circulate within a closed community, according to strict regulations, without those in possession being dispossessed by this very distribution" (225). As for the *Cortegiano*, it is understood that the discourse is self-referential. To demonstrate a concept, it is often sufficient to name a person in the text that illustrates the concept or that has illustrated it in the past, for everybody to understand. See, e.g., the reference to Roberto da Bari for gracefulness in dancing (1, 27) or in causing laughter (2, 49). At times the allusion is to absent people whose qualities or faults are known by everybody. Even for witty remarks reactions are uniform (in regard to regional puns, e.g., everybody agrees that Florentines are more brilliant than Venetians).

19. Floriani does not hesitate to define this new role for woman at court as decidedly feminist because women are subjects of the debate (149–50). He then urges us not to "underestimate the significance of those pages in which the value of woman's presence in society is represented in new terms, not only as a presence able to stir up virile energies but also as an autonomous way of being of a person marked by generally human features [connotati generalmente umani]" (150). Thus, for Floriani, *Il libro del cortegiano* is feminist because women stir up virile energies (as usual, women have the function of go-betweens) and because they have a place in the text, thanks to their human features. With such a defender, it would be appropriate to quote Pio's complaint over the Magnifico's lack of energy (or logic) in championing her sex: "Now we can't at all understand your way of defending us" (3, 17, 233).

20. In this context, see Felman's rereading of this article. It is also worth noticing that neither the piece on "Femininity" nor the one on "Female Sexuality" generated a need in Freud for a corresponding study of masculinity.

21. See Lacan, *Four Fundamental Concepts*. De Lauretis rationalizes: this "all amounts to saying that woman, *as* subject of desire or of signification, is unrepresentable; or better, that in the phallic order of patriarchal culture and in its theory, woman is unrepresentable except as representation" (*Technologies,* 20).

22. See Kelly-Gadol, 46. On the relationship between a despotic ruler and a subjected courtier, see Javitch, "*Il Cortegiano.*"

CHAPTER 2

1. On the doubly determined nature of ideologies, in the sense that they express the class views and the interests of the group that produces them, see Bourdieu, "Symbolic Power," 116.

2. The association of women with affectation and mask was fashionable during the Renaissance. For example, both Agnolo Firenzuola in *Dialogo della bellezza delle donne* and Alessandro Piccolomini in *Raffaella* write on cosmetization. Female dissimulation, in the sense that women always wear a mask and femininity is always an artifact, is also a basic Lacanian concept (taken from Joan Rivière). On the subject of woman-mask and on the processes of masking and transvesting, see also Doane, "Film and the Masquerade"; and Chapter 7 below on Fiordispina.

3. Cicero used a similar argument in *Orator* when he assimilated two contrasting types of woman, the made-up and the natural woman, to the Asiatic (artificial) and the Attic (simple) style (23: 78.8–79.8). Ferroni links Cicero's insight to the concept of *sprezzatura* ("Sprezzatura," 143–45). The made-up woman is, of course, unable to appreciate the *grazia/sprezzatura* concepts on which the courtier has to build his image.

4. According to Bakhtin (*Rabelais and His World*), the grotesque parts of the body are those literally open to the others' gaze: "the open mouth, the genital organs, the breast, the phallus, the potbelly, the nose" (26). The classical body, decidedly enclosed, corresponds to "palaces, churches, institutions, and private homes" (154) and to the classical language of our fathers. On this subject, see Russo; Stallybrass and White; and Miles, *Carnal Knowing*. On further use of the grotesque vis-à-vis women in Castiglione, see Chapter 3 below on jokes.

5. If the disciplined body is expressive of a class ideology, prescribed behavior has decidedly political implications. For the importance every society gives to dress, speech, and behavior, see Bourdieu, *Outline;* and Foucault, *History of Sexuality* and *Power/Knowledge.* On the construction of a docile female body, see Silverman, "*Histoire d'O.*"

6. My comments owe much to the studies on films and on the image of women in visual arts by Mulvey; Doane, *The Desire to Desire;* and Plaza.

7. On Alexander's reputation for magnanimity and prodigality in the medieval tradition, with a list of exempla, see Cary, esp. 86–91 and 209–18. Alexander's magnanimity, so much praised in French troubadour and courtly love poetry, was in any case always perceived as prodigality from a philosophical point of view. In Italy, Dante, Boccaccio, Petrarch, and Machiavelli, at one point or another, refer to Alexander's largess. Versions of the story of Campaspe have numerous variants. There are two sources: Istros, *frag.* 48; and Muller (F. H. G., I, 424) and Aelian, *Var. Hist.*, 10: 2, where the story is about Eubotas.

8. Girard is the most influential theorizer of triangular desire (*Deceit, Desire*). For him the rivalry between a subject and his rival—a conflictual one because they both desire the same object—lowers the intrinsic worth of the desired object at the expense of the desiring duo, one the double

of the other. For a critique of the Girardian inability to make room for woman as desiring subject, and thus for woman as autonomous being, see Moi.

9. In her work, Sedgwick has extensively examined "the routing of homosocial desire through women" (49). The value of the feminine presence in *Il libro del cortegiano* reflects, I think, precisely a desire to reinforce this male libidinal trust, which is tendentially homosexual but purposely situated within a larger heterosexual environment. See also Irigaray for a definition of sexual relationships as "hom(m)osexuelles" (*This Sex*).

10. The example of Zeuxis comes from Cicero, *De Invent.* II, I, and is reproduced almost verbatim. See Barocchi, 1534. The example is also in other treatises on women (e.g., Capella's). See Patrizi. On Ariosto's use of Zeuxis in his description of female beauty, see Chapter 5 below on Olimpia.

11. Barocchi, 1530. See also Hulse, 86–88. The letter, which bears no date and no signature, was probably written in 1514. Ideal femininity thus should be imaginable in order to be reproducible. Any reproduction, however, has to idealize the real. In this context, see Panofsky, 47–65; and Lee, *Ut Pictura Poesis*, 7–11. For a discussion of *Il libro del cortegiano* as "ritratto di pittura," see Rebhorn, 61–79; and Hanning, "Castiglione's Verbal Portrait."

12. "Many portraits of unknown beautiful women," Cropper writes, "are now characterized as representations of ideal beauty in which the question of identity is immaterial. No unidentified male portrait, on the other hand, is ever said to be a beautiful representation made for its own sake" ("Beauty of Woman," 178). See also G. Pozzi for a study of the relationship between perfect femininity in poetry and its translation in painting.

13. The natural and scholastic philosophical theories argued to defend or accuse the female sex are taken from Greek and Latin *auctoritates*. For example, Aristotle's *De generatione animalium* is brought in for the distinction woman/coldness and man/warmth, and Xenophon's *Oeconomicus* is used to explain the need for woman's education in the roles of wife and mother. Xenophon's theories were to be fully revived in the early Renaissance by Leon Battista Alberti, who in the third book of his influential *I libri della famiglia* (1435) went a long way to circumscribe woman's protobourgeois social boundaries.

14. To summarize the table published in the appendix to a re-edition of the *Cortegiano* (I am using that published in 1547 and quoted by Guidi, "Reformulations," 145), the courtier and the court lady share nobility, beauty, prudence, and knowledge of letters, dance, music, and painting. As is characteristic of their sex, women should have goodness, good manage-

ment skills, honesty, affability, and pleasant, entertaining manners. Men should have a lively mind, boldness, loyalty, magnanimity, moderation, and nimbleness. They should also have knowledge of duels, fighting, running, jumping, and hunting and be familiar with a number of different languages (Spanish and French).

15. On paradoxical treatments of women's superiority in the Renaissance, see Daenens.

16. To Boccaccio, Guidi adds Christine de Pisan, *La cité des dames;* Alvaro de Luna, *De las virtuosas e claras mujeres;* the catalogue by Diego de San Pedro, *Carcel de amor;* and perhaps Alonso de Carthagene, *De las mujeres illustres* ("De l'amour," 42). Given the similarities, Woodbridge (71–72) advances the hypothesis that Castiglione also knew Agrippa's *De nobilitate.*

17. Lipking (361) argues that the reason Castiglione offers so many examples is that women and wit are difficult to define theoretically; thus he prefers illustration to explanation.

18. Jordan (*Renaissance Feminism,* 83) rightly suggests that the reason the duchess quiets Cesare Gonzaga when he expounds on her imposed widowhood is that his hidden suggestion for her to take a lover would benefit only the courtier while implicitly undermining her own position at court as wife and duchess.

19. For Lacan, the subject's misrecognition in the proffered image is more closely tied with issues of desire, difference, and absence. Subjectivity in the Lacanian individual is more shifting and the self more divided than in the Althusserian individual.

20. For a study of Ottaviano's intervention, see Rebhorn, chap. 6; for a study of Bembo's, see Nelson. On Bembo's influence on Castiglione's style, see Floriani. The debate still rages on whether Book 4 of the *Cortegiano* unifies the general argument running through the first three books or moves away from it. For the argument in favor of unity, see Ryan; and Trafton; for that against, see Burckhardt; and Lipking.

21. Nelson defines Bembo's position as more optimistic and less loaded with compromises than Ficino's. Zorzi-Pugliese (119) finds irony in Castiglione's use of Ficinian love theory. She also notices that there is no discussion of the possibility that women may experience divine love themselves. The link between Neoplatonism and courtly ideology is well established; see Vasoli, 77–78.

CHAPTER 3

1. Bergson insists that decorum is essential in laughing, since laughter can sour.

2. "Humor is difficult to combat," Linda Woodbridge writes, "because

he who protests, even against a cruel jest, can always be accused of not being able to take a joke. The charge that feminists have no sense of humor has arisen from feminist protests against misogynistic jokes" (32).

3. The self-deprecation often present in women's humor testifies more to a masochistic than to a hostile penchant in women. Apte writes: "In public domains women seem generally not to engage in: verbal duels, ritual insults, practical jokes, and pranks, all of which reflect the competitive spirit, and the aggressive and hostile quality, of men's humor; slapstick; institutionalized clowning; and institutionalized joking relationships with female kin" (69). Radical changes in forms of humor since the Renaissance are possible, of course, but unlikely; therefore, I think that a study such as this one would apply to any period. See also Lakoff for a study of women's language and verbal inhibitions in public forums.

4. Although Cicero's presence is pervasive, Bibbiena keeps some distance from him by adding a third category, that of practical jokes, to the two enunciated by Cicero: polished pleasantries embedded in narrative form and *dicta,* pungent remarks. For more on Cicero, see Valmaggi. Castiglione draws also from Quintilian's *Institutio oratoria;* from humanist texts by G. Pontano (*De sermone*) and G. Poggio Bracciolini (*Facetiarum liber*); from contemporary texts such as those by A. Cornazzaro, *Quod de proverbiorum origine inscribitur* (1503) and *Proverbii* (1525), and by A. Mainardi, *Motti e facezie* (1515) and *Facezie, piacevolezze, fabule e motti* (1516). In this context, Cian's and Maier's comments in their respective editions of the *Cortegiano* are indispensable. The *Cortegiano* also became a source of jokes and witticisms. Montaigne, for example, merges Bracciolini and Castiglione to create a pun on women's obstinacy, in the case of the woman who kept making the sign for "scissors" to her husband after she had lost the capacity to say the word itself. The episode is in Book 3 of the *Cortegiano.* Later examples of treatises on jokes during the Renaissance are L. Domenichi, *Facezie et motti arguti,* 1548; G. Fracastoro, *De sympathia et antipathia rerum,* 1546; and V. Maggi, *De ridiculis,* 1550. See Ossola, *Dal "Cortegiano" all'"Uomo di Mondo",* 50–51 for a reconstruction of the figure of Castiglione as author "de ridiculis," and Floriani (137–39) for references to Ciceronian sources. For more on witticism in the humanist tradition, see Pullini; for an overview of paradoxes, see Colie; for a more general approach to dirty jokes via Freud, but with a more sociological emphasis, see Legman; for a theory of the comic and the laughter, see Olbrechts-Tyteca.

5. For a reconstruction of the fortune of jokes in the five manuscripts of *Il libro del cortegiano,* see Guidi, " 'Festive narrazioni,' " 173–74.

6. This calculation was made by Mulas (105).

7. For similar points, see Rebhorn, 141; and Guidi, " 'Festive narrazioni,' " 185.

8. Among the very few articles briefly touching on jokes in the *Cortegiano,* see Shapiro, "Mirror and Portrait"; and Woodhouse, chap. 4.

9. For more on Aristotle, see *De partibus animalium.*

10. Mehlman questions the possibility that an innocent joke can exist and asks whether all jokes are not somehow tendentious.

11. Interestingly, Freud thinks that innocent jokes can provoke only moderate laughter. Dirty jokes, on the other hand, should cause a hearty, resounding laugh.

12. In Freud's words, "A joke will allow us to exploit something ridiculous in our enemy which we could not, on account of obstacles in the way, bring forward openly or consciously; once again, then, the joke *will evade restrictions and open sources of pleasure that have become inaccessible.* It will further bribe the hearer with its yield of pleasure into taking sides with us without any very close investigation" (*Jokes,* 103).

13. On the politics of looking, see, e.g., Mulvey; Doane, "Film and the Masquerade"; and Silverman, *Subject of Semiotics.*

14. On the concept of womanliness as a masquerade, see Rivière; Lacan, "Meaning of the Phallus"; Irigaray, *This Sex;* Doane, "Film and the Masquerade"; and Finucci. See also Chapter 7 below on Fiordispina.

15. For a study of sumptuary laws in Italy and their social implications, see Hughes, "Sumptuary Law." Virulent attacks on female adornment and makeup are of course a misogynist staple. See, e.g., Tertullian. Castiglione may also have been familiar with Clement of Alexandria, possibly in a Latin translation. Ariosto also plays up the connection of makeup and female artifice. Traveling on the moon, Astolfo "saw great quantities of bird-lime for ensnaring: your charms, good ladies" (34, 81).

16. Affectation as the result of excessive emphasis on behavior was a common topic. Alberti in *De iciarchia,* for example, expounded on it.

17. "What does a nude signify?" John Berger asks. "To be naked is to be oneself. To be nude is to be seen naked by others and yet not recognized for oneself. . . . To be naked is to be without disguise which, in that situation, can never be discarded" (53–54). See also Saunders. For Clark (*The Nude*), a nude body is a re-formed body, that is, a body minus its sensibility. For more on female nakedness and nudity, see Chapters 4 and 5 below on Angelica and Olimpia, respectively.

18. There is no trace of shame of nudity in Adam, however. In the painting, Eve covers her genitals in shame, but Adam covers his eyes because it was through them that he was tempted to sin.

19. For an overview of philosophical ideas on womanhood during the

Renaissance, see MacLean, 1–24; Kelso; and Jordan, *Renaissance Feminism*.

20. For a thorough study of homosocial desire in English literature, see Sedgwick. On the connection between jokes and the homosocial contract in Freud, see Gallop, 33–39.

21. The episode is also found in Cicero's *De oratore* (II, 68), but Castiglione modernizes it.

22. "Ethnographic accounts of women playing practical jokes or pranks on each other or on men in everyday social interactions," Apte writes, "seem almost nonexistent. On the other hand, men seem to play practical jokes not only on other men but also on women" (70). Examples of the last are fully represented in the *Cortegiano,* as we shall see. For a study of the metaphor of play in Boccaccio, see Mazzotta, *The World at Play.*

23. On the subject of the naive, Freud writes: "Naive *remarks* are, of course, better suited for comparison with jokes than naive actions, since remarks and not actions are the usual form in which jokes are expressed" (*Jokes,* 182). The explanations in the text are somewhat unclear because Freud tends to use the same examples that earlier illustrated the mechanism of the joke-work.

24. In Freud's words, "The person who is the victim of the injury, pain . . . might obtain *humorous* pleasure, while the unconcerned person laughs from *comic* pleasure" (*Jokes,* 228). See also his short essay "Humor."

25. Bloch's reading of the French fabliaux follows the same line of reasoning: "The comic tale works not, as Freud (and Bergson) would have it, only to subvert the social, but to reinforce it as well. . . . Behind every beating is a lesson to be learned; and behind every castration, a reimposition of the law" (120).

CHAPTER 4

1. Both Tomalin (*Fortunes* and "Bradamante and Marfisa") and Robinson concentrate on female warriors. As for Angelica, things may be changing. Santoro's study in *L'anello* (57–81) and Shemek's "That Elusive Object" are innovative and perceptive.

2. For a reading of the *Furioso* as independent from the *Innamorato* and other earlier romance epics, see Calvino, "Presentazione." My own reading of Angelica as a narcissistic, indifferent woman would not work for Boiardo's Angelica, who is both pursuer and pursued.

3. The number of romance narratives published during the Renaissance was enormous and well explains Ariosto's fascination with the genre. Beer speculates that no fewer than 500,000 copies of these narratives were in circulation in Italy between 1470 and 1600. Quest and *entrelacement* are

the main romance themes Ariosto employed. On the relationship between the *Furioso* and medieval romances, see Del Corno Branca.

4. See, e.g., Alberti's influential treatise, *Della famiglia*. On the Renaissance desire to normatize individuals' behaviors and family relationships, see Ariès; Klapisch-Zuber; and Stone. See also the Introduction and Chapter 8 below.

5. For more on horses, horsing around, and the pair Angelica/mare ("giumenta"), see Giamatti, "Sfrenatura"; and Dalla Palma, *Le strutture*.

6. Zatti (chap. 2) emphasizes that what actually ends is simply the search for objects of desire, which then becomes a search for knowledge. For Quint, the movement away from romance and toward epic closure starts with the destruction of Atlante's palace, which in the first version of the *Furioso* came in the exact middle canto ("The Figure of Atlante," 87). See also Parker, *Inescapable Romance;* Tylus; Bruscagli; Fichter; and Saccone, *Il "soggetto."* Donato, on the other hand, argues for open-endedness, as does Chiampi, who writes that women's unwillingness in the *Furioso* to consider themselves objects of exchange precludes resolution and closure. Since Ariosto posits desire as always self-regenerating, Chiampi (20–23) goes on, his epic is necessarily open-ended.

7. For Girard, desire has a sex, and this sex is male. In Jacobus's words, "eliminating the narcissistic woman, Girard also eliminates sexual difference, since in his scheme there is only male desire which the woman mimics" (136).

8. The ring comes straight from Boiardo, who proposes it early in Book 2 of *Orlando innamorato*. The original reference is to the ring of Gyges the Lydian in Plato's *Republic*. In the *Furioso* the ring initially belongs to Angelica; it is subsequently taken away from her and then returned after a number of interesting detours. During the time that she does not have it, she experiences misfortune after misfortune, until she loses her kingdom (11, 5). As Ariosto explains, Brunello stole Angelica's ring in the *Innamorato;* Melissa in the *Furioso* urges Bradamante to do the same to Brunello (3, 69). Bradamante accomplishes the task and sends the ring to Ruggiero via Melissa. Ruggiero's unintentional return of the ring to Angelica before battling with the sea monster brings this narrative motif full circle.

9. See Girard in *Deceit, Desire* and *Things Hidden,* and Moi's critique of Girard's blindness to woman's desire. For a reading of desire as not triangular but circular vis-à-vis Angelica, see Shemek, "That Elusive Object."

10. On the connection between dazzlement and madness, as opposite to truth, light, and classical reason, see Foucault, *Madness,* 108.

11. See, e.g., Javitch, "Rescuing Ovid," 92 *n*10.

12. Ruggiero is described as Perseus. He comes on a winged horse (Perseus used winged sandals), has a magic reflecting shield like that of Perseus, and a magic ring assuring invisibility like Perseus's cap of Hades. The medieval sources are Manilio and Valerio Flacco. A later source is Pontano.

13. On the difference between nakedness and nudity, see Berger, 54. For a description of a realistically rendered naked body in the *Furioso,* see, e.g., Orlando's frenzied undressing at the onset of his folly (23, 133). For more on women's nudity, see Chapter 5 below.

14. See, in this context, Mulvey; Bryson; and Williams. See also my discussion of Renaissance perspective in Chapter 5 on Olimpia below.

15. As will become clear in my study of Olimpia, I read the Andromeda story as a master myth of feminization and domestication.

16. Angelica is given the chance to talk at length on another occasion, in Canto 1. Her discourse there, however, is a reaction to Sacripante's in that she tries to identify with the Angelica he has just evoked. She identifies so well, in fact, that soon after, she becomes the prime object of his cupidity for "tanto ben" (1, 57).

17. See also Silverman, *Acoustic Mirror,* 28; and De Lauretis, *Alice Doesn't.*

18. For a study of the myth from Ovid to medieval allegorizers to Ariosto, see Javitch, "Rescuing Ovid"; and Shapiro, *Poetics of Ariosto.* For a more general use of the myth, see Munich.

19. In the inscription that will cause Orlando's madness, Medoro speaks of "commodità" in reference to Angelica's stay in the cave: "De la commodità che qui m'è data / io povero Medor ricompensarvi / d'altro non posso, che d'ognor lodarvi" ("I, poor Medor, cannot repay you for your indulgence otherwise than by ever praising you" [23, 108]). This sense of *commodità* seems much less related to reward than it may appear to at first sight. For a similar view, see Weaver, 405 *n*23. For a literal translation of *commodità* into "commodity," see Giamatti, "*Sfrenatura,*" 35.

20. On the myth of a female phallus that allows man to disavow castration, see Mannoni, 9–34. On woman's becoming the phallus, which makes her reach "a state of narcissistic autonomy," see Grunberger, 75. In Lacanian psychoanalysis, woman is the phallus and man has the phallus in the sense that, since the phallus is the signifier of the desire of the other, woman—as object of desire for man—by being the phallus confirms to man that he has it. See Lacan, "Meaning of the Phallus," 83. For further discussion of this topic, see Chapter 7 below on Fiordispina.

21. For more on disavowal as central to the structure of fetishism, see Deleuze, 31.

22. An interesting episode occurs at the very moment that Angelica

unexpectedly appears before Sacripante in Canto 1. Ariosto writes that no mother was ever as happy to see a son she feared dead as Sacripante was when he saw Angelica. In this scenario, Sacripante turns into a woman, and Angelica becomes a man. More precisely, he becomes a mother, and Angelica a lost son. Since mothers offer children a feeling of wholeness, primordial harmony, and presymbolic plenitude, this transcodification of a regressive maternal fantasy illustrates with a vengeance Sacripante's refusal of separation and loss. For John Newman, Sacripante's character-ization as a mother derives from the *Aeneid*. In a similar scenario, Aeneas first meets his mother, Venus, dressed as a huntress, and then meets Dido. Angelica's sudden appearance and greeting changes Sacripante's position to that of Aeneas's mother, Venus (323). Newman also points out that Sacripante assumes a feminine position when in his "Verginella" song he quotes the girls' chorus (62) and not the youths' chorus from Catullus.

23. Regarding the construction of woman in the cult of the female star, Mulvey writes: "Fetishistic scopophilia builds up the physical beauty of the object, transforming it into something satisfying in itself. . . . [It] can exist outside linear time as the erotic instinct is focused on the look alone" (21–22).

24. As Barthes points out, "In any man who utters the other's absence *something feminine* is declared" (*A Lover's Discourse*, 14).

25. The author addresses the expression to himself: "Ma tosto far, come vorrei, nol posso; / che 'l male è penetrato infin all'osso" ("I cannot do so as quickly as I should wish, for the disease has eaten me to the bone" [24, 3]). Thus, he establishes the brotherhood of all erring—that is, all inevitably erring—and foolish lovers. For further references to Virgil, see Fichter; Carne-Ross; and Marinelli, *Ariosto and Boiardo*.

26. See Laplanche and Pontalis, 475, on this *mise en scene* of desire. Freud writes that neurotics often fall prey to foreboding thoughts they think will come true ("The Uncanny," 239–40).

27. On the connection of this dream with the experience of satisfaction analyzed by Freud, see Saccone, *Il "soggetto,"* 228, 236. Ariosto substitutes Petrarch's "to see" ("vedermi") ("do not hope ever to see me on earth" [*Rime sparse*, 250]) with a more striking "to enjoy" ("gioirne," 8, 84).

28. Earlier, the same metaphor of a pine tree serves as a disempow-ered phallic image for Sacripante when he loses face and also his "giostra" with Bradamante (1, 65). A pine tree, moreover, is also the first item that Orlando destroys in his rampage (23, 134). For more on the pine tree as a sexual image and specifically as an image related to Pinabello, see Mancini, 177.

29. As Freud writes, "It is not true that, after the child has made his ob-servation of the woman, he has preserved unaltered his belief that women

have a phallus. He has retained that belief, but he has also given it up. . . . We can now see what the fetish achieves and what it is that maintains it. It remains a token of triumph over the threat of castration and a protection against it. It also saves the fetishist from becoming a homosexual, by endowing women with the characteristic which makes them tolerable as sexual objects" ("Fetishism," 154). The belief that the fetishist can only be male is central to Freud's position. Recently, Kofman has appropriated fetishism for women in *The Enigma* and, more recently, in her rereading of Freud through Derrida in "Ça Cloche." Here Kofman (112) reclaims for women's purposes a strategy that uses Derrida's undecidability. A fetishistic oscillation between knowing and denying knowledge, she argues, allows women to oscillate between dominant and non-dominant positions with no privileging of the phallus. On this subject, see also Berg.

30. On the decorative value of the fetishized object, Smirnoff writes: "The fetish is not simply an adjunct: amulet, trinket, talisman, juju, but also a *decoration*—as well an embellishment as a distinction—for it provides the subject with the insignia of his status" (323).

31. In Erasmus's *Praise of Folly*, the open Silenus box reveals the dichotomous faces of reality: wisdom and folly. For a reading of Orlando's madness in the context of Seneca's and Erasmus's views on madness, see Mazzotta, "Power and Play." On the connection of the figure of Erasmus's Silenus to Ariosto, see Chesney, 199. On the connections among the Virgilian Dionysian-Silenus, the Platonic/Erasmian Silenus, and the Ariostan Orlando-Silenus, see Ascoli, *Ariosto's Bitter Harmony*, 342–44, 348–51.

32. Boiardo's Orlando knows the point well: "If Rinaldo finds the beautiful virgin in the woods—I know full well what a rogue he is—she will not escape him as a maiden" (*Innamorato* 1, 2, 25).

33. The characterization of the Medusa occupies a good number of lines. Ariosto also makes use of medieval allegorizers (e.g., Fulgentius's *Mythologies*). In this context, see Shapiro, *Poetics of Ariosto*. The myth of the Medusa was formed as early as the seventh century B.C. For a study of the myth in Greek mythology, see Tyrrell; and L. Schneider.

34. For Ariosto's demystification and trivialization of Dantean transcendental meanings, see Javitch, "The *Orlando furioso*"; and Parker, *Inescapable Romance*, chap. 1. See also Segre, 51–83. Ariosto's Medusa is more Dantesque (a desire for something perceived as deadly or as the personification of death) than Petrarchan (a desire that fascinates no matter how dangerous the threat of being petrified, e.g., "Medusa and my error have made me a stone" [*Rime sparse*, 366]). See also Mazzotta, *Dante*, on the references to Medusa in Dante and in medieval allegorizers. Ascoli (*Ariosto's Bitter Harmony*) notices the allusions to the Medusa in the *Furioso* but ex-

amines only the link between Pegasus (born from the dying Medusa) and the hippogryph. Haddad studies the Medusan petrification of Orlando in Canto 23 after he reads Angelica and Medoro's inscription. For further references to this myth, see Chapters 5 and 6 below.

35. For more on Proteus's "sexual barbarism," see Giamatti, "Proteus Unbound," 468–70. See also L. Schneider on Medusa's punishment. On at least one other occasion in the *Furioso*, the Marganorre episode in Canto 37, women are punished for the sins of men. Marganorre's wrath toward women, in fact, would better be directed toward his two sons, who break the laws of hospitality and mock marital faithfulness. On the other hand, there is the Orco who eats only men, in the episode of Norandino in Canto 17. This does not mean that the Orco spares women, for he keeps them prisoner. But whereas freedom for women in the Angelica and the Olimpia stories can come only through men's help (Ruggiero rescues the former, Orlando the latter), here the men engineer their own escape. Ironically, the problem during their flight comes from Lucina, Norandino's wife. She is subsequently punished the Angelica-Olimpia way: tied to a rock and exposed to the elements (17, 60). Once again men rescue a chained female beauty (in this case, Mandricardo and Gradasso), and she is reunited with her husband.

36. Berlusconi (78) goes further and sees in Orlando's immersion an anticipation of his subsequent immersion into folly and reabsorption into sand and earth. The episode also recalls Jonah's immersion.

37. Beer (54–55) traces the parallel between the characterization of Orlando and Nebuchadnezzar back to Orlando's dream in Canto 8. Both men have premonitory dreams in which their future folly is staged. Both men also miraculously regain their sanity.

38. Rinaldo's return to normalcy is predicated by his own characterization in the epic. As critics have not failed to notice, Rinaldo is a prudent, pragmatic, and thoughtful knight—the perfect everyman. As such, he deserves to return home and live happily. To wit, he understands the lesson implied in the marriage tales during his trip to Italy and refuses to drink from the magic goblet in Canto 43. See Santoro, *Letture ariostesche*, for a description of Rinaldo as *homo prudens*; and Wiggins, *Figures*, for a reading of Rinaldo as "gran pedone."

39. This is illustrated by Sacripante's tortuous thoughts in Canto 1. After having celebrated the proper worth of the "verginella," he asserts that a maiden loses her value in the heart of all other knights after she has been possessed. As a result, she can be loved only by the one who possesses her first (1, 44). Immediately afterward, however, he revises this conclusion and wonders why the others win and he has to die of deprivation. Thus, he decides to keep loving and pursuing Angelica no matter what

he thought earlier. For a Girardian reading of triangular desire vis-à-vis Angelica, see Donato, 37, and more generally Zatti.

40. For a study of Bradamante's exemplary quest, see especially Marinelli, *Ariosto and Boiardo*. For a study of her "feminine" characterization, see Chapter 8 below. Unlike Angelica, Bradamante already belongs fully to her society: her brother, Rinaldo, is one of the worthiest French paladins, and she herself is well liked by the emperor.

41. As Saccone notes, all heroic characters in the *Furioso* are knights except Cloridano and Medoro ("Cloridano e Medoro," 92 *n*38). For a dismissal of Medoro's heroism, though perhaps exaggerated, see Wiggins, *Figures*, 180–81.

42. Besides the knights' search for Angelica as the elusive ideal of womanhood, there are other searches in the text for the explanation of the mystery of femininity. Rinaldo's refusal to test his wife's faithfulness, Rodomonte's quest for an understandable woman, and Astolfo's and Jocondo's hunt for female fidelity reiterate woman's inner difference while emphasizing man's incessant attempt to grasp and categorize her. Zatti (chap. 2) sees this type of quest as very much present in the second part of the *Furioso*. Looking for the absolute example of female faithfulness, Ariosto states that he himself plans to go to any length and to use any means necessary to explain woman with tongue and pen, in verse and prose ("con lingua e con inchiostro, e in verso e in prosa," 27, 124). The obsessiveness of this explanation of femininity is confirmed by Ariosto's borrowing from Petrarch's famous Canzone 23 ("with paper and ink"), a poem centering on the inner destructive potential of love and of the beloved.

CHAPTER 5

1. Bacchelli (617) concurs with Segre in emphasizing the new heroic dimensions that the Olimpia story gives the figure of Orlando. For Larivaille (21), the additions to the 1532 edition emphasize the heroes' personal adventures and de-emphasize the role of war and strife.

2. The situation mirrors that of Rinaldo called to the rescue of Ginevra's honor in Canto 4. In both cases, figures of authority but not of physical might (an old man for Olimpia, monks for Ginevra) ask the help of a Christian hero in a quest. He accepts in the name of knightly honor, solves the problem, and moves on (supposedly) to more important enterprises. See also Dalla Palma, *Le strutture*.

3. Ariosto experimented with calling Olimpia Hispulla or Artulla before settling on his first choice, Olimpia. Her beloved, Bireno, was originally named Pruteno. See Debenedetti, XXII. Rajna (*Le fonti*) is unable

to find a specific source for the first part of the Olimpia story. He compares Olimpia to Judith, since both women take vengeance upon men through beheading. Several mythological references exist for the second part. Rajna settles on Ariadne (in Ovid's *Heroides*, X), on Hercules's saving of Hesione, and on Perseus's saving of Andromeda in Ovid's *Metamorphoses*. For the first Olimpia, Gilardino elaborates on a German source, the *Kudrunlied*.

4. To make Oberto's arrival better fit the narrative, Ariosto added an octave (11, 11) that shows Orlando's enterprise at Ebuda to be the result of a promise made to a woman he encountered before becoming engrossed with Olimpia's problems. See Debenedetti, 5.

5. See Durling; and Wiggins. Saccone ("Prospettive," 64–66) sees faith as a key structuring factor, specifically in the additions to the third edition. On faith as a continually challenged concept, see Bonifazi, 81–120. Ascoli (*Ariosto's Bitter Harmony*, 284) and Zatti (100) argue for a balance between faith and compromise. Brand (*Ludovico Ariosto*, 176–77) sees Olimpia's characterization as constituting, in Ariosto, a shift away from the rendering of earlier women as faithless (Angelica) or plainly wicked (Alcina).

6. Santoro (*L'anello*, 101) is an exception among the critics. He does not reproach Olimpia for singlemindedness but rather emphasizes the importance of rationality in her behavior. See also Brand, *Ludovico Ariosto*, 68–70.

7. Olimpia's psychological makeup can easily fit the classification of masochist, of course, but I disagree with the reasons given for her behavior. Musacchio's view ("L'Olimpia," 105) is that Olimpia is masochistic because she has no mother and her father is overindulgent. The more the father pleases her, the more guilt she feels. Bireno sees through Olimpia's constant need to punish herself, the critic writes, and abandons her for a less complicated woman. It is only after her experience in Ebuda that Olimpia finally becomes normal.

8. Dollimore (*Radical Tragedy*, 258) argues for an extension of the threat that the Other poses to the bourgeois to other categories of identities (race, sexuality, class). Barthes defines the process of inoculation as modern: "One immunizes the contents of the collective imagination by means of a small inoculation of acknowledged evil; one thus protects it against the risk of a generalized subversion. This *liberal* treatment would not have been possible only a hundred years ago. Then, the bourgeois Good did not compromise with anything, it was quite stiff. It has become much more supple since: the bourgeoisie no longer hesitates to acknowledge some localized subversions" (*Mythologies*, 150–51).

9. On woman as phallus-substitute, see Mulvey, 7.

10. In this sense, Drusilla in the Marganorre episode replicates Olimpia

in that she murders the husband imposed on her on their wedding day. The retribution for the husband's murder is authorial in the case of Olimpia and paternal in Drusilla (her father-in-law punishes her through dismemberment). Marganorre also punishes women by sadistically slitting their throats on the tombs of his two sons. Both Olimpia and Drusilla decide to commit suicide by jumping into the sea. Olimpia tries three times but fails (10, 26); Drusilla almost succeeds (37, 57). When they have no power, they similarly pretend ("simular," "simuli," "simula") to agree to the wedding: Olimpia bows to Cimosco's will (9, 36); Drusilla to Tanacro's (37, 59). Both women plot their vengeance in the same fashion: Olimpia vows that to go without first avenging herself would be more bitter than all the hurt she suffered (9, 36); Ariosto says of Drusilla that her face affected peace but her heart cried out for revenge (37, 60). "Marganor il fellon" (37, 47) resembles Cimosco, who is "il più d'ogn'altro fello" (9, 42). Both men are associated not only linguistically with the phallus (in Italian "fallo," and thus "fello," and "fellon") but also metonymically with phallic objects: a cannon for Cimosco ("il cavo ferro," 9, 73) and a tower for Marganorre ("la rocca in cima al sasso," 37, 80).

11. A recent movie seems to reenact this distinction. Critics of *Thelma and Louise* have chastised Louise, the killer of Thelma's would-be rapist, not for the murder per se, but for its gratuitousness. Louise kills the man not to stop Thelma's rape but for what he says after Thelma has already been released, a word that is sufficiently angering that she suddenly discharges her gun. In other words, Louise would have been in the right to kill the man to save Thelma from rape (the topos of the unprotected woman defended in a manly way—through a gun), but she is in the wrong for taking vengeance for what he—and other boorish men—may have done to her and her gender.

12. "To decapitate = to castrate," Freud writes bluntly ("Medusa's Head," 273). On the displacement upward, see Ferenczi.

13. There is plenty of blood in the *Furioso*, Gilardino (442) argues, but this murder is too bloody and out of character, and Ariosto refuses to use his typical irony to justify it.

14. This scene of Olimpia in bed particularly incensed Neo-Aristotelian commentators, who found the description inopportune. The danger of sexual assertiveness by woman is illustrated at length in the episode of Alcina's "demasculinization" of Ruggiero in Canto 7.

15. The episode of the Mankilling women in Cantos 19–20 further illustrates this point. The "immoral" world of these self-sufficient women is redressed by another woman, Marfisa, wielding a phallic instrument, her sword, upon which she swears to take care of the problem. Guidon Selvaggio, moreover, is sure that his wife will help him escape, even

though it means she must betray her group, because, he explains, she wants to have him for herself. Again, women are represented as having no loyalty toward each other when a man comes into the picture.

16. The story of Ariadne, daughter of Ninos, can be found in Catullus's Poem 64 and throughout Ovid's work: in *Heroides* 10 in the form of a love letter from the abandoned woman to her unfaithful husband, in *Metamorphoses* 8, and also in *Ars amatoria* 1. Ariosto's imitation of the story is not limited to the plot but extends to specific lines taken almost verbatim from Ovid. See, e.g., his rendering of Ariadne's awakening or his comparison of the bereaved woman's stillness to stones. For two suggestive studies of imitation in the Renaissance, see Greene ("The humanist poet is not a neurotic son crippled by a Freudian family romance, which is to say he is not in Harold Bloom's terms Romantic. He is rather like the son in a classical comedy who displaces his father at the moment of reconciliation"; *The Light in Troy*, 41); and Quint, *Origin and Originality*. Through a reading of the lunar episode in the *Furioso*, Quint argues that Ariosto revindicates total poetic autonomy for himself. In an examination of Ariosto's use of alternately authoritative and invalidating sources (e.g., Turpin), Zatti (193) elaborates on the poet's technique of *contaminatio* of models from the tradition. For a study of the connection between Ariosto and Ovid, see Hanning, "Ariosto, Ovid"; and Javitch, "The Imitation." In "Rescuing Ovid," Javitch shows that the Ariostan reworkings of Ovidian myths are closer to the original, playful, irreverent Latin version than to the allegorizations that in the Middle Ages moralized Ovid's stories. In "The *Orlando Furioso*," Javitch lists a number of similarities between the two authors that point forward to an altogether new appreciation and rereading of Ovid in the Renaissance. In "The Imitation," Javitch also studies Ariosto's borrowings from Catullus's Poem 64, of which *Heroides* 10 is considered a parodic imitation. Like Catullus's Ariadne, Olimpia is a paragon of faithfulness victimized by a faithless beloved. Pavlock (128, 154) notices that the attribution of faithfulness to women, rather than men, is a Catullan addition. As for the Olimpia episode, she acknowledges the use of Ovidian irony in the rendering of the scene and faults Olimpia for her irresponsibility and for speaking as a prisoner of contrived literary conventions and courtly mannerisms.

17. Ariosto certainly saw Titian's *Bacchus and Ariadne*, which was completed in 1523 and displayed in Alfonso d'Este's Camerino. See Gould, 3.

18. In this sense she is closer to Ovid's Ariadne than to Catullus's, whose response foreshadows madness.

19. The description of Orlando's killing of the Orca is close to the description of Hercules's overpowering of the sea monster in Valerius Flaccus's *Argonautica* 2, 515–17. See also Chapter 4 above on Angelica. For

more on the myth, see Apollodorus, *Library* 2, 2, 4; and Ovid, *Metamorphoses* 4, vv. 706–29. In Ariosto's retelling, the myth turns into the story of one man, who feels wronged, taking vengeance on another man, whom he had previously wronged by raping his daughter, through the bodies of, once again, women.

20. Freud lists rescue of the beloved, especially of a beloved seemingly in need of guidance and a more virtuous life, as a powerful male fantasy ("A man rescuing a woman from the water in a dream . . . amounts to making her his own mother"; "Special Type," 174). Man then identifies with the father as a paternal figure. For a discussion of rescue fantasies, see Geha.

21. The myth of Halcyone, who killed herself after she heard that her husband Ceyx—who had left her, although unwillingly, to help his brother—had tragically died at sea, is evoked in premonitory fashion even before Olimpia realizes that she has been abandoned (10, 20). Halcyone represents another example of unending, faithful, wifely love. She is changed into a bird.

22. See Barkan, "Diana and Actaeon," for an exhaustive reading of the myth; and Mazzotta, "The *Canzoniere*." See also Chapter 7 below on Fiordispina.

23. I rely here on Mulvey's insights on visual pleasure. See also Silverman, *Subject of Semiotics*, 222–25. For more on fetishism, see Chapter 4 above on Angelica.

24. The pun here, "membra"/"rimembra," is also taken from Petrarch's Canzone 23.

25. See Edgerton; and Snyder.

26. Interestingly, Ariosto had frozen Olimpia's body on the rock in the earlier canto (10, 34) and left her there until he could come back to conclude her story.

27. See Jay; Berger; and Bryson. Although the woman represented in Titian's *Venus of Urbino* looks back at the onlooker, she is an idealization of femininity and not a portrait of likeness. See Goffen (697 *n*21). Because she functions as allegory of marriage, this woman can be given an assertive role.

28. The gaze always belongs to the other, not to the subject being looked at. "In the scopic field," Lacan writes, "the gaze is outside, I am looked at, that is to say, I am a picture. . . . The gaze is the instrument through which . . . I am *photo-graphed*" (*Four Fundamental Concepts*, 106). Criticism regarding the gendered politics of looking is extensive; see, e.g., Mulvey; De Lauretis, *Alice Doesn't*; Silverman, *Subject of Semiotics*; and Doane, *The Desire to Desire*. For a rebuttal of the argument of women's passivity within the scopic regime, see Schwartz.

29. Another association is more provocative in this context, since it

seems to fit perfectly the doll-like characterization of Olimpia that I have pursued, a characterization that casts woman as "the uncanny stranger on display" in Cixous's words ("Laugh of the Medusa," 250). In his study of Manet's *Olympia*, Bernheimer points out that the protagonist of the text Freud studied in his essay on the uncanny was also named Olympia, a doll "at once human and nonhuman, alive and dead, whole yet dismemberable, female yet not" (19). Freud ("The Uncanny," 231) works on the connection between seeing and power, eye and phallus.

30. On the distinction between a nude body and a naked body, see Berger. Renaissance art used this new obsession with seeing rather than touching extensively. It was fueled partly by the spread of printing presses, which made books readily available at relatively low cost, and partly by the growth of illustrated texts.

31. Lodovico Dolce referred to Ariosto as "un Titiano" because of the palette of colors he used in representation. See also Hanning, "Ariosto, Ovid." Galileo (87–88) compared Ariosto to a painter who smooths and rounds surfaces in oil painting for a final, harmonious representation. Notwithstanding his painterly representations, Ariosto claims that writers are intrinsically better than painters since painters have remained famous through the centuries, thanks to writers ("mercè degli scrittori," 33, 1) who kept their memory alive. Ariosto's reference is to Greek artists such as Parrhasius, Apollodorus, Apelles, and the ubiquitous Zeuxis. As for modern painters, he cites many but faults them for their inability to paint the future. Unlike them, in fact, he—a writer—can revolutionize time by prophetically "painting" the French invasions of Italy (Canto 33). For a study of the connections between Ariosto and contemporary painters, with a detailed bibliography, see Gnudi; and Ceserani. Ariosto is most usually linked to Dosso Dossi, Titian, and Raphael. His epic has been illustrated by, among others, Fragonard and Doré. For a study of the use of Ariosto's motifs in painting (the encounter between Angelica and Medoro, the inscriptions on the tree, etc.), see Lee, *Names*. On Renaissance connections between poetry and painting, see Lee, *Ut Pictura Poesis*. On female bodies described through Petrarchan topoi, see Cropper, "On Beautiful Women"; and Pozzi.

32. See Ginzburg for some observations on the use of high cultural codes (usually from mythological examples taken from Ovid or from Renaissance rewritings of Ovidian material) to represent erotic female subjects in Titian. The resurgence of Ovid was most evident in the 1520's, precisely the time of the writing of the *Furioso*.

33. On the practice of blazoning women's parts as a way of taking possession of them, see Parker, *Literary Fat Ladies*, 131; and Vickers, "Diana Described" and " 'This Heraldry.' "

34. In painting, it was exactly the look back at the spectator-voyeur

that was deemed so scandalous in Manet's *Olympia*. For recent rereadings of female nudity and how nudity signifies in art, see Bryson; Berger; Saunders; and Betterton.

35. I disagree, in this context, with Pavlock's reading of the final scene. "Desire," Pavlock writes, "does not seem to be transformed by the fear of exile or death but merely gets transferred to the next available object, in this case Oberto" (184). Nothing in the narrative suggests that Olimpia desires Oberto. She simply accepts him because she has learned her lesson; or, perhaps, does not really accept him, but has finally become practical.

CHAPTER 6

1. This number is from Dalla Palma, *Le strutture*, 139. Little is known about the sources for the episode. Rajna (*Le fonti*, 227–33, 458–63) mentions Apuleius's *The Golden Ass* for the section in the cave; the French romance *Palamedès* (f. 334, f. 532) for the octaves covering Odorico's treason; Boccaccio's episode of Alatiel (*Decameron*, Day 2, Novella 7) for Isabella's voyage from her father's house and the shipwreck. From Boccaccio also comes Zerbino's name (a dialectical spelling of Gerbino), whose story in the *Decameron* (Day 4, Novella 4) resembles the love story between Isabella and Zerbino. Doralice's choice of another man comes from *Tristan* (I, f. 42) and *Palamedès*. Isabella's choice of death originates from a story in Francesco Barbaro's *De re uxoria*.

2. For more on sources for and adaptations of Lucretia's story, see Donaldson. For a study of her characterization in Salutati, see Jed; for the same in Shakespeare, see Vickers, " 'This Heraldry.' " Other oft-cited examples of women choosing self-inflicted martyrdom to avoid rape can be found in Christian exegesis (e.g., Pelagia).

3. See Di Cesare for a reading of the classical and scriptural references in the scene.

4. Describing the assault on Paris, Ariosto compares Rodomonte to a serpent ready for action after a lengthy winter hibernation (17, 11), a simile that repeats Virgil's description of Pyrrhus roaming through a wildly destroyed Troy (*Aeneid* 2, 469–75). Rodomonte is also compared to Turnus (like him, he will be killed by the "right" dynast, Ruggiero-Aeneas) and is linked to Nembrot, who built the unfinished Tower of Babel (14, 119), as Rodomonte will leave his own tower, unfinished, next to Isabella's mausoleum. On the linking of Saracens to devils in the Carolingian cycle, see Comfort. Marinelli gives two references for Rodomonte's name that connect him to demons, although Ariosto stops short of dehumanizing him: "There is the curious similarity of his name to that of Rhadamanthus, the infernal judge of Greek myth; and also to that of the fallen angel in

Wolfram von Eschenbach's *Parzival*, 'Radamant' " (*Ariosto and Boiardo*, 56). Earlier, in connection with the episode of Dalinda, Ariosto had compared a woman killer to an infernal spirit (5, 3).

5. As Greenblatt argues, "Self-fashioning is achieved in relation to something perceived as alien, strange, or hostile. This threatening Other —heretic, savage, witch, adulteress, traitor, Antichrist—must be discovered or invented in order to be attacked and destroyed" (*Renaissance Self-fashioning*, 9).

6. The latter is illustrated in the cuckold story that Rodomonte hears at the inn at which he spends the night just before his encounter with Isabella. Stories of cuckoldry are usually told for misogynistic purposes; man's lopsided representation of woman as an unreliable, unfaithful, and uncaring human being victimizing him usually ends with her disposal. On the other hand, man's desire to know about his mate's infidelities is obsessive because of what it can reveal about him to his male friends. By ridiculing her, however, he can retaliate against her capacity for mocking him and putting him in the position where he usually puts her, that of object of a discourse. At the same time, if men are victims—which is what stories of cuckoldry imply—the problem rests no longer with them, their behavior, or their inadequacies (an assumption threatening to their sexuality), but with women. Since all men are equally fooled, these stories eventually reinforce feelings of camaraderie among them. In this case, the twin examples of a queen choosing a dwarf and of a wife choosing an unkempt servant over the two most handsome men in the world are illuminating illustrations of men's fear of women's sexuality. The two women do not cuckold their husbands for worthy rivals, the teller implies; instead, their betrayal is the unavoidable result of their nature. Not surprisingly, stories told by men for men reinforce rather than question male narcissism and transform women into what best fits male fantasies. Rodomonte does not lack for vitriolic words for describing them: "Troublesome, arrogant, spiteful, unloving, faithless, foolish, brazen, cruel, wicked, thankless, you are born into the world for a perpetual plague" (27, 121).

7. For a similar view, see Wiggins, *Figures*, 56. Also see Durling, 55–56, for a rebuttal of the accusation of fickleness regarding Doralice.

8. As Durling explains, "It is untrue that women are more changeable than men in the poem; it is man in general who is flux, like all things. The instability of earthly goods has a principal embodiment in the women of the poem because they are a principal object of desire" (175).

9. The distinction between the two kinds of love for woman, one focusing on the soul, the other on the body, is widely known. Both require a hierarchy in gender positions: man is the subject/activator; woman

the object/recipient. In both cases male narcissism remains firmly in place. On Petrarchan echoes in the Rodomonte story, see Weaver, 392.

10. Ariosto plays with the pun on "above" ("sopra") for men and "below" ("sotto") for women more than once, as when he assesses Ruggiero's status at the end of the epic both in bed and in the field (46, 100). But, more interestingly, he also uses it in rationalizing why, in the past, poets have kept their female colleagues out of the halls of fame: they "would never allow women the upper hand, but did their utmost to keep them down, as though the fair sex's honour would cloud their own, as mist obscures the sun" (37, 3).

11. This attitude is quite common among knights collecting spoils of war. When Mandricardo sees Marfisa dressed as a woman, he decides to conquer her to give her to Rodomonte in what he thinks amounts to a quasi-even exchange for Doralice. Thus, he jousts with Marfisa's companions, routs them, and claims her as his property. Marfisa refuses with perfect logic: he could have her if she had been under the protection of other knights, but since she takes care of her own safety, he should engage her directly (26, 79).

12. See Sanday, 85.

13. In Greek tragedy, Loraux (61) emphasizes, these coincidences are not merely fortuitous. Men rarely die from wounds on their necks; rather, their most vulnerable parts, according to Loraux (54), are the side and the liver.

14. Ariosto reads the myth through Apollodorus's *Library* 2, 4; Fulgentius's *Mythologies*, already in print at the turn of the sixteenth century; Boccaccio's *De genealogie* 14, 10; Pierre Bersuire (Petrus Berchorius); and, of course, Ovid's *Metamorphoses*, Book 4, 5 (which offers the most common recounting).

15. Zeus's transformation into a shower of gold for seductive purposes is also recounted by Homer in the *Iliad* 14, 319–20; and by Horace in *Odes* 3, 16, 1. On the comparison of Danaë to a virginal figure, see Graves, 1:238.

16. For a study of rape in mythology, see Zeitlin.

17. For a reading of the second part of the Perseus story culminating in the rescue of Andromeda, see Chapter 5 above on Olimpia.

18. For the classical linkings in psychoanalysis of the decapitated Medusa with castration, see Freud, "Medusa's Head." See also Hertz; McGann; and L. Schneider. For further references, see Chapters 4 and 5 above on Angelica and Olimpia.

19. As John Freccero argues in discussing the Medusan power, "Its threat is the threat of idolatry. In terms of mythological exempla, petrification by the Medusa is the real consequence of Pygmalion's folly" ("Medusa," 13).

20. Freud ("The Infantile Genital Organization") links the head of the Medusa with the mother's genitals and Athena *cum* shield with unapproachability. See also "Medusa's Head," 273.

21. In *The Freudian Body*, Bersani argues for the creative potential that sublimation of a dangerously hurt sexuality eventually offers. In "The Laugh of the Medusa," Cixous comments on man's need to transform a monstrous, Medusan (sexual) female into a positive (asexual) one ("She is not deadly. She is beautiful and she's laughing," 255).

22. Entombment returns Isabella to her starting point, since she was imprisoned in a cave before Orlando's arrival. Caves are feminine enclosures in the *Furioso*, the most obvious case being the cave inhabited by Merlino, in which Bradamante learns of the dynastic future she will put into motion. For more on tombs and enclosures, see Chesney, 158; and Ascoli, *Ariosto's Bitter Harmony*, 371.

23. As Lacan was to say, "The body as ultimate signified is the cadaver or stone phallus" ("Le corps comme signifié dernier, c'est le cadavre ou le phalle de pierre"). The French quotation comes from an unpublished seminar paper by Lacan entitled "La relation d'objet" (Dec. 5, 1956), cited in David-Menard, 191.

24. The indispensable text on homosocial desire is Sedgwick's.

25. On the collector's reasons for subsuming "the environment to a scenario of the personal," see Stewart, 162–63.

26. A reversal of this custom takes place at the conclusion of the Marganorre episode. After defeating him, Bradamante and Marfisa inscribe a new law in the column previously used to assert Marganorre's law. They also add his armor, shield, and helmet (37, 119). Rather than being an emblem of man's power, as it was for Rodomonte, here the accoutrement symbolizes man's utter powerlessness.

27. On the melancholic's eroticization of the lost object, see Agamben, 27.

28. Abraham and Torok connect introjection to mourning (the mourner takes stock of his loss of the loved one) and incorporation to melancholia (the mourner refuses to come to terms with his grief). See also Lacan's reading of Freud's term "incorporation" ("Desire," 37). By foregrounding gender, Schiesari rewrites melancholia as male and shows how the appropriation of the poetics of melancholia/mourning varies with the gender of the mourner.

CHAPTER 7

1. On degli Agostini's continuation of the story, see Bruscagli. The numbering of the octaves quoted is his. On twins in contemporary texts

(e.g., Bibbiena's *La Calandria* written in 1513), see Ferroni, "Sprezzatura." Rajna (*Le fonti*) writes that the *Menaechmi* had a number of runs in theaters in Ferrara, specifically in 1486, 1491, and 1493. On sources of sex changes used for the sake of a ruse, see Rajna, "Ricciardetto." He mentions a medieval poem, Guillaume de Blois's *Alda*, as a source for male cross-dressing and speculates that Ariosto might have inserted the Fiordispina-Ricciardetto story later in the process of composition. As is often the case for Renaissance heroes, Ricciardetto's love story is further elaborated by another author, Giovampietro Civeri, in *Ricciardetto innamorato* (Venice: Agostino Zoppini e nipoti, 1595). The book is listed in Beer's "Appendice II" (362), a chronological survey of epic romances printed between 1470 and 1600. As for Fiordispina, considered a personification of *impudicitia* by the Renaissance moralist and allegorist Orazio Toscanella (*Bellezze del "Furioso,"* Venice, 1574), she turns out to be just that in her reincarnation as Malecasta in Spenser's *The Fairie Queene*, a name strongly pointing to her supposed lack of, or lack of desire for, chastity. Surprisingly though, Fiordispina's lament about unnatural love resurfaces in an altogether different context in Spenser in Britomart's avowal of love for Arthegall (3, 2, 30–47). The episode of Fiordispina's searching for the "tool" in Bradamante that would allow her to gratify her desire can also be found in *The Fairie Queene* (3, 2, 60–66), where Malecasta prowls in Britomart's bed, thinking to find a man, only to discover that the guest will resort to the sword to foil her attempt at seduction. See Alpers, 37–80, 180–85. Wiggins notices that Spenser is ambivalent toward Ariosto and tends to present his borrowings from the Italian master as moral rewritings; for example, in the Fiordispina episode he manages "to make Ariosto seem the proponent of hedonistic promiscuity and penis worship" ("Spenser's Anxiety," 85), which is for Spenser one way of reading Ariosto minus his pervasive irony. Fiordispina's surprise and rejoicing at her bedmate's sexual transformation (" 'If this is a dream,' she cried, 'keep me asleep for good,' " 25, 67) has echoes in Shakespeare's *Twelfth Night* ("If it be thus to dream, still let me sleep," IV.i.62), another tale of sexual gyrations.

2. On transgression of dress codes, see Jardine. On sumptuary laws in Italy, see Hughes, "Sumptuary Laws." For an analysis of inversion and perversion, see Dollimore, "Subjectivity." Belsey ("Disrupting Sexual Difference") argues that cross-dressing opened up new possibilities for definitions of gender. Focusing on the theater, Levine writes that transvestism challenged the notion of a fixed gender with the perception that it was not. This unfixed gender was, of course, seen as monstrous. For a study of transvestism in romances, see Schleiner.

3. See Davis's chapter "Women on Top." The public was also accustomed to seeing cross-dressing on stage in England, where boys routinely

played women's roles. In Italy, however, theatrical companies often consisted of related individuals, and women were frequently used as actresses. Orgel ("Nobody's Perfect," 9) notes that Italian companies performing in England naturally used their actresses, although English women were not ordinarily allowed to perform on stage.

4. Silverman ("Fragments," 139) points out that men used clothes in exhibitionistic ways until the end of the seventeenth century, when material and size ceased to correspond to status. Hollander argues that for a time in the early sixteenth century men's bodies were portrayed in suggestive poses with "decolletage and flowing hair" (208) in the front, and colorful stockings emphasizing the rear. In some paintings (e.g., Mantegna's *Martyrdom of Saint Christopher*), the lacings holding the stockings were even left partially undone to project a stronger sexual appeal (235). As for today, women's cross-dressing is so common that it is hardly possible to talk of female disguise; see Barthes, *The Fashion System*, 257. Things have not changed too much for men, however; they put on women's clothes only with some sense of comic relief in mind and with the understanding that such clothes simply suggest a temporary, freely chosen aberration. There is indeed plenty of power still attached to the simple act of choosing one's clothes and what sex to imitate.

5. According to Irigaray (*This Sex*, 133), women masquerade to be part of man's desire, but this eventually leads them to relinquish their own desire. See also Heath, "Joan Rivière"; and Doane, "Masquerade Reconsidered," 44, for two readings of Rivière's position. Doane ("Film and the Masquerade") defines the masquerade as an act of resistance, an active way for a woman to destabilize expectations of what she should be. The female masquerade, then, does not constitute a submission to a dominant ideology, but a way to create a position of resistance because it helps to undermine the usual representation of femininity. For a reading of the masquerade in Ariosto as it relates to Dalinda and Gabrina, see Finucci. For a reading of the masquerade through Bakhtin, see Russo.

6. For more on the concepts of masculinism and masculinity, see Britton.

7. Paradoxically, in Canto 36 Ferraù—uncertain whether the warrior who unhorsed him is Bradamante or Ricciardetto—decides it is Bradamante precisely because of her proven superiority in combat (36, 13).

8. Following Aristotle (*De generatione animalium*) and Galen, and up until the eighteenth century, male and female reproductive organs were thought to be homologous, with female organs imagined as inverted versions of the male (they could not come out for lack of heat). The standard being masculine, a hierarchical placement followed. The female, it was thought, contributed no seed because of her coldness; moreover, fluid dis-

charge, if any, appeared only, as one would expect, in the most feminine types ("it occurs in the fair-skinned and feminine of appearance as a rule, not in the dark and masculine-looking," *De generatione animalium* I, 49). See Jordan, *Renaissance Feminism*, 29–34; Laqueur; Greenblatt, "Fiction and Friction"; and MacLean.

9. Freud also elaborates on penis envy in "The Taboo of Virginity," 205, where he connects penis envy to women's hostile reaction toward men following their first sexual intercourse.

10. See J. Rose, *Sexuality*, 66. The distinction between penis and phallus has been the object of great critical interest. For Gallop, "The penis is what men have and women do not; the phallus is the attribute of power which neither men nor women have. But as long as the attribute of power is a phallus which can only have meaning by referring to and being confused with a penis, this confusion will support a structure in which it seems reasonable that men have power and women do not" (127). See also Sprengnether, 156–58; and Butler, 44–48. On the differentiation of the phallus as natural and the phallus as ideologically and culturally constructed, see Ebert, 32–33.

11. "For want of a stake," Montrelay argues, "representation is not worth anything" (234). The construction of a stake for woman, a task that Irigaray and Kristeva have tried to accomplish, has been criticized as essentialist; see Doane, "Woman's Stake."

12. For a more detailed examination of Bradamante's femininity, see Chapter 8 below. That the unwilling submission to a haircut, as in the Biblical story of Samson and Delilah, is castrating for man is evident in the episode of the monster Orrilo in Canto 15. Orrilo is able to reconstitute his body, no matter how many parts have been cut off, by simply picking up and putting back in place the truncated elements. The end comes when Astolfo, after cutting his head, shears his hair from side to side and thus severs the fatal hair ("crine fatal") that guaranteed the monster's invincibility and immortality (15, 78–88).

13. Ricciardetto's opportunism is far from the posture of a courtly lover. In courtly love literature such gratifications are out of the question, given the different social class and marital status of the lady and her suitor.

14. In Bibbiena's *La calandria*, whose plot of cross-dressings and exchanges of identities has a number of similarities to the present episode, Fulvia discovers that Santilla, who should be a man (Lidio) dressed as his twin sister, Santilla, is indeed Santilla herself, a woman. This makes Fulvia despair at the sign of such a visible lack: "privo si trova di quel che più si brama" (he lacks what is most wanted). Brand ("Ariosto's Ricciardetto," 125) doubts that Ariosto could have known *La calandria*, first performed in Urbino in 1513 and then in Rome in 1514, although both presentations took place before Ariosto wrote this episode.

15. See Jacqueline Rose, "Introduction II," esp. 46–48 (in Mitchell and Rose, *Feminine Sexuality*), for a reading of Lacan in this context; and Baudrillard for a reading of Freud ("Freud was right: there is but one sexuality, one libido—and it is masculine. Sexuality has a strong, discriminative structure centered on the phallus, castration, the Name-of-the-Father, and repression. There is none other. There is no use dreaming of some non-phallic, unlocked, unmarked sexuality," 6).

16. "Desire is quite independent from the objects it seeks and is in no way determined by the value or desirability of the latter," Donato writes. In the Fiordispina incident, he continues, "the systematic inversion of the sexual roles shows how amorous relationships are subordinated to a problem of desire rather than the latter being an immediate consequence of a natural attraction" (38).

17. I am aware that this is a generalization and that there is more at stake in this issue. Fiordispina is represented as a hunting Diana, which means not only that she represents woman but also that she stands for whatever man sees as dangerous in woman. (As the Actaeon myth shows, Diana's sacred virginity leads to man's dismemberment as retaliation for an unlawful, voyeuristic seeing.) Likewise, Bradamante appears as a woman on the grass, but there is also a long tradition of sleeping male knights both in pastoral and in Breton literature. For the purpose of my argument, however, I choose to simplify the problem.

18. See Bellour; and Lemoine-Luccioni, *La robe* ("The cases of female fetishism are rare and always doubtful. The reason is a simple one: woman does not have a penis; she is therefore not exposed to the threat of castration, at least not in the same fashion as man does," 124).

19. As Ebert puts it, "Bigenderism is a strategic or *quasi*-bigenderism that can only be partially and temporarily enacted. Individuals are permitted to occupy bigendered subject positions—to take on *limited* attributes of the other gender—only to the degree that is specifically required by current relations of production and only so far as the primacy of male gender is not substantially threatened" (36).

20. Cross-dressing excites men, not women, who choose to dress in pants for practical reasons and not for sexual titillation; see Millot, 104.

21. See also her *Speculum*.

22. For more in this context, see Adams, "Representation" and "Per Os"; Kofman, *The Enigma of Woman*; and Silverman, "Masochism." For a study of the concept of bisexuality, see Laplanche and Pontalis.

23. For Merleau-Ponty (see "The Body," in his *Phenomenology*), the body is not constituted naturally, but historically. This point is useful in establishing that although it is true that all individuals as a species are biologically marked, it is only through time that they become gender-specific. See also Butler; Scott; and De Lauretis, *Technologies*.

24. For a study of transsexualism along Lacanian lines, see Millot. For a study of androgyny (positive and negative) in the Renaissance, see Jordan, *Renaissance Feminism*, 136–37; Woodbridge, 140–41; and Silberman. For a reading of female impersonation as convenient to men, see Miller, "I's in Drag."

25. For more on the myth, see C. Freccero, 149, and Silberman. Freud's connection of water, birth, and maternity is well known: "Birth is regularly expressed in dreams by some connection with water: one falls into the water or one comes out of the water—one gives birth or one is born" ("Symbolism in Dreams," 160).

26. The imitation is at times quite clear. See, e.g., octaves 35–37 in Ariosto and Ovid, *Metamorphoses* 9, vv. 727–36 (" 'What will become of me?' / She said, 'Possessed by love unheard of, love / So monstrous, so unique? . . . / Cows never yearn for cows, nor mares for mares; / The ewe follows the ram, the hind her hart; / So the birds mate, so every animal; / A female never fires a female's love.' "

27. See Vickers's reading of the myth ("Diana Described") in the context of the famous Petrarchan Canzone 23, "Nel dolce tempo della prima etade." See also Mazzotta's study ("The *Canzoniere*") of Petrarch's shifting identificatory positions between Diana and Actaeon. For another reading of the myth in Ariosto, see Chapter 5 above on Olimpia.

28. See Ruggiero on governmental interventions in Venice to discipline sexuality and prosecute fornication during the Renaissance. Ricciardetto's sin of concupiscence had been judged of minor consequence (23, 57). The Magnifico, in Book 3 of the *Cortegiano*, says the same about men's profligacy: "We have granted ourselves the license by which we want the same sins that are trivial and sometimes even praiseworthy when committed by men to be so damnable in women that they cannot be punished enough, save by a shameful death or at least everlasting infamy" (3, 38, 244).

CHAPTER 8

1. For a reading of Marfisa as serious *guerriera* and Bradamante as comic, see Tomalin, "Bradamante and Marfisa"; and idem, *Fortunes*.

2. There is a similar celebration of Bradamante's female progeny later in Canto 13, 56–73. There, however, rather than offering a list drawn from myth, fiction, and history, as in the case of the male descendents in Canto 3, Ariosto makes a few exemplary women suffice for all the unmentioned ones in order to speed matters ("ch'a fin ne vegna," 13, 58).

3. See Klapisch-Zuber; Ariès; Hay and Law; and Kelly-Gadol. Goldthwaite notices a considerable increase in the building of family palaces (usually housing a single conjugal family), a reflection of the movement

in that period toward a nuclear family sharing living arrangements. In a study of the Florentine *catasto*, Herlihy and Klapisch-Zuber (297) arrive at the same conclusions. The monogamous family rests on unquestionable paternity, since it distributes property along patrilineal lines. As a consequence, women's chastity acquires extreme importance. Women's position within the household during the fifteenth and sixteenth centuries seems to have been domesticated more than ever, for wives were both institutionally and ideologically subordinated to their husbands. Concern for lineage reduced the size and responsibility of the conjugal family as younger sons were cast off and younger daughters were sent to nunneries. Since the aristocracy would not marry its daughters below their rank, the sixteenth century saw an increase in dowries to three times their level of the previous century. Hughes ("Representing the Family," *n27*; see also 26–28) writes that as many as 44 percent of young women were disposed through forced monacation in the seventeenth century, the time when this custom was most visible. For more on some of these points, see Hamilton. On the connections between work and sexual discipline, and between public and private that came to the forefront with the rise of the middle class, see Elias, 161–91; and Foucault, *History of Sexuality*. On the eroticization of the household during the Renaissance, see Stone. See also the Introduction to this book.

4. Greenblatt writes: "This whole conception of individuation seems to me bound up with Renaissance conception of the emergence of male identity. . . . If a crucial step in male individuation is separation from the female, this separation is enacted inversely in the rites of cross-dressing" ("Fiction and Friction," 93). On female cross-dressing, see also K. Newman, "Renaissance Family Politics"; Jardine; Howard, "Crossdressing"; M. Rose; and more generally, Chapter 7 above on Fiordispina.

5. On homosexuality in the Renaissance, see Saslow. On sexual habits and sexual crimes of the period in Venice and for legal interventions to regulate them, see Ruggiero.

6. For a study of treatises, see Jordan, *Renaissance Feminism*; Kelso; Kelly-Gadol; and Fahy. The most cherished wifely virtues were chastity and silence. Ariosto was familiar with a number of treatises on women. He knew Castiglione's text at the very least, along with Mario Equicola's *De mulieribus* (1501). (Like Ariosto, Equicola was at the Este court in Ferrara.) In her introductory remarks, Woodbridge argues that misogynistic attitudes toward women in literary texts should not necessarily stand as reflections of the real state of women in society or of the author's real feelings on the issue. For some of these topics, see Chapter 2 above.

7. See Quint, "The Figure of Atlante," 80; Parker, *Inescapable Romance*, 37; Ascoli, *Ariosto's Bitter Harmony*, 376; and Zatti, chap. 1. The shift from

open-endedness (typical of romances) to closure (typical of epic narratives) seems to take place in the middle of the *Furioso* with the destruction of Atlante's palace and the death of Pinabello. A number of critics, such as Donato, however, see the *Furioso* as open-ended, or at least as having an unsatisfactory ending. As for the *Innamorato*, there is a general agreement that this romance epic does not proceed structurally toward closure (see Marinelli, *Ariosto and Boiardo*, 75–76).

8. In the third *Furioso*, many choices seem to parallel middle-class values (e.g., Bradamante refuses to disobey her parents, and Ruggiero agrees that he is worth little without a crown), and the individual knight no longer gets involved in adventures that reaffirm his own individuality. For Moretti (96), the world of the 1532 *Furioso* is a world of strict social conventions fostering negativity in human behavior.

9. See, e.g., MacLean, 57, 66, 84. Kelso essentially is of the same opinion. I would argue that women's cross-dressing is a literary topic precisely because it was often only a literary fantasy.

10. Tasso writes in *Apologia*: "This appropriateness is not in the *Furioso*, where Ruggiero is more loved than he loves and Bradamante loves more than she is loved. She pursues Ruggiero, tries to free him from prison, and performs all those tasks and operations that would appear more appropriate in a knight who wants to acquire the love of his woman, even allowing for the fact that she is a warrior; whereas Ruggiero does nothing to gain the love of Bradamante, seems to care little for her, and shows little esteem of her. This would not be so unseemly were the poet not pretending that from this love and this marriage the Princes of Este were to derive" (132).

11. A booklet attached to an edition of the *Furioso* and titled *Pareri in duello* (Venice: Valvassori, 1566) examines the praxis of the different duels of the *Furioso*. According to this text, there is no reason for the armed encounter between Bradamante and Sacripante in Canto 1 because Sacripante has nothing to settle with Bradamante (10). The duel between Ruggiero and Rodomonte in the last canto, however, is the most justified because it closely follows the rules of honor governing jousts (564). See Hempfer, 317. Thus Bradamante is unwittingly deprived of the right of victory for the only joust she engages in without the magic spear or the help of Melissa (apart from her later duel with Pinabello, which has catastrophic consequences for Ruggiero), because the duel is useless according to chivalric rules.

12. Swords are not as important to women as they are to men. As McLucas ("Ariosto," 61–72) notices, men often name them (Orlando's is called Durindana, Ruggiero's Balisarda) or go to war to retrieve them (Mandricardo is obsessed with Orlando's sword). Ariosto even modifies

Bradamante's name from its uneven spelling in Boiardo ("Brandimante" or "Brandiamante") in order to eradicate any phallic association from it.

13. McLucas ("Amazon," 41–42) attributes Ariosto's unwillingness to have his women suffer injury or death in battle to three causes: (1) Ariosto might not take them seriously as warriors; (2) Ariosto does not want a wound to stain women's beauty and appearance; (3) Ariosto does not want to portray women as humiliated. I agree that all three are plausible when taken together. However, other women die in the *Furioso* outside combat, and their death is neither aesthetically nor morally plausible (e.g., Gabrina's macabre hanging and Isabella's bloody beheading). Women are not to be wounded in combat because combat is a temporary activity for them, I submit, and real wounds for women, those that in narrative make characters grow and understand, must come from other, more important areas in life, often the result of biological drives. The connotations of honor, which are always at stake for men in combat, change when applied to women.

14. In some instances, not only does Bradamante seem to have the phallus, but Ariosto also makes puns about her having it. After she defeats them, the three Northern kings decide to punish themselves for their failure ("punir lor fallo," 33, 76); when she meets Rodomonte, she chastises him for wanting others to make penance for his fault ("penitenza del tuo fallo," 35, 42). *Fallo* in Italian means not only "fault" but also "phallus" and "penis."

15. For a reading of the Mankilling women episode, see Roche; for a reading of the Marganorre episode, see Ascoli's "Cotextual Ironies."

16. Amazons are connected to incorrect femininity but not to aberrant sexuality. See Schleiner ("While there is a long tradition, going back to Greek historians, of presenting Amazons as 'monstrous' in many ways . . . lesbianism is not usually part of that tradition," 614).

17. Both Bradamante and Marfisa are botched Amazon figures in their comic endings. Throughout the mythical tradition, Amazons are wounded and killed by the male hero, who often pierces their breasts in an appropriate gesture of denial of woman's difference. Tasso, for one, is closer to the tradition in his choice of the method of Clorinda's death. On Marfisa as a recast Camilla, see Roche. For a study of the theme of wounded Amazons in Tasso's epic, see Bellamy. Javitch ("The *Orlando Furioso*," 1029) suggests that Ariosto rewrites Virgil but also deflates the grandeur of his heroes, even as he imitates Ovid in earnest. Javitch believes that Ariosto was already aware that the two Latin poets were promoting a radically different view of Augustan ideology: Virgil's was moral, solemn, ordered, and passionless; Ovid's was witty, irreverent, revisionary, and subversive. Ariosto's mood is clearly closer to Ovid's playfulness than to

Virgil's ponderousness. Fichter argues that neither Ariosto's treatment of the epic nor his treatment of history is specifically Virgilian, even in those passages in which Ariosto consciously uses Virgilian tones and settings. See also Parker, *Inescapable Romance.*

18. In this sense, the wedding of Bradamante and Ruggiero resembles that of Lavinia and Aeneas in the continuation of the *Aeneid* by Maphaeus Vegius, "Thirteenth Book of the *Aeneid.*"

19. Momigliano (140) argues that Canto 44 is one of the worst in the *Furioso* precisely because the bourgeois motive is unpoetic. For a view closer to mine, see Benson. In light of this canto, it may be argued that there is indeed a woman who is powerful throughout the *Furioso*, a woman whose will is very much taken into account. This woman is Beatrice, Bradamante's mother, who insists that her daughter marry a landed nobleman in order to remain within her class. Beatrice is indeed powerful, but I would suggest that she is powerful because she is a mother, not because she is a woman. As a wife, a woman owes as much obedience to her husband as children owe to their father. But as a mother, she is also respected by her children, who owe obedience to her. A powerful mother, however, can be threatening because she can challenge male privileges by having a voice in the exchange of daughters in marriage. Thus, Beatrice as a mother is not characterized in positive terms in the *Furioso*, and Ariosto refuses to give a mother, empowered or disempowered, to any other female character in his narrative, although they all have fathers. Even Marfisa finds herself with a putative father, Atlante.

20. No outside approval, priest, ceremony, witness, or banns were needed for two consenting adults to marry until the church came to regulate the matter during the sixteenth century and punished or excommunicated those who chose to do otherwise. See Ozment, 25–44. On nuptial rites in Tuscany up to the Counter-Reformation, see Klapisch-Zuber, 178–212. Ruggiero argues that the uncertainty about what kind of consent determined a lawful union meant for many lower-class couples that they could have a sexual relationship and postpone the ceremonial wedding to a later date. As can easily be imagined given the property involved, restrictions were especially relevant for higher-class families. According to Ruggiero, Venetian courts often intervened on matters of unlawful fornication brought to their attention, but higher-class families had their cases tried directly in the upper courts to underline the importance of the matter for social and economic reasons. Ariosto clearly emphasizes obedience to paternal and maternal will.

21. This outcome points forward to the pair's last joust, one in which Ruggiero again defeats Rodomonte in the name of moral superiority (see Dalla Palma, *Le Strutture*, 173–74). For a comprehensive reading of the

Innamorato, see Franceschetti. For a specific reading of this episode, see Marinelli, *Ariosto and Boiardo*.

22. On this topic, see Giamatti, *Spenser*; and Shepherd. As Robinson (179 *n*27) also notices, the story recalls Achilles's discovery of Penthesilea's sex when her helmet is lifted.

23. The same sequence of the unhelmeted woman warrior receiving a wound on the neck at a moment of amorous dialogue also occurs in Tasso's Tancredi/Clorinda episode (3, 29–30). Clorinda will die in a subsequent duel after being mortally wounded in her breast. For more on women's necks and throats, see Chapter 6 above on Isabella.

24. In a postmodern rewriting of this scene in *Il cavaliere inesistente*, Calvino ironically displaces from top to bottom the act of seeing a woman's face and of falling in love, as Rambaldo/Ruggiero chooses to admire different cheeks in Bradamante. He starts to love her at the very moment he sees her squatting for the purpose of urinating (49). See M. Schneider for some considerations on Bradamante's characterization in Calvino (she is promiscuous now and will become a nun writing the story of her adventures). Unlike Ruggiero, Rambaldo appears emasculated.

25. On the connection between seeing and power, eye and phallus, and its reverse, blindness and castration, all notions tied to the explanation of the Oedipus complex, see Freud, "The Uncanny," 231.

26. The tradition of seeing the face as a book to read and decipher is a long one. Stewart (128) cites Dante's famous collapsing of the notion of reading a face with literal alphabetization when the word OMO "constructs" a universal, human (man's) face in the *Commedia*.

27. See also Lacan, *Le seminaire XX*. For a reading of Lacan in this context, see Silverman, *Subject of Semiotics*; and Lemaire. For applications of the Lacanian castration complex to the visual field, see J. Rose, *Sexuality*; Mulvey; and Lurie.

28. Like many love stories in the latter part of the *Furioso* (e.g., Fiammetta, Adonio), this is a story of fidelity and of fear of cuckoldry. See Brand, *Ludovico Ariosto*, 78. Pool (187) finds the insertion redundant and a step backward in Bradamante's evolution.

29. In this sense, Ariosto corrects Ricciardetto's previous statement on the subject in Canto 25. There Ricciardetto constructs gender difference precisely from hair length and identifies himself as a man thanks to his cropped hair; here Bradamante questions the reliability of such an identification.

30. On Bradamante's madness aroused by love, see Weaver.

31. In the *Furioso*, Ullania is forgotten after being last seen in the city of Marganorre, a fact that Debenedetti (XXVIII) laments since Ariosto rarely leaves characters stranded.

32. See Segre, 34. For a structural reading of these octaves, see Casadei, 61–71. On the interweaving of ekphrasis and encomium, see Shapiro, *Poetics of Ariosto*, chap. 6.

33. See Debenedetti, XXIX; for the text of the 20 deleted stanzas, see pp. 145–48 of the same text. Merlino's frescoes come from Boiardo's *Innamorato* 2, 25, 42–56. There Brandimarte sees a fresco made of four scenes celebrating the past adventures and present glory of the Estes up to Alfonso, Ariosto's last patron. Hulse uses the narrated set of frescoes as a starting point for his study of the relationship between literature and painting (*paragone*) in the Renaissance.

34. For a study of the fragment and the story of its conservation, see Debenedetti's introduction. The fragment (in bad state) is kept today at the Biblioteca Nazionale in Naples (MS no. 352). Ariosto's attention to closure is also evident in his decision to omit the *Cinque canti* from the *Furioso*.

35. For a reading of the Olimpia/Ariadne story, see Chapter 5 above on Olimpia. For an examination of Cassandra's tapestry, see Ascoli, *Ariosto's Bitter Harmony*, 380–92; and Perry.

Bibliography

Abraham, Nicolas, and Maria Torok. "Introjection-Incorporation: Mourning *or* Melancholia." In Lebovici and Widlocher, eds., 3–16.

Adams, Parveen. "Per Os(cillation)." *Camera Obscura* 17 (1988): 7–29.

———. "Representation and Sexuality." *m/f* 1 (1978): 65–82.

Agamben, Giorgio. *Stanze: La parola e il fantasma nella cultura occidentale.* Turin: Einaudi, 1977.

Alberti, Leon Battista. *The Family in Renaissance Florence.* Trans. Renée New Watkins of *I libri della famiglia.* Columbia: University of South Carolina Press, 1969.

Alpers, Paul. *The Poetry of the "Fairie Queene."* Princeton: Princeton University Press, 1967.

Althusser, Louis. *For Marx.* Trans. Ben Brewster. New York: Pantheon, 1969.

———. "Ideology and Ideological State Apparatuses (Notes Towards an Investigation)." In idem, *Lenin,* 127–86.

———. *Lenin and Philosophy and Other Essays.* Trans. Ben Brewster. New York: Monthly Review Press, 1971.

———. "A Letter on Art in Reply to André Daspre." In idem, *Lenin,* 221–27.

Apollodorus. *The Library.* 2 vols. Ed. and trans. J. Frazier. Cambridge, Mass.: Harvard University Press, 1961.

Apte, Mahadev. *Humor and Laughter: An Anthropological Study.* Ithaca, N.Y.: Cornell University Press, 1985.

Ariès, Philippe. *Centuries of Childhood: A Social History of Family Life.* Trans. Robert Boldick. New York: Knopf, 1962.

Ariosto, Ludovico. *Cinque canti.* Ed. Lanfranco Caretti. Turin: Einaudi, 1977.

———. *Orlando furioso.* Ed. Giuliano Innamorati. Bologna: Zanichelli, 1967.

———. *Orlando furioso.* Ed. Marcello Turchi. Milan: Garzanti, 1974.

——. *Orlando Furioso*. Trans. Guido Waldman. Oxford: Oxford University Press, 1983.

——. *The Satires of Ludovico Ariosto*. Trans. Peter DeSa Wiggins. Athens: Ohio University Press, 1976.

Aristotle. *Aristotle's De Partibus Animalium I and De Generatione Animalium I*. Trans. B. M. Balme. Oxford: Clarendon Press, 1972.

——. *Aristotle's Politics*. Grinnell, Ia.: Peripatetic Press, 1986.

Ascoli, Albert. *Ariosto's Bitter Harmony: Crisis and Evasion in the Italian Renaissance*. Princeton: Princeton University Press, 1987.

——. "Cotextual Ironies: Sexual Politics and Poetics in *Orlando Furioso*." Unpublished essay.

Augustine. *City of God*. Ed. D. Knowles. Harmondsworth, Eng.: Penguin, 1972.

Bacchelli, Riccardo. *La congiura di Don Giulio d'Este*. Milan: Mondadori, 1958.

Bakhtin, Mikhail. *The Dialogic Imagination: Four Essays*. Ed. Michael Holquist. Austin: University of Texas Press, 1981.

——. *Rabelais and His World*. Trans. Helene Iswolki. Cambridge, Mass.: MIT Press, 1968.

Barbaro, Giovanni. *De re uxoria* (On wifely duties). Paris, 1513, 1533. Trans. B. Kohl, R. Witt, and E. Welles as *The Earthly Republic: Italian Humanists on Government and Society*. Philadelphia: University of Pennsylvania Press, 1978.

Barberi-Squarotti, Giorgio. "Nei dintorni del *Furioso*." In idem, *Fine dell'idillio: Da Dante a Marino*. Genoa: Melangolo, 1978, 105–16.

Barkan, Leonard. "Diana and Actaeon: The Myth as Synthesis." *English Literary Renaissance* 10 (1980): 317–59.

——. *The Gods Made Flesh: Metamorphosis and the Pursuit of Paganism*. New Haven: Yale University Press, 1986.

Barocchi, Paola, ed. *Scritti d'arte del Cinquecento*, vol. 2. Milan and Naples: Ricciardi, 1973.

Barrett, Michele. *Women's Oppression Today*. London: New Left Books, 1980.

Barthes, Roland. *The Fashion System*. New York: Hill & Wang, 1983.

——. *A Lover's Discourse*. Trans. Richard Howard. New York: Hill & Wang, 1978.

——. *Mythologies*. Trans. Alan Bass. London: Routledge & Kegan Paul, 1978.

Baudrillard, Jean. *Seduction*. Trans. Brian Singer. New York: St. Martin's Press, 1990.

Beer, Marina. *Romanzi di cavalleria: "Il Furioso" e il romanzo italiano del primo Cinquecento*. Rome: Bulzoni, 1987.

Bellamy, Elizabeth J. *Translations of Power: Narcissism and the Unconscious in*

Epic History. Ithaca, N.Y.: Cornell University Press, 1992.

Bellour, Raymond. "Psychosis, Neurosis, Perversion." *Camera Obscura* 3–4 (1979): 104–32.

Belsey, Catherine. "Constructing the Subject: Deconstructing the Text." In Judith Newton and Deborah Rosenfelt, eds., *Feminist Criticism and Social Change: Sex, Class and Race in Literature and Culture*. London: Methuen, 1985, 45–64.

——. *Critical Practice*. New York: Methuen, 1980.

——. "Disrupting Sexual Difference: Meaning and Gender in the Comedies." In John Drakakis, ed., *Alternative Shakespeares*. London: Methuen, 1985, 166–90.

——. *The Subject of Tragedy: Identity and Difference in Renaissance Drama*. New York: Methuen, 1985.

Benson, Pamela. "A Defense of the Excellence of Bradamante." *Quaderni d'Italianistica* 4 (1983): 135–53.

Berg, Elizabeth. "The Third Woman." *Diacritics* 12 (1982): 11–20.

Berger, John. *Ways of Seeing*. Harmondsworth, Eng.: Penguin, 1977.

Bergson, Henri. *Le Rire*. Paris: Presses Universitaires de France, 1950.

Berlusconi, Giovanna. "L'*Orlando furioso* poema dello spazio." In E. Girardi, ed., *Studi sull'Ariosto*. Milan: Vita e Pensiero, 1977, 39–130.

Bernheimer, Charles. "The Uncanny Lure of Manet's *Olympia*." In Diane Hunter, ed., *Seduction and Theory: Readings of Gender, Representation, and Rhetoric*. Urbana: University of Illinois Press, 1989, 13–27.

Berni, Francesco. *Rifacimento*. Venice: Giunta, 1545.

Bersani, Leo. *The Freudian Body: Psychoanalysis and Art*. New York: Columbia University Press, 1986.

Bertoni, Giulio. *La biblioteca estense e la cultura ferrarese ai tempi del duca Ercole I*. Turin: Loescher, 1903.

Betterton, Rosemary, ed. *Looking on: Femininity in the Visual Arts and the Media*. London: Pandora, 1987.

Bibbiena (Dovizi, Bernardo). *La calandria*. Padua: Antenore, 1985.

Bloch, Howard. *The Scandal of the Fabliaux*. Chicago: University of Chicago Press, 1986.

Boch, Gisela, and Giuliana Nobili, eds., *Il corpo delle donne*. Bologna: Transeuropa, 1988.

Boiardo, Matteo. *Orlando innamorato*. 2 vols. Ed. Angelandrea Zottoli. Milan: Mondadori, 1937.

Bologna, Corrado. "Le mutazioni del *Furioso*." In Alberto Asor Rosa, ed., *Letteratura Italiana VI*. Turin: Einaudi, 1986, 680–98.

Bonadeo, Alfredo. "Olimpia." *Italica* 45 (1958): 47–58.

Bonifazi, Neuro. *Le lettere infedeli: Ariosto, Leopardi, Manzoni*. Rome: Officina Edizioni, 1975.

Boose, Lynda. "The Family in Shakespeare Studies; or—Studies in the

Bibliography

Family of Shakespeareans; or—The Politics of Politics." *Renaissance Quarterly* 40 (1987): 707–42.

Bourdieu, Pierre. *Outline of a Theory of Practice*. Trans. R. Nice. Cambridge, Eng.: Cambridge University Press, 1977.

―――. "Symbolic Power." In Denis Gleeson, ed., *Identity and Structure: Issues in the Sociology of Education*. Driffield, Eng.: Nafferton Books, 1977, 112–19.

Braidotti, Rosi. "Modelli di dissonanza: donne e/in filosofia." In Patrizia Magli, ed., *Le donne e i segni: Scrittura, linguaggio, identità nel segno della differenza femminile*. Urbino: Il Lavoro Editoriale, 1985, 23–37.

Brand, C. P. "Ariosto's Ricciardetto and Fiordispina." In Gerhard Schmidt and Manfred Tietz, eds., *Stimmen der Romania: Festschrift für Theodor Elwert zum 70. Geburtstag*. Wiesbaden: Heymann Verlag, 1980, 121–33.

―――. *Ludovico Ariosto: A Preface to the "Orlando Furioso."* Edinburgh: Edinburgh University Press, 1974.

Britton, Andrew. *Masculinity and Power*. Oxford: Basil Blackwell, 1989.

Brown, Judith. "A Woman's Place Was in the Home: Women's Work in Renaissance Tuscany." In Ferguson et al., eds., 206–24.

Brownlee, Kevin, and Marina Scordilis Brownlee, eds. *Romance: Generic Transformation from Chretien de Troyes to Cervantes*. Hanover, N.H.: University Press of New England, 1985.

Bruni, Lionardo. "De studiis et litteris." In *Vittorino da Feltre and Other Humanist Educators*. Ed. and trans. W. H. Woodward. New York: Columbia University, Teachers College, 1963, 119–33.

Bruscagli, Riccardo. "'Ventura' e 'inchiesta' fra Boiardo e Ariosto." In Cesare Segre, ed., *Ludovico Ariosto: Lingua, stile e tradizione*. Milan: Feltrinelli, 1976, 107–36.

Bryson, Norman. *Vision and Painting: The Logic of the Gaze*. New Haven: Yale University Press, 1983.

Burckhardt, Jacob. *The Civilisation of the Renaissance in Italy*. Trans. S. G. C. Middlemore. London: Penguin, 1990.

Burgin, Victor. "Geometry and Abjection." In James Donald, ed., *Psychoanalysis and Cultural Theory: Thresholds*. New York: St. Martin's Press, 1991, 11–26.

Burgin, Victor, et al., eds. *Formations of Fantasy*. London: Methuen, 1986.

Butler, Judith. *Gender Trouble: Feminism and the Subversion of Identity*. New York: Routledge, 1990.

Calvino, Italo. *Il cavaliere inesistente*. Turin: Einaudi, 1972.

―――. *Mr. Palomar*. Trans. William Weaver. New York: Harcourt, Brace & Jovanovich, 1985.

―――. "Presentazione." In *Orlando furioso di Ludovico Ariosto, raccontato da Italo Calvino*. Turin: Einaudi, 1970, ix–xxvi.

Capellanus, Andreas (André le chapelain). *The Art of Courtly Love.* Trans. John Parry. New York: Norton, 1969.

Carne-Ross, D. S. "The One and the Many: A Reading of *Orlando Furioso*, Cantos 1 and 8." *Arion* 5 (1966): 195–234; *Arion* n.s. 3 (1976): 146–219.

Cary, George. *The Medieval Alexander.* Cambridge, Eng.: Cambridge University Press, 1956.

Casadei, Alberto. *La strategia delle varianti: Le correzioni storiche del terzo Furioso.* Lucca: Pacini Fazzi, 1988.

Castiglione, Baldassarre. *Il libro del cortegiano.* Ed. Ettore Bonora. Milan: Mursia, 1972.

———. *Il libro del cortegiano.* Ed. V. Cian. Florence: Sansoni, 1894.

———. *Il libro del cortegiano.* Ed. B. Maier. Turin: Utet, 1973.

———. *The Book of the Courtier.* Trans. George Bull. Harmondsworth, Eng.: Penguin, 1967.

———. *Lettere inedite e rare.* Ed. Guglielmo Gorni. Milan and Naples: Ricciardi, 1969.

Cavalluzzi, Raffaele. "'Rotti gli incanti e disprezzata l'arte' (Ariosto, *Cinque canti*) nel sistema della corte: Sintomi della coscienza infelice." *Lavoro critico* 33 (1984): 159–90.

Ceserani, Remo. "Ludovico Ariosto e la cultura figurativa del suo tempo." In Gian Paolo Biasin, Albert Mancini, and Nicholas Perella, eds., *Studies in the Italian Renaissance: Essays in Memory of Arnolfo B. Ferruolo.* Naples: Società Editrice Napoletana, 1985, 145–66.

Chemello, Adriana. "Donna di palazzo, moglie, cortigiana: Ruoli e funzioni sociali della donna in alcuni trattati del Cinquecento." In Prosperi, ed., 113–32.

Chesney, Elizabeth. *The Countervoyage of Rabelais and Ariosto: A Comparative Reading of Two Renaissance Mock Epics.* Durham, N.C.: Duke University Press, 1982.

Chiampi, Thomas. "Angelica's Flight and the Reduction of the Quest in the *Orlando Furioso*." *Canadian Journal of Italian Studies* 4 (1980): 1–25.

Chiappelli, Fredi. "Ariosto, Tasso e la bellezza delle donne." *Filologia e critica* 10 (1985): 325–41.

Chittolini, Giorgio, ed. *La crisi degli ordinamenti comunali e le origini dello stato del Rinascimento.* Bologna: Mulino, 1979.

Chojnacki, Stanley. "The Power of Love: Wives and Husbands in Late Medieval Venice." In Mary Erler and Mary Kowaleski, eds., *Women and Power in the Middle Ages.* Athens: University of Georgia Press, 1988, 126–48.

Cicero, Marcus Tullius. *Orator (De oratore).* Trans. H. M. Hubbell. In T. E. Page et al., eds., *Cicero: Brutus and Orator.* London: Heinemann, 1929.

Cixous, Helene. "The Laugh of the Medusa." In Elaine Marks and Isabelle de Courtivron, eds., *New French Feminisms*. Amherst: University of Massachussetts Press, 1980, 245–64.

Clark, Kenneth. *The Nude: A Study in Ideal Art*. London: John Murray, 1956.

Colie, Rosalie. *Paradoxia epidemica: The Renaissance Tradition of Paradox*. Princeton: Princeton University Press, 1966.

Comfort, W. W. "The Saracen in Italian Epic Poetry." *PMLA* 59 (1944): 882–910.

Cottom, Daniel. "The Enchantment of Interpretation." *Critical Inquiry* 11 (1985): 574–94.

Croce, Benedetto. *Ariosto, Shakespeare e Corneille*, vol. 2. Bari: Laterza, 1968.

Cropper, Elizabeth. "On Beautiful Women, Parmigianino, *Petrarchismo*, and the Vernacular Style." *Art Bulletin* 56 (1976): 376–94.

———. "The Beauty of Woman: Problems in the Rhetoric of Renaissance Portraiture." In Ferguson et al., eds., 175–90.

Cuccaro, Vincent. *The Humanism of Ludovico Ariosto: From the "Satire" to the "Furioso."* Ravenna: Longo, 1981.

Daenens, Francine. "Superiore perchè inferiore: Il paradosso della superiorità della donna in alcuni trattati italiani del Cinquecento." In Vanna Gentili, ed., *Trasgressione tragica e norma domestica: Esemplari di tipologie femminili della letteratura europea*. Rome: Edizione di Storia e Letteratura, 1983, 11–50.

Dalla Palma, Giuseppe. "Una cifra per la pazzia d'Orlando." *Strumenti critici* 9 (1975): 367–79.

———. *Le strutture narrative dell' "Orlando furioso."* Florence: Olschki, 1984.

David-Ménard, Monique. *Hysteria from Freud to Lacan*. Trans. Catherine Porter. Ithaca, N.Y.: Cornell University Press, 1989.

Davis, Nathalie Zemon. *Society and Culture in Early Modern France*. Stanford: Stanford University Press, 1975.

Debenedetti, Santorre. *I frammenti autografi dell' "Orlando furioso."* Turin: Chiantore, 1937.

De Lauretis, Teresa. *Alice Doesn't: Feminism, Semiotics, Cinema*. Bloomington: Indiana University Press, 1984.

———. "The Female Body and Heterosexual Presumption." *Semiotica* 67 (1987): 259–79.

———. *Technologies of Gender: Essays on Theory, Film and Fiction*. Bloomington: Indiana University Press, 1987.

Del Corno Branca, Daniela. *L'"Orlando furioso" e il romanzo cavalleresco medievale*. Florence: Olschki, 1973.

Deleuze, Gilles. *Coldness and Cruelty*. Trans. J. McNeil. In Gilles Deleuze and Leopold von Sacher-Masoch, *Masochism*. New York: Zone Books, 1989.

De Rougemont, Denis. *Love in the Western World*. New York: Pantheon, 1956.

De Sanctis, Francesco. *Storia della letteratura italiana*, vol. 2. Milan: Feltrinelli, 1964.

Diamond, Elin. "Brechtian Theory / Feminist Theory: Toward a Gestic Feminist Criticism." *Drama Review* 32 (1988): 82–94.

Di Cesare, Mario. "Isabella and Her Hermit: Stillness at the Center of the *Orlando Furioso*." *Mediaevalia* 6 (1980): 311–32.

Diefendorf, Barbara. "Family Culture, Renaissance Culture." *Renaissance Quarterly* 40 (1987): 661–81.

Dionisotti, Carlo. "La letteratura italiana nell'età del concilio di Trento." In idem, *Geografia e storia della letteratura italiana*. Turin: Einaudi, 1967, 183–204.

———. "Niccolò Liburnio e la letteratura cortigiana." *Lettere italiane* 14 (1962): 33–58.

Doane, Mary Ann. *The Desire to Desire*. Bloomington: Indiana University Press, 1987.

———. "Film and the Masquerade: Theorising the Female Spectator." *Screen* 23.3–4 (1982): 74–88.

———. "Masquerade Reconsidered: Further Thoughts on the Female Spectator." *Discourse* 11.1 (Fall–Winter 1988–89): 42–54.

———. "Woman's Stake: Filming the Female Body." In Constance Penley, ed., *Feminism and Film History*. New York: Routledge, 1988, 216–28.

Dolce, Ludovico. *Dialogo della Pittura di M. Ludovico Dolce, intitolato L'Aretino*. Venice, 1557. Reprinted in Paola Barocchi, ed., *Trattati d'arte del Cinquecento fra Manierismo e Controriforma*, vol. 1. Bari: Laterza, 1960.

Dollimore, Jonathan. *Radical Tragedy: Religion, Ideology and Power in the Drama of Shakespeare and His Contemporaries*. Chicago: University of Chicago Press, 1984.

———. "Subjectivity, Sexuality and Transgression: The Jacobean Connection." *Renaissance Drama* n.s. 17 (1986): 53–81.

Donaldson, Ian. *The Rapes of Lucretia: A Myth and Its Transformations*. Oxford: Clarendon Press, 1982.

Donato, Eugenio. " 'Per selve e boscherecci labirinti': Desire and Narrative Structure in Ariosto's *Orlando Furioso*." In Parker and Quint, eds., 33–62.

DuBois, Page. *Centaurs and Amazons: Women and the Pre-history of the Great Chain of Being*. Ann Arbor: University of Michigan Press, 1982.

Durling, Robert. *The Figure of the Poet in Renaissance Epic*. Cambridge, Mass.: Harvard University Press, 1965.

Ebert, Teresa. "The Romance of Patriarchy: Ideology, Subjectivity and Postmodern Cultural Theory." *Cultural Critique* 10 (1988): 19–57.

Eco, Umberto. "An *Ars Oblivionalis*? Forget it!" *PMLA* 103 (1988): 254–61.

Edgerton, Samuel. *The Renaissance Rediscovery of Linear Perspective*. New York: Basic Books, 1975.

Eisenstein, Elizabeth. *The Printing Press as an Agent of Change: Communications and Cultural Transformations in Early Modern Europe*. Cambridge, Eng.: Cambridge University Press, 1979.

Elias, Norbert. *The Civilizing Process*, vol. 1; *The History of Manners*. Trans. Edmund Jephcott. New York: Pantheon Books, 1978.

Engels, Friedrich. *The Origin of the Family, Private Property, and the State*. New York: International Publishers, 1942.

Erasmus, Desiderius. *The Praise of Folly*. Trans. H. H. Hudson. Princeton: Princeton University Press, 1941.

Fahy, Conor. "Three Early Renaissance Treatises on Women." *Italian Studies* 11 (1956): 30–55.

Felman, Shoshana. "Rereading Femininity." *Yale French Studies* 61 (1981): 19–44.

Ferenczi, Sandor. *Further Contributions to the Theory and Technique of Psychoanalysis*. London: Hogarth Press, 1926.

Ferguson, Margaret, Maureen Quilligan, and Nancy Vickers, eds. *Rewriting the Renaissance: The Discourse of Sexual Difference in Early Modern Europe*. Chicago: University of Chicago Press, 1986.

Ferroni, Giulio. "Da Bradamante a Ricciardetto: Interferenze testuali e scambi di sesso." In Costanzo Di Girolamo and Ivano Paccagnella, eds., *La parola ritrovata*. Palermo: Sellerio, 1982, 137–59.

———. "Sprezzatura e simulazione." In Ossola, ed., 119–47.

Fichter, Andrew. *Poets Historical: Dynastic Epic in the Renaissance*. New Haven: Yale University Press, 1982.

Finucci, Valeria. "The Female Masquerade: Ariosto and the Game of Desire." In idem and Regina Schwartz, eds., *Desire in the English and Italian Renaissances: Psychoanalytic Readings of Literary Texts*. Forthcoming, 1993.

Flieger, Jerry Aline. "The Purloined Punchline: Joke as Textual Paradigm." In Robert Con Davis, ed., *Lacan and Narration: The Psychoanalytic Difference in Narrative Theory*. Baltimore: Johns Hopkins University Press, 1983.

Floriani, Piero. *Bembo e Castiglione: Studi sul classicismo del Cinquecento*. Rome: Bulzoni, 1976.

Fonte, Moderata (Modesta Pozzo). *Il merito delle donne*. Ed. Adriana Chemello. Venice: Eidos, 1988.

Foucault, Michel. *The Archaeology of Knowledge and the Discourse of Language*. Trans. Alan Sheridan. London: Tavistock, 1972.

———. *Discipline and Punish: The Birth of the Prison*. Trans. Alan Sheridan. New York: Pantheon, 1977.

————. *The History of Sexuality*, Vol. 1, *An Introduction*. Trans. Robert Hurley. New York: Random House, 1978.

————. *Madness and Civilization*. Trans. Richard Howard. New York: Random House, 1965.

————. *Power/Knowledge: Selected Interviews and Other Writings*. Ed. Colin Gordon. New York: Pantheon, 1980.

————. "The Subject and Power." In Brian Willis, ed., *Art After Modernism: Rethinking Representation*. New York: Museum of Contemporary Art, 1984, 417–32.

Franceschetti, Antonio. *L' "Orlando Innamorato" e le sue componenti tematiche e strutturali*. Florence: Olschki, 1975.

Freccero, Carla. "The Other and the Same: The Image of the Hermaphrodite in Rabelais." In Ferguson et al., eds., 145–58.

Freccero, John. "The Fig Tree and the Laurel: Petrarch's Poetics." *Diacritics* 5 (1975): 34–40.

————. "Medusa: The Letter and the Spirit." *Yearbook of Italian Studies* 1972: 1–18.

Freud, Sigmund. "Analysis Terminable and Interminable." 1937. *Standard Edition* [hereafter, *SE*] 23 (1964): 216–53.

————. "A Child Is Being Beaten: A Contribution to the Study of the Origin of Sexual Perversions." 1919. *SE* 17 (1955): 179–204.

————. "Creative Writers and Day-dreaming." 1908. *SE* 9 (1959): 143–53.

————. "The Ego and the Super-ego (Ego Ideal)." In *The Ego and the Id*. 1923. *SE* 19 (1961): 28–39.

————. "Female Sexuality." 1931. *SE* 21 (1961): 225–43.

————. "Femininity." 1933. *SE* 22 (1964): 112–35.

————. "Fetishism." 1927. *SE* 21 (1961): 152–57.

————. "Fragments of an Analysis of a Case of Hysteria." 1905 [1901]. *SE* 7 (1953): 3–122.

————. "Humor." *International Journal of Psychoanalysis* 9 (1928): 1–6.

————. "The Infantile Genital Organization of the Libido (An Interpolation into the Theory of Sexuality." 1923. *SE* 19 (1961): 141–45.

————. *Inhibitions, Symptoms and Anxiety*. 1926. *SE* 20 (1959): 77–172.

————. *Jokes and Their Relation to the Unconscious*. 1905. Trans. James Strachey. New York: Norton, 1960.

————. "Medusa's Head." 1922, 1940. *SE* 18 (1955): 273–74.

————. "Mourning and Melancholia." 1917 [1915]. *SE* 14 (1957): 242–58.

————. "On Narcissism: An Introduction." 1914. *SE* 14 (1957): 69–102.

————. "Some Psychical Consequences of the Anatomical Distinction Between the Sexes." 1925. *SE* 19 (1961): 248–58.

————. "A Special Type of Choice of Object Made by Men: Contribution to the Psychology of Love, I." 1910. *SE* 11 (1957): 165–75.

————. *The Standard Edition of the Complete Psychological Works of Sigmund Freud*. Trans. and ed. James Strachey. 24 vols. London: Hogarth Press, 1953–74.

————. "Symbolism in Dreams." 1916. In *Introductory Lectures on Psychoanalysis*. *SE* 15 (1961): 149–69.

————. "The Taboo of Virginity: Contributions to the Psychology of Love, III." 1918 [1917]. *SE* 11 (1957): 193–208.

————. "Three Essays on the Theory of Sexuality." 1905. *SE* 7 (1953): 125–243.

————. "The Uncanny." 1919. *SE* 17 (1955): 219–52.

Frye, Northrop. *Anatomy of Criticism*. Princeton: Princeton University Press, 1957.

Galilei, Galileo. *Scritti letterari*. Ed. Alberto Chiari. Florence: Le Monnier, 1943.

Gallop, Jane. *Thinking Through the Body*. New York: Columbia University Press, 1988.

Geertz, Clifford. *The Interpretation of Cultures: Selected Essays*. New York: Basic Books, 1973.

Geha, Richard. "For the Love of Medusa: A Psychoanalytic Glimpse into Gynecocide." *Psychoanalytic Review* 62 (1975): 49–77.

Ghinassi, Ghino. "Fasi dell'elaborazione del *Cortegiano*." *Studi di filologia italiana* 25 (1967): 155–96.

Giamatti, Bartlett. "Proteus Unbound: Some Versions of the Sea God in the Renaissance." In Peter Demetz, Thomas Greene, and Lowry Nelson, eds., *The Disciplines of Criticism: Essays in Literary Theory, Interpretation, and History*. New Haven: Yale University Press, 1968, 437–75.

————. "*Sfrenatura*: Restraint and Release in the *Orlando Furioso*." In Scaglione, ed., 31–39.

————. *Spenser: From Magic to Miracle*. Ed. Herschel Baker. Cambridge, Mass.: Harvard University Press, 1971.

Gilardino, Sergio Maria. "Per una reinterpretazione dell'Olimpia ariostesca: I contributi della filologia germanica." In Vittore Branca, ed., *Rinascimento: Aspetti e problemi attuali*. Florence: Olschki, 1982, 429–44.

Ginzburg, Carlo. "Tiziano, Ovidio e i codici della figurazione erotica nel '500." In *Tiziano e Venezia*. Vicenza: Neri Pozza, 1980, 125–35.

Girard, René. *Deceit, Desire and the Novel: Self and Other in Literary Structure*. Trans. Y. Freccero. Baltimore: Johns Hopkins University Press, 1965.

————. *Things Hidden Since the Foundation of the World*. Trans. S. Bann and M. Metteer. Stanford: Stanford University Press, 1987.

Gnudi, Cesare. "L'Ariosto e le arti figurative." In *Atti dei Convegni Lincei*. Rome: Accademia Nazionale dei Lincei, 1975, 331–400.

Goffen, Rona. "Renaissance Dreams." *Renaissance Quarterly* 40 (1987): 682–706.

Goldthwaite, Richard. "The Florentine Palace as Domestic Architecture." *American Historical Review* 77 (1972): 977–1012.

Gorni, Guglielmo. "Il rovescio del *Cortegiano* e le lettere del Castiglione." *Paragone* 354 (1979): 63–75.

Gould, Cecil. *The Studio of Alfonso d'Este and Titian's "Bacchus and Ariadne."* London: National Gallery, 1970.

Gramsci, Antonio. *Selections from the Prison Notebooks.* Ed. and trans. Quintin Hoare and Geoffrey Smith. New York: International Press, 1971.

Graves, Robert. *The Greek Myths.* 2 vols. Harmondsworth, Eng.: Penguin, 1955.

Greenblatt, Stephen. "Fiction and Friction." In *Shakespearean Negotiations: The Circulation of Social Energy in Renaissance England.* Berkeley: University of California Press, 1988, 66–93.

———. "Psychoanalysis and Renaissance Culture." In Parker and Quint, eds., 210–24.

———. *Renaissance Self-fashioning: From More to Shakespeare.* Chicago: University of Chicago Press, 1980.

Greene, Thomas. "The Flexibility of the Self in Renaissance Literature." In Peter Demetz, Thomas Greene, and Lowry Nelson, eds., *The Disciplines of Criticism: Essays in Literary Theory, Interpretation, and History.* New Haven: Yale University Press, 1968, 241–64.

———. "*Il Cortegiano* and the Choice of a Game." In Hanning and Rosand, eds., 1–15.

———. *The Light in Troy: Imitation and Discovery in Renaissance Poetry.* New Haven: Yale University Press, 1982.

Grendler, Paul. *Critics of the Italian World, 1530–1560: Anton Francesco Doni, Nicolò Franco, and Ortensio Lando.* Madison: University of Wisconsin Press, 1969.

———. *Schooling in Renaissance Italy: Literacy and Learning, 1300–1600.* Baltimore: Johns Hopkins University Press, 1989.

Grunberger, Bela. "Outline for a Study of Narcissism in Female Sexuality." In Janine Chasseguet-Smirgel, ed., *Female Sexuality: New Psychoanalytic Views.* Ann Arbor: University of Michigan Press, 1970, 68–83.

Guidi, José. "De l'amour courtois à l'amour sacré: La condition de la femme dans l'oeuvre de Baldassar Castiglione." In A. Rochon, ed., *Images de la femme dans la littérature italienne de la Renaissance: Préjugés misogynes et aspirations nouvelles.* Paris: Université de la Sorbonne Nouvelle, 1980, 9–80.

————. " 'Festive narrazioni,' 'motti' et 'burle' (beffe): L'art des facéties dans *Le Courtisan.*" In A. Rochon, ed., *Formes et significations de la beffa dans la littérature italienne de la Renaissance.* Paris: Université de la Sorbonne Nouvelle, 1975, 171–210.

————. "Reformulations de l'idéologie aristocratique au XVIᵉ siècle: Les différentes rédactions et la fortune du *Curtisan.*" In Jean Toscan et al., eds., *Réécritures,* vol. 1. Paris: Université de la Sorbonne Nouvelle, 1983, 121–84.

Gundersheimer, Werner. *Ferrara: The Style of a Renaissance Despotism.* Princeton: Princeton University Press, 1973.

Haddad, Miranda. "Ovid's Medusa in Dante and Ariosto: The Poetics of Self-confrontation." *Journal of Medieval and Renaissance Studies* 19 (1989): 211–25.

Hamilton, Roberta. *The Liberation of Women: A Study of Patriarchy and Capitalism.* London: George Allen & Unwin, 1978.

Hanning, Robert. "Ariosto, Ovid and the Painters: Mythological Paragone in *Orlando Furioso* X and XI." In Scaglione, ed., 99–116.

————. "Castiglione's Verbal Portrait: Structure and Strategies." In Hanning and Rosand, eds., 131–41.

Hanning, Robert, and David Rosand, eds. *Castiglione: The Ideal and the Real in Renaissance Culture.* New Haven: Yale University Press, 1983.

Hay, Denys, and John Law. *Italy in the Age of the Renaissance, 1380–1530.* London: Longman, 1989.

Heath, Stephen. "Difference." *Screen* 19.3 (1978): 51–112.

————. "Joan Rivière and the Masquerade." In Burgin et al., eds., 45–61.

————. *Questions of Cinema.* Bloomington: Indiana University Press, 1981.

Hempfer, Klaus. "Un criterio di validità per interpretazioni: L'epica cavalleresca italiana del Rinascimento." *Intersezioni* 4 (1984): 289–320.

Herlihy, David. "Deaths, Marriage, Births, and the Tuscan Economy." In R. D. Lee, ed., *Population Patterns in the Past.* New York: Academic Press, 1977, 135–64.

Herlihy, David, and Christiane Klapisch-Zuber. *Tuscans and Their Families: Study of the Florentine Catasto of 1427.* New Haven: Yale University Press, 1985.

Hertz, Neil. "Medusa's Head: Male Hysteria Under Political Pressure." *Representations* 4 (1983): 27–54.

Higonnet, Margaret. "Speaking Silences: Women's Suicide." In Susan Suleiman, ed., *The Female Body in Western Culture: Contemporary Perspectives.* Cambridge, Mass.: Harvard University Press, 1986, 68–83.

Hollander, Anne. *Seeing Through Clothes.* New York: Viking, 1975.

Howard, Jean. "Crossdressing, the Theatre, and Gender Struggle in Early Modern England." *Shakespeare Quarterly* 39 (1988): 418–40.

—————. "The New Historicism in Renaissance Studies." *English Literary Renaissance* 16 (1986): 13–43.

Hughes, Diane Owen. "Representing the Family: Portraits and Purposes in Early Modern Italy." *Journal of Interdisciplinary History* 17.1 (1986): 7–38.

—————. "Sumptuary Laws and Social Relations in Renaissance Italy." In John Bossy, ed., *Disputes and Settlements: Law and Human Relations in the West*. Cambridge, Eng.: Cambridge University Press, 1983, 66–99.

Hulse, Clark. *The Rule of Art: Literature and Painting in the Renaissance*. Chicago: University of Chicago Press, 1990.

Irigaray, Luce. *Speculum of the Other Woman*. Trans. G. Gill. Ithaca, N.Y.: Cornell University Press, 1985.

—————. *This Sex Which Is Not One*. Trans. Catherine Porter. Ithaca, N.Y.: Cornell University Press, 1985.

Jacobus, Mary. "Is There a Woman in This Text?" *New Literary History* 4 (1982): 117–41.

Jameson, Fredric. "Magical Narratives: Romance as Genre." *New Literary History* 7 (1975): 135–63.

—————. *The Political Unconscious: Narrative as a Socially Symbolic Act*. Ithaca, N.Y.: Cornell University Press, 1981.

Jardine, Lisa. *Still Harping on Daughters: Women and Drama in the Age of Shakespeare*. Totowa, N.J.: Barnes & Noble, 1975.

Javitch, Daniel. "*Il Cortegiano* and the Constraints of Despotism." In Hanning and Rosand, eds., 17–28.

—————. "The Imitation of Imitations in *Orlando Furioso*." *Renaissance Quarterly* 38 (1985): 215–39.

—————. "The *Orlando Furioso* and Ovid's Revision of the *Aeneid*." *MLN* 99 (1984): 1023–36.

—————. *Proclaiming a Classic: The Canonization of "Orlando Furioso."* Princeton: Princeton University Press, 1991.

—————. "Rescuing Ovid from the Allegorizers: The Liberation of Angelica, *Furioso* X." In Scaglione, ed., 85–98.

Jay, Martin. "Scopic Regimes of Modernity." In Hal Foster, ed., *Discussions in Contemporary Culture*, vol. 2. Seattle: Bay Press, 1988, 3–23.

Jed, Stephanie. *Chaste Thinking: The Rape of Lucretia and the Birth of Humanism*. Bloomington: Indiana University Press, 1989.

Jerome. *Commentariorum in Jonam Prophetam Liber Unus*. Corpus Christianorum Series Latina, vol. 76. Turnhout: Brepals, 1969, 390–91.

Jones, Ann Rosalind. "Nets and Bridles: Early Modern Conduct Books and Sixteenth-Century Women's Lyrics." In Nancy Armstrong and Leonard Tennenhouse, eds., *The Ideology of Conduct: Essays in Literature and the History of Sexuality*. New York: Methuen, 1987, 39–72.

Jordan, Constance. "Feminism and the Humanists: The Case of Sir Thomas Elyot's *Defence of Good Women.*" In Ferguson et al., eds., 242–58.

———. *Renaissance Feminism: Literary Texts and Political Models.* Ithaca, N.Y.: Cornell University Press, 1990.

Kelly-Gadol, Joan. *Women, History and Theory: The Essays of Joan Kelly.* Illinois Press, 1956.

Kennedy, William. "Ariosto's Ironic Allegory." *MLN* 88 (1973): 44–67.

Kerrigan, William, and Gordon Braden. *The Idea of the Renaissance.* Baltimore: Johns Hopkins University Press, 1989.

Klapisch-Zuber, Christiane. *Women, Family and Ritual in Renaissance Italy.* Trans. Lydia Cochrane. Chicago: University of Chicago Press, 1985.

Kofman, Sarah. "Ça cloche." In Philippe Lacoue-Labarthe and Jean-Luc Nancy, eds., *Les fins de l'homme: A partir de Jacques Derrida.* Paris: Galilée, 1981, 83–116.

———. *The Enigma of Woman: Woman in Freud's Writing.* Trans. Catherine Porter. Ithaca, N.Y.: Cornell University Press, 1985.

Kristeva, Julia. "On the Melancholic Imaginary." In Shlomith Rimmon-Kenan, ed., *Discourse in Psychoanalysis and Literature.* London: Methuen, 1987, 104–23.

Kuhn, Annette. "Structures of Patriarchy and Capital in the Family." In idem, ed., *Feminism and Materialism: Women and Modes of Production.* London: Routledge & Kegan Paul, 1978, 42–67.

Lacan, Jacques. "Desire and the Interpretation of Desire in *Hamlet.*" In Shoshana Felman, ed., *Literature and Psychoanalysis. The Question of Reading: Otherwise.* Baltimore: Johns Hopkins University Press, 1982, 11–52.

———. *Ecrits: A Selection.* Trans. Alan Sheridan. New York: Norton, 1977.

———. *The Four Fundamental Concepts of Psychoanalysis.* Trans. Alan Sheridan. New York: Norton, 1977.

———. "God and the *Jouissance* of the Woman." In Mitchell and Rose, eds., 137–48.

———. "The Meaning of the Phallus." In Mitchell and Rose, eds., 74–85.

———. *Le séminaire XX: Encore* (1972–73). Paris: Seuil, 1975. Excerpts in Mitchell and Rose, eds., 137–61.

Lakoff, Robin. *Language and Woman's Place.* New York: Harper & Row, 1975.

Landino, Cristoforo. *Scritti critici e teorici.* 2 vols. Ed. Roberto Cardini. Rome: Bulzoni, 1974.

Laplanche, Jean, and Jean-Bertrand Pontalis. *The Language of Psycho-analysis.* Trans. D. Micholson-Smith. New York: Norton, 1973.

Laqueur, Thomas. "Orgasm, Generation, and the Politics of Reproductive Biology." *Representations* 14 (1986): 1–41.

Larivaille, Paul. *Syntaxe dramatique et syntaxe narrative dans le Roland Furieux.* Paris: Université Paris X, 1977.

Lebovici, Serge, and Daniel Widlocher, eds., *Psychoanalysis in France.* New York: International University Press, 1980.

Lee, Rensselaer. *Names on Trees: Ariosto into Art.* Princeton: Princeton University Press, 1977.

———. *Ut Pictura Poesis: The Humanist Theory of Painting.* New York: Norton, 1967.

Legman, Gershon. *Rationale of the Dirty Joke.* New York: Bell, 1975.

Lemaire, Anika. *Jacques Lacan.* Trans. David Macey. Boston: Routledge & Kegan Paul, 1977.

Lemoine-Luccioni, Eugénie. *La robe: Essai psychanalytique sur le vêtement.* Paris: Seuil, 1983.

Levine, Laura. "Men in Women's Clothing: Antitheatricality and Effeminization from 1579 to 1642." *Criticism* 28 (1986): 124–43.

Lipking, Lawrence. "The Dialectic of *Il Cortegiano.*" *PMLA* 81 (1966): 355–62.

Loraux, Nicole. *Tragic Ways of Killing a Woman.* Cambridge, Mass.: Harvard University Press, 1987.

Lurie, Susan. "The Construction of the 'Castrated Woman' in Psychoanalysis and Cinema." *Discourse* 4 (1981–82): 52–74.

Lythe, Guy, and Stephen Orgel, eds. *Patronage in the Renaissance.* Princeton: Princeton University Press, 1981.

MacLean, Ian. *The Renaissance Notion of Woman: A Study in the Fortunes of Scholasticism and Medical Science in European Intellectual Life.* Cambridge, Eng.: Cambridge University Press, 1980.

Mancini, Albert. "Personaggi della poesia cavalleresca: Cavalieri e villani nell'*Orlando furioso.*" In I. Bertoni, ed., *Civiltà della parola.* Milan: Marzorati, 1989, 171–88.

Mannoni, Octave. *Clefs pour l'imaginaire ou l'autre scène.* Paris: Seuil, 1969.

Marinelli, Peter. *Ariosto and Boiardo: The Origins of "Orlando Furioso."* Columbia: University of Missouri Press, 1987.

———. "Shaping the Ore: Image and Design in Canto 1 of *Orlando Furioso.*" *MLN* 103 (1988): 31–49.

Marx, Karl. *Capital.* Trans. Ben Fowkes. Harmondsworth, Eng.: Penguin, 1976.

Mazzacurati, Giancarlo. "Baldassar Castiglione e la teoria cortigiana: Ideologia di classe e dottrina critica." *MLN* 83 (1968): 16–60.

———. "Il 'cortegiano' e lo 'scolare.' " In idem, *Il Rinascimento dei moderni: La crisi culturale del XVI secolo e la negazione delle origini.* Bologna: Mulino, 1985, 261–95.

———. "La negazione delle origini." *Intersezioni* 2 (1982): 275–308.

Mazzotta, Giuseppe. "The *Canzoniere* and the Language of the Self."

Studies in Philology 75 (1978): 271–96.

———. *Dante, Poet of the Desert: History and Allegory in the "Divine Comedy."* Princeton: Princeton University Press, 1979.

———. "Power and Play in the *Orlando Furioso.*" Unpublished paper.

———. *The World at Play in Boccaccio's "Decameron."* Princeton: Princeton University Press, 1986.

McGann, Jerome. "The Beauty of the Medusa: A Study in Romantic Literary Iconology." *Studies in Romanticism* 11.1 (1972): 3–25.

McLucas, John. "Amazon, Sorceress, and Queen: Women and War in the Aristocratic Literature of Sixteenth Century Italy." *Italianist* 8 (1988): 33–55.

———. "Ariosto and the Androgyne: Symmetries of Sex in the *Orlando Furioso.*" Ph.D. dissertation, Yale University, 1983.

Mehlman, Jeffrey. "How to Read Freud on Jokes: The Critic as *Schadchen.*" *New Literary History* 6 (1974–75): 439–61.

Merleau-Ponty, Maurice. *The Phenomenology of Perception.* Trans. Colin Smith. Boston: Routledge & Kegan Paul, 1962.

Miles, Margaret. *Carnal Knowing: Female Nakedness and Religious Meaning in the Christian West.* Boston: Beacon Press, 1989.

———. "Nudity, Gender, and Religious Meaning in the Italian Renaissance." In Doug Adams and Diane Apostolos-Cappadona, eds., *Art as Religious Studies.* New York: Crossroad, 1987, 101–16.

Miller, Nancy. "The Exquisite Cadavers: Women in Eighteenth-Century Fiction." *Diacritics* 5 (1975): 37–43.

———. "I's in Drag: The Sex of Recollection." *Eighteenth Century* 22 (1981): 47–57.

Millot, Catherine. *Horsexe: Essai sur le transexualisme.* Paris: Point Hors Ligne, 1983.

Mitchell, Juliet, and Jacqueline Rose. *Feminine Sexuality: Jacques Lacan and the Ecole Freudienne.* New York: Norton, 1982.

Moi, Toril. "The Missing Mother: The Oedipal Rivalries of René Girard." *Diacritics* 12 (1982): 21–31.

Molinaro, Julius. "Sin and Punishment in the *Orlando Furioso.*" *MLN* 89 (1974): 35–46.

Momigliano, Attilio. *Saggio sull' "Orlando furioso."* Bari: Laterza, 1973.

Montrelay, Michele. "Inquiry into Femininity." In Toril Moi, ed., *French Feminist Thought: A Reader.* Oxford: Blackwell, 1987, 227–49.

Montrose, Louis. "The Elizabethan Subject and the Spenserian Text." In Parker and Quint, eds., 303–34.

Moretti, Walter. *L'ultimo Ariosto.* Bologna: Patron, 1977.

Mulas, Luisa. "Funzione degli esempi, funzione del *Cortegiano.*" In Ossola, ed., 97–117.

Mulvey, Laura. *Visual and Other Pleasures*. Bloomington: Indiana University Press, 1989.

Munich, Adrienne. *Andromeda's Chains: Gender and Interpretation in Victorian Literature and Art*. New York: Columbia University Press, 1989.

Musacchio, Enrico. *Amore, ragione e follia: Una rilettura dell' "Orlando Furioso."* Rome: Bulzoni, 1983.

———. "L'Olimpia dell'Ariosto." *Proceedings of the Pacific Northwest Conference on Foreign Languages* 21 (1970): 102–10.

Mykyta, Larysa. "Lacan, Literature and the Look: Woman in the Eye of Psychoanalysis." *Substance* 39 (1983): 49–57.

Neely, Carol Thomas. "Constructing the Subject: Feminist Practice and the New Renaissance Discourses." *English Literary History* 18 (1988): 5–18.

Nelson, John Charles. *Renaissance Theory of Love*. New York: Columbia University Press, 1958.

Newman, John. *The Classical Epic Tradition*. Madison: University of Wisconsin Press, 1986.

Newman, Karen. "Renaissance Family Politics and Shakespeare's *The Taming of the Shrew.*" *English Literary Renaissance* 16 (1986): 86–100.

Nietzsche, Friedrich. *Beyond Good and Evil*. Trans. W. Kaufmann. New York: Random, 1966.

Olbrechts-Tyteca, Lucie. *Il comico del discorso: Un contributo alla teoria generale del comico e del riso*. Milan: Feltrinelli, 1977.

Orgel, Stephen. "Nobody's Perfect: Or Why Did the English Stage Take Boys for Women?" *South Atlantic Quarterly* 88 (1989): 7–29.

Ossola, Carlo. *Dal "Cortegiano" all' "Uomo di mondo."* Turin: Einaudi, 1987.

———. "*Il libro del Cortegiano*: Cornice e ritratto." *Lettere italiane* 31 (1979): 517–33. Reprinted in Ossola, *Dal "Cortegiano,"* 27–42.

———, ed. *La corte e il cortegiano*, Vol. 1, *La scena del testo*. Rome: Bulzoni, 1980.

Ovid. *Heroides X & XII*. In Florence Verducci, *Ovid's Toyshop of the Heart: Epistulae Heroidum*. Princeton: Princeton University Press, 1985, 236–43.

———. *Metamorphoses*. Trans. A. D. Melville. Oxford: Oxford University Press, 1986.

Owens, Craig. "The Discourse of Others: Feminists and Postmodernism." In Hal Foster, ed., *The Anti-Aesthetic: Essays on Postmodern Culture*. Seattle: Bay Press, 1983, 57–82.

Ozment, Steven. *When Fathers Ruled: Family Life in Reformation Europe*. Cambridge, Mass.: Harvard University Press, 1983.

Pacteau, Francette. "The Impossible Referent: Representations of the Androgyne." In Burgin et al., eds., 62–84.

Padoan, Giorgio. "L'*Orlando furioso* e la crisi del Rinascimento." *Lettere italiane* 25 (1975): 286–307.

———. " 'Ut Pictura Poesis': Le 'pitture' di Ariosto, le 'poesie' di Tiziano." In idem, *Momenti del Rinascimento veneto*. Padua: Antenore, 1978, 347–70.

Panofsky, Erwin. *Idea: A Concept in Art Theory*. Trans. Joseph Peake. Columbia: University of South Carolina Press, 1968.

Papagno, Giuseppe, and Amedeo Quondam, eds., *La corte e lo spazio: Ferrara estense*. 3 vols. Rome: Bulzoni, 1982.

Parker, Patricia. *Inescapable Romance: Studies in the Poetics of a Mode*. Princeton: Princeton University Press, 1979.

———. *Literary Fat Ladies: Rhetoric, Gender, Property*. London: Methuen, 1987.

Parker, Patricia, and David Quint, eds., *Literary Theory / Renaissance Texts*. Baltimore: Johns Hopkins University Press, 1986.

Patrizi, Giorgio. "*Il libro del cortegiano* e la trattatistica sul comportamento." In Alberto Asor Rosa, ed., *Letteratura italiana*, Vol. 3, *Le forme del testo*. Turin: Einaudi, 1984, 855–90.

Patterson, Lee. *Negotiating the Past: The Historical Understanding of Medieval Literature*. Madison: University of Wisconsin Press, 1987.

———. "On the Margin: Postmodernism, Ironic History, and Medieval Studies." *Speculum* 65 (1990): 87–108.

Pavlock, Barbara. *Eros, Imitation, and the Epic Tradition*. Ithaca, N.Y.: Cornell University Press, 1990.

Perry, Alexander S. "The Poet's Craft: The Tapestry Metaphor in Ariosto and Spenser." Ph.D. dissertation, Columbia University, 1982.

Petrarch, Francesco. *Petrarch's Lyric Poems: The Rime sparse and Other Lyrics*. Trans. and ed. Robert Durling. Cambridge, Mass.: Harvard University Press, 1976.

Pico della Mirandola, Giovanni. *De dignitate hominis* (Oration on the dignity of man). In Ernst Cassirer et al., eds., *The Renaissance Philosophy of Man*. Chicago: University of Chicago Press, 1948.

Piromalli, Antonio. *La cultura a Ferrara al tempo di Ludovico Ariosto*. Rome: Bulzoni, 1975.

Plaza, Monique. "Pouvoir 'phallomorphique' et la psychologie de 'la femme.' " *Questions féministes* 1 (1977): 91–119.

Plett, Heinrich. "Aesthetic Constituents in the Courtly Culture of Renaissance England." *New Literary History* 14 (1983): 597–621.

Poe, Edgar Allan. "The Philosophy of Composition." In *The Works of Edgar Allan Poe*, vol. 1. New York: A. C. Armstrong and Son, 1884, 259–70.

Pollock, Griselda. *Vision and Difference: Femininity, Feminism and Histories of Art*. London: Routledge, 1988.

Pool, Franco. *Interpretazione dell' "Orlando furioso."* Florence: La Nuova Italia, 1968.

Pozzi, Giovanni. "Il ritratto della donna nella poesia d'inizio Cinquecento e la pittura di Giorgione." *Lettere italiane* 31 (1979): 3–30.

Pozzi, Mario. *Trattatisti del cinquecento.* Milan and Naples: Ricciardi, 1978.

Prosperi, Adriano, ed. *La corte e il cortegiano,* vol. 2, *Un modello europeo.* Rome: Bulzoni, 1980.

Pullini, Giorgio. *Burle e facezie del Quattrocento.* Pisa: Nistri-Lischi, 1958.

Quint, David. "The Boat of Romance and Renaissance Epic." In Brownlee and Brownlee, eds., 178–202.

———. "Epic and Empire." *Comparative Literature* 41 (1989): 1–32.

———. "The Figure of Atlante: Ariosto and Boiardo's Poem." *MLN* 94 (1979): 77–91.

———. *Origin and Originality in Renaissance Literature.* New Haven: Yale University Press, 1983.

Quondam, Amedeo. "La 'forma del vivere': Schede per l'analisi del discorso cortigiano." In Prosperi, ed., 15–68.

Ragland-Sullivan, Ellie. "Dora and the Name-of-the-Father: The Structure of Hysteria." In Marleen Barr and Richard Feldstein, eds., *Discontented Discourses: Feminism / Textual Intervention / Psychoanalysis.* Urbana: University of Illinois Press, 1989, 208–40.

Rajna, Pio. *Le fonti dell' "Orlando furioso."* Florence: Sansoni, 1900.

———. "Ricciardetto e Fiordispina." In John Fitzgerald et al., eds., *Todd Memorial Volumes: Philological Studies,* vol. 2. Freeport, N.Y.: Books for Libraries Press, 1930, 91–105.

Rebhorn, Wayne. *Courtly Performances: Masking and Festivity in Castiglione's "Book of the Courtier."* Detroit: Wayne State University Press, 1978.

Resta, Giuseppe. "Ariosto e i suoi personaggi." *Rivista di psicoanalisi* 3 (1957): 59–83.

Rivière, Joan. "Womanliness as a Masquerade." In Burgin et al., eds., 35–44.

Robinson, Margaret. *Monstrous Regiment: The Lady Knight in Sixteenth-Century Epic.* New York: Garland, 1985.

Roche, Thomas. "Ariosto's Marfisa or Camilla Domesticated." *MLN* 103 (1988): 113–33.

Rose, Jacqueline. "Paranoia and the Film System." In Constance Penley, ed., *Feminism and Film Theory.* New York: Routledge, 1988, 141–58.

———. *Sexuality in the Field of Vision.* London: Verso, 1986.

Rose, Mary Beth. *The Expense of Spirit: Love and Sexuality in English Renaissance Drama.* Ithaca, N.Y.: Cornell University Press, 1988.

Ruggiero, Guido. *The Boundaries of Eros: Sex Crime and Sexuality in Renaissance Venice.* New York: Oxford University Press, 1985.

Russo, Mary. "Female Grotesques: Carnival and Theory." In Teresa De Lauretis, ed., *Feminist Studies / Critical Studies*. Bloomington: Indiana University Press, 1986, 213–29.

Ryan, Lawrence. "Book Four of Castiglione's *Courtier*: Climax or Afterthought?" *Studies in the Renaissance* 19 (1972): 156–79.

Saccaro Battisti, Giuseppa. "La donna, le donne nel *Cortegiano*." In Ossola, ed., 219–49.

Saccone, Eduardo. "Cloridano e Medoro, con alcuni argomenti per una lettura del primo *Furioso*." *MLN* 83 (1968): 67–99.

———. "Prospettive sull'ultimo *Furioso*." *MLN* 98 (1983): 55–69.

———. *Il "soggetto" del "Furioso" e altri saggi tra quattro e cinquecento*. Naples: Liguori, 1974.

———. "Trattato e ritratto: L'introduzione del *Cortegiano*." *MLN* 93 (1978): 1–21.

Sanday, Peggy Reeves. "Rape and the Silencing of the Feminine." In Tomaselli and Porter, eds., 84–101.

Santoro, Mario. *L'anello di Angelica: Nuovi saggi ariosteschi*. Naples: Federico & Ardia, 1983.

———. *Letture ariostesche*. Naples: Liguori, 1973.

Sartre, Jean-Paul. *Being and Nothingness*. Trans. Hazel Barnes. New York: Washington Square, 1966.

Saslow, James. *Ganymede in the Renaissance: Homosexuality in Art and Society*. New Haven: Yale University Press, 1986.

Saunders, Gill. *The Nude: A New Perspective*. London: Herbert Press, 1989.

Scaglione, Aldo. "Cinquecento Mannerism and the Use of Petrarch." In D. B. Hardison, ed., *Medieval and Renaissance Studies*. Chapel Hill: University of North Carolina Press, 1971, 122–55.

Scaglione, Aldo, ed. *Ariosto 1974 in America*. Ravenna: Longo, 1976.

Schiesari, Juliana. "The Gendering of Melancholia: Torquato Tasso and Isabella di Morra." In Marilyn Migiel and Juliana Schiesari, eds., *Refiguring Woman: Perspectives on Gender and the Italian Renaissance*. Ithaca, N.Y.: Cornell University Press, 1991, 233–62.

Schleiner, Winfried. "Male Cross-dressing and Transvestism in Renaissance Romances." *Sixteenth Century Journal* 19 (1988): 605–19.

Schneider, Laurie. "Ms. Medusa: Transformations of a Bisexual Image." *Psychoanalytic Study of Society* 9 (1981): 105–53.

Schneider, Marilyn. "Calvino: Erotic Metaphor and the Hermaphroditic Solution." *Stanford Italian Review* 2.1 (1981): 93–118.

Schwartz, Regina. "Rethinking Voyeurism and Patriarchy: The Case of *Paradise Lost*." *Representations* 34 (1991): 85–103.

Scott, Joan W. "Gender: A Useful Category of Historical Analysis." *American Historical Review* 91 (1986): 1053–75.

Sedgwick, Eve Kosofski. *Between Men: English Literature and Male Homosocial Desire*. New York: Columbia University Press, 1985.

Segre, Cesare. *Esperienze ariostesche*. Pisa: Nistri-Lischi, 1966.

Shapiro, Marianne. "Mirror and Portrait: The Structure of *Il Libro del Cortegiano*." *Journal of Medieval and Renaissance Studies* 5 (1975): 37–61.

———. *The Poetics of Ariosto*. Detroit: Wayne State University Press, 1988.

Shemek, Deanna. "Of Women, Knights, Arms, and Love: The *Querelle des Femmes* in Ariosto's Poem." *MLN* 104 (1989): 68–97.

———. "That Elusive Object of Desire: Angelica in the *Orlando Furioso*." *Annali d'Italianistica* 7 (1989): 116–41.

Shepherd, Simon. *Amazons and Warrior Women: Varieties of Feminism in Seventeenth Century Drama*. New York: St. Martin's Press, 1981.

Silberman, Lauren. "Mythographic Transformations of Ovid's Hermaphrodite." *Sixteenth Century Journal* 19 (1988): 643–52.

Silverman, Kaja. *The Acoustic Mirror: The Female Voice in Psychoanalysis and Cinema*. Bloomington: Indiana University Press, 1988.

———. "Fragments of a Fashionable Discourse." In Tania Modleski, ed., *Studies in Entertainment: Critical Approaches to Mass Culture*. Bloomington: Indiana University Press, 1986, 139–52.

———. "*Histoire d'O*. The Construction of a Female Subject." In Carole Vance, ed., *Pleasure and Danger: Exploring Female Sexuality*. London: Routledge and Kegan Paul, 1984, 320–49.

———. "Masochism and Male Subjectivity." *Camera Obscura* 17 (1988): 31–66.

———. *The Subject of Semiotics*. New York: Oxford University Press, 1983.

Smirnoff, Victor. "The Fetishistic Transaction." In Lebovici and Widlocher, eds., 303–31.

Snyder, Joel. "Picturing Vision." *Critical Inquiry* 6 (1980): 499–526.

Speroni, Sperone. "Il dialogo della cura familiare." In M. Pozzi, ed., *Trattati d'amore del 500*. Bari: Laterza, 1980.

Sprengnether, Madelon. *The Spectral Mother: Freud, Feminism and Psychoanalysis*. Ithaca, N.Y.: Cornell University Press, 1990.

Stallybrass, Peter, and Allon White. *The Politics and Poetics of Transgression*. Ithaca, N.Y.: Cornell University Press, 1986.

Stati, Sorin. *Il dialogo*. Naples: Liguori, 1982.

Stewart, Susan. *On Longing: Narratives of the Miniature, the Gigantic, the Souvenir, the Collection*. Baltimore: Johns Hopkins University Press, 1984.

Stoller, Robert. *Sex and Gender*, vol. 1. London: Hogarth Press, 1968.

Stone, Lawrence. *The Family, Sex and Marriage in England, 1500–1800*. New York: Harper & Row, 1977.

Tasso, Torquato. *Apologia del S. Torquato Tasso in difesa della sua "Gerusalemme liberata" a gli Accademici della Crusca*. Ferrara, 1586. Reprinted in idem,

Opere, vol. 5. Ed. Bruno Maier. Milan: Rizzoli, 1965.

————. *Gerusalemme liberata*. Ed. Bruno Maier. Milan: Rizzoli, 1982.

————. *Prose*. Ed. Ettore Mazzali. Milan: Ricciardi, 1959.

Tertullian, Quintus Septimius. "On the Apparel of Women." In Alexander Roberts and James Donaldson, eds., *The Ante-Nicene Fathers*, vol. 4. Buffalo: Christian Literature, 1897.

Todorov, Tzvetan. "Freud sur l'énonciation." *Langages* 17 (1970): 34–41.

Tomalin, Margaret. "Bradamante and Marfisa: An Analysis of the *Guerriere* of the *Orlando Furioso*." *Modern Language Review* 71 (1976): 540–52.

————. *The Fortunes of the Warrior Heroine in Italian Literature*. Ravenna: Longo, 1982.

Tomaselli, Sylvana, and Roy Porter, eds., *Rape*. Oxford: Basil Blackwell, 1986.

Trafton, Dain. "Structure and Meaning in the *Courtier*." *English Literary Renaissance* 2 (1972): 283–97.

Turchi, Marcello. "Sui personaggi del *Furioso*." *La rassegna della letteratura italiana* 79 (1975): 129–45.

Tylus, Jane. "The Curse of Babel: The *Orlando Furioso* and Epic (Mis)-Appropriation." *MLN* 103 (1988): 154–71.

Tyrrell, William. *Amazons: A Study of Athenian Mythmaking*. Baltimore: Johns Hopkins University Press, 1984.

Valmaggi, Luigi. "Per le fonti del *Cortegiano*." *Giornale storico della letteratura italiana* 14 (1889): 72–93.

Vasoli, Cesare. *La cultura delle corti*. Bologna: Cappelli, 1980.

Vernant, Jean-Pierre. *Myth and Society in Ancient Greece*. Trans. J. Lloyd. Brighton, Eng.: Harvester Press, 1980.

Vickers, Nancy. "Diana Described: Scattered Woman and Scattered Rhyme." In E. Abel, ed., *Writing and Sexual Difference*. Chicago: University of Chicago Press, 1982, 95–109.

————. " 'This Heraldry in Lucrece' Face." *Poetics Today* 6 (1985): 171–84.

Virgil. *Virgil's Aeneid*. Trans. C. H. Sisson. London: Carcanet, 1986.

Weaver, Elissa. "Lettura dell'intreccio nell'*Orlando Furioso*: Il caso delle tre pazzie d'amore." *Strumenti critici* 11 (1977): 384–406.

Weber, Samuel. "Laughing in the Meanwhile." *MLN* 102 (1987): 691–706.

————. *The Legend of Freud*. Minneapolis: University of Minnesota Press, 1982.

Whigham, Frank. "Interpretation at Court: Courtesy and the Performer-Audience Dialectic." *New Literary History* 14 (1983): 623–39.

Wiggins, Peter DeSa. *Figures in Ariosto's Tapestry: Character and Design in the "Orlando Furioso."* Baltimore: Johns Hopkins University Press, 1986.

————. "Spenser's Anxiety." *MLN* 103 (1988): 75–86.

Williams, Linda. "Film Body: An Implantation of Perversions." In Philip Rosen, ed., *Narrative, Apparatus, Ideology*. New York: Columbia University Press, 1986, 507–34.

Wittig, Monique, and Sande Zeig. *Lesbian Peoples: Material for a Dictionary*. New York: Avon Books, 1979.

Woodbridge, Linda. *Women and the English Renaissance: Literature and the Nature of Womankind, 1540–1620*. Urbana: University of Illinois Press, 1984.

Woodhouse, J. R. *Baldesar Castiglione: A Reassessment of "The Courtier."* Edinburgh: Edinburgh University Press, 1978.

Zancan, Marina. "La donna e il cerchio nel *Cortigiano* di B. Castiglione: Le funzioni del femminile nell'immagine di corte." In idem, ed., *Nel cerchio della luna: Figure di donna in alcuni testi del XVI secolo*. Venice: Marsilio, 1983, 13–56.

Zanette, Emilio. *Conversazioni sull' "Orlando furioso."* Pisa: Nistri-Lischi, 1958.

Zatti, Sergio. *Il "Furioso" fra epos e romanzo*. Lucca: Pacini Fazzi, 1990.

Zeitlin, Froma. "Configurations of Rape in Greek Myth." In Tomaselli and Porter, eds., 122–51.

Zorzi-Pugliese, Olga. "Variations on Ficino's *De Amore*: The Hymns to Love by Benivieni and Castiglione." In Konrad Eisenbichler and Olga Zorzi-Pugliese, eds., *Ficino and Renaissance Platonism*. Ottawa: Dovehouse, 1986, 113–21.

Index

In this index an "f" after a number indicates a separate reference on the next page, and an "ff" indicates separate references on the next two pages. A continuous discussion over two or more pages is indicated by a span of page numbers, e.g., "57–59." *Passim* is used for a cluster of references in close but not consecutive sequence.

Library of Congress Cataloging-in-Publication Data

Finucci, Valeria.
    The lady vanishes : subjectivity and representation in Castiglione
and Ariosto / Valeria Finucci.
        p.   cm.
    Includes bibliographical references and index.
    ISBN 0-8047-2045-2 (alk. paper) :
    1. Ariosto, Lodovico, 1474–1533. Orlando furioso.   2. Ariosto,
Lodovico, 1474–1533—Characters—Women.   3. Castiglione,
Baldassarre, conte, 1478–1529. Libro del cortegiano.   4. Women in
literature.   5. Courts and courtiers.   6. Women—Italy—History—
Renaissance, 1450–1600.   I. Title.
PQ4572.A3W645   1992
851'.3—dc20   91-44808
                                                          CIP

⊗   This book is printed on acid-free paper